Beyond Combat

Beyond Combat

Essays in
Military History
in Honor of
Russell F. Weigley

Edited by
Edward G. Longacre
and
Theodore J. Zeman

American Philosophical Society
Philadelphia   2007

*Transactions of the
American Philosophical Society
Held at Philadelphia
For Promoting Useful Knowledge
Volume 97, Part 4*

Copyright © 2007 by the American Philosophical Society for its Transactions series, Volume 97. All rights reserved.

ISBN-13: 978-0-87169-974-9

US ISSN: 0065-9746

Library of Congress Cataloging-in-Publication Data

Beyond combat : essays in military history in honor of Russell F. Weigley / edited by Edward G. Longacre and Theodore J. Zeman.
     p. cm.—(Transactions of the American Philosophical Society held at Philadelphia for promoting useful knowledge, ISSN 0065-9746 ; v. 97, pt. 4)
  Includes bibliographical references and index.
  ISBN 978-0-87169-974-9 (paper)
1. United States—History, Military—19th century. 2. United States—History, Military—20th century. 3. United States—Historiography. 4. Weigley, Russell Frank. 5. Historians—United States—Biography. 6. Weigley, Russell Frank—Bibliography. I. Longacre, Edward G., 1946– II. Zeman, Theodore J., 1965–

E181.B585 2007
355.00973—dc22
                                                             2007040571

[Of] arms and the man I sing.
  —Virgil, *The Aeneid*

Contents

	Foreword	ix
	Introduction *Dennis Showalter*	1
1.	Flexing the Sable Arm: Emancipation, Black Troops, and Hard War *James Paradis*	5
2.	"The Great Question of the Campaign Was One of Supplies": A Reinterpretation of Sherman's Generalship during the 1864 March to Atlanta in Light of the Logistic Strategy *J. Britt McCarley*	26
3.	The United States Navy and the Genesis of Maritime Education *Jennifer L. Speelman*	65
4.	The Ambassador's Troops: U.S. Military Attachés and Military Intelligence, 1885–1920 *John F. Votaw*	83
5.	Leadership Prerequisites: Colonel Conrad S. Babcock and Command Development during World War I *Douglas Johnson*	104
6.	The Battle for Uniform Votes: The Politics of Soldier Voting in the Elections of 1944 *Christopher DeRosa*	129
7.	Eisenhower As Ground-Forces Commander: The British Viewpoint *G. E. Patrick Murray*	153
8.	Operation Rollup: The U.S. Army's Rebuild Program during the Korean War *Peter S. Kindsvatter*	187

9. "Justice with Courage": Considerations on the Weakness of British Imperial Power
    Adam Norman Lynde   201

Select Bibliography of Published Works and Conference Papers Written by Russell F. Weigley   245

Contributors   255

Index   259

Foreword

"The 'new military history' is new in its concern for military history as a part of the whole of history, not isolated from the rest, for the military as a projection of society at large, for the relationships of the soldier and the state, for military institutions and military thought."[1] So wrote Russell Frank Weigley, one of the most accomplished and respected military historians of the latter half of the twentieth century. Professor Weigley's influence on military history extends beyond academics to the military sphere. His books and articles have influenced military thought and professional military education. His lectures have been heard in university classrooms and service academies throughout the United States and Europe. Yet although many are familiar with his writings and teachings, most know relatively little about the man himself: the events that inspired him to become a historian and the varied interests he pursued outside the classroom. What follows is a brief biography that may help the reader understand the teacher, the author, and the mentor who touched the lives of so many both on and beyond the college campus.

Weigley was born on July 2, 1930, in Reading, Pennsylvania. His nearly lifelong interest in military history—especially the history of the American Civil War—was an inheritance. His middle name honored his great-great uncle, Francis Adam Weigley, who served in the 7th Pennsylvania Volunteer Cavalry from 1861 to 1864. Francis Weigley died of wounds in a Confederate prison but not before he sent his brother, Jacob (Russell Weigley's great-grandfather), letters that resonated with succeeding generations of the family. Living only ninety miles from the battlefield of Gettysburg, the Weigley family traveled there every year throughout Russell Weigley's childhood and adolescence. The images that the place evoked stirred the youngster to study its history. As a youth, he spent the summer mowing the lawn at Reading's Charles Evans Cemetery, where he tended the grave of a noted Union cavalry commander, Major General David McMurtrie Gregg. Weigley took an interest in Gregg's life and, eventually, military history in general.

---

1. Russell F. Weigley, ed., *New Dimensions in Military History: An Anthology* (San Rafael, CA: Presidio, 1975), 11.

In 1948 Weigley graduated from Reading High School and began studying for his bachelor's degree at the local institution of higher learning, Albright College. He had planned to study law, but during his junior year a history professor persuaded him to enter that field instead. Weigley not only excelled immediately in his new discipline but also developed a facility for mathematics. He found that working complex trigonometry and calculus equations sharpened his mind and thus made him a better student of history.

In 1952 Weigley graduated from Albright with straight A's, only the third or fourth student to achieve that distinction. He then entered the graduate program in history at the University of Pennsylvania, where he received his master's degree in 1953. At once he began studying for his doctorate under the supervision of Roy F. Nichols, whose antebellum political study, *The Disruption of American Democracy*, had received the Pulitzer Prize for history four years earlier. In 1956, after only two and a half years of study, Weigley was awarded the PhD. During the next two years he served as a history instructor at the University of Pennsylvania. One of his colleagues, Richard Dunn, recalls that the new man gained a reputation as the "Young Turk" of the faculty, whose infectious commitment to the teaching of history motivated his colleagues and helped improve the department's curriculum.

While working on his doctorate, Weigley made daily trips by train to and from his hometown. During one such commute he met his future wife, Emma Seifrit, also a resident of Reading, who was studying for her master's degree in nutrition at Drexel Institute of Technology (later Drexel University). The chance meeting would lead to a long and loving marriage. No wonder the fledgling historian developed an abiding interest in trains and took every opportunity to ride them when traveling.

In 1958, Professor Weigley began teaching American intellectual history at Drexel Institute. He was extremely fond of the course and hoped to teach it in his later career at Temple University. Regrettably, the demands placed on him to lecture in military history left him no time to do so. While he was at Drexel, his first book, *Quartermaster General of the Union Army*, based on the doctoral dissertation he had produced under Professor Nichols, was published. For many years it remained the only full-length biography of Montgomery C. Meigs, who managed the supply system that supported the Northern war effort. The volume remains an important tool for understanding the logistical system of the Union forces.

In 1962, Weigley was appointed associate professor of history at Temple University. That year his second book, *Towards An American Army: Military Thought from Washington to Marshall*, was released to great acclaim. It established his reputation as analyst and interpreter of the role of the military in American society. One of his former students, Marc Gallicchio, remembers how the professor would warn his students that military history was not an idyll for buffs but a serious subject worthy of rigorous inquiry. Weigley was determined that they come to understand the ways in which the American military had influenced the life of a fundamentally antimilitaristic nation. An examination question with which his students would become familiar was: "Discuss how the United States has attempted to reconcile the existence of a military establishment with republican institutions."

Russ Weigley and Emma Seifrit were married on July 27, 1963. They took up permanent residence in Philadelphia, a city both had come to love. They purchased a house in Center City within walking distance of Temple; in later years Russ proudly noted that he had never driven to work. Emma, who received her doctorate from New York University in 1971 and later taught at Penn, also enjoyed the accessibility of their Center City home, which soon became a gathering place for students, colleagues, and friends.

In 1964 Weigley became chairperson of Temple's history department. Two years later he was granted tenure and promoted to full professor. Although deeply involved in his teaching, he indulged many other interests, one of the foremost being baseball. He had played the game as a youngster and had become a fan of both of Philadelphia's major league teams: the hapless but lovable Phillies and the more elite and successful Athletics. He never completely recovered from the Athletics' move to Kansas City in 1955. Over the years he considered developing a course on baseball as a mirror of American society but never found the time to do so. His talent for mathematics enabled him to master the records and statistics of the sport, and he unfailingly marked a player's passing in his well-worn copy of *The Baseball Encyclopedia*.

His hometown sports allegiances were long-lasting and sometimes painful. Herbert Ershkowitz, a fellow professor at Temple, remembers riding with Weigley when returning from a meeting of the Pennsylvania Historical Association during which Weigley listened intently to a Phillies' playoff game. When it became obvious that the team would lose, he abruptly turned off the radio. Russ couldn't stand to hear his team go down to defeat. He once declared that to be a Phillies' fan was the acid test of loyalty. Rooting for a team that lost so often and so abjectly was a frustrating experience but one that built character and fostered a sense of commitment. When he attended a game between the Phillies and the Oakland Athletics soon after interleague play began, he found himself torn between his allegiance to the Phillies and his fondness for the club that had broken his heart not by losing but by leaving town for greener pastures, larger crowds, and gaudier uniforms.

Baseball was not the only sport Weigley followed intently. He became a fan of Big Five basketball in Philadelphia. He and Emma attended as many games at the Palestra as their busy schedules permitted. He also occupied a Municipal Stadium (and later a Veterans Stadium) seat during the annual Army-Navy football game, which he often attended in company with one of his former graduate student, Colonel Jerry Comello of the U.S. Army. It was this variety of interests that made Weigley such a fascinating person to talk to and learn from.

For one academic year, 1967–68, Weigley served as a visiting professor at Dartmouth College in Hanover, New Hampshire. During this period his *History of the United States Army*, a volume in the Macmillan Wars of America series, was published. The book details the growth and development of the U.S. Army from the small defense force of an insular nation to the highly polished weapon of a major world power. The book appeared as the United States found its global military commitments on the rise; thus, the author's analysis of the army's relationship to American society at large was especially timely. Weigley noted that the tortuous course and political complexity of the still-unfolding war in Vietnam had begun to strain the nation's civil-military bonds, and he suggested that unless the nation as a whole united in support of the conflict, victory was unattainable. Events would prove him correct.

When the young professor joined the Temple faculty, military history was not part of the curriculum. For that matter, the course that covered the Civil War was a superficial overview of battles and campaigns with little attempt to place the conflict in a political or social context. No offering explored the part played by the military in the growth and modernization of the nation or gave serious attention to military strategy or policy. Thus, Weigley had to develop from scratch a course embracing these and other themes that he considered integral to an appreciation of war and war makers. He firmly believed that only by studying war in all its aspects could a nation find ways to avoid it.

His growing reputation as an interpreter of strategy, tactics, and policy won him the respect and admiration of military educators. In 1973–74 he occupied the Harold Keith Johnson Chair as Visiting Professor of Military History at the U.S. Army Military History Institute (USAMHI), Carlisle Barracks, Pennsylvania. His association with the USAMHI and the Army War College of which it was a part provided a further spur to his reputation while enabling him to forge enduring relationships with colleagues, both military and civilian. One friend acquired at Carlisle was Dr. Richard J. Sommers, the USAMHI's archivist/historian. Among other memories, Sommers recalls their shared passion for collecting toy soldiers and wargaming with them. He recalls, too, the insignia-laden neckties they sported in each other's company:

> Every time we met over all those years—scores of occasions, really—our gaze first fixed on each other's cravat, as, for instance, I would see him wearing a powder blue tie with white shakos, and he would espy my brown tie with two kepis, one Federal and one Confederate. To symbolize my appreciation for all that he contributed to *Richmond Redeemed* [Sommers's

1981 study of a critical period in the Petersburg Campaign], I gave him a navy blue tie (rather his favorite color, I daresay) full of mounted knights with drawn swords—the only kind of armored warfare, I made clear to him, that was worthy of study. Relatively more recent soldiers in armor, British Royal Horse Guards, adorned the medium blue tie with which I thanked him for addressing the Harrisburg Civil War Round Table in April of 1986.

Such symbols suggest still stronger significance, beyond even professional interest and profound gratitude and personal friendship. Civil War soldiers said it best, when referring to some other unit or some other commander whose steadfast reliability on the battlefield they knew that they could count on when committed to combat. "He'll do to tie to," the soldiers would say. So too with the Great Scholar and the Good Friend Russ Weigley: "He'll do to tie to."

Weigley's ability to win and hold friends would characterize him throughout his life. As he became more prominent in the history community, he refused to develop a sense of self-importance or become distant or unapproachable. In many ways he was a private person, as is every gentleman worthy of the name. He never thrust himself upon others, never burdened students or colleagues with his personal cares and concerns. Still, when permitted sustained contact with him, a person would come away with a sense not only of knowing something of the eminent scholar, the dedicated teacher, but of having touched, and been touched by, his essential humanity: his patience and kindness, his unpretentiousness, his wit, his perceptivity, and his genuine interest in and concern for those who shared his world.

Beginning in the 1970s, Weigley devoted an increasing amount of time to rearing his children. On April 26, 1973, he and Emma were blessed with the birth of a son, Jared. Three years and one month later, Jared was joined by a sister, Catherine. The Weigleys spent many days squiring their children not only to playgrounds and soccer fields but also to historical sites and theaters showing movies that the parents considered educational as well as entertaining. Jared Weigley, who would go on to a career as a film producer and writer, remembers his father as an avid movie buff. Realistic images of military operations, such as offered by Stanley Kubrick's World War I classic *Paths of Glory*—the elder Weigley's favorite film—influenced his literary depictions of combat.

The year 1973 saw the publication of Weigley's most influential work, *The American Way of War: A History of United States Military Strategy and Policy*. The book, which attained high standing in both military and academic circles, examines "the development of American military strategy and tactics, both in theory and practice, integrating the concept of strategy as a political, economic, diplomatic, and psychological means for attaining war aims with the actual application of strategic thought in war."² The study explores the operations of George Washington's little army, which was forced to fight a war of attrition; the tactics of the larger volunteer armies of the Union and Confederacy, whose commanders sought in vain a Napoleonic-style victory of annihilation; the guerrilla techniques of the Indian-fighting U.S. Army; and the military-political strategy practiced by the huge multinational forces that waged the great wars of the twentieth century. In the book's later chapters Weigley stresses that the emergence of nuclear weapons has both facilitated and complicated the quest for decisive military victory. He warns of the peculiar difficulties posed by low-intensity conflict and the insurgency tactics of the enemy that America fought in Southeast Asia, factors that appear to call for a sweeping review of U.S. military policy.

The American Way of War not only won great acclaim for its author but, by increasing his stature in the profession, placed greater demands on his time and labor. Weigley's course "The Military and American Society" prompted Reserve Officer Training Corps directors at other institutions to send their students to Temple. His graduate classes induced many officers stationed at Carlisle to make the three-hour trip to Philadelphia to study under him. Despite the increased graduate-level workload, he continued to teach undergraduate courses. At about this time, a review of history department policies recommended that, as befit his status, he should be required to teach only graduate students. A former colleague, Mark Haller, recalls that Weigley was affronted by the gesture and refused to give up his undergraduate courses, much to the appreciation of those who took them.

All who studied under Weigley were struck by his ability to lecture long and clearly without recourse to notes. His grasp of the course material was astounding; even the most obscure questions brought a prompt and learned response. One student remembers a classmate inquiring about one of innumerable U.S. Army regulations. Weigley floored the student not only by thoroughly explaining the regulation but by providing from memory a full citation of its source. Many of the talks that Weigley gave at universities, public forums, and military service schools were delivered sans notes. This remarkable proficiency also characterized the discourses he delivered in houses of worship. On the Sunday closest to the Fourth of July, he would preach at Philadelphia's First Unitarian Church, effortlessly meshing historical and religious lessons without referring to a single note. In one sermon that remains vivid in his family's mind, he contended that the Gettysburg Address superseded the Declaration of Independence as the great statement of American ideals. In composing the Gettysburg Address, he believed, Abraham Lincoln had established a moral order that

---

2. Russell F. Weigley, *The American Way of War: A History of United States Military Strategy and Policy* (New York and London: Macmillan, 1973), dust jacket copy.

guided the nation ever afterward. Although Weigley impressed his audiences with the sagacity of his observations, by dispensing with notes he left no written record of his lectures and sermons. We are left only with what he published, a rich legacy to be sure but one that might have been richer still.

In 1981, Weigley's study of the campaigns of 1944–45 in France and Germany, *Eisenhower's Lieutenants*, was published to wide acclaim. Its descriptions of combat are so vivid that many readers supposed that Weigley himself had experienced it. Among those so impressed was another Philadelphia historian, Professor David Burton of Saint Joseph's College (now Saint Joseph's University). Burton, who had served in Europe as an infantryman during the Battle of the Bulge and was wounded as the Allies advanced into Germany, greatly admired his colleague's ability to convey the horrors of warfare as faced by the common soldier. He agreed with Weigley that combat shaped the way wars were conducted but that it was important to understand how the military functioned within the society that developed the policies under which it fought.

A volume that Weigley edited, published in 1982, bespoke his love for the city he called home. *Philadelphia: A 300-Year History* had special meaning for him, having begun under the editorship of his mentor at Penn. When Roy Nichols fell seriously ill, his most accomplished student took over the project. Russ was quickly confronted by daunting obstacles: some of those who had been engaged to contribute essays had died; others had failed to complete their work for other reasons. Although forced to recommission some contributions and to rewrite others that failed to meet his exacting standards, he shepherded the book to its completion. By the date of its publication it had evolved into a work of which he and those who had benefited from his editorial skills could be justly proud.

In 1985 Weigley was named Distinguished University Professor, one of the first Temple faculty members so honored. Despite the ever-increasing demands made upon him by his teaching duties and off-campus contributions to his profession, he continued to find the time to help those who depended on him—undergraduates and grad students alike—for guidance. Many of the latter were not typical PhD candidates but rather were professionals, including army officers who under other advisors would not have progressed beyond the master's degree. Regardless of their background and educational experience, Weigley encouraged his students to realize their full potential and to strive for the doctorate that many of them coveted. Better than they themselves, in many cases, he possessed an intuitive knowledge of his students' capabilities. His time-consuming commitment to them often meant a corresponding lack of time devoted to his writing projects and speaking commitments, yet he never subordinated their interests to his own.

The personable relations that Weigley established with his students extended beyond the classroom, even beyond the campus. He regularly entertained them in his Center City home where, at the conclusion of every semester, he would treat them to music, convivial conversation, and Fish House Punch, a tasty libation served in Philadelphia since the Colonial period. He took pride in preparing this memorable concoction while being careful to warn against imbibing too freely lest one fall victim to its deceptively potent effects.

Professor Weigley's love of drawing, which he had indulged since early youth, was demonstrated in the artwork that adorned the personalized Christmas cards he sent to former students, relatives, and friends. A talented cartographer, he drew the base maps that illuminated the military operations detailed in some of his books. He had an abiding interest in music as well; for forty years Emma and he held season tickets to the renowned Philadelphia Orchestra.

Weigley served in many administrative and editorial capacities beyond those he shouldered at Temple. For many years he was active in the affairs of the Pennsylvania Historical Association and served as its president from 1975 to 1978. From 1983 until his death he was councilor of the association; edited its journal, *Pennsylvania History*; and chaired its publications committee. In 1974–79 and 1987–91 he was a member of the Department of the Army's historical advisory committee. From 1991 until his death he sat on the Board of Directors of the American Committee on the History of the Second World War, and from 1977 to 2004 he occupied a similar position in the World War II Studies Association. These and other professional attachments demanded increasing time and attention, but he refused to neglect his students. One of them, Thomas English, remembers visiting him at his home to discuss a reading assignment. The telephone rang, and Weigley excused himself to answer it but quickly returned to his guest. When English indicated that he gladly would have waited until Weigley could properly attend to the call—a matter, English surmised, of some importance—his host would not hear of it: the student had an appointment with him and thus first claim to his attention. According priority to his students no matter the situation was an immutable core value of Russell Weigley.

In 1989 Weigley was awarded the prestigious Samuel Eliot Morrison Prize, presented at the annual meeting of the American Military Institute. The accompanying citation read: "To Dr. Russell F. Weigley, Temple University, for his large body of contributions to American military history in research and writing, reflecting a spectrum of scholarly activity contributing greatly to the field."[3] He continued to prove himself worthy of such accolades. In 1991 his study of a seminal period in European military history, *The Age of Battles: The Quest for Decisive Warfare from Breitenfeld to Waterloo*, was released. An examination of strategy and tactics from the early seventeenth century through the Napoleonic Wars, the volume demonstrates that in the case of every European army other

---

3. *American Military Institute Headquarters Gazette*, Summer 1989, 2.

than Great Britain's, the quest for decisive military action and the attempt to make warfare a true extension of political policy had produced battlefield failure, social upheaval, and economic ruin. The work was widely praised by critics at home and abroad and was the recipient of an Outstanding Book Award from the Society for Military History.

Other honors followed in rapid succession. In 1992 Weigley became the eighth holder of the U.S. Marine Corps Command and Staff College Foundation Chair of Military Affairs. The following year he was elected to membership in the American Philosophical Society, a Philadelphia institution of unequaled prestige. Concurrently, he achieved the status of 33rd Degree Freemason, the highest post one could attain in that international fraternity. Friends and associates suggested that he also apply for entrance into Mensa, an organization whose members sported advanced IQs. Although he possessed the necessary qualifications, he rejected the suggestion out of hand, believing the group not only exclusionary but also elitist and snobbish.

As the 1990s drew to a close, Professor Weigley decided to retire from full-time teaching. He desired to spend more time with his family and to travel with Emma to places that his professional commitments had prevented them from visiting. He also wished to devote more attention to his writing, including the completion of a sequel to *The Age of Battles* covering European warfare through the end of World War I. Already, too, he had began work on a military-political-social study of the American Civil War, the conflict that, more than fifty years earlier, had instilled in him an avid interest in American history. As he confided to his students on more than one occasion, he considered himself, first and foremost, a Civil War historian despite the wide-ranging scope of his interests and the works he had published on various subjects.

The announcement of Weigley's retirement in 1998 prompted Temple to name him Distinguished University Professor Emeritus. The school sponsored a retirement colloquium in his honor during which several of his former students presented papers that reflected the breadth and depth of their mentor's influence. Retirement tributes were also paid him by the Pennsylvania legislature, the Army War College, and the United States Military Academy.

In retirement Weigley kept almost as busy as when carrying a full teaching load. He and Emma took a cruise to Alaska and a train ride across Canada. They also made an excursion from Philadelphia's 30th Street Station to Reading and back, a journey that evoked memories of the day they had met forty years earlier. Back home, he kept active by teaching one graduate course each semester while also tending to his duties as codirector of the Center for the Study of Force and Diplomacy, an organization he had founded at Temple in concert with Professor Richard Immerman, then-chairperson of the history department. In fulfillment of its mission, the center brought together students and former students to speak, write, exchange ideas, and share interdisciplinary expertise on issues military and diplomatic. Somehow Weigley also found the time to supervise the doctoral progress of graduate students and to deliver papers before numerous professional, academic, civic, and fraternal organizations.

In 2000, Weigley published what would prove to be his final book, *A Great Civil War: A Military and Political History, 1861–1865*. With this volume he came full circle from his days as a grad student and young professor, when his interests had centered on America's most divisive and critical conflict. The work, as was true of all that had preceded it, demonstrated his perfectionist bent. According to his wife, he wrote the main draft in longhand on a legal-size pad. The deliberate pace with which he composed enabled him to produce a finished product even before he transferred it to paper via the typewriter. His former students, who benefited from the care with which he critiqued their research papers and dissertations, can testify to the precision with which he turned out his finely wrought prose. He would react sharply whenever he encountered split infinitives, missing commas, and dangling participles. He expected his students to research and write with the same care, diligence, and thoroughness that characterized his own work, qualities he considered hallmarks of his profession.

In common with its many predecessors, *A Great Civil War* met with wide acclaim and earned prestigious honors. Dick Sommers, for one, was gratified that his friend had returned to his thematic roots. For years Sommers's friend had "tolerated my gentle chiding as he strayed into pre–Civil War conflicts and even my merciless upbraiding as he degenerated into the twentieth century of *Eisenhower's Lieutenants*. He understood my delight that for his magnum opus he came home to the Straight and Narrow to write *A Great Civil War*." In 2001 the book received the Lincoln Prize, which honors extraordinary contributions to the study of the Civil War period. The award constituted a crowning achievement of sorts, one that validated and rewarded a long, fruitful, and distinguished career.

Weigley did not consider that career at an end. Up to the time of his death on March 3, 2004, he gathered materials for yet another book of Civil War history, this one specific to the battle that had claimed his attention as a youth: Gettysburg. Having conducted years of research on the subject and having made innumerable visits to that battlefield, often in company with family, friends, and students, he believed himself capable of producing a fresh interpretation of that oft-chronicled yet much-misunderstood engagement.

As always, however, Weigley found that he could not devote himself full-time to a single project, even one that increasingly vied for his attention. Professional commitments and personal interests called him to Europe, where he and Emma found time to explore the battlefields of France and Britain. While in England, he also toured cultural sites and visited the haunts of favorite historical and literary personages including King Arthur, Robin Hood, and Sherlock Holmes. Upon returning home, Weigley resumed his Gettysburg research, a project interrupted yet again by his work on professional panels including the National World War II Memorial Committee, of which he was the sole civilian member. It was shortly after his return from Washington following a planning session of this committee that he succumbed to a fatal heart attack. He was seventy-three years old.

The untimeliness of Weigley's passing left virtually everyone who knew him grief-stricken. A memorial service held at Temple University the following May permitted former colleagues, students, and friends to pay tribute to the many contributions he had made to his college, his city, and his profession. The service was attended by an overflow group, many of whom attempted to put into words their respect for his professional attainments, their appreciation of his mentoring skills, and their gratitude at having shared his world. The occasion was crowned by a moving tribute delivered by his first doctoral student, John Alexander, OP, a member of the faculty of Providence College. Father Alexander's benediction remains vivid in the minds of those in attendance that day:

> The most famous speech in American history was delivered at a memorial service. Lincoln's Gettysburg Address, which Russ analyzed so well in *A Great Civil War*, summons a new birth of self in the face of loss as it articulates the range of human emotions from grief to hope to gratitude.
>
> Let us take a moment to express our gratitude for Russ. Gratitude for his dedication as a teacher and a scholar. Gratitude for his patience and tolerance. Gratitude for his compassion and kindness. Gratitude for the love that he brought to everything he did.
>
> His enthusiasm for history was contagious. His sincere humility as an outstanding scholar was an example. Speaking as one of his students, and for so many of his students, it was a blessing to have Russ for a teacher, mentor, and friend. How many of us, when we come to challenging choices in teaching and scholarship think, "What would Russ do?" And his example encourages us to do the best we can, as he always did.
>
> We your students, your colleagues, your friends, and your family are grateful for your presence in our lives. Your presence lives with us and summons in us a new birth of commitment that we may hear, as you have heard, those words of benediction: "Well done, my good and faithful servant. . . . Enter the kingdom prepared for you from the foundation of the world."

This book would not have reached fruition without the assistance of many people deserving of the editors' gratitude. First and foremost we thank the Weigley family—Emma, Jared, and Catherine—for sharing with us facts and anecdotes that illuminate aspects of the life of their husband and father hitherto unknown or little understood. We also thank Professor Dennis Showalter of Colorado College, one of Russ Weigley's closest friends in the profession, who contributed the thorough and insightful introduction to this volume. We are equally indebted to Professor Gregory J. W. Urwin of Temple University, whose editorial assistance, patient advice, and moral support kept this project on course through rough seas. Our appreciation likewise goes to Dave Burton and Dick Sommers for their illuminating recollections of their dear friend. Our gratitude, in fact, encompasses all of Russ's friends, students, and fellow faculty members who recorded their appreciation of his personal qualities and professional accomplishments. Thanks, too, to John McNulty for supplying the epigraph for this volume and to Ann Longacre for clerical assistance. Finally, we thank Russell Frank Weigley for the instruction, guidance, and friendship he offered us over a period gratifyingly lengthy and regrettably brief.

Edward G. Longacre
Newport News, Virginia

Theodore J. Zeman
Philadelphia, Pennsylvania

Introduction

Dennis Showalter

"Is there anything this guy doesn't know?" That question was part of the title of a paper presented at the 1999 symposium honoring Russ Weigley on his retirement from Temple University. It specifically reflected the first impression he made on one of his many graduate students. But in one form or another it also aphorized the respect that Professor Weigley enjoyed in the global community of scholars, not only military historians but also researchers in other fields who benefited from his perceptive insights, measured judgments, and, not least, his personal graciousness and professional generosity.

Military history differs significantly from most other historical specialties in that it resists extreme specialization. In part this is a function of academic programs that find room for general courses on war and society more readily than the narrowly focused offerings characterizing the rest of the discipline's curriculum. But it reflects as well the discipline's continued commitment to what might be called the greater, rather than the lesser, intellectual world. Its leading figures, those most often spoken of with respect in private as well as publicly, are characterized by wide intellectual range as both teachers and scholars.

Russell Weigley exemplified and epitomized that breadth. His major works structured fields from the nature of American military thought and practice (*The American Way of War*) through the relationship of force structure and command in the D-Day campaign (*Eisenhower's Lieutenants*) to the nature of early modern battle (*The Age of Battles*). But his proudest legacy was the work of his graduate students. Many dozens of men and women completed PhDs under his supervision. They went on to a broad spectrum of careers and lives: professors and administrators, professional soldiers and government historians, museum directors and independent scholars. What they shared was a mentoring that runs through their work like a red thread: respect for their sources, their subjects, and the English language. Russ was a mortal foe of dissertation prose! That in turn amounts to respect for their readers, a respect shaping this cutting-edge anthology.

The contributors to this volume were solicited with a view to demonstrating Professor Weigley's range of interest and influence. A major theme of his own scholarship, both overtly and as subtext, was adaptability in both individuals and institutions: the ability to expand perspective to meet requirements. That ability is central to three essays from three seminal periods of American military history. Britt McCarley highlights logistics as the central element of Union general William T. Sherman's conduct of the Atlanta Campaign of 1864. Responding to criticism of Sherman as a barely adequate battle captain, McCarley demonstrates that tactics played a secondary role in Sherman's approach. His primary and immediate concern, operating in a region barely removed from subsistence agriculture, was to maintain his army's supplies while denying his Confederate opponents. In the wider context of national policy, that meant holding casualties and costs to a minimum during an election year. Sherman succeeded brilliantly on both levels, strengthening the Union's will to war, ensuring President Abraham Lincoln's reelection, and setting the stage for the final thrust into the Confederacy's remaining heartland: the March to the Sea.

Fifty years later an American Expeditionary Force (AEF) created virtually from whole cloth found itself in the middle of a war whose parameters had been set for years. Effective midlevel command—brigades, regiments, and battalions—was at a corresponding premium. Douglas Johnson shows that the frequently criticized rigidity imposed by the AEF's commander, General John J. Pershing, created relative uniformity, which in turn enabled officers to establish acceptable—albeit seldom remarkable—levels of competence at successively higher levels of command. The system might not have been optimal, but it was functional.

In a tour de force exercise of considering the other side of the hill, Patrick Murray critiques the British perspective on Dwight Eisenhower as the ground-forces commander of the Grand Alliance. His definition is important. British prime minister Winston Churchill, Chief of Staff Alan Brooke, and 21st Army Group commander Bernard Montgomery accepted Eisenhower as an adequate supreme commander. The focus of their criticism was his refusal as ground commander to concentrate forces for a single thrust to Berlin. Murray's Eisenhower is tough, shrewd, and complex, no mere "chairman of the board" but a strategist whose broad-front approach reflected a clear understanding of the political and operational limits of the Berlin option. Eisenhower may have been a small-town boy from Kansas, but from D-Day to the end of the war in Europe he successfully focused and harnessed his talents to meet a challenge that no American general had ever faced.

An arguably even better way of evaluating a military system's effectiveness is in terms of its capacity for self-evaluation, self-development, and, when necessary, self-reform. John Votaw introduces this aspect by analyzing the development of U.S. military attachés and observers from ad hoc appointments based heavily on personal wealth and social graces to central and systematic participants in the U.S. intelligence system. Votaw convincingly demonstrates that the process reflected the energy, the initiative, and the developing professionalism of the attachés' more than systematic initiatives from higher military or civilian levels. What he calls the "rigorous self-analysis" of the military and naval intelligence services was not derailed even by the collective lack of interest after World War I. When in the late 1930s foreign aggression again became a serious issue, the attaché system was in place to respond.

Reform is not always a matter of ideas and policies. In the early stages of the Korean War, the U.S. Army was short of equipment in every category from tanks to field radios. Its response, as presented by Peter Kindsvatter, included a major self-help project, Operation Rollup. Initiated desultorily in 1948 before the war's outbreak and greatly expanded as the fighting intensified, rollup involved salvaging—scavenging might be more accurate—the million tons and more of vehicles and equipment abandoned across the western Pacific after World War II. The material was sorted, collected, and shipped to Japan, where plants and workers left idle since 1945 rebuilt and refurbished it for shipment to Korea. This variant of the regional cargo cults may have belied America's standing as the world's dominant industrial power. It also proved cost-effective. It gave Japan's economy welcome stimulation, and it helped keep American forces in the field during the Korean War's critical early months, a muddy-boots response to a practical challenge.

Russell Weigley insisted that effective command and planning for a country such as the United States, with its heritage of small standing forces and national mobilizations, involved close and systematic links between the military and society. Jennifer Speelman describes the U.S. Navy's nineteenth-century contributions to formal, institutional education for a merchant marine with a heritage of blue-water pragmatism and personal experience. Stephen B. Luce played a central role in developing state-level nautical schools, whose curricula initially emphasized seamanship and navigation and then began incorporating engineering and mechanics as well.

National mobilization for major wars produced significant tensions in a peacetime army that tended toward hierarchy, homogeneity, and intimacy. Christopher DeRosa shows that the question of soldiers voting in the presidential election of 1944 both challenged the army's institutional insularity and began a process of redefining U.S. citizenship by affirming short-term citizen service as a norm. An army initially dubious about administrating an election became during the Cold War an enthusiastic supporter of voting in uniform as an affirmation not merely of democratic citizenship but of service in a military itself fundamentally democratic, in its own way!

James Paradis surveys another aspect of the relationship between armed forces and society in the United States by considering government and military policies on the use of black soldiers in the Civil War. His story is likely to be the most familiar one to readers of this work, at least in outline form. Paradis economically reestablishes the initial reluctance of both the federal government and the Union Army to accept black volunteers and the issues leading to that policy's breakdown at the sharp end of military operations. The interrelated problems of establishing effective control of occupied territory, depriving the Confederacy of an essential resource, and administering the increasing numbers of refugee slaves combined to make putting blacks in uniform a least-worst solution that significantly shaped the Union victory, if not the postwar Reconstruction. It is worth noting that in many cultures military units identified with minorities are often fiercely defended by those minorities as a signifier of their identity. The Scots regiments of the British Army are the most familiar example, and the class regiments of India represent the best example. American blacks from the beginning, however, have regarded segregated units as a stepping stone to full participation in the military system. In turn, the contemporary U.S. Army's 9th and 10th Cavalry and the newly reconstituted 24th Infantry celebrate their Buffalo Soldier heritage in a multiethnic context.

The final essay in this anthology may seem at first glance to stand alone. But in fact Adam Lynde's analysis of the ideas and experiences that shaped British perceptions of civil-military relations in the crucial years of the eighteenth century both shows the importance of British precedents in establishing American models of civil-military relations and establishes the significant differences between the two approaches. Lynde highlights the British conviction that civic order was best secured by integrating civil and military spheres: restricting commissions as army officers to the landed-property classes and allowing those officers to sit in Parliament. This is a fundamental contrast to the American principle of isolating the armed forces, clearly demarcating their sphere of responsibility from that of the civil authority. In turn, Lynde argues, civil-military interactions in strategic planning were much more synergistic than the U.S. model, particularly as Britain's interests and its armed forces expanded during the century. Neither approach, however, has proved a panacea; assumptions based on presumed tradition can be as misleading as they are alluring. And in presenting the importance of pragmatism as opposed to dogmatism, of hands-on scholarship as opposed to a priori reasoning, Lynde's essay affirms the fundamental principles of Russell Weigley's distinguished career.

1
Flexing the Sable Arm
Emancipation, Black Troops, and Hard War

James Paradis

As the American Civil War began, few people could have envisioned the fratricidal carnage and physical devastation to come. Few indeed could have foreseen that this conflict would strike down suddenly the centuries-old institution of slavery and thrust nearly two hundred thousand black men into the armed forces of the United States.

At the beginning of the war, the United States followed a policy that historians Mark Grimsley and Ethan S. Rafuse refer to, respectively, as "conciliation" and "moderation." Northerners reasoned that Southerners were their countrymen before the war and would be countrymen again once the conflict was won and the nation restored. Many Americans including President Abraham Lincoln wanted to avoid any harsh actions against those in rebellion in order to effect an amicable reunification as free of bitterness and resentment as possible. They aimed to crush the Confederate Army, but they wished to leave civilians unmolested and to keep intact the economic and social structure of the South, slavery included.[1]

At the war's outset Lincoln embraced this approach. He counseled against "radical and extreme measures, which may reach the loyal as well as the disloyal." He also wanted the war to end quickly so that it would not "degenerate into a violent and remorseless revolutionary struggle." His general in chief, Winfield Scott, planned to avoid bloody conflict, defeating the South by blockading its coast and taking control of the Mississippi River. Scott's successor, Major General George B. McClellan, even more strongly supported the kid-glove approach. According to McClellan, not only should the constitutional, civil, and political rights of Southern civilians be protected, but "the people of the South should understand that we are not making war upon the institution of slavery, but if they submit to the Constitution and Laws of the Union they will be protected." He declared that the armed forces of the United States must by their actions prove the government to be "benign and beneficent." Any other policy might "render impossible the reconstruction of the Union."[2]

Through the early months of the war, the Lincoln administration's policy of moderation ruled out draconian military measures and actions that would hurt Southern civilians, many of whom were presumed to be loyal to the Union. Had the U.S. military achieved final victory in the first year of the contest, it is unlikely that it would have resorted to hard war. The government would have implemented no radical policies and would have made no assault on slavery. The want of military success forced the government's hand.

Between the first year of the Civil War and its concluding twelve months, the conflict was transformed dramatically from a war of civility to a remorseless war of exhaustion. The change came, however, in stages. Congressional legislation and executive actions employing the hard hand of war seemed to mirror the fortunes of the Union armed forces in the Eastern theater of operations. The North suffered a humiliating defeat at First Bull Run (or First Manassas) in July 1861. Barely two weeks after this debacle, Congress passed the first Confiscation Act, which authorized the emancipation of the slaves of rebels as well as those slaves who had been forced to assist Confederate war efforts. The patience of Lincoln and Congress began to dissipate as the policy of leniency and restraint failed to achieve its purpose. Lincoln announced that "those enemies must understand that they cannot experiment for ten years trying to destroy the government, and if they fail still come back into the Union unhurt."[3]

Lincoln reevaluated his commitment to a conciliatory policy. McClellan did not. The general in chief reasserted his faith in restraint and rejected tampering with slavery. His attitude raised questions about his commitment to decisive victory, and his inactivity prompted Congress and the president to act more decisively themselves.

McClellan took charge of the Army of the Potomac in July 1861. Eight months later he still had not advanced his army toward the enemy and had given no hint of a plan to do so. On March 11, 1862, Lincoln removed him as general in chief, retaining him as commander of the Army of the Potomac. On March 13, Congress passed an article of war that forbade military officers, under penalty of court-martial, from returning fugitive slaves to rebel owners.

McClellan finally revealed his plans and began to implement his offensive operations. By April, however, his so-called Peninsula Campaign had bogged down at Yorktown, Virginia, where his nearly one hundred thousand troops had been halted by some seventeen thousand Confederates. Lincoln exhorted him: "It is indispensable to *you* that you strike a blow. . . . *But you must act.*" He might have added that if the general failed to apply military force, the president and Congress would do so with governmental policy. Congress continued chipping away at slavery, abolishing the institution in the District of Columbia.

McClellan's army eventually reached the outskirts of Richmond, but a series of Confederate assaults drove it from the enemy capital to the banks of the James River. The campaign having fizzled, the army began withdrawing from the Peninsula, and Congress acted again, banning slavery in all U.S. territories. It also passed a second Confiscation Act authorizing the seizure of property of all persons in rebellion and declaring their escaped slaves free men and women. On the same day, Congress revised the Militia Act to permit employment of blacks in the military.

These developments show that the Lincoln administration had entered a twilight period, no longer conciliatory toward the Confederacy but stopping short of hard war. During this interval, which Grimsley calls a time of "pragmatic" action, a series of practical decisions, made to meet changing exigencies, brought about progressive modification of war policy.[4]

Although the words and actions of the Lincoln administration on the subject of emancipation and African American troops appear inconsistent and contradictory, the president maintained a kind of consistency throughout the war. Lincoln's policy becomes clear when viewed in the light of his paramount objective: winning the war.

Horace Greeley chided the president in 1862 over his failure to act against slavery. Lincoln's famous reply includes the oft-quoted statement: "My paramount object in this struggle is to save the Union and is not either to save or to destroy slavery. If I could save the Union without freeing any slave I would do it, and if I could save it by freeing all the slaves I would do it; and if I could save it by freeing some and leaving others alone I would also do that. What I do about slavery, and the colored race, I do because I believe it helps save the Union, and what I forbear, I forbear because I do not believe it would help to save the Union. I shall do less whenever I shall believe what I am doing hurts the cause, and I shall do more whenever I shall believe doing more will help the cause."[5]

The administration's military policy can best be understood by replacing the words "save the Union" with "win the war." Neither could occur without the other, and the achievement of either would accomplish both. The policy of Lincoln's administration toward black soldiers rested consistently on this guideline: whatever helps win the war is approved, whatever impedes victory is rejected. The pragmatism of this approach reflected the nature of the transitional stage in the shift from a war of restraint to a hard war.

When Lincoln first revealed to his cabinet his intent to free slaves in the rebellious states, his proposal won the group's approval. Secretary of State William H. Seward, although a passionate foe of slavery, counseled the president to delay the release of the proclamation until a more opportune time. Recent military reverses had left the federal government in an unfavorable situation. Such a pronouncement made at that time, in a position of weakness, would look like an act of desperation. Lincoln took Seward's advice and waited. The president finally issued the preliminary Emancipation Proclamation in the wake of the Union's strategic victory at Antietam.[6]

Some have suggested that, in fact, this document freed no slaves. Lincoln's severest critics even suggest that he had no intention of freeing any slaves and desired that slavery continue. Both of these views are demonstrably incorrect. Many slaves had fled from Confederate territory to the refuge of Union lines. Before the Emancipation Proclamation, they remained fugitives and the lawful property of those who claimed to own them. The only reason they were not returned to their owners was that this particular type of property was being used to construct fortifications and otherwise aid the Rebel cause. They were held by Union forces not as free men and women, but as human entrenching tools seized from the enemy. After the proclamation took effect in January 1863, they became forever free.

The cynical claim that Lincoln planned to take no action against slavery would only be true if he planned to follow the issuance of the Emancipation Proclamation by sitting back and losing the war. The point missed by these critics is that Lincoln did not plan to lose the war. He planned to win the war, and, as he sometimes had to explain to his generals, winning the war meant driving forward into enemy territory. The Union Army advanced as an army of liberation, empowered as such by the Emancipation Proclamation.

Evaluations of Lincoln's proclamation vary widely. A few historians have questioned the sincerity of the president's commitment to act against slavery. Lerone Bennett Jr. has asserted that the proclamation freed no one and that Lincoln had no intention or desire to disrupt the institution of slavery. Bennett contends that "Lincoln supported the enslavement of four million slaves and opposed abolitionists who wanted to free them," and he calls Lincoln "the common enemy of the slave and the ally . . . of their tormentors and murderers." Many other historians have defended the Emancipator as a political realist, praising the effectiveness of his policies. Allen C. Guelzo pronounces the proclamation "the End of Slavery in America."[7]

The longer the war continued, the more closely linked became the aims of union and emancipation. No matter how much Lincoln may have personally desired to set every slave free, he was realistic enough to understand that he would free none if he failed to win the war. After issuing the preliminary Emancipation Proclamation (and after the fall 1862 elections), Lincoln confirmed his commitment to waging hard war by firing the two generals most wedded to moderation, George B. McClellan and Don Carlos Buell.

Even after Northern strategists abandoned limited war and embraced a hard war policy, they still had reasons to hesitate regarding emancipation. While military victory might well mean the end of slavery, the opposite would not necessarily be true. Declaring an end to slavery would bring no military victory. On the contrary, if such a declaration undermined public support for the war in the loyal states, chances for military success would greatly diminish.

When Lincoln declared the Southern slaves free, he also declared an end to limited war and raised hard war to a new level. Both Southerners and conservative Northerners charged that Lincoln sought to incite servile insurrection with his proclamation. The document itself supports this charge by including a plea to the people thus liberated "to abstain from all violence, unless in necessary self-defense." These words carried a false ring to Southerners, who envisioned hundreds of Nat Turners rampaging through their countryside. The fact that Lincoln included this passage indicates that he thought it might very well happen. Southern outrage intensified with the additional passage that called for the enlistment of blacks into the armed forces of the United States. To Southerners this provided proof of Lincoln's intent not only to incite slaves to kill Southern whites but also to systematically arm blacks and train them to kill. In Southerners' minds, Lincoln's actions were tantamount to raising the black flag: it transcended even hard war and amounted to atrocity. The Union raised hard war to a new level, and the Confederacy would respond in kind. A Northern newspaper opposing the use of black troops warned that "if the United States elects to employ barbarian means and agencies against the South, they must expect barbarian usage in return."[8]

Union Major General David Hunter urged full use of the "sable arm" to bring hard war to the enemy. Hunter advocated "a general arming of all the negroes and a general destruction of all the property of the slaveholders." He asked permission to march an army "through the heart of Georgia, Alabama, and Mississippi to New Orleans, arming all the Negroes and burning the house and property of every slaveholder. A passage of this kind would create such a commotion among the negroes that they themselves could be left to do the rest of the work. I am a firm believer in the maxim that 'slaveholders have no rights a negro is bound to respect.'"[9]

As willingness to punish the South grew, so too did Northern willingness to use black troops to do it. With a new justification for the war effort, "emancipation helped establish the moral groundwork for hard war." Moreover, "black enlistment made the Emancipation Proclamation irrevocable."[10]

Conventional wisdom has produced the image of Lincoln striving to overcome the prejudice of Northern whites against arming blacks. In fact, the first challenge that Lincoln faced was overcoming his own prejudice against enlisting black men. On July 22, 1862, when the president first shared with his cabinet his intent to declare emancipation, the arming of African Americans was no part of his plan. Secretary of the Treasury Salmon P. Chase recorded in his diary: "The question of arming slaves was brought up and I advocated it warmly. The president was unwilling to adopt this measure."[11]

Lincoln did, however, give thought to future employment of black troops. About the same time that he revealed his preliminary Emancipation Proclamation to the cabinet, he penned a memorandum that stated:

> To recruiting of free negroes, no objection.
> To recruiting slaves of disloyal owners, no objection.
> To recruiting slaves of loyal owners, *with their consent*, no objection.
> To recruiting slaves of loyal owners *without* their consent, objection, *unless the necessity is urgent.*[12]

On August 4, 1862, Lincoln told a delegation that he was "not prepared to go the length of enlisting negroes as soldiers. He would employ all colored men offered as laborers but would not promise to make soldiers of them." On September 13, in reply to a memorial from a group of Chicago Christians urging emancipation, the president conceded that emancipation might help, but he dismissed the value of black soldiers: "I also concede that emancipation would help us in Europe, and convince them that we are incited by something more than ambition. I grant further that it would help *somewhat* at the North, though not so much, I fear, as you and those you represent imagine. Still, some additional strength would be added in that way to the war. And then unquestionably it would weaken the rebels by drawing off their laborers, which is of great importance. But I am not so sure we could do much with the blacks. If we were to arm them, I fear that in a few weeks the arms would be in the hands of the rebels; and indeed thus far we have not had arms enough to equip our white troops."[13]

Lincoln's belief that arms given to black soldiers would soon be in the hands of the rebels reveals his conviction that African American soldiers could not be victorious on the battlefield. It also suggests that if placed in a combat situation, such troops would either throw down their weapons and run away or be easily captured by the enemy. Lincoln went on to state another major concern: "I will mention another thing, though it meet only with your scorn and contempt: There are fifty thousand bayonets in the Union armies from the Border Slave States. It would be a serious matter if, in consequence of a proclamation such as you desire, they should go over to the rebels." The president often emphasized the essential necessity of retaining the loyalty of the Border States. He even reportedly commented that while he hoped that God was on his side, he *must* have Kentucky.[14]

One of the problems that Lincoln faced in establishing and following a consistent policy regarding the employment of African Americans as soldiers was the decentralized nature of both government and military responsibility. While Washington might establish one policy, state governments might choose to set their own policy. Since the states, not the federal government, raised most of the troops serving in the Union Army, Washington exercised little control over enlistment requirements. To further complicate matters, individual commanders in the field, responding to circumstances and the need for additional manpower, might act on their own in adopting policies within their bailiwick.

An odd brand of liberation played out in South Carolina, where David Hunter ordered his troops to sweep up all local slaves of military age and dragoon them into the army. Russell F. Weigley observes that the frequent impressments of slaves into the Union Army demonstrated the inherent conflict between liberty and war: "Still, while war may have been the only feasible instrument with which to strike the fetters from the victims of American slavery, war so much tends to manufacture fetters of its own that it is a most unsatisfactory means for advancing the cause of liberty, even when waged by an Abraham Lincoln."[15]

Even before Lincoln's proclamation, Union military leaders acted to employ the sable arm that Frederick Douglass had been urging the government to use. In 1862, in the Union-occupied coastal region of South Carolina, General Hunter assembled former slaves into a body of soldiers whom he uniformed and armed. This unit became the vanguard of the 1st South Carolina Infantry (African Descent), the first regiment of African American troops in the Civil War. Eventually command of the regiment passed to Colonel Thomas Wentworth Higginson, who had given financial and moral support to John Brown. Higginson's book *Army Life in a Black Regiment* would become a classic of Civil War literature. When conservative U.S. congressmen heard of this action and demanded to know if Hunter was raising a regiment of fugitive slaves, the general's wry reply delighted abolitionists and outraged those conservative congressmen: "No regiment of 'fugitive slaves' has been or is organized in this department. There is, however, a fine regiment of persons whose late masters are 'fugitive rebels,' men who everywhere fly before the appearance of the national flag, leaving their servants behind them to shift as best they can for themselves. So far, indeed, are the loyal persons composing this regiment from seeking to avoid the presence of their late owners that they are now, one and all, working with remarkable industry to place themselves in a position to go in full and effective pursuit of their fugacious and traitorous proprietors."[16]

On August 25, 1862, even before the preliminary Emancipation Proclamation was released, Secretary of War Edwin M. Stanton authorized Brigadier General Rufus Saxton to "arm, uniform, equip, and receive into the service of the United States such number of volunteers of African descent as you may deem expedient, not exceeding 5,000." Stanton also permitted Saxton to "detail officers to instruct them in military drill, discipline, and duty, and to command them." Later that year, the War Department took a more aggressive approach when it ordered Brigadier General Thomas West Sherman to "avail yourself of the service of any persons, whether fugitives from labor or not, who may offer them to the National

Government. You will employ such persons in such services as they may be fitted for—either as ordinary employees, or if special circumstances seem to require it, in any other capacity, with such organization (in squads, companies, or otherwise) as you may deem most beneficial to the service." Yet the next line in these instructions—very likely added by Lincoln—modified this order: "This, however, not being a general arming of them for military service."[17]

In July 1862 the U.S. Congress overhauled the seventy-year-old Militia Act, changing the section that excluded blacks from the military and empowering Lincoln to organize and employ African Americans "for any military or naval service for which they be found competent." Lincoln's Emancipation Proclamation, which took effect on January 1, 1863, formally authorized the organization and participation of African Americans as soldiers in the Army of United States.[18]

Many units were formed under this authority. James H. Lane, Kansas senator and general of his state's militia, organized the 1st Regiment of Kansas Colored Infantry. If anyone stood for unleashing hard war it was Lane, who was ruthless in his treatment of Southern sympathizers. The 1st Kansas fought Confederate forces in engagements at Sherwood and Bush Creek. On July 2, 1863, while fighting raged at Gettysburg, the 1st Kansas engaged a force of Texans and their American Indian allies at Cabin Creek in the Cherokee Nation, the future state of Oklahoma.

One of the most unusual military organizations of the war was composed of black volunteers from New Orleans. Free blacks as well as slaves had fought in defense of that city, first for the French in 1727 and later for the Spanish. They fought for the Patriot cause in the American Revolution and in 1812 helped Andrew Jackson defend New Orleans. With this long history of loyal service, it is not surprising that the State of Louisiana, upon seceding from the Union, accepted the enlistment of free black men. The Louisiana Native Guard included black officers as well as enlisted men.[19]

When New Orleans fell to Union forces early in the war, the Native Guard was ordered to evacuate the city along with the rest of its Confederate defenders. The black soldiers, however, did not obey this order and instead offered their services to Union Major General Benjamin F. Butler, the occupation commander in New Orleans. Earlier in the war while commanding forces at Fort Monroe, Virginia, Butler had found a loophole by which he could circumvent the Fugitive Slave Law. When Confederate officers, under a flag of truce, requested the return of their slaves who had fled to the Union lines, Butler claimed the fugitives as contraband of war, thus setting a precedent. From that time on, Union officers would refuse to return fugitives, and the term "contraband" came to be synonymous with escaped slaves.

In New Orleans, Butler found a novel way around government restrictions on enlisting blacks. The government had recently announced that former Confederate soldiers who swore an oath of allegiance to the United States could be enlisted in the Union forces. Because this directive did not specify race, on August 22, 1862, Butler officially decreed that these black "former Confederates" be enlisted in the Volunteer Service of the United States.[20]

Black troops raised in South Carolina and Kansas continued their active campaigning. Those blacks raised in New Orleans, later designated the Corps d'Afrique, attacked and besieged Port Hudson, a Confederate stronghold on the Mississippi River. Their valorous but futile assault on those formidable works rivaled the more famous attack of the 54th Massachusetts Infantry on Battery Wagner, South Carolina, which fell to the Union on July 9, 1863. At Milliken's Bend, Louisiana, during June 5–7, 1863, another new unit of black recruits, inexperienced in battle, repulsed a series of vigorous attacks by veteran Confederates. Then or soon afterward, black troops fought successfully in various theaters from the Carolina coast to the Mississippi River and beyond.[21]

Most black units did not see action in the major campaigns of the war but instead took part in sideshows or did garrison and guard duty behind the lines. Some commanders decided to keep blacks out of harm's way for fear of the brutal treatment they would receive if taken prisoner. Other field leaders not only hesitated to employ soldiers of color but displayed an aversion to commanding them. William T. Sherman admitted that "I cannot bring myself to trust Negroes with arms in positions of danger and trust."[22]

As commander of the Army of the James from late 1863 until January 1865, Benjamin Butler stood in stark contrast to Sherman and other Negrophobes. He actively sought to bring African American units under his command, even offering to swap inexperienced white regiments for veteran black outfits. Eventually he organized his United States Colored Troops (USCT) into the XXV Corps, the first and only American army corps composed exclusively of black units. This command was soon broken up, however, and one of its divisions was sent to North Carolina to assist in the capture of Fort Fisher, which defended the port of Wilmington.

Butler demonstrated a willingness, even an eagerness, to employ the USCT in key situations. He not only assigned black units to defensive positions but allowed them to spearhead offensive operations as well. He also organized African Americans into cavalry and artillery units despite the opposition of the War Department.[23]

Compared to other Union armies, the Army of the James included far fewer generals with West Point training or experience in previous wars. This helps to justify its designation as "the preeminent civilian army of its day." Although plagued by a history of failure, Butler's army could also boast of significant triumphs on the battlefield. Its dramatic storming and capture of the Dimmock Line, the elaborate outer defenses of Petersburg, Virginia, laid that key city open to capture. The taking and holding of Fort Harrison rendered Richmond vulnerable and eventually led to its evacuation. In both of these cases the failure of higher echelons to follow up the army's gains left the fruits of its success unclaimed.[24]

The mid-1863 invasion of the North by Robert E. Lee's Army of Northern Virginia compelled Pennsylvania governor Andrew G. Curtin to call for volunteers, regardless of race, to defend the Keystone State. In Philadelphia, black volunteers quickly filled an entire company. The enthusiasm shown by the African-American community that summer echoed the excitement once shown throughout the North in April 1861, when the first call for all-white troops sounded. This new martial fever served to drown out the increasing opposition to the war, even as protest and riots against the draft spread throughout the North, most notably in the streets of New York.

When the Philadelphia volunteers reached Harrisburg, however, the commander of the local military department, Major General Darius N. Couch, rebuffed them. Declaring that he was authorized to accept only sixty-day volunteers, he rejected outright the thirty-day men who had reached the state capital. Although Couch also refused short-term white volunteers, the spurned blacks believed that race had been a factor in this decision. Washington agreed; shortly afterward, Secretary of War Stanton telegraphed Couch to accept volunteers "regardless of race." The snubbed Philadelphia soldiers formed the core of Company A, 3rd Regiment of United States Colored Infantry, the first regiment of black troops raised in Pennsylvania. The 3rd Regiment was the first of eleven regiments to be trained at Camp William Penn, just outside Philadelphia.[25]

As the Bay State raised the 54th and 55th Regiments of Massachusetts Infantry, it created a bonus for itself. These newly raised units could be counted against their state's quota. Each state was required to meet a quota of enlistments imposed by the federal government. Failure to meet this quota would force state officials to conscript enough citizens to make up the difference. Elected officials dreaded the thought of taking a politically unpopular action and welcomed this avenue of escape.

Unfortunately, Massachusetts did not have enough black males of military age to constitute any significant military unit. To fill their ranks, the state sent agents to other states that had significant black populations. Massachusetts's agents heavily mined Pennsylvania, particularly Philadelphia, the largest black community in the Free States. To avoid arousing local suspicion, under cover of night they shepherded their recruits in small groups onto northbound trains.

Other states did not ignore what was happening in Massachusetts. They also began recruiting elsewhere. This cross-border recruiting bore the potential for serious conflicts. Lincoln took the opportunity to weigh in on this conflict when he received a message from Governor John Andrew of Massachusetts, perhaps his staunchest ally among the war governors. Andrew complained that fugitives from slavery desiring to travel northward to his state were being forcibly detained in the Washington area. He appealed to the president to intervene. Lincoln, no doubt with tongue in cheek, sent the governor the following reply:

> Yours of the 12th was received yesterday. If I were to judge from the letter, without any external knowledge, I should suppose that all the colored people South of Washington were struggling to get to Massachusetts; that Massachusetts was anxious to receive and retain the whole of them as permanent citizens; and that the United States Government here was interposing and preventing this. But I suppose these are neither really the facts, nor meant to be asserted as true by you. Coming down to what I suppose to be the real facts, you are engaged in trying to raise colored troops for the U.S. and wish to take recruits from Virginia, through Washington, to Massachusetts for that object; and the loyal Governor of Virginia, also trying to raise troops for us, objects to your taking his material away while we, having to care for all, and being responsible alike to all, have to do as much for him, as we would have to do for you, if he was, by our authority, taking men from Massachusetts to fill up Virginia regiments. No more than this has been intended by me or, as I think, by the Secretary of War. There may have been some abuses of this, as a rule, which, it known, should be prevented in future.[26]

The federal government would prevent these abuses in the future by terminating state-designated black regiments. From that point on, all units of African Americans would be organized under the auspices of the Bureau of United States Colored Troops (BUSCT). From the beginning, federal authorities required that the commissioned officers leading these units be white. While this requirement clearly reflected the lack of confidence in the competence of blacks to be officers, several other factors figured in this decision. The opportunity for advancement in rank attracted white volunteers. Presenting these new opportunities for whites helped reduce prejudice, both within the army and on the home front, against raising such units. Rarely did Democrats become officers in these regiments. For the most part, Republicans, who tended to favor a hard war policy, volunteered for these assignments.[27]

The BUSCT set a relatively high standard for would-be officers. Becoming an officer in this department required the successful completion of a test of competency. No other department in the army required such an examination for candidates to become officers. Problems arose as a high percentage of candidates failed the test. To increase the success rate, the BUSCT troops established a school to help prepare candidates to take the exam. This school, established at 1210 Chestnut Street in Philadelphia, served as the first officers' candidate school.

The president took a personal interest in appointing good men to lead these units. He approved of setting a high standard for officers of USCT regiments. He did show irritation, however, when a potential officer, a good man whom Lincoln wanted to see appointed, was rejected for not meeting the test requirements. The commander in chief revealed more than a little frustration with this red tape when he sent Secretary Stanton a terse note:

My dear Sir:

I personally wish Jacob R. Freese, of New-Jersey to be appointed a Colonel for a colored regiment and this regardless of whether he can tell the exact shade of Julius Caesar's hair. Yours truly

A. Lincoln[28]

The impressive performance of black men on the battlefield overcame the president's initial skepticism. He was transformed into an enthusiastic supporter of USCTs. In August 1863 he wrote that some of his most successful generals believed that the policies of emancipation and employment of colored troops "constitute the heaviest blow yet dealt to the rebellion." As he wrote to his future vice president, Andrew Johnson, "the colored population is the great *available* and yet *unavailed* of force for restoring the Union. The bare sight of fifty thousand armed, and drilled black soldiers on the banks of the Mississippi, would end the rebellion at once. And who doubts that we can present that sight, if we but take hold in earnest?"[29]

The president linked winning the war, saving the Union, and using black troops. He confessed in an April 1864 letter that although he at first opposed the policies of emancipation and the arming of African Americans, "I was, in my best judgment, driven to the alternative of either surrendering the Union, and with it, the Constitution, or of laying strong hand upon the colored element." He went on to admit that "I claim not to have controlled events, but confess plainly that events have controlled me." He reinforced his affirmation five months later when he declared that "any different policy in regard to the colored man, deprives us of his help. And this is more than we can bear. We can not spare the hundred and forty or fifty thousand now serving us as soldiers, seamen, and laborers. This is not a question of sentiment or taste, but one of physical force which may be measured and estimated as horse-power and Steam-power are measured and estimated. Keep it and you can save the Union. Throw it away, and the Union goes with it."[30]

By June 1864 the Army of the Potomac began to besiege Petersburg, Virginia. Capturing Petersburg would cut off the Confederate capital at nearby Richmond from its vital rail connection to the south and would all but assure that city's fall. Black troops from Butler's Army of the James assaulted and captured the outer defenses of Petersburg, and then the Army of the Potomac arrived and took over the operation. The ranking officer on the scene, Major General William "Baldy" Smith, hesitated, giving the Confederate defenders time to reinforce their thin inner line with troops hastily dispatched to that point from Lee's army. As a result, a Union assault with white troops the following day failed to carry the enemy lines. Both sides settled in for a siege. Having botched an early opportunity to storm the city, Ulysses S. Grant's army faced a frustrating siege against defenses that grew daily more formidable.

A group of coal miners serving in the Union army devised a scheme to break through the Confederate defenses. By tunneling below the no-man's-land between the armies and under the Rebel works, they could place a massive charge of explosives that, when detonated, would blast a gap in the enemy's line through which the Union troops could charge. Their suggestion progressed up the chain of command to the IX Corps commander, Major General Ambrose E. Burnside. Burnside secured permission to carry out the plan from Major General George Gordon Meade, the army's commander, and from Grant, the general in chief. Originally, Burnside's plan called for Brigadier General Edward Ferrero's division of black soldiers to spearhead the assault. Grant and Meade later forced Burnside to change the plan and allow a white division to lead the assault. Because the change came only hours before the explosion, the lead white division did not receive sufficient preparation and instruction in how to exploit the breach. Hence, when the assault came, many of the white troops marched into the crater caused by the blast rather than charging around it. The Confederates were able to recover, counterattack, and trap the Union troops in the horrid pit. At this unpromising point, the black troops originally designated to lead the action were thrown into the already-failed assault, with disastrous results. They were killed not only during the attack on the crater but also after the fighting ended, as some Confederates refused to take black prisoners.

Grant called the failed assault "the saddest affair I have witnessed in the war. Such opportunity for carrying fortifications I have never seen and do not expect again to have." The resulting embarrassment provoked Congress, through the Joint Committee on the Conduct of the War, to investigate the debacle. During his testimony, General Grant revealed his belief that the plan would have succeeded if he had used his black troops as originally planned. He justified his decision, however, explaining that "I agreed with General Meade in his objection to that plan. General Meade said that if we put the colored troops in front, (we had only that one division) and if it should prove a failure, it would then be said, and very properly, that we were shoving those people ahead to get killed because we did not care anything about them. But that could not be said if we put white troops in first."[31]

Historians have taken Grant at his word, that he feared the public would accuse the high command of treating the black troops as cannon fodder because it did not really care about them. This explanation, though, does not have a clear ring of truth. Why would there be a greater outcry from the all-white electorate about blacks being killed rather than whites? With the possible exception of the more strident abolitionists, this seems unlikely. Moreover, the appalling losses suffered by the 54th Massachusetts in its futile assault the previous year evoked no protest, not even from the black community.

Other explanations seem more likely. Grant may have simply lacked faith in black soldiers. He had commanded white troops throughout the war, and he knew what they could accomplish. Command of African American troops had only recently passed to him, and he may have lacked confidence in their abilities. Grant also might have been motivated not by the specter of what would happen if the assault failed but by concern for the consequences should it succeed. In the latter event, the black troops would have to be given credit for breaching the Confederate lines. A breakthrough at Petersburg would mean the collapse of Richmond. While the demise of the Confederate capital would bring rejoicing for the North, it would be a blow to the morale of Northern whites in the army and on the home front. What a humiliation it would be after more than three years of bloody battle by white troops if blacks were to make the effort that brought on the fall of the Rebel capital and the end of the war. This consideration may better explain Grant's decision not to use the USCT in the Petersburg operation.

The fate of African American prisoners at Petersburg was another issue with which the Lincoln administration had to deal. The Confederate Congress refused to treat captured black soldiers as prisoners of war. They were considered agents of servile insurrection, subject to execution or enslavement. Confederate President Jefferson Davis branded white officers in charge of black regiments as "outlaws," roughly equivalent to the modern concept of war criminals, and singled them out for harsh treatment. Davis's secretary of war, James A. Seddon, made an even more severe pronouncement by recommending that "the negro [captives] be executed as an example." General P. G. T. Beauregard declared, "Let the execution be with the garrote." President Davis, concerned about possible retaliation, intervened with a restrained official policy. The unspoken solution employed by individual Confederates, however, would be a combination of showing no quarter and committing what Allan Nevins called "secret murder."[32]

Confederate refusal to exchange captured black soldiers as prisoners of war drove Grant to suspend prisoner exchanges. This led to obscenely overcrowded and undersupplied prisoner facilities and the nightmare transformation of POW pens into death camps. Grant continued suspension of prisoner exchanges because they benefited the enemy and allowed the South to prolong resistance.

Cessation of prisoner exchanges, originating in conflict over black troops, became part of Grant's war of exhaustion. Once again African American involvement influenced the increasingly hard hand of war.

The Lincoln administration had no choice but to respond to Confederate threats to murder or enslave those blacks who had risked all to fight in the Union Army. Black troops were as much Lincoln's soldiers as any other men, and he was obligated to look after them. The president decided to threaten retaliation. He stated that for any black soldiers executed, an equal number of Confederate prisoners of war would be put to death, and for each Union captive remanded to slavery, a Confederate prisoner would be put to hard labor. Lincoln had little choice but to make this announcement if he wanted to retain black volunteers.

At least one Union commander in the field implemented his own system of retribution. Benjamin F. Butler heard reports that captured black soldiers had been put to work building Confederate fortifications. The fortifications to which they were assigned included some that were under fire from Union guns. Butler was at that time supervising the digging of a canal at Dutch Gap, a peninsula along the James River. Black troops had been assigned to this difficult and distasteful work. Confederate artillery made the work perilous as well by lobbing shells onto the site. With permission from Grant, Butler put Southern prisoners to work on the canal and notified the Confederates that they would remain there under fire from their own forces until captured black soldiers received the treatment due prisoners of war. Robert E. Lee contacted Grant directly and assured him that the black POWs had been removed from the offending assignment. Grant then ordered Butler to release the Confederate prisoners from canal duty.[33]

Controversy over Lincoln's policy in this area arose not so much over what he said but rather over what he and his administration did or did not do. Numerous reports of mistreatment, including the murder of African American prisoners, came from places such as Saltville, Virginia; Poison Springs, Arkansas; and Olustee, Florida. Yet no Confederate prisoners were ever executed in response to the many alleged cases of Southerners carrying out their threats to harm black captives.

The most notorious of these episodes was the Fort Pillow Massacre in Tennessee. On April 12, 1864, Confederate forces under Major General Nathan Bedford Forrest attacked and captured a fort garrisoned by black and white volunteers from Tennessee. Both of these groups engendered emotional revulsion in Confederates. Many reports told of Confederates committing atrocities after the fort had fallen, including refusing to accept the surrender of black soldiers and killing some of them along with their white officers. When word of the massacre reached Secretary of War Stanton, he immediately ordered Major General William T. Sherman, the ranking officer in that theater, to assign a competent officer to investigate the allegations. Sherman appointed Brigadier General Mason Brayman, a former railroad lawyer, who began his investigation on April 16. Brayman needed only one day of testimony to inform Sherman of "proof of horrid barbarities in ways without example."[34]

Congress also responded with remarkable speed. Only ten days after the battle, a congressional delegation including Ohio senator Benjamin F. Wade traveled to Fort Pillow and began its fact-finding investigation. The testimony given during this inquest showed clearly that overzealous Confederates had indeed violated the rules of war in their treatment of prisoners.[35]

This situation put the Lincoln administration in a quandary. The federal government had threatened to execute one Confederate for each Union prisoner of war murdered, but could it follow through on its threat? On May 3, Lincoln sent to his cabinet members a memo asking each to prepare and submit his written opinion as to the course of action the administration should take. The cabinet debated, weighing the options and expressing widely differing points of view. Secretary of State Seward wanted to demand that the Confederate government explain or disavow the massacre and promise that such acts would not be repeated. In the meantime, Seward suggested, the United States should set aside a number of Southern prisoners as hostages to be held until the Confederates gave a satisfactory reply.

Secretaries Chase, Stanton, and Gideon Welles agreed with Seward's recommendation. Stanton also insisted that General Forrest himself and all members of his command involved in the Fort Pillow affair be excluded from amnesty and prisoner exchange. The United States should also demand that the Confederate government hand over all suspects, said Stanton, who went on to suggest that unless the rebels complied with these demands (a highly doubtful prospect), punitive action should be taken against the hostages. On the other hand, the conservative attorney general, Edward Bates, rejected retaliation as "wholly unjustifiable in law and conscience," since the hostages themselves had not committed any crimes. The federal government could not justifiably punish them for the crimes of others. Secretary of the Interior John P. Usher agreed with Bates but insisted that members of Forrest's command, if taken prisoner, should be "set aside for execution." Yet Usher feared that with Grant's big offensive, the Overland Campaign of 1864, about to begin, it would be wise to avoid "any extreme action." Postmaster General Montgomery Blair also supported the conservative approach.[36]

In April, upon hearing the first rumors of a massacre at Fort Pillow, Lincoln spoke in Baltimore, the city with the largest black community in the nation. He talked tough on the issue, stating his belief that the reports were probably true and that if they proved so "the retribution shall surely come. It will be matter of grave consideration in what exact course to apply the retribution; but in the supposed case, it must come." By mid-May the president had directed Secretary Stanton to inform the insurgents, through proper military channels, that in the absence of a satisfactory response from Richmond by the first day of July, "it will be assumed by the government of the United States, that said captured colored troops shall have been murdered, or subjected to Slavery, and that said government will, upon said assumption, take such action as may then appear expedient and just."[37]

The voices of caution prevailed, however, and the Lincoln administration took no reciprocal punitive action against Confederate prisoners. Northern politics may also have influenced the outcome. A presidential election loomed only months away. The opposition favored peace at almost any cost. For Lincoln, losing the election meant losing the war, and Lincoln's paramount object was winning this war. Retaliation would mean that Lincoln would have to execute at random a considerable number of Confederate prisoners. The Northern public might well reject the idea that a large number of otherwise innocent white Confederates be slain in response to allegations that some blacks had been killed. Unionists from the border states, along with conservatives throughout the North, would denounce such retaliation. Killing an equal number of whites to avenge blacks would play into the hands of the Democratic opposition, whose spokesmen were already characterizing Lincoln as an extremist favoring racial equality and carrying on a war that slaughtered thousands of whites to free blacks.

In his Baltimore speech, Lincoln stressed that "there seems to be some anxiety in the public mind whether the government is doing its duty to the colored soldier, and to the service, at this point." He reassured the audience that he intended to give each black soldier "all the protection given to any other soldier." At the same time, he tried to explain his practical dilemma. His succinct statement could have served as the theme of his policy toward blacks: "The difficulty is not in stating the principle, but in practically applying it."[38]

Although neither the government nor the military took official action in retaliation for the reported massacre at Fort Pillow and maintained silence with regard to black soldiers, it tacitly supported a policy of revenge. No significant government official or military officer either cautioned blacks against personal acts of retaliation or condemned any reported instance of African American troops taking retribution into their own hands. If the arming of black troops raised the bar with respect to the ferocity of the war, the Confederate response of refusing quarter raised it again. Cries of "Remember Fort Pillow!" and "No Quarter!" began to ring out from black fighting men.

The most notable example of black troops embracing a new level of hard war occurred during the spring 1865 operation against Fort Blakely, outside Mobile, Alabama. A Union observer stated that the rebel defenders ran toward the white Union troops to surrender "to save being butchered" by the colored troops. The observer went on to declare that the black troops "did not take a prisoner. They killed all they took to a man." Confederate witnesses supported this claim. Several white officers, including chaplains, refuted these charges. One chaplain asserted as "a credible truth" his statement that "no one was injured by any colored soldier after resistance had ceased." Another officer insisted that "it is a fact that every officer of the colored troops will testify that not a rebel soldier was shot by the darkies after they had surrendered." Although these officers earnestly rejected the enemy's charges, they could only testify to what occurred within their line of sight. Most likely, scattered cases of prisoner abuse, perhaps including homicide, took place at Fort Blakely.[39]

Abraham Lincoln's policies regarding emancipation, the use of black troops, and the employment of hard war suggest a remarkable streak of single-mindedness. The president never deviated from his paramount objective: saving the Union through winning the war however he had to do it. Regardless of circumstances, public opinion, or pressures to the contrary, he always kept his eyes on the prize. When a limited war of conciliation failed to bear fruit, Lincoln willingly took off the gloves. From that point on, the hard hand of war and the sable arm struck as one and delivered the relentless blows that brought Union victory.

Notes

1. Mark Grimsley, *The Hard Hand of War: Union Military Policy toward Southern Civilians, 1861–1865* (New York: Cambridge University Press, 1995), 2–4, 7–11, 23, 31–33; Ethan S. Rafuse, *McClellan's War: The Failure of Moderation in the Struggle for the Union* (Bloomington: Indiana University Press, 2005), 1–3, 5–6, 98, 104–5, 111, 113, 115, 121–22, 126, 148–50.

2. Rafuse, *McClellan's War*, 157, 247.

3. Grimsley, *Hard Hand of War*, 92; Roy P. Basler et al., eds., *The Collected Works of Abraham Lincoln*, 9 vols. (New Brunswick, NJ: Rutgers University Press, 1953), 5:344–45.

4. Grimsley, *Hard Hand of War*, 3–4, 213–14; James M. McPherson, *Ordeal by Fire: The Civil War and Reconstruction*, 3rd ed. (New York: McGraw-Hill, 2001), 293.

5. Basler, *Collected Works of Lincoln*, 5:388–89.

6. Ibid., 337n.

7. Lerone Bennett Jr., *Forced into Glory: Abraham Lincoln's White Dream* (Chicago: Johnson Publishing, 2000), 13; Allen C. Guelzo, *Lincoln's Emancipation Proclamation: The End of Slavery in America* (New York: Simon & Schuster, 2004), 8, 227–30.

8. Derek W. Frisby, "'Remember Fort Pillow!' Politics, Atrocity, Propaganda, and the Evolution of Hard War," in Gregory J. W. Urwin, ed., *Black Flag over Dixie: Racial Atrocities and Reprisals in the Civil War* (Carbondale: Southern Illinois University Press, 2004), 122.

9. Grimsley, *Hard Hand of War*, 212; *The War of the Rebellion: A Compilation of the Official Records of the Union and Confederate Armies*, 4 series, 70 vols. in 128 (Washington, DC: U.S. Government Printing Office, 1880–1901), Series III, 3:740 (hereafter cited as OR).

10. Michael Fellman, Lesley J. Gordon, and Daniel E. Southerland, *This Terrible War: The Civil War and Its Aftermath* (New York: Pearson, 2003), 145; Grimsley, *Hard Hand of War*, 213; Guelzo, *Lincoln's Emancipation Proclamation*, 219.

11. Basler, *Collected Works of Lincoln*, 5:337.

12. Ibid., 338.

13. Ibid., 357, 423.

14. Ibid., 423.

15. Russell F. Weigley, *A Great Civil War: A Military and Political History, 1861–1865* (Bloomington: Indiana University Press, 2000), 185–86.

16. OR, I, 6:264; Dudley T. Cornish, *The Sable Arm: Negro Troops in the Union Army* (Lawrence: University Press of Kansas, 1987), 32–47; Thomas Wentworth Higginson, *Army Life in a Black Regiment* (Boston: Houghton Mifflin, 1870); Noah Andre Trudeau, *Like Men of War: Black Troops in the Civil War, 1862–1865* (Boston: Little, Brown, 1998), 15–16; William A. Gladstone, *Men of Color* (Gettysburg, PA: Thomas Publications, 1993), 7–10.

17. OR, I, 14:377; OR, III, 2:152–53; Cornish, *Sable Arm*, 80.

18. OR, III, 5:654; Cornish, *Sable Arm*, 46–47.

19. Gladstone, *Men of Color*, 12.

20. OR, III, 2:436–37; Cornish, *Sable Arm*, 66; Trudeau, *Like Men of War*, 23–46; Gladstone, *Men of Color*, 12–13.

21. Lawrence Lee Hewitt, "An Ironic Route to Glory: Louisiana's Native Guards at Port Hudson," in John David Smith, ed., *Black Soldiers in Blue: African American Troops in the Civil War Era* (Chapel Hill: University of North Carolina Press, 2002), 78–106; Richard Lowe, "Battle on the Levee: The Fight at Milliken's Bend," in Smith, *Black Soldiers in Blue*, 78–106; Arthur W. Bergeron Jr., "The Battle of Olustee," in Smith, *Black Soldiers in Blue*, 136–49; Cornish, *Sable Arm*, 144–45; Trudeau, *Like Men of War*, 46–59.

22. Trudeau, *Like Men of War*, 276.

23. Edward G. Longacre, *Army of Amateurs: General Benjamin F. Butler and the Army of the James, 1863–1865* (Mechanicsburg, PA: Stackpole, 1997), 51, 243–44.

24. Ibid., xi; Trudeau, *Like Men of War*, 220–27, 284–300; William Glen Robertson, "From the Crater to New Market Heights: A Tale of Two Divisions," in Smith, *Black Soldiers in Blue*, 169–99.

25. OR, 1, 27, 2:211–12; "The Military Movement," *Philadelphia Public Ledger*, June 18, 1863; "The Military Movements," *Philadelphia Public Ledger*, June 19, 1863; "Parade of Colored Troops," *Philadelphia Public Ledger*, June 20, 1863; "Enthusiastic Meeting of Colored Men," *Philadelphia Press*, June 25, 1863; Russell F. Weigley, "Emergency Troops in the Gettysburg Campaign," *Pennsylvania History* 25 (1958): 39–57; Gladstone, *Men of Color*, 109; Frank H. Taylor, *Philadelphia in the Civil War, 1861–1865* (Philadelphia: The City, 1913), 188, 243, 351; Frederick M. Binder, "Pennsylvania Negro Regiments in the Civil War," *Journal of Negro History* 37 (1952): 386–88; James M. Paradis, *Strike the Blow for Freedom: The 6th United States Colored Infantry in the Civil War* (Shippensburg, PA: White Mane, 1998), 8–10; James M. Paradis, *African Americans and the Gettysburg Campaign* (Lanham, MD: Scarecrow, 2005), 36–38; Harry C. Silcox,

"Nineteenth Century Philadelphia Black Militant: Octavius V. Catto (1839–1871)," *Pennsylvania History* 44 (1977): 59–62; Wilbur S. Nye, *Here Come the Rebels!* (Baton Rouge: Louisiana State University Press, 1965), 224–25, 228, 232, 299, 339.

26. Louis F. Emilio, *A Brave Black Regiment: History of the Fifty-fourth Regiment of Massachusetts Volunteer Infantry* (Boston: Boston Book Company, 1894), 9; Paradis, *Strike the Blow for Freedom*, 5–6; Basler, *Collected Works of Lincoln*, 7:191.

27. Joseph T. Glatthaar, *Forged in Battle: The Civil War Alliance of Black Soldiers and White Officers* (New York: Free Press, 1990), 17; John McMurray, *Recollections of a Colored Troop* (Brookville, PA: Privately printed, 1916), 8.

28. Taylor, *Philadelphia in the Civil War*, 188–89; Basler, *Collected Works of Lincoln*, 7:11.

29. Basler, *Collected Works of Lincoln*, 6:149–50, 408–9.

30. Ibid., 7:282; 8:2.

31. G. T. Beauregard, "Four Days of Battle at Petersburg," in Robert Underwood Johnson and Clarence Clough Buel, eds., *Battles and Leaders of the Civil War*, 4 vols. (New York: Century Company, 1887–88), 4:540–44; William H. Powell, "The Battle of the Petersburg Crater," in Johnson and Buel, *Battles and Leaders of the Civil War*, 4:545–60; Charles H. Houghton, "In the Crater," in Johnson and Buel, *Battles and Leaders of the Civil War*, 4:561–62; Henry Goddard Thomas, "The Colored Troops at Petersburg," in Johnson and Buel, *Battles and Leaders of the Civil War*, 4:563–67; Ulysses S. Grant, *Personal Memoirs of Ulysses S. Grant*, 2 vols. (New York: Charles H. Webster, 1885–86), 2:292–98, 307–15; Cornish, *Sable Arm*, 272–78; Trudeau, *Like Men of War*, 220–51; *Report of the Committee on the Conduct of the War on Attack on Petersburg, on the 30th Day of July, 1864* (Washington, DC: U.S. Government Printing Office, 1865), 5; OR, I, 40, 1:17.

32. Allan Nevins, *The War for the Union*, 4 vols. (New York: Scribner, 1960), 2:520–22; *Journal of the Confederate Congress*, 3:386–87; Weigley, *Great Civil War*, 189; OR, I, 22:964–65; OR, II, 4:21–22, 945–46.

33. OR, I, 42, 2:959; OR, I, 42, 3:216–17; OR, II, 6:594–600; Nevins, *War for the Union*, 2:521–22; Benjamin F. Butler, *Autobiography and Personal Reminiscences of Major-General Benj. F. Butler: Butler's Book* (Boston: A. M. Thayler, 1892), 599–605; McMurray, *Recollections of a Colored Troop*, 46; Horace Montgomery, "A Union Officer's Recollections of the Negro As a Soldier," *Pennsylvania History* 28 (1961): 174–75; Brainerd Dyer, "The Treatment of Colored Troops by the Confederates, 1861–1865," *Journal of Negro History* 20 (1935): 273–86; Richard J. Sommers, "The Dutch Gap Affair: Military Atrocities and the Rights of Negro Soldiers," *Civil War History* 21 (1975): 51–64.

34. OR, I, 32, 3:395.

35. Gregory J. W. Urwin, "Warfare, Race, and the Civil War in American Memory," 1–18; Anne J. Bailey, "A Texas Cavalry Raid: Reaction to Black Soldiers and Contraband," 19–33; Howard C. Westwood, "Captive Black Union Soldiers in Charleston: What to Do?" 34–51; James G. Hollandsworth Jr., "The Execution of White Officers from Black Units by Confederate Forces during the Civil War," 52–64; David J. Coles, "'Shooting Niggers Sir': Confederate Mistreatment of Union Black Soldiers at the Bat-

tle of Olustee," 65–88; Gregory J. W. Urwin, "'We *Cannot* Treat Negroes . . . As Prisoners of War:' Racial Atrocities and Reprisals in Civil War Arkansas," 132–52; Weymouth T. Jordan Jr. and Gerald W. Thomas, "Massacre at Plymouth, April 20, 1864," 153–202; Bryce A. Suderow, "The Battle of the Crater: The Civil War's Worst Massacre," 203–9; all in Urwin, *Black Flag over Dixie*. For Fort Pillow, see Albert Castel, "The Fort Pillow Massacre: A Fresh Examination of the Evidence," *Civil War History* 4 (1958): 37–50; John Cimprich and Robert C. Mainfort Jr., "Fort Pillow Revisited: New Evidence about an Old Controversy," *Civil War History* 28 (1982): 293–306; Richard L. Fuchs, *An Unerring Fire: The Massacre at Fort Pillow* (Rutherford, NJ: Fairleigh Dickinson University Press, 1994), 57–139, 159–67; John Cimprich, "The Fort Pillow Massacre: Assessing the Evidence," in Smith, *Black Soldiers in Blue*, 150–68; Trudeau, *Like Men of War*, 156–69; and Glatthaar, *Forged in Battle*, 155–59.

36. Basler, *Collected Works of Lincoln*, 7:302–3, 328–29, 345–46.

37. Ibid., 345–46.

38. Ibid., 301–3.

39. OR, I, 32, 3:364; Cornish, *Sable Arm*, 177; Glatthaar, *Forged in Battle*, 157–58; Trudeau, *Like Men of War*, 46–47; Fuchs, *Unerring Fire*, 145–48; Mark Grimsley, "'A Very Long Shadow:' Race Atrocity and the American Civil War," in Urwin, *Black Flag over Dixie*, 231–46.

2
"The Great Question of the Campaign Was One of Supplies"
A Reinterpretation of Sherman's Generalship during the 1864 March to Atlanta in Light of the Logistic Strategy

J. Britt McCarley

Supplies are the great question.
Sherman to Grant, April 24, 1864

The Atlanta Campaign would simply have been impossible without the use of the railroads from Louisville ... to Atlanta.
Sherman, Memoirs

That single stem of railroad, four hundred and seventy-three miles long, supplied an army of one hundred thousand men and thirty-five thousand animals ... from May 1 to November 12, 1864.
Sherman, Memoirs

I doubt if ever an army was better supplied than this.
Sherman, Campaign Report, September 15, 1864

YANKEE MAJOR GENERAL WILLIAM TECUMSEH ("Cump") Sherman of the Union Army harbored no doubts regarding his feats of generalship and logistics—in him the two were inextricably interwoven—during the 1864 Atlanta Campaign. Commentators since, including historians, have often battled with one another concerning the matter. A review of the significant historical literature on the subject serves as a starting point to bring this Sherman debate, one among many, back to the general's position that the combination of supply and leadership can go far toward achieving decisive results in a military campaign if not in the many—usually indecisive—battlefield collisions of arms that constitute it.

There was a time when the 1864 Atlanta Campaign was underrepresented in American Civil War scholarship and therefore underappreciated for its pivotal role in the conflict. That time has passed. After the 1882 publication of Jacob D. Cox's pro-Sherman *Atlanta* as part of Scribner's Campaigns of the Civil War series, no modern analytical, book-length, scholarly studies on the entire campaign appeared until the completion of two doctoral dissertations directed by Emory University's esteemed Bell Irvin Wiley. Neither dissertation was overly critical of Sherman: Richard M. McMurry's "The Atlanta Campaign, December 23, 1863 to July 18, 1864" (1967) or Errol M. Clauss's "The Atlanta Campaign, 18 July– 2 September 1864" (1965). Among published works, next came James Lee McDonough and James Pickett Jones's *War So Terrible: Sherman and Atlanta* (1987), which, like Cox's study before it, was favorable toward Sherman's generalship. Since the 1992 release of Albert E. Castel's *Decision in the West: The Atlanta Campaign of 1864*, however, scholars largely have taken either a negative or a neutral position on Sherman in the campaign. In order of publication, these studies are: Lee B. Kennett's *Marching through Georgia: The Story of Soldiers and Civilians During Sherman's Campaign* (1995), Richard M. McMurry's *Atlanta 1864: Last Chance for the Confederacy* (2000), and Stephen E. Davis's *Atlanta Will Fall: Sherman, Joe Johnston, and the Yankee Heavy Battalions* (2001). The much more numerous biographies of Sherman are, overall, no less critical of his generalship, and some even demonize him.[1]

Whether portrayed in positive, neutral, or negative terms, Sherman was, and is, the central character in the campaign. Forces under his command seized and held the initiative during the four months of marching and fighting that led to the fall of the vital city of Atlanta. Its capture boosted flagging Northern morale during that summer of great sacrifice and contributed substantially to President Abraham Lincoln's bid for reelection that fall. Lincoln's return to the White House meant that the North would prosecute the war unto the destruction of both the Southern Confederacy and the institution of chattel slavery. No less than nineteenth-century American-style social revolution and total war were in the bargain, and Sherman's success during the march to Atlanta helped make them reality. Yet the revisionist historians, especially Castel, McMurry, and Davis, claim that Sherman's conduct of operations in the Atlanta Campaign has been overrated and that Sherman as a soldier during the summer of 1864 has been oversold. To them Sherman was a less capable commander in North Georgia than had earlier been the accepted wisdom. They assert that his success during the campaign resulted from operating against such lackluster Confederate commanders as Joseph E. Johnston and John Bell Hood. The most recent contributions to the literature frequently strain to make a less-than-satisfactory point and often miss the mark regarding the summer triumph of Union arms. They appear to argue against the preponderance of good evidence to maintain that Sherman won primarily because his competition was inept.

While it is true that Johnston and Hood were not among the Confederacy's finest generals, Sherman nonetheless achieved much in his campaign for Atlanta. The march was especially well planned and executed. The Federals confronted and solved many operational puzzles. Not only did they operate, maintain, and repair an extensive railroad network to sustain the campaign, they also overcame problems posed by the region's geography and weather. All of this was no mean feat and cannot be explained by underrating the quality of Confederate leadership or devaluing Sherman's generalship. Finally, the Rebel Army of Tennessee was initially capably led at the corps and lower levels of command, and its veteran soldiers fought well and hard throughout the summer of 1864. Thus it is time for a more balanced corrective to the predominantly anti-Sherman character of recent Atlanta Campaign scholarship and time as well to place the pendulum of historical interpretation more toward a central position, somewhere between adoration and vilification.[2]

Sherman was an impressive sight, even allowing for posturing before the still new-fangled camera. Forty-four years old in the spring of 1864, he was tall and lean and had a thatch of unruly reddish hair and whiskers, the last looking more like glorified stubble than beard. His drawn, wrinkled brow and straight-set mouth bespoke determination and confidence but belied his normally agitated state. His overactive mind led him to talk constantly about a wide variety of subjects, not all of them military, and he waved his arms about as he spoke, scattering ashes from his ever-present cigar. Sherman's abundant energy determined his work habits. He slept little at night, relying more on catnaps to refresh him during the day. While awake he spent his time personally supervising his command and writing, always writing, often late into the night by the light of lamp or campfire to his wife, brother, and colleagues in arms. Although a major general of volunteers, Sherman did not usually dress like a general officer. He preferred the common soldier's sack coat and the civilian's black felt hat. His ceaseless activity and unpretentious dress led a commentator to note that he looked "rather like an anxious man of business than an ideal soldier, suggesting the exchange and not the camp." American poet Walt Whitman, noticing Sherman's untamed features more than his other traits, described him as a "bit of stern, open air made up in the image of a man." Another observer, seeing the whole Sherman and pondering how perhaps he mirrored the character of the Northern states generally, remarked that he was "the quintessence of Yankeedom." This was the Sherman of 1864.[3]

Earlier in the Civil War, Sherman had been anything but impressive. After undistinguished years as an army officer, businessman, attorney, and educator, he secured a colonelcy in the regulars at the outbreak of the war. More capably than most of his peers, he commanded an infantry brigade at First Bull Run, where, in his baptism by fire, his command suffered more casualties than all but one other brigade. Through family political connections, he was soon promoted to brigadier general of volunteers and obtained a transfer to Kentucky to take part in early efforts to keep the Bluegrass State in the Union fold. After reluctantly assuming command of that endeavor when his superior resigned, Sherman became frustrated and depressed over the many problems besetting his command. He made the mistake of venting his frustrations and revealing his volatile temperament to War Department officials, who concluded that he was "luny" and consequently arranged his transfer to Missouri. There, as well, the stress of command proved too much for Sherman to handle. Beset by these troubles, he took leave, joined his wife who had come to meet him, and returned with her to their home in Lancaster, Ohio. Seizing the opportunity to increase circulation and strike back at a general who was openly antipress, a Cincinnati newspaper ran an article labeling Sherman as "insane" and "stark mad." Other newspapers picked up the theme. The general's family fought back, though not with much initial success.[4]

Fortunately for Sherman, his former commander, Major General Henry W. Halleck, rejected the insanity charge and remained faithful to him. Halleck posted him to training recruits shortly after he returned to active duty in early 1862, even though Sherman had not fully recovered. Assigned command initially of an infantry division, he served under the victorious Major General Ulysses S. Grant in the Shiloh, Vicksburg, and Chattanooga campaigns. During those operations Sherman rehabilitated his damaged reputation; regained his self-confidence; obtained a major generalcy of volunteers; rose to command a division, then a corps, and finally an army; and along the way became Grant's most trusted subordinate and closest military friend. Grant's trust and confidence in Sherman were implicit. The two men had also become personal friends, transcending their official roles as commander and subordinate. As Grant's star rose, so rose Sherman's.[5]

As the winter chill of 1863–64 faded into spring warmth, Sherman's life and career as a soldier reached a milestone. In March 1864, Lincoln promoted Grant to the long-vacant grade of lieutenant general and appointed him general-in-chief of all the United States armies, giving him direction over the land war against the Confederacy. Before departing for the East, Grant named Sherman commanding general of the Military Division of the Mississippi, the primary command in the West, which eventually encompassed the departments and armies of the Tennessee, the Cumberland, the Ohio, and Arkansas, commanded, respectively, by Major Generals James B. McPherson, George H. Thomas, John M. Schofield, and Frederick Steele. At a meeting between Grant and Sherman in Cincinnati, Ohio, in mid-March, the two great western leaders discussed grand strategy for the coming campaign season. Grant's strategic design was for all the Federal armies simultaneously to assault the Confederacy across the entire war front, east and west. The previous Rebel advantage of using interior lines to shift troops to threatened points to parry uncoordinated Union thrusts—most conspicuously exercised in 1863 with troop movements by rail from Virginia to Georgia that culminated in the September Confederate victory at Chickamauga—would be nullified, and Southern armies, already lean in manpower, would be destroyed or at least neutralized in a final campaign of annihilation.[6]

When the generals parted company, Sherman traveled back to Nashville, Tennessee, to begin six weeks of preparing his armies. Using a special railroad car, beginning in late March he inspected his command. On his way through southeastern Tennessee and northeastern Alabama, he consulted his army commanders and determined the matériel resources each would need to take the field by early May. After conferring with his subordinates, Sherman concluded that "the great question of the [coming] campaign was one of supplies."[7] Understanding the magnitude of the logistical problem facing him and realizing the need for personal intervention, Sherman assumed personal direction of the railroads. They were his principal means of supply and communication, stretching along nearly one thousand miles of track from his base of operations on the Ohio River in Louisville, Kentucky; south to his chief depot in Nashville, Tennessee; and farther south to his forward depot in Chattanooga, Tennessee. Of the several railroads in the theater of operations, none was more important than the Western and Atlantic (W&A) Railroad. Its roughly one hundred miles of track, completed in the 1850s and the property of the State of Georgia, linked Chattanooga with Atlanta. The W&A supplied both Sherman and his Confederate opponents, the former from the north out of Chattanooga and the latter from the south out of Atlanta.

Initially the railroads were Sherman's greatest worry. He found the few available boxcars and flatcars crowded with soldiers, animals, unnecessary cargo, and unneeded and unwanted civilians. He directed that henceforth only ammunition, food, and other essential military supplies were allowed aboard the trains. All returning troops would walk to their units, along the way often herding cattle headed for the armies. Sherman found that the exhausted condition of the countryside had forced his commanders to issue army rations to local inhabitants or risk seeing them starve. He suspended rations to civilians, who raised a howl but managed to survive on their own. Through these reforms Sherman intended to accumulate enough supplies forward, especially at Chattanooga, to be ready for Grant's signal to begin the campaign. Even these severe measures, however, ultimately failed.

To better achieve his end of gathering enough logistical wherewithal to start the campaign, Sherman met in Nashville with his master of transportation, chief quartermaster, and chief commissary. After Sherman revealed that he would march with about one hundred thousand men and sixty thousand animals, the group concluded that 130 railroad cars, each carrying ten tons, would have to arrive daily in Chattanooga for supplies to accumulate. When the chief quartermaster explained that he did not have enough railroad engines and cars, Sherman immediately authorized him to hold in Louisville and Nashville all incoming rolling stock needed to finish the job. Before the campaign to Atlanta was over, cars and engines bearing the name of many Northern railroad companies operated along the tracks from Louisville to the Union front line. Special detachments of the U.S. Military Railroad Construction Corps, quartered along trunk lines and abundantly supplied with crossties, spikes, bridge timbers, and rails to repair breaks as quickly as possible, safeguarded the Federal railroad supply lines against disruption.

Sherman's occasionally heavy-handed methods worked. Depot warehouses bulged even before the campaign began. Those at Chattanooga alone contained enough supplies by early May to sustain Sherman's bluecoats for one month without resupply. Such enormous accumulations of food, ammunition, and clothing protected the Federals from the ever-present danger of having their iron lifelines cut by Rebel cavalry raiders or guerrilla units, the latter being especially abundant in the country that the Union railroads traversed. Regarding the military's seizure and use of private property, Sherman later acknowledged that "as much as to any other single fact, I attribute [to this policy] the perfect success which afterward attended our campaigns."[8] Allowing for pride in accomplishment and some hyperbole, the logistical record of the campaign supports his assertion.

Despite the positive results of his railroad reforms, Sherman remained unsatisfied. He was concerned especially with ensuring the mobility of combat troops. He had been in the field enough to know that the North's ability to outproduce the South in industrial goods had its disadvantages. Chief among these was the tendency for Union armies to be too heavily encumbered with impedimenta to capitalize on advantages achieved on the march or the battlefield. To counter this tendency, he severely limited the amount of baggage allotted to individuals or units. Junior officers and enlisted soldiers carried a heavy load: enough food and clothing to last five days in addition to their usual equipment. By effectively turning men into mules, Sherman intended to reduce extraneous field transportation. Company officers were allowed one pack horse or mule, and each regiment was authorized one wagon and one ambulance. Every brigade and division was permitted a supply train, but its wagons were limited to hauling food, ammunition, and uniforms. Only headquarters personnel and the wounded were allowed large tents.

While Sherman acknowledged that he could not completely enforce the orders concerning small-unit transportation and camp equipage, he set an example for his men. He and his headquarters staff traveled especially light, relying only on wall-tent flies for cover and no camp furniture. Major General Thomas, a long-serving and robust Regular Army officer, made no effort to curtail the excess tentage in his headquarters, which Sherman snidely referred to as "Thomas's Circus." Because Thomas was one of his trusted lieutenants, Sherman did not confront him on the issue. Referring to his efforts to strip his armies for action, Sherman wrote: "My entire headquarters transportation is one wagon for myself, aides, officers, clerks, and orderlies. I think this is as low down as we can get until we get flat broke, and thenceforward things will begin to mend. Soldiering as we have been doing for the past two years, with such trains and impediments, has been a farce, and nothing but poverty will cure it." As May arrived with warmer and longer days, Sherman's time for preparation drew to a close. Deficiencies remained in his command, mainly the nagging lack of horses in his cavalry units and the absence of the XVII Army Corps, two of whose four divisions were serving in the misguided Red River Campaign while the others were on veteran leave and unavailable for frontline duty for weeks to come. Overall, though, Sherman's reforms had succeeded. His armies now mirrored Sherman himself in appearance and temperament. Like him, they were lean and active and were eagerly awaiting the signal from the East to begin the campaign.[9]

For a month Sherman had known Grant's overarching intent for the blue columns slated for the 1864 marches. Grant's direction had come in an April 4 letter: "You I propose to move against Johnston's army, to break it up, and to get into the interior of the enemy's country as far as you can, inflicting all the damage you can against their war resources. I do not propose to lay down for you a plan of campaign, but simply to lay down the work it is desirable to have done, and leave you free to execute it in your own way." In an April 19 letter, Grant added that both he and Sherman should keep the enemy in their front constantly engaged so the Confederates could not use interior lines to concentrate against and possibly defeat one of the Union's main efforts. This is virtually all the guidance Grant gave Sherman for his march to Atlanta.[10]

British military historian John Keegan has praised Grant for writing clear and concise orders, which he seems to have done on this occasion as well. Grant's April 4 letter in effect instructed Sherman to pursue two strategies at once: a combat strategy and a logistic strategy. The former strategy aims to defeat an enemy principally through maneuver and battle. Victory on the battlefield can occur in one climactic, annihilative, incapacitating engagement or by degrees through attrition. The latter strategy focuses primarily on denying an enemy the logistical means to resist, which can also be achieved by marching and fighting. Sherman's earlier command experience amply proved that he was no battle captain. At First Bull Run he had committed his large brigade piecemeal, which may have cost the Federals one of their best opportunities to capture the key position of Henry Hill, win the war's first true battle, and possibly destroy the Southern rebellion at the outset.

Under Grant's command, at Shiloh in April 1862 Sherman failed to heed warnings of an impending Confederate assault and prepare his division for battle. At the beginning of the long Vicksburg Campaign, in late 1862, his attack at Chickasaw Bluffs was ill-advised and accordingly failed. Outside Chattanooga in November 1863, he mishandled an attempt to take a tactically significant stretch of Missionary Ridge. Sherman could not solely pursue a combat strategy; he lacked the battlefield talent to make it work. Grant's Atlanta Campaign instructions, however, were flexible, which may have been the result of his understanding of Sherman's tactical shortcomings. It remained to be seen whether Sherman possessed the martial acumen to plan and conduct a campaign that entailed moving, sustaining, and engaging corps and armies.

The primary objective of Grant's grand strategy was destroying the Southern armies, the Confederacy's center of gravity. Another target was the Rebel will to resist, encompassed in the ability and commitment of Southern civilians to assist in the war effort. At least since he commanded the Union garrison at Memphis, Tennessee, in March 1862, Sherman had believed that destroying the South's civilian-based war resources—a phenomenon known as hard war—would strike a double blow, crippling both Confederate military forces and civilian morale, from the totality of which the rebellious states could not recover. Grant thought likewise; the second part of his April 4 directions therefore allowed Sherman to exercise his own judgment about which course of action to follow. In responses to Grant dated April 10 and 24, Sherman indicated that he would send McPherson's army to operate toward Rome, Georgia, beyond the left of General Johnston's roughly fifty thousand-man Army of Tennessee, dug in along Rocky Face Ridge north and east of the railroad junction at Dalton. Sherman intended to threaten the W&A, Johnston's primary line of communication running south to Atlanta. Sherman mentioned in these same letters that crossing the Chattahoochee River, northwest of Atlanta, and moving directly against the city also would form part of his campaign.

Beyond these sketchy details of a logistic strategy aimed at the Confederate railroad and base of operations, Sherman did not reveal how he planned to fulfill his mission. Would he first employ a combat strategy by seeking a decisive set-piece battle with Johnston and then march triumphantly and unopposed to Atlanta? Or would he sidestep Johnston, reach toward the rich logistical treasures of Atlanta's railroads and factories, and force the Rebel commander to fight a decisive engagement for the Confederate lines of communication? If Sherman chose the latter course, how would he guard his own vulnerable lifeline, stretching all the way to Louisville? Considering his tactical ineptitude, perhaps Sherman could pursue only the latter part of his orders, a logistic strategy, as his likeliest path to victory.[11]

In early May 1864, the synchronized Union campaigns against the Confederacy began. As the two parts of the main effort, Grant entered the tangled Wilderness of northern Virginia on May 5, and Sherman approached the bastion of Rocky Face Ridge on May 7. At Rocky Face, Johnston awaited the Federal assault in positions whose strength more than compensated for his nearly two-to-one numerical disadvantage. The disparity—about one hundred thousand Federals opposed by some fifty thousand Confederates—was not decisively large. In offensive operations against a capable and well-led foe fighting from improved positions on advantageous ground, an attacking force generally will require a three-to-one margin in manpower to have a reasonable chance of winning. Johnston had had months to perfect his positions around Dalton.

In keeping with his own deficiencies as a battle captain, Sherman elected to hold the Rebels in front with Thomas's and Schofield's armies. He sent his old Army of the Tennessee, now under McPherson, south as his flying column through unguarded Snake Creek Gap with orders to tear up the W&A in Johnston's rear. This might force the Confederates to withdraw rather than be separated from Atlanta's warehouses. After being reinforced by Thomas, McPherson was to pounce on the Southerners' flank as they retreated. McPherson therefore was to execute a wide turning movement, a tactic that sought, often by threatening enemy communication lines, to maneuver a defender from prepared positions for a fight in the open field. Envelopment, by contrast, looked to sweep closely around an opponent's flank and pry him out of position through battle from a more favorable angle than a frontal assault. Turning movements, as executed by Sherman throughout the march to Atlanta, were a holdover from the old Napoleonic *la manoeuvre sur les derrières.*

In one of the Civil War's most famous lost opportunities, however, McPherson hesitated when his vanguard encountered unexpected resistance on May 9 at Resaca on the railroad east of Snake Creek Gap's opening onto the Oostanaula River valley. Johnston retreated to preserve his supply line. McPherson's detractors have claimed that he timidly approached the railroad and too quickly withdrew into the gap when he discovered a brigade of reinforcing Confederate cavalry. Nearly a full Rebel infantry corps of around fifteen thousand reinforcements was a little farther south, of which McPherson was ignorant, so his caution may be interpreted as prudent. The enduring significance of the Snake Creek Gap–Resaca maneuver—however much it might have been a missed opportunity—is that Sherman, the logistic strategist, set his course for one of the best examples in military history of striking the enemy's line of communication in a series of turning movements at the operational level as the surest way to win rather than hammering his front line at the tactical level. In short, Sherman had seized and would continue to hold the initiative by fixing the Confederates in place with frontal pressure (rather than a head-on assault) and then flanking the enemy's position, a method and routine he followed during the entire course of the Atlanta Campaign. In the May 14–15 Battle of Resaca, Sherman also initiated the combat strategy of the campaign. However, costly Federal attacks succeeded only in drawing Southern attention from Union attempts to cross the Oostanaula farther downstream. After the engagement, Sherman returned to the logistic strategy and constructed a pontoon bridge downriver at Lay's Ferry, threatening the Confederate rail line.[12]

Johnston, his communications threatened again, withdrew across the Oostanaula and continued south beyond Gravelly Plateau, eventually reaching Cassville, where confusion and dissension among his corps commanders led him to retreat over the Etowah River and by May 20 to occupy well-fortified positions in the Allatoona Mountains. These positions centered on Allatoona Pass, overlooking the narrow floodplain of the Etowah and protecting the railroad to Atlanta. Unwilling to conduct a river crossing under fire and frontally assault strong earthworks, Sherman elected again to turn Johnston's position. Following several days of repairing the railroad up to his position and resting and resupplying his troops, Sherman began his southward march afresh. With ten days' supplies in their wagons, the bluecoats crossed the Etowah at numerous points downstream near Kingston and entered tangled forests the likes of which the Federals had not seen in this campaign. Sherman's immediate objective was the crossroads of Dallas, about twenty miles to the southwest. Johnston discovered the move and established his army in a blocking position generally behind Pumpkinvine Creek, east of Dallas, and north to New Hope Church. Along this line for a week, Northerners and Southerners clashed in a series of chaotic engagements, with the fiercest at New Hope Church on May 25 and two days later at Pickett's Mill. These were the Atlanta Campaign's equivalent to the confusion—but not the slaughter—of Virginia's Battles of the Wilderness and Spotsylvania. Although Sherman unwisely employed the combat strategy twice in the Dallas area and failed, he did not persist, for his own line was stretched thin with a gap vulnerable to Confederate counterattack near the Pickett's Mill positions.

As the availability of rations in Sherman's ranks diminished due to the onset of heavy rains and consequent supply transportation problems, he conducted a gradual leftward extension until he approached the railroad south of the fortified lines at Allatoona. As the Yankees conducted this retrograde operation, Johnston attacked Sherman for the first time in the campaign, albeit on a small scale, at Dallas on May 28. Although the indecisive fighting did not significantly alter the course of events, it did indicate that Johnston was beginning to move himself, or be moved by pressure from the Confederate government, more toward committing the Army of Tennessee to pitched battle, perhaps even one with decisive possibilities. For the time being, however, Johnston had no choice but to withdraw again, this time to the vicinity of Big Shanty along the W&A north of Kennesaw

Mountain, with his right attached to the railroad at Brush Mountain and his left anchored on Lost Mountain, ten miles to the southwest. Even considering the recent reinforcement of Johnston's army to around seventy thousand with the assimilation of two infantry divisions from the Army of Mississippi, this line was still too long for the combined Rebel forces to defend. Although it inflicted much hardship on his common soldiers, Sherman had applied his logistic strategy to lever Johnston out of an impregnable position at Allatoona Pass. Through the first half of June, as Sherman pressured new Southern positions and as Johnston steadily withdrew to shorter and more easily defended lines anchored on mountains, torrential rains came and altered the campaign's character for several weeks.[13]

On the night of June 18–19, Johnston slipped into the six miles of fortified works about the twin peaks of Kennesaw Mountain, a still shorter and much more easily defended line. For two weeks already the rains had fallen, rendering into quagmires the primitive roads that Sherman's quartermasters used to haul supplies to the front lines. Muddy and seemingly bottomless roads not only slowed supply wagons but, more critically, prevented blue-coated flanking columns from turning Johnston's left to threaten the W&A behind Rebel lines. Sherman worried lest inactivity in his armies give Johnston an opportunity to unleash the Southern cavalry against the Yankee railroad. During the campaign, Johnston repeatedly importuned the Confederate government to launch a large and determined mounted raid on Sherman's supply lines but to no avail. To keep his adversary busy and away from endangering his own line of communication, Sherman sent his rain-soaked troops to probe Johnston's entire front. The effort against the Southern left ended in stalemate in the Kolb Farm fight on June 22. Again Johnston's forces lashed out at their Union adversaries, sustaining more casualties but halting Sherman's probing activities for the moment.

On that day the weather began clearing, but it took several more days for the roads to harden enough for Sherman to again employ McPherson's flying column. During these first warm and dry days in weeks, as Schofield's army extended the Union right and forced Johnston to thin the Southern line to parallel the Federal fieldworks, Sherman decided to change his customary stratagem. During the last few days, he had become frustrated, irritable, and impatient over the slowed pace of operations and was also concerned about the apparent recent Confederate turn more toward the tactical offensive. In discussions with his lieutenants, he concluded—although Thomas disagreed—that since he had stretched his lines as far as he could, the Confederates must have weakened theirs to match him. If he strongly assaulted the Rebel center at two points, Sherman continued, he might achieve a surprise breakthrough and hold one half of Johnston's army in check while he defeated the other half with the bulk of the Union forces and threatened the railroad to Atlanta at the same time. It was an ambitious plan. A Southern loss could be decisive. Also motivating Sherman was his belief that Union troops had become too dependent on flanking marches and that a stand-up fight would remind them what war and this campaign were about. On June 24, the Yankee chieftain issued his attack orders.

Early on the morning of June 27, the day of the assault, Federal artillery bombarded the Confederate line, and bluecoat infantry began uphill charges against brown-clad foes well protected by trenches and little damaged by the barrage. For several hours fighting continued near Thomas's center at Dead Angle and along McPherson's front upon the slopes of Big and Little Kennesaw and adjoining Pigeon Hill. Nowhere along the Southern line did Northerners breach the main defenses, and in the failed effort about three thousand Federals were killed or wounded, compared to Confederate losses of about seven hundred. It was the Atlanta Campaign's closest equivalent to the quick and bloody early June Battle of Cold Harbor in Virginia.

Although Sherman eventually accepted responsibility for the sanguinary repulse at Kennesaw, he rationalized his failure. In deciding to assault Johnston frontally, he overruled objections from two of his three army commanders. On the surface, Sherman's decision seems senseless. Did he not comprehend the effect of combining rifled weaponry and trenches and the resulting ascendancy of the defense, especially considering that by this time he knew the relative cost to the Federal forces of the frontal assaults in the Wilderness and at Spotsylvania and Cold Harbor? Quite the contrary was the case. Although no paragon of military professionalism by prewar standards, Sherman understood the realities of the Civil War battlefield; ignorance cannot explain his Kennesaw debacle. Rather, it was his frustration and impatience over the stalemated situation in the trenches since June 19 that accounted for Sherman's failure eight days later. He also thought of the two times recently when the Confederates had attacked his formations and intended through a direct Union assault to foil Johnston's apparent decision to go over to the attack if circumstances warranted. The Yankee leader's increasingly unpleasant mood during the siegelike operations along the Kennesaw line overcame his good sense. Moreover, Sherman at Kennesaw, like Lee at Gettysburg the year before, believed that the enemy had strengthened his flanks at the expense of his center, which appeared to be vulnerable to direct assault. Events proved both leaders to be wrong. Frontal assaults against foes entrenched or occupying advantageous ground were nearly impossible as a means of triumph. If it ever existed, the age of decisive war-winning victories reached on single battlefields in as little as one day had passed.

At Kennesaw, Sherman resorted to a combat strategy like the one suggested in the first part of Grant's April 4 instructions. Similar to Resaca the month before, Sherman failed to break up Johnston's army. Sherman proved again that he was no battle captain. Later, however, he demonstrated a quality not shared by every Civil War general. Sherman learned from Kennesaw that direct charges on field fortifications were too costly, and he did not repeat this scenario except when at least tactical victory seemed assured. After all, he had experienced firsthand at First Bull Run the price to be paid for a frontal assault, and after being reminded of it three years later he did not want to pay that butcher's bill again.

Now his fretful mind turned back to his old flanking game. During the June 27 attacks, portions of Schofield's army moved past Johnston's left and got into position to threaten the W&A railroad. After Sherman consulted his army commanders and accumulated enough supplies to quit his railroad for several days, he withdrew McPherson's troops from the left and sent them on the night of July 2 far to the right, beyond the area Schofield had seized. Johnston discovered the move, gave up the heights of Kennesaw, and began racing for the Chattahoochee River, the last water barrier before Atlanta. The Rebel chieftain won the race, and his weary columns, after briefly resisting at Smyrna Station and Ruff's Mill, occupied a seemingly impenetrable line along Nickajack Creek on the north bank of the Chattahoochee. Sherman was ignorant of the line's existence, and he did not expect Johnston to defend again, as he had done at Resaca, with a major river directly in the rear of the Southern line. Considering his army's recent past, Sherman refused to launch a major assault against the Nickajack defenses. Instead he looked to his flanking ploy, but rather than throwing his accustomed right hook he planned one from the left side.

On July 8, Schofield's troops conducted a surprise river crossing of the rain-swollen Chattahoochee beyond the Federal left near the mouth of Soap Creek. Union cavalry seized unguarded river passages farther upstream at Roswell the next day. The movements to gain the south bank of the Chattahoochee cost Sherman no casualties, rare in a war whose glacial progress too often was measured in killed and wounded. With the security of his river line compromised, Johnston fell back to the south bank, burning all his bridges. For most of the next week, the rest of the Union army crossed the Chattahoochee, fortified the Atlanta side of the river, and prepared for the decisive engagements to seize the Gate City of the South.[14]

Just before his columns crossed the Chattahoochee, Sherman, in one of his nearly daily telegraph reports to Army Chief of Staff Halleck in Washington, foreshadowed his next moves against Atlanta. "All the regular crossing-places are covered by forts, apparently of long construction; but we shall cross in due time, and instead of attacking Atlanta direct, or any of its forts," Sherman wrote, "I propose to make a circuit, destroying all its railroads. This is a delicate movement and must be done with caution."[15] At last on Atlanta's doorstep, he did not plan to batter his way into the city. He had learned the lesson of Kennesaw and intended to adhere to the logistic strategy. Following rest and resupply, on July 17 Sherman's three armies began a general advance in the form of a giant right wheel with Decatur, six miles east of Atlanta, and the Georgia Railroad as the immediate objectives.

The same day, Confederate President Jefferson Davis, exasperated by Johnston's ceaseless withdrawals and never-ending excuses for them, replaced him with one of his corps commanders, Lieutenant General John Bell Hood, who had been scheming for the job for months through connections in the Richmond government. Johnston had yielded territory and failed to bring Sherman to a decisive engagement. Hood, always eager to fight, had no choice but to attack. Johnston's conduct of the campaign left no other viable options, and Davis had fired Johnston for not quickly attacking to save Atlanta once the campaign moved south of the Chattahoochee. Despite his battle-shattered and impaired body, the result of wounds received in 1863 at Gettysburg and Chickamauga, Hood was promoted on July 18 to the temporary grade of general to exercise army command. Sherman soon got word of the change in Southern leadership. Not knowing Hood himself, he consulted two of Hood's West Point classmates, McPherson and Schofield, who informed Sherman of Hood's nature. Sherman later wrote that he "inferred that the change of commanders meant 'fight.'"[16]

By July 20, McPherson had reached the Georgia Railroad at Decatur, and his troops began tearing up track on both sides of the town, the purpose of which was to eliminate the possibility of Hood's reinforcing Lee in Virginia by rail or the reverse in Georgia. That day, Hood launched the first of his sorties from Atlanta's encircling fortifications. North of the city, he intended to envelop the Union left in the vicinity of Peachtree Creek, drive the bluecoats away, and destroy them. Starting now, Hood sought decisive battle. At the least, he wanted to prevent the Yankees from wrapping their infantry columns completely around the citadel of Atlanta, breaking all of its sustaining railroads, and forcing the defenders to withdraw, surrender, or in their entirety march out into the open and fight a set-piece battle with the larger Federal forces for possession of the city. The Battle of Peachtree Creek should have put Sherman on his guard. He knew what Confederate tactics would be, yet he relaxed his vigil during the next maneuvers.[17]

The following day, Sherman instructed McPherson to send his XVI Army Corps, which had been forced out of formation as the Union lines shortened upon approaching Atlanta, to the Georgia Railroad east of the city to finish destroying the track. Sherman alerted McPherson to be ready to shift his army west of Atlanta to wreck the Macon and Western (M&W) Railroad, the last supply artery of any consequence serving the city. On July 22, Sherman sent Brigadier General Kenner Garrard's cavalry division, which had been guarding the Union left, on a raid east of Decatur to Covington to further ruin the Georgia Railroad. Although Sherman received warning that the Confederates might attack, he had become lost in planning his next wheel against the M&W and did not place troops to guard McPherson's now open left flank. Moreover, by his own admission he was deceived into thinking that the Confederate withdrawal on July 22, actually part of Hood's plan for the next battle, meant that Hood was evacuating

Atlanta. Fortunately, McPherson himself took precautions. Before receiving Sherman's instructions regarding the XVI Corps, McPherson had the foresight to move that corps to cover the Federal left.

Late on the morning of July 22, Sherman and McPherson stood before the Augustus Hurt (or Howard) House, north of the Georgia Railroad on an eminence called Copenhill and in the immediate rear of the Union front line, considering Hood's combative nature, the near certainty that he would attack again, and the resulting need now more than ever for caution to characterize the Federal approach to Atlanta. The two Northern commanders were also discussing bombarding the city from lofty Bald Hill, which McPherson's troops had seized the day before. About that time reports arrived revealing Confederate movement beyond the Union left. Straightaway, McPherson and his staff took to their mounts and rode off in that direction. Soon Sherman heard firing from the area of McPherson's left, and shortly the same sound came from McPherson's distant rear near Decatur, where the Army of the Tennessee's supply trains had gathered. So began the Battle of Bald Hill or, popularly and inaccurately, the Battle of Atlanta. Again Hood had sortied from the city. He sent a portion of his army on a long nighttime march and was striking the Federal left, which McPherson earlier had tried to protect. In an enveloping march that Hood himself likened after the war to a similar one by Lieutenant General Thomas J. "Stonewall" Jackson in 1863 at Chancellorsville, Virginia, Hood aimed to strike the left flank and rear of McPherson's army, roll up the entire Yankee line, and drive Sherman away from Atlanta. Hood also sent a large cavalry force to Decatur to destroy McPherson's supply wagons. Although both elegant and ambitious, Hood's plan nonetheless failed partly because the several Southern thrusts that day were unsynchronized, thus giving the Northerners time to parry each one in turn. Confederate infantry killed McPherson early in the battle as he rode toward his endangered flank, but his men held their ground and repelled all of Hood's assaults. At day's end, the largest and costliest battle of the Atlanta Campaign had ended. Rebel losses overall amounted to fifty-five hundred, Union casualties to about four thousand. Hood was living up to his reputation as a fighter, but to no avail. Sherman's armies remained on Atlanta's doorstep.

Despite Northern victory in the Battle of Bald Hill, Sherman's part in the action was disappointing. He mismanaged the defense of his armies' left, proving again that he was no battle captain. Furthermore, he became so engrossed in his mental calculations for the next grand wheeling movement that he failed to learn the lesson of Peachtree Creek or heed his lieutenants' warning about Hood's fighting instincts. Sherman was simply lucky that McPherson had placed the XVI Corps in what proved to be the actual battle line before orders arrived directing it back to the Georgia Railroad. The Yankee chieftain was fortunate also that McPherson convinced him to keep the XVI Corps right where it was, for that unit prevented the Unionists from being struck fully in the rear. Moreover, the absence of Garrard's cavalry deprived Sherman of eyes with which to watch the Federal left, eyes that surely would have spotted danger before it turned into a surprise attack. Sherman's mental detachment on the eve of Bald Hill seemed to confirm one of the early criticisms leveled at him during the time that reporters had called him crazy. Because of his gross exaggerations in 1861 of Confederate strength in Kentucky, journalists had labeled him a visionary, and his intellectual wanderings prior to Hood's second sally from Atlanta's defenses tended to validate that charge. If Sherman was a visionary, however, he was at least a skillful one. Now he envisioned a march culminating his logistic strategy by severing the M&W. Two days after Bald Hill, a message from Grant warned of the possibility that reinforcements were on their way to Hood from General Lee, the latter then confronting the Yankee besiegers of Petersburg, Virginia. Sherman scrapped his plan to rest the armies and dispatched them at once to the west side of Atlanta to begin the great left wheel.

The Army of the Tennessee led the way under Major General Oliver O. Howard, whom Sherman, with Grant in approval, had appointed to replace the fallen McPherson. Howard's promotion to army command occasioned great controversy among Sherman's lieutenants, none more than Major General Joseph Hooker, the XX Army Corps commander, who maintained that because his date of rank made him the most senior officer present (except for Sherman) and because he had commanded the Army of the Potomac the year before, he should receive McPherson's command. Sherman concluded, however, that the one-armed, pious Howard was the most capable soldier available to direct the complex movements of an army, and the commanding general's choice prevailed. Major General John A. Logan, Illinois politician turned XV Army Corps commander, had assumed direction of the Army of the Tennessee immediately after McPherson's death and led it capably during the remainder of the Battle of Bald Hill. It was Logan, not Hooker, whom Sherman actually passed over in favor of Howard for McPherson's command. Logan later accused Sherman of cronyism for selecting Howard, a fellow West Point graduate. Sherman did not deny the charge and probably was guilty at least of lacking political sensitivity in the matter.[18]

On July 28, Howard's columns headed for the M&W. Remembering the previous week's experience, Sherman sent a division from Thomas's army to support Howard's right and guard against another Confederate envelopment. Howard's troops halted on a high ridge with a clear view of Atlanta. All along this line the Federals began constructing their customary hasty barricades while awaiting orders to continue south or resist the next charge from Atlanta's fortifications. Hood did not keep them waiting long. He sent the battered remnants of two of his three infantry corps on what he planned to be the successful version of the flanking march that had failed six days earlier.

The Rebel assaults this time fell almost exclusively on Logan's corps, which occupied the southern end of Howard's line in the vicinity of a Methodist meetinghouse called Ezra Church. The Confederate attacks lacked coordination and vigor, due in part to Hood's absence from the battlefield. Southerners briefly enveloped Howard's open right flank. Reinforcements from Howard's own army repulsed the Rebels, all without the infantry division Sherman had dispatched to the scene, which did not arrive because it lacked both a good map and a competent guide who knew the local roads. All of the Confederate assaults struck the Northern line piecemeal and frontally, and Logan's men slaughtered their assailants. The victory left Logan feeling redeemed after not being selected for army command. Hood's vigorous counterattacks were now bleeding his own army white and draining the Southern fighting spirit.[19]

In late July, as the Union infantry moved west of Atlanta, Sherman launched the first in a month-long series of cavalry raids designed to sever Hood's last rail line sooner than Yankee foot soldiers could. Each time, however, these mounted versions of the logistic strategy failed. One effort did so spectacularly. Major General George Stoneman secured Sherman's permission to raid the M&W and then ride farther south and free the more than thirty thousand Federal prisoners held in the Georgia camps at Macon and Andersonville. Beyond vague notions of then possibly riding to the Florida coast, Stoneman did not say what he planned to do with these pitiful, starving wretches once he had freed them. Sherman gave no more firm direction than generally to indicate that as many of the prisoners as possible should be brought back to the Union forces at Atlanta. Stoneman disobeyed orders by skipping his primary mission and heading first for the prisoners. Confederate cavalry defeated and scattered reinforcing Union horsemen south of Atlanta, captured Stoneman, and imprisoned him at Macon.

Hoping to exploit this success, Hood sent most of his cavalry under Major General Joseph Wheeler in early August to cut the W&A, Sherman's railroad supply line north to Chattanooga. The Rebel raiders managed to scare Sherman and temporarily broke the railroad at several points, but they failed for the same reasons as the Union cavalry. Horsemen during the Atlanta Campaign, Northern and Southern, did not prosecute the destruction of railroads with the same purpose and thoroughness as their infantry comrades. Whenever cavalry raiders were threatened, their horses quickly carried them to safety. After causing minimal damage, Hood's cavalry left the W&A and veered into East Tennessee. Sherman drew an easy breath. His vital railroad again was safe. From as early as March until well past the end of the Atlanta Campaign, Confederate cavalry, primarily led by the notorious and talented Major General Nathan B. Forrest, bedeviled Sherman and the several combined infantry and cavalry forces he sent to destroy these Rebel raiders. Although Forrest won handily on June 10 at Brice's Cross Roads, Mississippi, he failed overall to interrupt the flow of supplies in Sherman's logistical network.[20]

Following the fighting at Ezra Church, Sherman wanted to continue his left wheel against Atlanta's west side by cutting the single rail line connecting the city with East Point. There the M&W and the Atlanta and West Point (A&WP) Railroad merged from the south and southwest, respectively, for the final run five miles north to the city. Sherman believed that capturing East Point would culminate his logistic strategy by severing the joined railroads. He combined Schofield's XXIII Army Corps and the XIV Army Corps of Thomas's army into a task force and directed it to cross a branch of Utoy Creek and seize the railroad. After Ezra Church, Hood hurriedly extended his fieldworks southwestward to East Point. From its start on August 2, the Union offensive faltered, partly because much of the Union cavalry was conducting raids and was unavailable for screening duty. Also, Schofield and the XIV Corps commander failed to work in harmony, leading to the latter's resignation. The Federal drive stumbled, giving the Rebels time to set their defense, and finally halted on August 7 well short of the rail line. Northern losses far exceeded Southern casualties. Sherman canceled the grand wheel to envelop the Confederate left and cut the combined railroads. Into August he maintained his position and contented himself with bombarding Atlanta.[21]

As August ended, Sherman continued to endure failed cavalry raids, unsuccessful fighting against the Southern left, and the apparently ineffective shelling of Atlanta. Having as he did such active habits of mind and body, he found intolerable the inherent tedium of a siege. As he wrote to Halleck, "I am too impatient for a siege." Siege warfare, with its sorties from and attacks upon fortified positions, emphasized Sherman's tactical ineptitude. In letters to his wife and brother as the campaign proceeded, he fixated more and more on possessing Atlanta to complete his logistic strategy. To Halleck he vowed to "make the inside of Atlanta too hot to be endured," and to Howard he urged: "Let us destroy Atlanta and make it a desolation." Sherman intended to culminate his campaign with more marching and flanking, not trench warfare and frontal assaults. Ironically, Hood had already aided Sherman by earlier dispatching most of Wheeler's cavalry on the fruitless raid against the Yankee railroads.[22]

In mid-August, Sherman issued general orders for the last march of the campaign. Inconclusive bombardment and failed cavalry raids convinced Sherman that to have Atlanta he needed to maneuver his infantry. He developed a plan to leave one corps to guard the reconstructed Chattahoochee River railroad bridge and a nearby supply depot, while the rest of his force, with him in command, completed the "desolating circle around Atlanta" by severing the M&W, the city's last rail connection to the Confederacy and resupply. Sherman had tried a version of this stratagem in May during his march south of the Etowah River to Dallas, and in the June stalemate before Kennesaw Mountain he had contemplated something like what he was now about to do. Earlier, when Johnston had commanded the Confederates at Dallas and Kennesaw, the Rebel army was stronger and more spirited. Since then, Hood's sorties had thinned the Southern ranks, and too little Confederate cavalry remained nearby to monitor Federal movements in any direction.[23]

Sherman wired Halleck on August 24: "I will be all ready and will commence the movement round Atlanta by the south to-morrow night, and for some time you will hear little of me." The next day the bluecoats, except the corps detailed to protect the Chattahoochee bridge, vacated their entrenchments before Atlanta, withdrew southwestward to a staging area, and prepared to conduct the decisive turning movement to lever Hood out of the city. Sherman directed his columns first to the A&WP, the extension of which into Alabama Major General Lovell H. Rousseau's Federal cavalry raiders had interrupted in July. Now Union infantry thoroughly destroyed the A&WP in a manner that cavalry could not duplicate. Foot soldiers separated rails from ties, made roaring fires from the ties, and placed the rails across the flames. Once a rail became red hot in the center, infantrymen grabbed the cool ends, ran to a nearby tree or telegraph pole, and wrapped the whole thing tightly in a circle, twisting the rail's hot surface and ruining it. Federals called these destroyed rails, among other labels, Sherman's Neckties.

On August 31, the blue columns reached their objective, the M&W south of East Point and north of Jonesboro, and began destroying that line in the same fashion. Atlanta was now isolated. Meanwhile, Hood and his lieutenants, with little cavalry to screen Sherman's baffling withdrawal, concluded that Wheeler's raid must have forced Sherman back to protect his railroad lifeline. Later, the Confederate commanders reasoned that the Yankees were indeed headed for the M&W, but they failed to identify the immediate objective. Was it East Point, Rough and Ready, or Jonesboro? When the last appeared to be the target, Hood dispatched a task force of two Rebel infantry corps under Lieutenant General William J. Hardee to protect the M&W. The Southern move was an empty gesture, as Sherman already had cut Atlanta's last railroad.[24]

That fact notwithstanding, Hardee's task force, entrenched now before Jonesboro, attacked Howard's hilltop position west of the town on August 31. Late and uncoordinated, the Rebel assaults failed to repulse Howard. The next day, Thomas and Schofield also bore down on Hardee from the north. Arriving on the scene, Sherman concluded that a rare chance availed to destroy most of Hood's army. He ordered a direct assault on September 1 against the Confederates defending Jonesboro and sent two Union columns east and south to deny the Rebels' avenues of retreat from the town, "hoping thus to capture the whole of Hardee's corps," as Sherman explained. The Federal attack gained ground, but the several corps in the area failed to coordinate once Sherman shifted his attention to destroying the railroad north of Jonesboro. Both encircling maneuvers failed, and Hardee escaped after nightfall. Resorting again to the combat strategy on the second day at Jonesboro but not following through, Sherman missed an opportunity to achieve his stated objective and incurred losses three times as large as those of the Confederates. Nonetheless, the Yankee chieftain came tantalizingly close to a decisive battlefield victory, even if against only a detachment of Hood's battered army. Still, where were the rest of the Rebel troops?[25]

During the night of September 1–2, while his armies rested following the Battle of Jonesboro, Sherman recalled being "so restless and impatient that I could not sleep." He was right to worry. As he awaited daylight, he heard explosions from the direction of Atlanta and feared for the safety of the Union troops left to guard the Chattahoochee railroad bridge. Unknown to Sherman, Hood was evacuating the city and destroying public property useful to the Federals, especially the many railroad cars containing his reserve ordnance stores. The next morning, the corps that Sherman had detailed to protect the river depot and railroad span marched to Atlanta and accepted the city's surrender from its mayor. Due to another missed opportunity for Sherman—he occupied a central position between scattered Confederate formations—Hood's army reunited during the night, withdrew south of Jonesboro to Lovejoy's Station, and built strong fieldworks. To no avail, the Federals probed the new Rebel line for several days. The Atlanta Campaign was finally over. For the Union, it ended with the great supply prizes—Atlanta and its railroads—in hand, with the Army of Tennessee effectively broken up, with the war-sustaining resources of the Gate City substantially damaged, and with Sherman's logistic strategy achieved. Now Sherman could march his weary legions into the city for much-needed rest and refitting even as he contemplated his next move.[26]

Sherman wired Washington the good news: "So Atlanta is ours, and fairly won." But how should his victory be evaluated? Union generalship in the Atlanta Campaign was manifestly Sherman's generalship. While he sought the council of his subordinate commanders—Thomas, McPherson, Schofield, and Howard—Sherman himself led his army group to victory during the late spring and summer of 1864. Although Grant gave him the enormous, dual task of destroying Johnston's army and impairing Confederate war-making ability in Georgia, the general in chief left the operational details to Sherman's judgment. Consequently, Sherman employed principally a logistic strategy and only occasionally replaced or supplemented it with a combat strategy. For him the logistic strategy played to his strengths. He had practiced a similar approach during his early 1864 Meridian Campaign in Mississippi, and that experience had stood him in good stead in Georgia.[27]

Sherman was unexcelled, if not unparalleled, as an organizer, administrator, and logistician. The thoroughness of his preparation for the campaign bore witness to that. To be sure, his logistical success in Georgia was built on Grant's achievements in the Chattanooga, Tennessee, area in 1863–64, which in turn rested on the accomplishments of Major General William S. Rosecrans in central Tennessee in 1863 and those of then-Major General Grant in north-central Tennessee in 1862. Nonetheless, as Albert Castel has maintained, Sherman's efforts in organization, administration, and supply constitute "the greatest logistic achievement of the war." Sherman was indeed no battle captain, a fact he understood well enough to avoid the tactical offensive as his primary military policy, Kennesaw Mountain notwithstanding. In fact, the slaughter pen of Kennesaw was the exception in the campaign that proved the rule about Sherman's tactical ineptness. In launching the June 27 assaults on the Kennesaw line, he intended to fight the campaign's decisive battle but failed. Otherwise, Sherman largely sought to deny the Rebels their railroad lifelines through flanking marches aimed at lines of communication. To paraphrase Sherman, the great question of the Atlanta Campaign unmistakably was supplies: providing the North's and denying the South's.[28]

Ironically, Johnston and Hood saved Sherman from himself on the tactical level, the former by always withdrawing and preventing Sherman from engaging in decisive battle (Kennesaw, again, excepted) to break up the Confederate Army of Tennessee and the latter by adopting the offensive-defensive to save Atlanta itself and instead breaking up his own army. By the end of the campaign, Hood's army was about the same size it had been under Johnston in early May, but it was a pale imitation of its former self, especially due to the inexperience that hindered it at command levels of the corps and, to some degree, the division. Despite his ingrained impatience, Sherman on the march to Atlanta was the essence of military discretion (Kennesaw, again, excluded). He refrained from needless and wasteful frontal assaults intended to annihilate his foe, with Resaca, New Hope Church, Pickett's Mill, Utoy Creek, and the second day at Jonesboro not rising to that standard. In the end, Sherman was better than his Confederate opponents at balancing annihilation and attrition.[29]

Besides capturing Atlanta and effectively destroying the Army of Tennessee, Sherman's logistic strategy saved lives, at least Northern lives. His legions knew this and accordingly held him in high regard. On the strategic and operational (but only occasionally the tactical) offensive, his resort to turning movements and envelopments rather than head-on attacks cost nearly thirty-two thousand Federal casualties as against some thirty-five thousand Confederate losses incurred on the strategic and operational defensive. Continuous operations—the daily fighting, from small-scale skirmishes to large-scale battles—also contributed to the high combined casualties. The higher Southern figures ensued largely from Hood's frequent tactical sorties around Atlanta, a policy that ruined his army's military effectiveness by draining its fighting spirit and bringing to positions of greater responsibility leaders of lesser experience.[30]

Despite the combined loss of sixty-seven thousand that resulted from the struggle for the Gate City, Sherman accomplished his mission without the casualties suffered by Grant in the East. There the Army of the Potomac pursued similar objectives, that is, destroying Lee's army and capturing the Confederate capital. By mid-June, with the start of the actions along the Petersburg, Virginia, line, Grant's marches and battles had cost the Federals more than sixty-five thousand casualties, close to the Atlanta Campaign's combined total of Union and Confederate losses. Rebel casualties in Virginia during the same period approached thirty-seven thousand troops, more than Sherman, Johnston, or Hood suffered on the way to Atlanta. Moreover, at this point Lee's army had just begun nearly a year of grinding, attrition-based warfare until, exhausted, it retreated to Appomattox Court House, Virginia, in the war's closing weeks and surrendered. In Georgia, Sherman admittedly was lucky to fight Johnston, who would not attack him on a large scale, and then Hood, who had no choice but to assault the Unionists and give them victory on the combat side of the ledger. Hood at least made Sherman work to win, something Johnston had never done. At the highest levels, the long-standing Davis-Johnston schism so divided Southern councils that the Rebel high command failed to work together to meaningfully threaten Sherman's logistics. One result was that Confederate cavalry raids in the West never coalesced above a piecemeal level, and the threat they might have posed to Sherman's advance went by the boards. Even if the more than 140-year-old debate over Southern leadership during the march to Atlanta never reaches a conclusion, one thing is certain: Sherman outgeneraled both Johnston and Hood.[31]

Finally, Sherman's generalship in the Atlanta Campaign stands out as a striking and especially instructive example of using principally the logistic strategy, aided occasionally by the combat strategy, to achieve military objectives at a reasonable cost, a delicate balancing of means and ends. Historian Edward Hagerman has argued that in this combination of strategies Sherman "en route to Atlanta provided one emerging face of modern warfare." Other more direct methods, such as frequent head-on assaults or set-piece open-field battles, would have claimed more lives and consumed more national treasure than the North generally, or the Republican Party specifically, could accept in the presidential election year of 1864. Sherman's speedy and comparatively inexpensive victory at Atlanta assured Abraham Lincoln's reelection. Anything more costly, combined with Grant's protracted bloodletting in the East, might have meant defeat for the Republicans at the polls and a major setback for the fragile Northern will to pursue the war to total victory. More the product of carefulness than audaciousness, Sherman's resounding triumph in the Atlanta Campaign does not rank him as a great battlefield captain, but he may be counted among the strategic and operational Great Captains of military history, one who may never have won a decisive battle but, more important, never lost a decisive campaign.[32]

Notes

1. In the order of appearance in the first paragraph above, full citations of the Atlanta Campaign studies are Jacob D. Cox, *Atlanta* (New York: Scribner, 1882); Richard M. McMurry, "The Atlanta Campaign: December 23, 1863 to July 18, 1864" (PhD diss., Emory University, 1967); Errol M. Clauss, "The Atlanta Campaign, 18 July–2 September 1864" (PhD diss., Emory University, 1965); James L. McDonough and James P. Jones, *War So Terrible: Sherman and Atlanta* (New York: Norton, 1987); Albert Castel, *Decision in the West: The Atlanta Campaign of 1864* (Lawrence: University Press of Kansas, 1992); Lee B. Kennett, *Marching through Georgia: The Story of Soldiers and Civilians during Sherman's Campaign* (New York: HarperCollins, 1995); Richard M. McMurry, *Atlanta 1864: Last Chance for the Confederacy* (Lincoln: University of Nebraska Press, 2000); and Stephen E. Davis, *Atlanta Will Fall: Sherman, Joe Johnston, and the Yankee Heavy Battalions* (Wilmington, DE: Scholarly Resources, 2001). The voluminous primary and secondary sources on the Atlanta Campaign cannot be reproduced here in their entirety. Most of the works cited above contain useful but incomplete source notes or bibliographies. Dated by recent scholarship but another serviceable place to start is Stephen E. Davis and Richard M. McMurry, "A Reader's Guide to the Atlanta Campaign," and Stephen E. Davis, "A Look at the Latest Literature, 1984–1989," 109–10, both in J. Britt McCarley, *The Atlanta Campaign: A Civil War Driving Tour of Atlanta-Area Battlefields* (Atlanta: Cherokee, 1989). Book-length Sherman biographies, in order of publication, include Basil H. Liddell Hart, *Sherman: Soldier, Realist, American* (New York: Dodd, Mead, 1929); Lloyd Lewis, *Sherman: Fighting Prophet* (New York: Harcourt, Brace, 1932); Earl Schenck Miers, *The General Who Marched to Hell: William Tecumseh Sherman and His Relentless Atlanta Campaign and Fiery March through Georgia* (New York: Knopf, 1951); James M. Merrill, *William Tecumseh Sherman* (Chicago: Rand-McNally, 1971); John Bennett Walters, *Merchant of Terror: General Sherman and Total War* (Indianapolis: Bobbs-Merrill, 1973); Charles Royster, *The Destructive War: William Tecumseh Sherman, Stonewall Jackson, and the Americans* (New York: Knopf, 1991); Charles E. Vetter, *Sherman: Merchant of Terror, Advocate of Peace* (Gretna, LA: Pelican, 1992); John F. Marszalek, *Sherman: A Soldier's Passion for Order* (New York: Free Press, 1993); Michael Fellman, *Citizen Sherman: A Life of William Tecumseh Sherman* (New York: Random House, 1995); Stanley P. Hirshson, *The White Tecumseh: A Biography of General William T. Sherman* (New York: Wiley, 1997); and Lee B. Kennett, *Sherman: A Soldier's Life* (New York: HarperCollins, 2002). For the appropriate criticism that Liddell Hart's biography in particular has drawn, see Albert Castel, "Liddell Hart's *Sherman*: Propaganda As History," *Journal of Military History* 67 (2003): 405–26. On the Civil War military relationship between Sherman and Lieutenant General Ulysses S. Grant, see Edward G. Longacre, *General Ulysses S. Grant: The Soldier and the Man* (New York: Da Capo, 2006); Charles B. Flood, *Grant and Sherman: The Friendship That Won the Civil War* (New York: Farrar, Straus and Giroux, 2005); Brooks D. Simpson, *Ulysses S. Grant: Triumph over Adversity* (Boston: Houghton Mifflin, 2000); Joseph T. Glatthaar, *Partners in Command: The Relationships between Leaders in the Civil War* (New York: Free Press, 1994); and William S. McFeely, *Grant: A*

Biography (New York: Norton, 1981). A still-useful set of articles summarizing Sherman's military career is Albert E. Castel, "W. T. Sherman: The Life of a Rising Son," *Civil War Times Illustrated* 18 (July 1979): 4–7, 42–46; 18 (August 1979): 12–22; 18 (October 1979): 10–21. Sherman's activities and ideas can be followed in William T. Sherman, *Memoirs of General W. T. Sherman* (New York: Library of America, 1990); William T. Sherman and John Sherman, *Sherman Letters: Correspondence between General and Senator Sherman from 1837 to 1891*, by Rachel S. Thorndike (New York: Scribner, 1894); William T. Sherman, *Home Letters of General Sherman*, ed. Mark A. DeWolfe Howe (New York: Scribner, 1909); and William T. Sherman, *Sherman's Civil War: Selected Correspondence of William T. Sherman, 1860–1865*, ed. Brooks D. Simpson and Jean V. Berlin (Chapel Hill: University of North Carolina Press, 1999).

2. For specific examples of Castel's, McMurry's, and Davis's interpretations, see Castel, *Decision in the West*, 181–82, 208, 260–62, 283–85, 343–44, 387–89, 392–93, 411, 413–14, 454–61, 539–42, 563–65, 567–68, 570–71; McMurry, *Atlanta 1864*, 49, 65, 73, 111, 180–83; and Davis, *Atlanta Will Fall*, 71–72, 136, 197–200. In publication order, a representative sample of the periodical literature evincing an anti-Sherman interpretation of the Atlanta Campaign includes Errol M. Clauss, "Sherman's Failure at Atlanta," *Georgia Historical Quarterly* 53 (1969): 321–29; Richard M. McMurry, "The Atlanta Campaign of 1864: A New Look," *Civil War History* 22 (1976): 5–15; and Albert E. Castel, "Prevaricating through Georgia: Sherman's *Memoirs* As a Source on the Atlanta Campaign," *Civil War History* 40 (1994): 48–71. A rebuttal to Castel's article is John F. Marszalek, "Sherman Called It the Way He Saw It," *Civil War History* 40 (1994): 72–78. Two anti-Sherman interpretations from Union participants in the campaign are Henry Van Ness Boynton, *Sherman's Historical Raid: The Memoirs in the Light of the Record* (Cincinnati: Wilstach, Baldwin, 1875); and Henry Stone, "The Strategy of the Campaign," in Sydney C. Kerksis, Lee A. Wallace Jr., and Margie R. Bearss, eds., *The Atlanta Papers* (Dayton, OH: Morningside, 1980), 133–62. Finally, Boynton's work is considered a response to a work by a pro-Sherman Union participant, David P. Conyngham, *Sherman's March through the South with Sketches and Incidents of the Campaign* (New York: Sheldon, 1865). A pro-Sherman response to Boynton is C. W. Moulton, *The Review of General Sherman's Memoirs Examined, Chiefly in the Light of Its Own Evidence* (Cincinnati: Robert Clarke, 1875).

3. In order, the quotations in this paragraph are themselves quoted in T. Harry Williams, *McClellan, Sherman, and Grant* (New Brunswick, NJ: Rutgers University Press, 1962), 48; Shelby Foote, *Red River to Appomattox*, vol. 3, *The Civil War: A Narrative* (New York: Random House, 1974), 395; and Williams, *McClellan, Sherman, and Grant*, 50. Useful descriptions of Sherman's person can also be found in Marszalek, *Sherman: A Soldier's Passion for Order*, 13, 116–17, 147, 159, 168–69, 197, 204, 248, 289–90, 321, 363–64, 405, and in abundance in Lewis, *Sherman: Fighting Prophet*, passim.

4. In order, the quotations in this paragraph are themselves quoted in John F. Marszalek, *Sherman's Other War: The General and the Civil War Press* (Memphis, TN: Memphis State University Press, 1981), 62, 64. Marszalek develops the insanity theme regarding Sherman in ibid., 49–93. See also Marszalek, *Sherman: A Soldier's Passion for Order*, 162–67.

5. See Marszalek, *Sherman: A Soldier's Passion for Order*, 167–258, passim; John F. Marszalek, *Commander of All Lincoln's Armies: A Life of General Henry W. Halleck* (Cambridge, MA: Harvard University Press, 2004), 113–14. In addition to Flood, *Grant and Sherman*, and Glatthaar, *Partners in Command*, both passim, see also Longacre, *Grant: Soldier and Man*, 151, 194, 215–16, 226, 230, 251–52; Simpson, *Grant: Triumph*, 347–48, 377; and McFeely, *Grant: Biography*, 118–20, 177, 180–89.

6. Concerning Grant's and Sherman's formulation of the North's 1864 grand strategy, see Report, Lieutenant General Ulysses S. Grant, Commanding Armies of the United States, to Honorable Edward M. Stanton, Secretary of War, July 22, 1865, in *The War of the Rebellion: A Compilation of the Official Records of the Union and Confederate Armies*, 4 series, 70 vols. in 128 (Washington, DC: U.S. Government Printing Office, 1880–1901) (hereafter cited as OR), series I, vol. 38, 1:2–3; Report, Major General William T. Sherman, Headquarters Military Division of the Mississippi, to Major General Henry W. Halleck, Chief of Staff, Armies of the United States, September 15, 1864, in OR, I, 38, 1:61–62; Ulysses S. Grant, *Personal Memoirs of U.S. Grant* (New York: Webster, 1885–86), 368, 371, 380; Marszalek, *Sherman: A Soldier's Passion for Order*, 256–60. For Sherman's postwar description of the Union's 1864 grand strategy and a general description of the Atlanta Campaign from the Federal perspective, see William T. Sherman, "The Grand Strategy of the Last Year of the War," in Robert Underwood Johnson and Clarence Clough Buel, eds., *Battles and Leaders of the Civil War*, 4 vols. (New York: Century, 1887–88), 4:247–54. Grant and Sherman first met in December 1863 in Nashville, Tennessee, anticipating the need to craft a grand strategy for the North's 1864 land war against the Confederacy. Their March 1864 meeting in Cincinnati was to wrap up their earlier designs. For more see R. Steven Jones, *The Right Hand of Command: Use and Disuse of Personal Staffs in the Civil War* (Mechanicsburg, PA: Stackpole, 2000), 151, 157; Lewis, *Sherman: Fighting Prophet*, 328–32; and John R. Scales, *Sherman Invades Georgia: Planning the North Georgia Campaign Using a Modern Perspective* (Annapolis, MD: Naval Institute Press, 2006), passim. For Sherman and Grant, both native Ohioans without conspicuous prewar success, it must have been delicious irony to meet in Ohio's principal city and along the way to have become the two most powerful officers in the Union Army. For Sherman in particular, the feeling must have been all the more special since the newspaper that first labeled him as mad and insane was located in Cincinnati. Shortly before the campaign began, he formalized the composition of his army group in Special Orders No. 35, Headquarters Military Division of the Mississippi, April 25, 1864, in OR, I, 32, 3:496–97. See also Castel, *Decision in the West*, 62–68, 79–89; McMurry, *Atlanta 1864*, 1–5, 12–20; Davis, *Atlanta Will Fall*, 18–19; Kennett, *Marching through Georgia*, 3–9; McDonough and Jones, *War So Terrible*, 10–34; and Cox, *Atlanta*, 19–24. Two of Sherman's three named armies have benefited from recent histories: Larry J. Daniel, *Days of Glory: The Army of the Cumberland, 1861–1865* (Baton Rouge: Louisiana State University Press, 2004); and Steven E. Woodworth, *Nothing but Glory: The Army of the Tennessee, 1861–1865* (New York: Knopf, 2005). The Union armies of the Tennessee, the Cumberland, and the Ohio served together in Georgia under Sherman's personal command during the Atlanta Campaign and thus constituted an army group, to use a later generation's term. Shortly after the

campaign began, Steele's entire department was transferred out of Sherman's military division. Included in the Grant-Sherman grand strategic design, in addition to Sherman's march toward Atlanta, was a supporting operation, to be commanded by the politician Major General Nathaniel P. Banks, from New Orleans, Louisiana, to Mobile, Alabama. From there Banks was to operate in the direction of Atlanta, with the intent of impaling the western Confederates on the horns of a strategic dilemma over the availability of Southern resources in men and matériel with which to confront these two simultaneous and cooperating Federal threats. Had the campaigns followed their plans, Sherman and Banks would have drawn a line across the western Confederacy connecting Chattanooga with Mobile by way of Atlanta. Instead, Banks, with support from Lincoln and Halleck, launched the ultimately disastrous Red River Campaign in northern Louisiana. Its failure allowed the Confederates west of the Appalachian Mountains to concentrate more on Sherman's army group than on other Union forces in that region. For details, see Gary D. Joiner, *One Damn Blunder from Beginning to End: The Red River Campaign of 1864* (Wilmington, DE: Scholarly Resources, 2003); Arthur W. Bergeron Jr. and Gary D. Joiner, eds., *The Red River Campaign: Union and Confederate Leadership and the War in Louisiana* (Shreveport, LA: Parabellum, 2003); Edward Hagerman, *The American Civil War and the Origins of Modern Warfare: Ideas, Organization, and Field Command* (Bloomington: Indiana University Press, 1988), 276; Jones, *Personal Staffs*, 166; and Mark M. Boatner III, *The Civil War Dictionary*, rev. ed. (New York: David McKay, 1988), 685–89.

7. Sherman, *Memoirs*, 466.

8. Ibid., 469. On the pivotal role of railroads to Union operations during the campaign, see also Report, Sherman to Halleck, in OR, I, 38, 1:83.

9. The quotation in this paragraph is in Letter, Major General William T. Sherman, Headquarters Military Division of the Mississippi, to Brigadier General Montgomery C. Meigs, Quartermaster General, May 3, 1864, in OR, I, 38, 4:20. Regarding the logistical preparation of Sherman's armies for the Atlanta Campaign, see J. Britt McCarley, "'He Was So Well Provided for That He Could Sweep the World for Gain': The Supply of Sherman's Armies during the Atlanta Campaign, 1864" (MA thesis, Georgia State University, 1982), 25–51; Marszalek, *Sherman: A Soldier's Passion for Order*, 260–64; Castel, *Decision in the West*, 90–99, 112–20; McMurry, *Atlanta 1864*, 26–31, 32–36; Davis, *Atlanta Will Fall*, 18–24; Kennett, *Marching through Georgia*, 62–68; McDonough and Jones, *War So Terrible*, 34–45; and Cox, *Atlanta*, 24–25. On Union logistics in the campaign as a whole, see James J. Cooke, "Feeding Sherman's Army: Union Logistics in the Campaign for Atlanta," in Theodore P. Savas and David A. Woodbury, eds., *The Campaign for Atlanta and Sherman's March to the Sea*, 2 vols. (Campbell, CA: Savas-Woodbury, 1994), 1:97–114; James G. Bogle, "The Western and Atlantic Railroad in the Campaign for Atlanta," in Savas and Woodbury, *The Campaign for Atlanta and Sherman's March to the Sea*, 2:325–38; Hagerman, *Origins of Modern Warfare*, 278–83; Russell F. Weigley, *History of the United States Army*, enlarged ed. (Bloomington: Indiana University Press, 1984), 223–24; Christopher R. Gabel, *Railroad Generalship: Foundations of Civil War Strategy* (Fort Leavenworth, KS: U.S. Army Command and General Staff College, Combat Studies Institute, 1997), esp. 4–5; Duncan K. Major Jr. and

Robert S. Fitch, *Supply of Sherman's Army during the Atlanta Campaign* (Fort Leavenworth, KS: Army Service Schools Press, 1911), passim. For logistics in general during the Atlanta Campaign, see also Erna Risch, *Quartermaster Support of the Army* (Washington, DC: Center of Military History, 1962), 389–452, passim; James A. Huston, *The Sinews of War: Army Logistics, 1775–1953* (Washington, DC: Center of Military History, 1966), 234–36; Benjamin D. King, Richard C. Briggs, and Eric R. Criner, *Spearhead of Logistics: A History of the United States Army Transportation Corps* (Fort Eustis, VA: U.S. Army Transportation Center, 1994), 66–67; and Report, Sherman to Halleck, in OR, I, 38, 1:84. On Sherman's economical view of staffs and staff work, which often led to his functioning as his own chief of staff, see Jones, *Personal Staffs*, xv, 159–60.

10. The quotation in this paragraph is reproduced in Letter, Lieutenant General Ulysses S. Grant, Headquarters Armies of the United States, to Major General William T. Sherman, Commanding Military Division of the Mississippi, April 4, 1864, in Sherman, *Memoirs*, 489–90. Grant's April 19, 1864, letter to Sherman and a fair amount of Sherman's Atlanta Campaign military correspondence are reprinted in Sherman, *Memoirs*, 489–94. See also Report, Grant to Stanton, in OR, I, 38, 1:3.

11. John Keegan, *The Mask of Command* (New York: Viking Penguin, 1987), 198–202. Some of the inspiration for the distinction here between a logistic strategy and a combat strategy comes from Archer Jones, *Civil War Command and Strategy: The Process of Victory and Defeat* (New York: Free Press, 1992), 132, 138, 144–45, 152, 181–85, 207, 217, 232–33. Sherman's tactical misadventures can be reviewed in Marszalek, *Sherman: A Soldier's Passion for Order*, 140–246, passim. Concerning the North's development of hard war, see Mark Grimsley, *The Hard Hand of War: Union Military Policy toward Southern Civilians, 1861–1865* (New York: Cambridge University Press, 1995). Sherman's April 10 and 24, 1864, responses to Grant are reproduced in Letters, Major General William T. Sherman, Headquarters Military Division of the Mississippi, to Lieutenant General Ulysses S. Grant, Commanding Armies of the United States, April 10 and 24, 1864, in Sherman, *Memoirs*, 491–94. On the eve of the campaign and more fully expressing his intent to Grant, Sherman wrote: "I will first secure Tunnel Hill, then *throw McPherson rapidly on his* [Confederate General Johnston's] *communications*, attacking at the same time in front continuously and in force" (emphasis added). For the full text, see Message, Major General William T. Sherman, Headquarters Military Division of the Mississippi, to Lieutenant General Ulysses S. Grant, Commanding Armies of the United States, May 4, 1864, in OR, I, 38, 4:25. For Union strategy in the campaign as a whole, see Marszalek, *Sherman: A Soldier's Passion for Order*, 264–65; Castel, *Decision in the West*, 67–68; McMurry, *Atlanta 1864*, 49–58; Davis, *Atlanta Will Fall*, 20, 23; Kennett, *Marching through Georgia*, 5–14; McDonough and Jones, *War So Terrible*, 14–21, 89–91; and Cox, *Atlanta*, 19–22.

12. Regarding the Atlanta Campaign's opening couple of weeks, including the Union Army's much-analyzed and -debated initial march through Snake Creek Gap, see Marszalek, *Sherman: A Soldier's Passion for Order*, 264–65; Castel, *Decision in the West*, 121–86, 567–68; McMurry, *Atlanta 1864*, 54–74; Davis, *Atlanta Will Fall*, 34–51; Kennett, *Marching through Georgia*, 176–94, passim; McDonough and Jones, *War So Terrible*, 98–122; Cox, *Atlanta*, 29–48; and McCarley, "Supply of Sherman's Armies,"

52–60. For the Battle of Resaca specifically, see Philip L. Secrist, *The Battle of Resaca: Atlanta Campaign, 1864* (Macon, GA: Mercer University Press, 1998). Useful summaries of the many marches and battles constituting the Atlanta Campaign can be found in Boatner, *Civil War Dictionary*. Other helpful studies on the campaign include Ronald H. Bailey, *Battles for Atlanta: Sherman Moves East* (Alexandria, VA: Time-Life, 1985); Samuel Carter III, *The Siege of Atlanta, 1864* (New York: Bonanza, 1973); Jack H. Lepa, *Breaking the Confederacy: The Georgia and Tennessee Campaign of 1864* (Jefferson, NC: McFarland, 2005); John Cannan, *The Atlanta Campaign, May–November 1864* (Conshohocken, PA: Combined, 1991); Albert E. Castel, *The Campaign for Atlanta* (Philadelphia: Eastern National Park and Monument Association, 1996); David Evans, "The Atlanta Campaign: A Special Issue," *Civil War Times Illustrated* 28 (Summer 1989): 12–16, 18, 20–24, 28–30, 32–34, 36–38, 40–61; William R. Scaife, *The Campaign for Atlanta*, 4th ed. (Cartersville, GA: Scaife, 1993); William R. Scaife, *War in Georgia: A Study of Military Command and Strategy* (Atlanta: Scaife, 1994); and Edward P. Shanahan, *Atlanta Campaign Staff Ride Briefing Book* (Atlanta: Office of the Command Historian, U.S. Army Reserve Command, 1995). A compilation of common soldiers' experiences in the campaign is Richard A. Baumgartner and Larry M. Strayer, *Echoes of Battle: The Atlanta Campaign, an Illustrated Collection of Union and Confederate Narratives* (Huntington, WV: Blue Acorn, 1991). The geography of the Atlanta Campaign is among the most complex of the Civil War; useful travel literature includes McCarley, *The Atlanta Campaign*; Jim Miles, *Fields of Glory: A History and Tour Guide of the War in the West, the Atlanta Campaign, 1864*, 2nd ed. (Nashville, TN: Cumberland House, 2002); Philip L. Secrist, *Sherman's 1864 Trail of Battle to Atlanta* (Macon, GA: Mercer University Press, 2006); Dennis P. Kelly, *Kennesaw Mountain and the Atlanta Campaign* (Marietta, GA: Kennesaw Mountain Historical Association, 1990); Richard M. McMurry, "Atlanta Campaign: Rocky Face to the Dallas Line, the Battles of May 1864," *Blue and Gray Magazine* 6 (April 1989): 10–23, 46, 48–60, 62; Dennis P. Kelly, "Atlanta Campaign: Mountains to Pass, a River to Cross, the Battle of Kennesaw Mountain and Related Actions from June 10 to July 9, 1864," *Blue and Gray Magazine* 6 (June 1989): 8–18, 20–28, 30, 46, 48–60; and Stephen E. Davis, "Atlanta Campaign: Hood Fights Desperately, the Battle for Atlanta, Actions from July 10 to September 2, 1864," *Blue and Gray Magazine* 6 (August 1989): 8–18, 20–22, 25–26, 28–30, 32–34, 36–39, 45–47, 49–62. Concerning Sherman's two-to-one versus the preferred three-to-one numerical advantage in manpower, only a foolish commander (which Sherman was not), upon encountering such an odds ratio, would have adopted the tactical offensive throughout the campaign in pursuit of a single decisive battle. Prior to the campaign's start, in a confidential late April letter to Major General Schofield, Sherman maintained: "I do not propose rushing on him [Rebel General Johnston] *rashly until* I have in hand all the available strength of your, Thomas' and McPherson's armies" (emphasis added), in Confidential Letter, Major General William T. Sherman, Headquarters Military Division of the Mississippi, to Major General John M. Schofield, Commanding Department of the Ohio, April 24, 1864, OR, I, 32, 3:474. On Napoleon's *la manoeuvre sur les derrières* and its pre-Napoleonic antecedents, see David G. Chandler, *The Campaigns of Napoleon* (New York: Macmillan, 1966), 162–70; and Russell

F. Weigley, *The American Way of War: A History of United States Military Strategy and Policy* (New York: Macmillan, 1973), 78–79. The imbroglio over the Snake Creek Gap maneuver strikes me as much ado about remarkably little. Of Sherman's armies, Schofield's was too small and therefore unlikely to succeed in the fighting resulting from executing the plan as ordered, and Thomas's was too large and consequently unable to move with the alacrity needed to succeed in the effort. That left McPherson's as the organization best suited in size to achieve Sherman's expressed intent. The fault certainly does not lie with Thomas, whose earlier idea had inspired the plan, or with Sherman, who seized upon that concept and fashioned the campaign's opening moves around it. The fault lies squarely with McPherson, who did not follow Sherman's orders to break the railroad and only then withdraw to the gap to await reinforcements and exploit the opportunity to strike Johnston's flank while he was withdrawing. On the other hand and in complete fairness to McPherson, Sherman's April 25, 1864, Special Orders No. 35, especially Paragraph III, in which he sought in general to regulate the command, composition, supply, and movement of his army group (see full OR orders citation in note 6 above) did not clarify whether McPherson in the campaign's opening moves and fights should have acted more aggressively (which he did not do) or less so.

13. For the events between the Army of Tennessee's withdrawal across the Oostanaula River and its abandonment of the Allatoona Pass position, see Marszalek, *Sherman: A Soldier's Passion for Order*, 265–71; Castel, *Decision in the West*, 186–285; McMurry, *Atlanta 1864*, 75–103; Davis, *Atlanta Will Fall*, 51–79; Kennett, *Marching through Georgia*, 174, 180, 182–85; McDonough and Jones, *War So Terrible*, 122–78; Cox, *Atlanta*, 49–103; and McCarley, "Supply of Sherman's Armies," 60–77. Evidence from a common soldier concerning the degree of suffering by the Union Army during the actions at New Hope Church, Pickett's Mill, and Dallas in particular and along the various mountain lines including Kennesaw Mountain can be found in Rice C. Bull, *Soldiering: The Civil War Diary of Rice C. Bull, 123rd New York Volunteer Infantry*, ed. K. Jack Bauer (San Rafael, CA: Presidio, 1977), 114–27. If the Rebel Army of Tennessee's high command at Cassville had been unified and resolute, Sherman was prepared to engage in grand battle then and there, within the first two weeks of the campaign. Regarding Sherman's intent to give battle about May 18–19, see Report, Sherman to Halleck, in OR, I, 38, 1:65.

14. Concerning the actions along the mountain lines including Kennesaw and through the Union Army's crossing of the Chattahoochee River, see Marszalek, *Sherman: A Soldier's Passion for Order*, 271–76; Castel, *Decision in the West*, 285–344; McMurry, *Atlanta 1864*, 103–20; Davis, *Atlanta Will Fall*, 79–101; Kennett, *Marching through Georgia*, 71, 75, 79, 119, 139, 155, 164–65, 171–73, 180, 189; McDonough and Jones, *War So Terrible*, 177–200; Cox, *Atlanta*, 103–43; and McCarley, "Supply of Sherman's Armies," 77–83. Other useful sources on the Kennesaw phase of the campaign include, in whole or in part, Richard M. McMurry, *The Road Past Kennesaw: The Atlanta Campaign of 1864* (Washington, DC: National Park Service, 1972); Kelly, *Kennesaw Mountain and the Atlanta Campaign*; Richard A. Baumgartner and Larry M. Strayer, *Kennesaw Mountain, June 1864: Bitter Standoff at the Gibraltar of Georgia* (Huntington, WV: Blue Acorn, 1998); Royster, *Destructive War*, 296–320; Richard M. McMurry, "Kennesaw Mountain,"

Civil War Times Illustrated 8 (January 1970): 19–34; Hagerman, *Origins of Modern Warfare*, 293–95. Two common soldiers' accounts typical of the futility of the Union experience in the June 27 assaults against the Dead Angle and Little Kennesaw Mountain and adjacent Pigeon Hill, respectively, are Lyman S. Widney (Sergeant, 34th Illinois Volunteers), letter to his parents, June 30, 1864 (IL-1), and diary entries, June 27–July 3, 1864 (IL-1A), both in Letter and Diary Collection, Kennesaw Mountain National Battlefield Park, Marietta, Georgia; and Theodore F. Upson, *With Sherman to the Sea: The Civil War Letters, Diaries, and Reminiscences of Theodore F. Upson*, ed. Oscar O. Winther (Bloomington: Indiana University Press, 1958), 115–17. On the Federal soldiers' experiences at Kennesaw Mountain generally, see also Paddy Griffith, *Battle Tactics of the Civil War* (New Haven, CT: Yale University Press, 1989), 47–48, 84, 122, 131, 138, 149, 153; and Earl J. Hess, *The Union Soldier in Battle: Enduring the Ordeal of Combat* (Lawrence: University Press of Kansas, 1997), 70–71. For Sherman's Kennesaw Mountain attack order, see Special Field Orders No. 28, Headquarters Military Division of the Mississippi, June 24, 1864, in OR, I, 38, 4:588. I make much of the Battle of Kennesaw Mountain for good reason. It was the only time during the Atlanta Campaign that Sherman set out deliberately to achieve a single decisive battlefield victory. He failed and never repeated the mistake. Regarding Sherman's ability to learn from Kennesaw, see Gerald F. Linderman, *Embattled Courage: The Experience of Combat in the American Civil War* (New York: Free Press, 1987), 136–37. At Kennesaw if nowhere else up to that point in the war, Sherman had just learned what Grant, despite his many, large, and lengthy battles fought in Virginia by late June 1864, had already known for some time: that neither a single day of battle nor any battle in its entirety was going to win this war. See McFeely, *Grant: Biography*, 183. On Gettysburg and First Bull Run, see Edwin B. Coddington, *The Gettysburg Campaign: A Study in Command* (New York: Scribner, 1968); Stephen W. Sears, *Gettysburg* (Boston: Houghton Mifflin, 2003); Ethan S. Rafuse, *A Single Grand Victory: The First Campaign and Battle of Manassas* (Wilmington, DE: Scholarly Resources, 2002); and David Detzer, *Donnybrook: The Battle of Bull Run* (New York: Harcourt, 2004). For more on the issue of decisive battle as Civil War generals came to understand it, especially as inspired by mistakenly Romantic notions associated with the example of Napoleon Bonaparte's 1805 Ulm campaign and its culmination in the climactic December 2 Battle of Austerlitz, see John A. Lynn, *Battle: A History of Combat and Culture* (Boulder, CO: Westview, 2003), 179–217; Chandler, *Campaigns of Napoleon*, 381–439, passim; Christopher Duffy, *Austerlitz 1805* (London: Seeley, 1977); Alistair Horne, *Napoleon: Master of Europe, 1805–1807* (New York: Morrow, 1979); Horne, *How Far from Austerlitz: Napoleon, 1805–1815* (New York: St. Martin's, 1996); David G. Chandler, *Austerlitz 1805: The Battle of the Three Emperors* (London: Osprey, 1990); Scott Bowden, *Napoleon and Austerlitz: The "Glory Years" of 1805–1807* (Chicago: Emperor's Press, 1997); Ian Castle, *Austerlitz, 1805: The Fate of Empires* (Oxford: Osprey, 2002); Castle, *Austerlitz: Napoleon and the Eagles of Europe* (Barnsley, UK: Pen and Sword, 2005); Robert Goetz, *1805: Austerlitz: Napoleon and the Destruction of the Third Coalition* (London: Greenhill, 2005); Frederick W. Kagan, *The End of the Old Order: Napoleon and Europe, 1801–1805* (Cambridge, MA: Da Capo, 2006); Robert A. Doughty and Ira D. Gruber, eds., *Warfare in the Western World: Military Operations from 1600 to 1871*, 2 vols. (Lexington,

MA: D. C. Heath, 1996), 1:215–22, 291–94, 392–98; Weigley, *American Way of War*, 77–152, passim; and Russell F. Weigley, *The Age of Battles: The Quest for Decisive Warfare from Breitenfeld to Waterloo* (Bloomington: Indiana University Press, 1991), 375–98, 536–43. For a corrective interpretation of Napoleon's improvised style of generalship and military genius, including the 1805 Ulm-Austerlitz Campaign, see Owen Connelly, *Blundering to Glory: Napoleon's Military Campaigns*, 3rd ed. (Lanham, MD: Rowman and Littlefield, 2006), 77–91. During their student days at the United States Military Academy at West Point from about the 1830s on, the academically talented cadets in particular learned about Napoleon and his campaigns from Professor Dennis Hart Mahan, also a West Point graduate, in the extracurricular Napoleon Club for both faculty and students, which Mahan himself founded. For details see Hagerman, *Origins of Modern Warfare*, 8, 34, 102, 108; Herman Hattaway and Archer Jones, *How the North Won: A Military History of the Civil War* (Urbana: University of Illinois Press, 1983), 12–13; and Stephen E. Ambrose, *Duty, Honor, Country: A History of West Point* (Baltimore: Johns Hopkins University Press, 1966), 138–39. Sherman was a West Point cadet from 1836 to 1840, during the period from 1832 when Mahan was on the academy's permanent faculty and sponsoring the club's activities. Also and in keeping with his intellectual talents, Sherman graduated sixth of forty-one cadets in the Class of 1840, putting him in the top 15 percent of his classmates. It is a reasonable inference, therefore, that Cadet Sherman would have known about, participated in, or been influenced by the Napoleon Club. For all the club might have taught him, however, Sherman possessed little if any tactical skill, but that did not prevent him from envisioning the potential for grand battle (i.e., the combat strategy), an often misunderstood Napoleonic legacy, at Cassville in mid-May 1864 and making a lackluster attempt to achieve it at Kennesaw Mountain in late June. With the Atlanta Campaign now at its approximate midpoint, it remained to be seen how Sherman would or could rebalance the combat and logistic strategies. See Sherman, *Memoirs*, 16, for his version of his standing as a student at West Point. By 1861, the Austerlitz of mid-nineteenth-century American military imagination had already shaped the way many Civil War generals, including Sherman, understood decisive battle during most of the war. In addition to the situation described above in the text proper, there is another plausible explanation for Sherman's resort at Kennesaw to the crudest of the combat strategies: a series of frontal assaults against entrenched defenders on high ground. The combination of Major General Nathaniel P. Banks's Red River Campaign in Louisiana, which began in early March 1864 and involved a portion of the XVII Army Corps, and furlough granted to the veteran Third and Fourth Divisions of that same corps altogether deprived Sherman of the services of Major General Francis P. Blair Jr.'s entire corps until June 8, when the Atlanta Campaign was just beginning to focus on Kennesaw Mountain. In his late April confidential letter to Schofield, Sherman had indicated that he had no intent of "rushing on him [the Confederates] rashly until I have in hand all the available strength." Although Sherman was prepared to fight grand battle at Cassville in mid-May, Johnston did not attack him until the Battles of Dallas on May 28 and Kolb's Farm on June 22. Johnston lost both indecisive engagements, but Sherman could not depend on Johnston's wearing down the Rebel army through simple attrition. Blair's two divisions came off leave and arrived north of Kennesaw at Acworth, compensating Sherman for his combat losses and detachments to protect his supply line thus far incurred during the campaign and bringing Federal strength up to about 112,000. Considering that Johnston's army had recently been reinforced to around 65,000 from the Gulf Coast area with at least the possibility of more reinforcements, especially since Banks was not campaigning in south Alabama as originally planned, Sherman decided to attack now while the Confederates were stretched thinly after Kolb's Farm, covering the lengthened Kennesaw line, because the Confederates, in his mind at least, surely must be vulnerable somewhere along the more than eight miles of fieldworks. For details see Confidential Letter, Sherman to Schofield, in OR, I, 32, 3:496–97; Report, Sherman to Halleck, in OR, I, 38, 1:67–70; Grant, *Personal Memoirs*, 382–83; Jones, *Personal Staffs*, 161.

15. Message, Major General William T. Sherman, Headquarters Military Division of the Mississippi, to Major General Henry W. Halleck, Chief of Staff, Armies of the United States, July 6, 1864, in OR, I, 38, 5:66.

16. Sherman, *Memoirs*, 544.

17. Regarding events from the crossing of the Chattahoochee River through the Battle of Peachtree Creek, see Marszalek, *Sherman: A Soldier's Passion for Order*, 276–77; Castel, *Decision in the West*, 344–83; McMurry, *Atlanta 1864*, 129–52; Davis, *Atlanta Will Fall*, 102–17, 127–36; Kennett, *Marching through Georgia*, 173, 174–75, 190; McDonough and Jones, *War So Terrible*, 200–218; Cox, *Atlanta*, 144–59; McCarley, "Supply of Sherman's Armies," 84–86. Still useful in understanding how civilians in particular experienced the actual fight for possession of the city of Atlanta is Adolph A. Hoehling, *Last Train from Atlanta* (New York: Yoseloff, 1958). On the fate of Atlanta's small Unionist civilian community as Sherman neared the city itself, see Thomas G. Dyer, *Secret Yankees: The Union Cirlce in Confederate Atlanta* (Baltimore: Johns Hopkins University Press, 1999), 155–212, passim.

18. Concerning the Union Army's approach to Atlanta from the east, the Battle of Bald Hill, and the fighting at Decatur, see Report, Sherman to Halleck, in OR, I, 38, 1:72–73; Grant, *Personal Memoirs*, 384; Marszalek, *Sherman: A Soldier's Passion for Order*, 277–79; Castel, *Decision in the West*, 383–414, 418–19; McMurry, *Atlanta 1864*, 152–55; Davis, *Atlanta Will Fall*, 136–48; Kennett, *Marching through Georgia*, 175–93, passim; McDonough and Jones, *War So Terrible*, 219–46; Cox, *Atlanta*, 160–81; McCarley, "Supply of Sherman's Armies," 86–87. For the cavalry expeditions associated with the Union Army's operations in the immediate vicinity of Atlanta, see David Evans, *Sherman's Horsemen: Union Cavalry Operations in the Atlanta Campaign* (Bloomington: Indiana University Press, 1999), 175–94. Regarding the controversy involving Sherman's passing over Logan for Howard, see McFeely, *Grant: Biography*, 177; John A. Logan, "The Dangerous West Point Monopoly," in Russell F. Weigley, ed., *The American Military: Readings in the History of the Military in American Society* (Reading, MA: Addison-Wesley, 1969), 77–85; Russell F. Weigley, *Towards an American Army: Military Thought from Washington to Marshall* (New York: Columbia University Press, 1962), 127–36; James P. Jones, *Black Jack: John A. Logan and Southern Illinois in the Civil War* (Carbondale: Southern Illinois University Press, 1995), 218–22; Gary Ecelbarger, *Black Jack Logan: An Extraordinary Life in Peace and War* (Guilford, CT: Lyons, 2005). In his memoirs, Hood cited the May 1–3, 1863, Battle of Chancellorsville, near Fredericks-

burg, Virginia, as his paradigm against which to measure the success of his offensive plan and maneuvers that resulted in the July 22 Battle of Bald Hill (also known as the Battle of Atlanta). Hood not only lost that battle, the largest of the Atlanta Campaign, but also suffered about 1,500 more casualties than Sherman. Moreover, Hood employed flimsy logic in choosing Chancellorsville as his pattern. Because of the peculiar circumstances leading to the battle, Hood was not involved. His infantry division had been in southeastern Virginia and eventually participated in the Siege of Suffolk. Still, for all the martial glory apparently associated with Lieutenant General Stonewall Jackson's May 2 successful flank attack against the exposed right flank of Major General Hooker's Army of the Potomac, the combined battle casualties for both sides at about thirty thousand were enormous. Jackson, mistaken with his staff for Union cavalry in the twilight of that day at Chancellorsville, was mortally wounded by his own men. For all that, the war was no closer to being decided except for attritioning General Lee's Army of Northern Virginia further toward eventual exhaustion. Hood, however, did participate, again as a division commander, in the late August 1862 Battle of Second Bull Run. There his participation in a corps-sized envelopment of the left flank of Union Major General John Pope's Army of Virginia on the battle's second day was conspicuous. The battle overall, however, was indecisive, as Pope's badly beaten but not incapacitated army fought a determined and skillful retrograde and escaped to the safety of large Union forces already protecting Washington, D.C. Perhaps if Hood had drawn on his actual experience and learned from it (a stretch, probably), he might have been less eager to continue sending his increasingly battered Army of Tennessee unsuccessfully against Sherman's flanks. For more see John B. Hood, *Advance and Retreat: Personal Experiences in the United States and Confederate States Armies* (New Orleans: Published for the Hood Orphan Memorial Fund by Pierre G. T. Beauregard, 1880); John J. Hennessy, *Return to Bull Run: The Campaign and Battle of Second Manassas* (New York: Simon and Schuster, 1993), 362–406; Stephen W. Sears, *Chancellorsville* (Boston: Houghton Mifflin, 1996); and Steven A. Cormier, *The Siege of Suffolk: The Forgotten Campaign, April 11–May 4, 1863* (Lynchburg, VA: Harold E. Howard, 1989). Doughty and Gruber, eds., *Warfare in the Western World*, 1, 392–98, draw a direct historical connection between the long-range frustration, ultimate indecision, and high butcher's bill of both 1805 Austerlitz and 1863 Chancellorsville, naming the phenomenon the Austerlitz Chimera because of the role of the imagination and unrealistic expectations in both examples, especially the post-1805 interpretation of Austerlitz as decisive and attempts by Union and Confederate generals during the Civil War to emulate Napoleon's greatest victory.

19. For Sherman's march to the west side of Atlanta and the Battle of Ezra Church, see Marszalek, *Sherman: A Soldier's Passion for Order*, 280; Castel, *Decision in the West*, 414–36; McMurry, *Atlanta 1864*, 155–59; Davis, *Atlanta Will Fall*, 148–54; Kennett, *Marching through Georgia*, 170, 182, 191, 196; McDonough and Jones, *War So Terrible*, 247–51, 256–64; Cox, *Atlanta*, 181–87; and McCarley, "Supply of Sherman's Armies," 87–89.

20. Concerning both the Union and Confederate cavalry raids, see Report, Sherman to Halleck, in OR, I, 38, 1:75–77. In the same report, Sherman even indicated that in thinking about and approving Stoneman's raid, there was "something most captivating

in the idea" (76). The only thing captive about the raid, however, was Stoneman himself and the troopers who surrendered with him. Otherwise, the entire effort was a dismal flop. See also Marszalek, *Sherman: A Soldier's Passion for Order*, 279–80, 282; Castel, *Decision in the West*, 436–43, 448–50, 469–75; McMurry, *Atlanta 1864*, 157–58, 164–67; Davis, *Atlanta Will Fall*, 149–50, 154–55, 167–74, 183; Kennett, *Marching through Georgia*, 128–47; McDonough and Jones, *War So Terrible*, 250–56, 285–90; Cox, *Atlanta*, 181–82, 188–89, 195–96; McCarley, "Supply of Sherman's Armies," 89–99, 101; Evans, *Sherman's Horsemen*, 204–7, 217–376, 404–67; and Jones, *Personal Staffs*, 157, 165, 169. Regarding Forrest's raids on Sherman's logistical network, see Edwin C. Bearss, *Forrest at Brice's Cross Roads and in North Mississippi in 1864* (Dayton, OH: Morningside, 1987).

21. For Sherman's failed Utoy Creek effort, see Marszalek, *Sherman: A Soldier's Passion for Order*, 280–82; Castel, *Decision in the West*, 448–69; McMurry, *Atlanta 1864*, 160–64; Davis, *Atlanta Will Fall*, 155–67; Kennett, *Marching through Georgia*, 125–28; McDonough and Jones, *War So Terrible*, 264–85; Cox, *Atlanta*, 188–95. My research indicates that the so-called Siege of Atlanta, usually asserted to have occurred between July 20 and August 17, 1864, was a nonevent. At no time during the Federal operations directly against the city did Sherman's forces entirely surround the place and completely cut if off from resupply, which fits the most widely accepted military definitions at the time of a siege. Among the best period definitions of siege are Henry W. Halleck, *Elements of Military Art and Science* (New York: Appleton, 1846), 368–77; and Henry L. Scott, *Military Dictionary* (New York: Van Nostrand, 1861), 551–59. Union bombardment was largely confined to fire, albeit heavy at times, from field-caliber guns with shot routinely not exceeding in weight about twenty pounds per round. Trying to conduct a siege with field guns alone, even a large number of them, could result in severe shortages of the very ammunition used to support the regular maneuvering and fighting of a field force such as Sherman's. In early August, Sherman summoned from Chattanooga four 4.5-inch siege and garrison guns, which arrived on August 10 and began firing the same day. For details on these guns, see Warren Ripley, *Artillery and Ammunition of the Civil War* (New York: Promontory, 1970), 165–66, 374. According to his official Report, Sherman to Halleck, in OR, I, 38, 1:79, Sherman "put [the guns] to work *night and day* and did execution on the city, causing frequent fires and creating confusion" (emphasis added). The Confederate works protecting Atlanta itself generally lay in an irregular circle about half a mile beyond the city's incorporation circle (about two miles in diameter), enclosing the greater part of the built-up area. The total area inside the circle of fieldworks and fortifications amounted to around 197 million square feet. In the same report, Sherman stated that to finally capture Atlanta his concluding maneuvers "involved the necessity of *raising* the siege of Atlanta" on August 18 (80, emphasis added). Figured generously, if the four Federal siege guns fired one round a minute for the eight days of the purported siege, then the ammunition expended would have totaled not more than 46,080 rounds distributed roughly over 197 million square feet, resulting in one round per roughly 4,300 square feet or one round inside every square in the area with sides measuring about 65 feet, hardly enough siegelike bombardment to cause heavy damage to the still young and low-density municipality of Atlanta, which photographs of

the city under Union occupation in the early fall of 1864 confirm. Structures near the city's protective earthworks, however, were substantially damaged by shellfire, which the period photographic record also establishes. The result is that the Siege of Atlanta was a siege in name only. A label more accurately reflecting the historical situation in and near the city during the period from about July 20 through August 17 would be "Actions before Atlanta's Trenches." In marked contrast, the 1781 Siege of Yorktown, Virginia, was a genuine siege and is easily counted among the world's most significant and influential military actions of any kind. There the clash of arms between the besieging Franco-American army and the besieged Anglo-German army proved to be the practical end of the War of American Independence with the surrender of the latter forces on October 19, 1781. The Franco-Americans under American lieutenant general George Washington lay classical siege to the Anglo-Germans under British lieutenant general Lord Charles Cornwallis. After nine days of siege proper, with one round fired approximately every sixty to ninety seconds from the roughly forty-three Franco-American siege-caliber guns—more than ten times the number of the same type of gun as the Union forces used at Atlanta—the Anglo-Germans had received an average of 10,800 rounds in an area measuring only 5.5 million square feet, which results in one round per roughly 510 square feet or one round inside every square in the area with sides measuring about 22 feet. Taking into consideration only the volume and total area distribution of siege artillery fire, the Franco-American fire at Yorktown was around eight times more concentrated than the Union fire at Atlanta. In short, the Franco-Americans (especially the French, who were the European masters of the art of the siege) in 1781 at Yorktown were serious about siege warfare; Sherman in 1864 at Atlanta was not, the fact of which he did not hide from superiors or subordinates. For more on 1781 Yorktown, see Jerome A. Greene, *The Guns of Independence: The Siege of Yorktown, 1781* (New York: Savas-Beatie, 2005); Lee B. Kennett, *The French Forces in America, 1780–1783* (Westport, CT: Greenwood, 1977), 144–45; David Chandler, *The Art of Warfare in the Age of Marlborough* (New York: Hippocrene, 1976), 234–71; and Christopher Duffy, *Fire and Stone: The Science of Fortress Warfare, 1660–1860* (London: Greenhill, 1975), 116–26.

22. In order, the quotations in this paragraph are in Message, Major General William T. Sherman, Headquarters Military Division of the Mississippi, to Major General Henry W. Halleck, Chief of Staff, Armies of the United States, August 7, 1864, in OR, I, 38, 5:409; ibid., 5:408; Message, Major General William T. Sherman, Headquarters Military Division of the Mississippi, to Major General Oliver O. Howard, Headquarters Department of the Tennessee, August 10, 1864, in ibid., 5:452. Regarding Sherman's letters to his wife and brother, see especially Sherman, *Home Letters*, 289–309, and Sherman, *Sherman Letters*, 234–40. Sherman responded with delight to Wheeler's Southern cavalry raid on his line of communication and not with dread as he often did when Confederate cavalryman Forrest appeared to threaten Sherman's railroad lifeline north to Chattanooga and beyond. Responding to Wheeler's raid, Sherman recalled in his official report that "I could not have asked for anything better [because] this detachment left me superior to the enemy in cavalry" (Report, Sherman to Halleck, in OR, I, 38, 1:79). Also on the same subject, see ibid., 83 and 88. Sherman worried much over what he perceived to be the slow pace of operations against Atlanta, but Grant in Virginia—where

the campaign to destroy General Lee's Rebel Army of Northern Virginia and seize the Confederate capital at Richmond, Virginia, had in fact bogged down in the trenches before nearby Petersburg—remained confident in Sherman and supportive of his progress thus far in destroying Hood's army and capturing Atlanta. For details see McFeely, *Grant: Biography*, 180–89.

23. The quotation in this paragraph is from Letter, Major General William T. Sherman, Headquarters Military Division of the Mississippi, to Lieutenant General Ulysses S. Grant, General in Chief, August 10, 1864, in OR, I, 38, 5:447. For Sherman's August 1864 plans to culminate his logistic strategy, which he labeled the grand movement, see Special Field Orders No. 57, Headquarters Military Division of the Mississippi, in OR, I, 38, 5:546. See also Marszalek, *Sherman: A Soldier's Passion for Order*, 281–82; Castel, *Decision in the West*, 468–75, 480–85; McMurry, *Atlanta 1864*, 167, 169; Davis, *Atlanta Will Fall*, 173–75; Kennett, *Marching through Georgia*, 198; McDonough and Jones, *War So Terrible*, 291–92; Cox, *Atlanta*, 196; McCarley, "Supply of Sherman's Armies," 99–101. Two days before Sherman issued Special Field Orders No. 57, Major General Schofield wrote him recommending a movement against the A&WP (intact to Columbus, Georgia, but broken in Alabama earlier in the summer by Rousseau's Union cavalry raid) and, more important, against the M&W directly south of Atlanta. For details see Letter, Major General John M. Schofield, Headquarters Army of the Ohio, to Major General William T. Sherman, Commanding Military Division of the Mississippi, August 14, 1864, in OR, I, 38, 5:498–99. Most significant, during the three months from the mid-May small-scale actions near Cassville, which did not result in actual battle, through the pitched battles right around Atlanta and the nonsiege of the city, all ending in mid-August, Sherman's martial ardor had gone from momentary expectation of grand battle (i.e., the combat strategy) to earnest commitment to grand movement (i.e., the logistic strategy) as his surest means of winning the campaign and seizing Atlanta if not actually breaking up Hood's now defensive-minded Confederate army. In other words, Sherman had completed a philosophical about-face from eagerness for battle to preference for maneuver. During the remainder of the war, only rarely did he stray from this policy and practice.

24. The quotation above is in Message, Major General William T. Sherman, Headquarters Military Division of the Mississippi, to Major General Henry W. Halleck, Chief of Staff, Armies of the United States, August 24, 1864, in OR, I, 38, 5:649. Concerning Rousseau's July 1864 cavalry raid in east-central Alabama, see David Evans, *Sherman's Horsemen*, 98–174. For the movement of the Federals to the vicinity of Jonesboro, see Marszalek, *Sherman: A Soldier's Passion for Order*, 282–83; Castel, *Decision in the West*, 485–98; McMurry, *Atlanta 1864*, 169–72; Davis, *Atlanta Will Fall*, 175–85; Kennett, *Marching through Georgia*, 198; McDonough and Jones, *War So Terrible*, 292–301; Cox, *Atlanta*, 196–201; McCarley, "Supply of Sherman's Armies," 101–3. On the Union soldiers' technique for destroying Confederate rail lines and producing Sherman's Neckties in the process, see Upson, *With Sherman to the Sea*, 123–24.

25. The quotation in this paragraph is in Sherman, *Memoirs*, 581. Regarding the Battle of Jonesboro, see Marszalek, *Sherman: A Soldier's Passion for Order*, 283; Castel, *Decision in the West*, 499–522, 570–71; McMurry, *Atlanta 1864*, 172–75; Davis, *Atlanta Will Fall*, 185–91; Kennett, *Marching through Georgia*, 188, 191–93, 203; McDonough

and Jones, *War So Terrible*, 301–7; Cox, *Atlanta*, 201–7; McCarley, "Supply of Sherman's Armies," 103.

26. The quotation in this paragraph is in Sherman, *Memoirs*, 581. Concerning the Confederate evacuation of Atlanta, the retreat to Lovejoy's Station, and the Union occupation of the Gate City, see Marszalek, *Sherman: A Soldier's Passion for Order*, 283; Castel, *Decision in the West*, 522–36; McMurry, *Atlanta 1864*, 174–76; Davis, *Atlanta Will Fall*, 191; Kennett, *Marching through Georgia*, 199–205; McDonough and Jones, *War So Terrible*, 307–13; Cox, *Atlanta*, 207–8; and McCarley, "Supply of Sherman's Armies," 103–4.

27. The quotation in this paragraph is in Message, Major General William T. Sherman, Headquarters Military Division of the Mississippi, to Major General Henry W. Halleck, Chief of Staff, Armies of the United States, September 3, 1864, in *OR*, I, 38, 5:777. For Sherman's 1864 Meridian Campaign in Mississippi, see Marszalek, *Sherman: A Soldier's Passion for Order*, 232–58, passim; Richard M. McMurry, "Sherman's Meridian Campaign," *Civil War Times Illustrated* 14 (May 1975): 24–32; Margie R. Bearss, *Sherman's Forgotten Campaign: The Meridian Expedition* (Baltimore: Gateway, 1987); and Buck T. Foster, *Sherman's Mississippi Campaign* (Tuscaloosa: University of Alabama Press, 2006).

28. The quotation in this paragraph is in Albert E. Castel, "W. T. Sherman: The Life of a Rising Son," *Civil War Times Illustrated* 18 (October 1979): 10. On how Sherman himself was engaged in sustaining Grant's 1862 Forts Henry and Donelson campaign, see Benjamin F. Cooling, *Forts Henry and Donelson: The Key to the Confederate Heartland* (Knoxville: University of Tennessee Press, 1987), 119, 161; and Flood, *Grant and Sherman*, 83, 87–89. As both a logistician and battlefield commander, Sherman was a throwback to the likes of Major General Nathanael Greene in the War of American Independence and Brevet Lieutenant General Winfield Scott in the Mexican-American War. Similar to Greene's focus on keeping his army adequately supplied in the Southern Campaign of 1780–81 and Scott's preference for flanking maneuvers instead of pitched battles during the 1847 march to Mexico City, Sherman's preoccupations on the way to Atlanta were also with supplies and operating against the Confederates' lines of communication. On Greene and Scott, see John Buchanan, *The Road to Guilford Courthouse: The American Revolution in the Carolinas* (New York: Wiley, 1997), 398–99; K. Jack Bauer, *The Mexican War, 1846–1848* (New York: Macmillan, 1974), 259–325, passim; Doughty and Gruber, *Warfare in the Western World*, 1:159–69, 317–22; Weigley, *American Way of War*, 27–37, 74–76.

29. There still is no better single source in the literature of U.S. military history at making the case for the presence of the traditional dichotomy between annihilation and attrition in the American experience than Weigley, *American Way of War*, esp. xvii–xxiii. Concerning the strategies of annihilation and attrition, see Hans Delbrück, *History of the Art of War within the Framework of Political History: The Modern Era*, vol. 4, trans. Walter J. Renfroe Jr. (Westport, CT: Greenwood, 1985). On Sherman's cautious tactics, see Hagerman, *Origins of Modern Warfare*, 293–97.

30. For the high regard that Sherman's men had for him, see Marszalek, *Sherman: A Soldier's Passion for Order*, 268–69. The two most authoritative discussions of aggregate

Union and Confederate casualties during the Atlanta Campaign are in McMurry, *Atlanta 1864*, 194–97, and Kelly, *Kennesaw Mountain and the Atlanta Campaign*, 59. Still, McMurry and Kelly disagree by several thousand Federal casualties. Because they are drawn from official sources and are more in keeping with the tone of the campaign, I have used Kelly's figures for Northern losses. See also Sherman, *Memoirs*, 607–8.

31. Regarding total Union and Confederate losses in Virginia from May 5 to June 18, 1864, see Mark Grimsley, *And Keep Moving On: The Virginia Campaign, May–June 1864* (Lincoln: University of Nebraska Press, 2002), 224–26; Gordon C. Rhea, *Cold Harbor: Grant and Lee, May 26–June 3, 1864* (Baton Rouge: Louisiana State University Press, 2002), 393; Noah A. Trudeau, *The Last Citadel: Petersburg, Virginia, June 1864–April 1865* (Boston: Little, Brown, 1991), 55. On the relative bloodlessness of the march to Atlanta, see Griffith, *Battle Tactics*, 50. For further discussion of Confederate leadership in the Atlanta Campaign beyond the now-standard campaign studies cited above in abundance, see Steven E. Woodworth, *No Band of Brothers: Problems of Rebel High Command* (Columbia: University of Missouri Press, 1999); David A. Coffey, *John Bell Hood and the Struggle for Atlanta* (Abilene, TX: McWhiney Foundation Press, 1998); Stephen E. Davis, "A Reappraisal of the Generalship of General John Bell Hood in the Battles for Atlanta," in Savas and Woodbury, *Campaign for Atlanta and Sherman's March to the Sea*, vol. 1; Richard M. McMurry, "A Policy So Disastrous: Joseph E. Johnston's Atlanta Campaign," in Savas and Woodbury, *Campaign for Atlanta and Sherman's March to the Sea*, vol. 2; Craig L. Symonds, *Joseph E. Johnston: A Civil War Biography* (New York: Norton, 1992); Steven E. Woodworth, *Jefferson Davis and His Generals: The Failure of Confederate Command in the West* (Lawrence: University Press of Kansas, 1990); Richard M. McMurry, *Two Great Rebel Armies: An Essay in Confederate Military History* (Chapel Hill: University of North Carolina Press, 1989); Richard M. McMurry, *John Bell Hood and the War for Southern Independence* (Lexington: University Press of Kentucky, 1982); Thomas L. Connelly and Archer Jones, *The Politics of Command: Factions and Ideas in Confederate Strategy* (Baton Rouge: Louisiana State University Press, 1973); Thomas L. Connelly, *Autumn of Glory: The Army of Tennessee, 1862–1865* (Baton Rouge: Louisiana State University Press, 1971); and Stanley F. Horn, *The Army of Tennessee* (Indianapolis: Bobbs-Merrill, 1941).

32. The quotation in this paragraph is in Hagerman, *Origins of Modern Warfare*, 277. Concerning the Atlanta Campaign's effect on the election of 1864, see John C. Waugh, *Reelecting Lincoln: The Battle for the 1864 Presidency* (New York: Crown, 1997); T. Harry Williams, *Lincoln and His Generals* (New York: Knopf, 1952), esp. 337–38; and Grant, *Personal Memoirs*, 390. Even considering his theory-peddling penchant for promoting Sherman as one of military history's Great Captains, see Basil H. Liddell Hart, *Strategy*, 2nd ed. (New York: Praeger, 1967), 149–51, 162. The summary analysis of Sherman's Atlanta Campaign generalship in these concluding paragraphs was also informed by Marszalek, *Sherman: A Soldier's Passion for Order*, 283–87; Castel, *Decision in the West*, 536–47, 561–65; McMurry, *Atlanta 1864*, 177–90, 204–8; Davis, *Atlanta Will Fall*, 197–200; Kennett, *Marching through Georgia*, 317–18; McDonough and Jones, *War So Terrible*, 319–21, 325–32; Cox, *Atlanta*, 208–17, passim; McCarley, "Supply of Sherman's Armies," 105–15; Russell F. Weigley, *A Great Civil War: A Military and*

Political History, 1861–1865 (Bloomington: Indiana University Press, 2000), 358–67; Herman Hattaway and Archer Jones, *How the North Won: A Military History of the Civil War* (Urbana: University of Illinois Press, 1983), 546–52, 563–64, 567–68, 576–77, 584–85, 593–99, 603–13, 622–25; Richard E. Beringer, Herman Hattaway, Archer Jones, and William N. Still Jr., *Why the South Lost the Civil War* (Athens: University of Georgia Press, 1986), 321–27.

3

THE UNITED STATES NAVY AND THE GENESIS OF MARITIME EDUCATION

Jennifer L. Speelman

IN THE SECOND HALF OF the nineteenth century, reform-minded officers in the U.S. Navy took part in a unique civil-military experiment in maritime education. Citing a symbiotic relationship between the navy and the merchant marine, seafarers from both the commercial and naval fleets joined forces between 1874 and 1902 to develop a formal system of nautical training for future merchant marine officers. In addition to their advocacy for the New Navy, such officers as Stephen B. Luce, Robert Phythian, French Ensor Chadwick, and William S. Sims played an active, if forgotten, role in establishing the three original state nautical schools: the New York Nautical School (established 1874), the Pennsylvania Nautical School (established 1889), and the Massachusetts Nautical Training School (established 1890). These schools represented a radical departure from the prevailing wisdom of learning the ropes at sea. Instead, in the rapidly transforming maritime world at the turn of the twentieth century, active-duty naval officers became school ship instructors in order to instill seamanship, engineering, and naval discipline into a new generation of merchant mariner officers.

The most articulate and effective spokesman for maritime education was Luce. He maintained a firm belief in education as a means of enhancing the personnel and professionalism of the naval service in a time of technological change and encouraged the officers around him to do the same.[1] Luce is best known for the 1863 publication of *Seamanship*, the first textbook of its kind used at the United States Naval Academy; the creation of the United States Naval Institute in 1873; and the founding of the United States Naval War College in 1884.[2] In addition, he wanted to apply his educational theories to the officers and men of the U.S. Merchant Marine, and he lobbied tirelessly in support of state nautical schools, the precursors of the United States Merchant Marine Academy. Like his more famous protégée, Alfred Thayer Mahan, Luce had carefully examined the relationship between commercial and military seagoing enterprise and national power and prestige. The call for commercial expansion at the end of the nineteenth century necessitated not only a larger merchant marine but also a larger navy to protect it.[3] Conversely, a country's merchant marine could serve a quasi-military function as a naval auxiliary for a modern navy. In particular, Luce saw the personnel of the merchant marine as a potential ready reserve of sailors for the navy in wartime.[4]

Luce and fellow naval officers had good reason to worry about the overall health of the merchant marine. In the antebellum period, American ships had handled two-thirds of the nation's foreign trade. That figure dropped to one-third after the Civil War and showed no signs of improvement in the following decades. Confederate commerce raiders, skyrocketing insurance rates, the collapse of the cotton trade, sale to foreign owners, and requisitioning by the Union Navy all factored into the short-term decline of the U.S. merchant fleet. However, something more fundamental lay at the heart of the problem. The advent of the British transatlantic steamers signaled the end of the American sailing packet's reign. Advances in steam engineering and iron construction left the American wooden shipbuilding industry behind, while at the same time scarce postwar capital went into internal improvements and western railroad construction rather than maritime enterprise.[5] America, it seemed, had gone west and abandoned the high seas.

Unable to compete with British steamers, American ship owners sold their vessels and got out of the business altogether. As the number of vessels in the U.S. registry declined, so too did the number of Americans willing to man them. Concerned about the influx of immigrants and foreigners into the navy and merchant marine, in 1872 Captain Luce ordered a statistical study of the crews of five naval ships serving in the Mediterranean Squadron. The results, reflecting similar manning problems in the merchant marine, revealed sailors from more than thirty-five different nationalities, with fewer than 46 percent of the total claiming to be native-born Americans. Naval officers of Anglo-American descent, like Luce, viewed these findings with alarm. They equated predominantly foreign-born crews with a host of shipboard dangers, including inadequate education, the inability to understand orders, low morale, high desertion rates, and a lack of loyalty to the American flag. Luce lamented the passing of the Yankee sailor and claimed that the present mix of seafarers was "inferior to those of almost every navy having the slightest pretensions of respectability."[6]

The solution to the manning problems, as Luce saw it, was the establishment of nautical schools. They would attract Americans back to the merchant service, help halt the overall decline of the service, reduce the appalling number of disasters at sea, safeguard vessels and cargo at sea, and restore pride in being an American sailor. Luce had been associated with formal naval education almost since its inception in 1845. As a member of the Class of 1849, he spent a year at the United States Naval Academy studying for his lieutenant's exam. Twenty-one years old at the time with seven years of service under his belt, he and his classmates proved a serious challenge to the administration. Charles Todorich referred to the "Oldsters" as "the most spirited, rambunctious, regulation-flouting group of men ever to grace Severn's shores."[7] In 1850 a significant reorganization of the academy took place, creating a curriculum emphasizing naval tactics and gunnery, seamanship, mathematics, natural philosophy (physics), English, and modern languages. A year later, a summer training cruise was added to the curriculum to give midshipmen more practical experience in seamanship and continued to be a prominent feature at the academy until 1909.[8]

This was the Naval Academy that Luce returned to in 1860–61 to become the assistant to the commandant. He was promoted in 1861 to head of its Department of Seamanship, a position he held until 1863. During this time, he became increasingly frustrated by the lack of professional literature covering basic aspects of seamanship. "Compared to the Army," he wrote, "with their wealth of professional literature, we may be likened to the nomadic tribes of the East who are content with the vague tradition of the past. Does it seem credible then, to this Institution that it should possess no textbook on the most important branch taught within these walls?"[9] Luce decided to research and write a comprehensive treatise on seamanship to solve this problem. However, the project proved too ambitious, and the Civil War prevented him from devoting his full attention to it, so that the end result was a synthesis of other sources.[10] Nevertheless, his *Seamanship*, first published in 1863, went through eight editions (five of them in ten years) and remained the primary text in the field until 1901.[11]

Luce's position at the Naval Academy gave him the opportunity to learn about the British model of maritime education. During the summer of 1863, Lieutenant Commander Luce accompanied the midshipmen on their transatlantic training cruise. While in England he gathered information about HMS *Conway* and HMS *Worcester*, nautical schools specifically designed to train merchant marine officers. In 1859, the Mercantile Marine Association of Liverpool had petitioned the Admiralty for a school ship. Numerous schools existed for the training of officers and men of the Royal Navy, but none existed for the merchant marine. The request was approved, and the frigate HMS *Conway* was provided for that purpose.[12] Given the success of the Liverpool school, Richard Green, a London ship owner, and William Munton Bullivant, a former sailor turned rope merchant, began to actively lobby the London maritime community to raise the funds necessary for operating a similar school on the Thames.[13] In 1862 the frigate HMS *Worcester* opened its doors as the Thames Marine Officers Training Ship and began accepting boys between the ages of twelve and fifteen for a two-year course of study. The curriculum included practical seamanship, navigation, nautical astronomy, and gunnery in addition to mathematics, mechanics, drawing, and

French. The Board of Trade stipulated that a graduation certificate from either school would count as one year of sea service, thus allowing cadets to take the Second Officer Examination after three years at sea.[14] While neither school included a training cruise in the curriculum, Luce was impressed. He observed that British sailors' "physique, intelligence, and seaman-like bearing surpassed any men we have seen on this side of the Atlantic for many years."[15] Upon his return, he began to actively encourage the establishment of nautical schools in the United States.[16] He cited as precedent the 1862 Morrill Land Grant Act (also known as the Agricultural College Bill) as federal legislation promoting a "liberal and practical education of the industrial classes in the several pursuits and professions of life."[17]

However, Luce's vision of maritime education did not become a reality until almost a decade later. In 1873, a group of New York merchants, underwriters, and ship owners had convinced the state legislature to pass "an Act to authorize the Board of Education for the City and County of New York to Establish a Nautical School." The state empowered the Executive Committee of the newly established New York State Nautical School to request a training ship from the U.S. Navy. Understandably hesitant to loan any of its vessels to a local government, Secretary of the Navy George M. Robeson refused to do so without the express consent of Congress.[18] The Executive Committee turned to Luce and asked him to draft federal legislation authorizing nautical schools and present it at the next session of Congress.[19]

Encouraged by the 1871 legislation requiring masters, mates, and engineers of steamers to obtain a certificate of competency from the Board of Steamboat Inspectors, Luce urged Congress to create a comprehensive system of maritime education, pointing out the limitations of the 1871 legislation. The examinations pertained only to officers serving on board steamships, not sailing vessels, and therefore failed to fully address questions of competency throughout the entire merchant marine. Although examined by the board in regard to engineering, the officers were not thoroughly examined in the subjects of seamanship and navigation, areas in which all merchant marine officers should have specialized knowledge.[20]

Luce believed that a successful system of maritime education should target sailors as early as possible in their career, boys between the ages of fourteen and seventeen.[21] This program of nautical instruction reflected Luce's educational philosophy and his own experiences as a fourteen-year-old midshipman in the U.S. Navy.[22] Well-trained boys were of greater value to the merchant and naval services than enlisted landsmen. "The latter," he wrote, "were generally too old to learn 'new tricks,' stiff jointed, and evinced little disposition to improve themselves."[23] To prepare these boys for the hardships and hazards of their profession, the curriculum include such vital elements as practical seamanship, navigation, and lifesaving as well as plenty of training cruises. Luce believed that "sailors can only be made at sea and on board sailing ships."[24]

His bill was titled "A bill to promote the efficiency of Masters and Mates in the Merchant Service, and to encourage the establishment of public Marine Schools." The final version included eighteen sections outlining the process for masters and mates to earn certificates of competency, penalties for sailing without a certificate or use of a fraudulent certificate, loans of naval vessels to serve as marine schools, assignment of naval officers as instructors, registration for boys attending marine schools, articles of indenture for boys to guarantee service until age twenty-one, requirements in ship tonnage corresponding to a prescribed number of boys on board, and inspection of marine schools by naval personnel.[25]

By February 1874, both the House and the Senate were considering nautical school legislation. Henry L. Dawes (R-MA) introduced the all-encompassing bill for Benjamin F. Butler (R-MA) in the U.S. House of Representatives as House Bill 1347. Aaron A. Sargent (R-CA), chairman of the Committee on Naval Affairs, introduced a second, abbreviated version of Luce's legislation as Senate Bill 176. Instead of a complete system regulating the training of merchant mariners, the Senate version merely gave the federal government authority to loan ships and naval officers to nautical schools if cities decided to establish them.[26] Dismayed, Luce undertook an intense lobbying campaign to ensure the passage of the more detailed House Bill 1347. He sent circular letters to the presidents of the General Boards of Trade throughout the country and called for the establishment of a federal agency devoted to the interest of ocean commerce, such as Great Britain's Board of Trade.[27]

Those efforts floundered. On June 20, 1874, the Senate approved the edited version of Luce's bill, known as the Marine Act of 1874, authorizing the establishment of nautical schools in the ports of New York, Boston, Philadelphia, Baltimore, Norfolk, and San Francisco and providing vessels and instructors on loan from the U.S. Navy.[28] Disappointed with the limitations of the legislation, Luce had nevertheless established the foundation for maritime education in the United States.

The Marine Act of 1874 marked the end of Luce's active involvement with the state nautical schools. It was now up to officers detailed to the school ships to take the concept from theory to practice. The first active-duty naval officers assigned to the New York Nautical School filled a variety of roles. Commander Robert L. Phythian, later superintendent of the Naval Academy between 1890 and 1894, came on board as superintendent. He was assisted by executive officer Lieutenant Commander George H. Wadleigh, senior instructor Lieutenant George W. De Long, junior instructor Lieutenant William H. Jacques, and physician and language arts instructor Passed Assistant Surgeon Daniel C. Burleigh.[29] The two-year course of instruction took place on USS *St. Mary's*, a 985-ton wooden sloop-of-war first launched in Washington, D.C., in 1844.[30] The vessel acted as classroom, dormitory, mess hall, and training ship for the roughly one hundred cadet-midshipmen who responded to the advertisements for maritime training. Although the New York Board of Education had been given the authority to administer and finance the starship, it was up to Superintendent Robert Phythian to design the curriculum, regulations, and daily schedule. One of his first actions was to hire a crew of twenty men (stewards, cooks, petty officers, and able seamen) to assist with the running of the ship. Ideally, as the cadet-midshipmen became more proficient, they would assume many of the responsibilities under the crew's guidance, but the crew would also act as instructors in the practical aspects of seamanship. This proved a more difficult task than expected, and Phythian complained that "great difficulty has been experienced in keeping up the complement. A large number have been shipped and discharged for incompetent or irregular habits. The men now on board seem to be well suited to their places, but a large majority of them are foreigners. It seems to me that no stronger argument in favor of the necessity of this school can be urged, than the fact that of the many who have applied for positions on board this ship, not six American seamen of fair capacity and good habits could be found."[31] Phythian echoed Luce's sentiments that the aim of maritime education was to attract native-born Americans into the merchant service. Typically, duty on board the *St. Mary's* lasted two years, but Commander Phythian remained on board three years. His tenure provided a stable and solid foundation for the fledgling nautical school.

Not surprisingly, Phythian used the Naval Academy at Annapolis as a model and created a curriculum that included basic academic subjects, practical seamanship, navigation, ordnance drill, and an annual training cruise. Cadet-midshipmen also studied arithmetic, reading, writing, spelling, grammar, penmanship, and geography as part of their general education. Practical seamanship included exercises in knotting and splicing, rowing boats, handling sails, and lifesaving drills. Luce's influence lingered, as his textbook *Seamanship* appeared in an edited version as *The Young Seamen's Manual* and became the standard book on ship handling.[32]

Navigation, the single most important skill necessary for rising from able seaman to mate, was eagerly sought out by cadets recognizing its benefit for future promotion. Cadet Washington L. Rodman studied hard as a cadet and continued to polish his navigation skills with Lieutenant Jacques after graduation during the winter of 1876–77. Rodman attended lectures and worked out problems using Nathaniel Bowditch's *The New American Practical Navigator* textbook, dead reckoning, chronometer, and watch comparisons. Rodman admitted to "having a very thorough course."[33]

The capstone of the maritime curriculum was a summer transatlantic training cruise in which the boys were asked to put into practice all they had learned while moored in New York Harbor. The general itinerary included stops in England, France, and Portugal. Few cadets were immune to the rigors of a transatlantic crossing under sail, and rough weather conditions brought more challenges to the already physically demanding task of handling a vessel under sail. Rodman wrote at the beginning of the 1876 practice cruise that "the boys are, with but with six or seven exceptions, woefully seasick, and the ship is in disgusting condition, and would be in great danger if a storm came up, for we could not get enough boys to handle her."[34] Upon the completion of two years of instruction, the cadet-midshipmen demonstrated their newly acquired maritime skills in both written and practical proficiency exams before receiving a graduation certificate.

After New York City, San Francisco announced that it would take advantage of the 1874 legislation. The U.S. Navy loaned USS *Jamestown* to its nautical school, but the West Coast experiment in maritime education ended abruptly in 1876. Still, naval officers remained convinced of the necessity of reviving the merchant fleet and training its mariners. In 1879 Lieutenant Commander French Ensor Chadwick visited the British maritime academies and sent a detailed report to the Bureau of Equipment and Recruiting thanking Captain Smith for providing information about the Thames Marine Training Ship in London. Since Luce's first visit, a total of seventeen maritime academies had been established for the training of merchant mariners in Great Britain, and in 1875 alone they boasted 1,306 graduates.[35] Compared to the solitary efforts of the New York Nautical School, limited by the size of USS *St. Mary's* to one hundred students, Chadwick believed that the United States would benefit from expanding its system of maritime education, especially along the lines of HMS *Worcester* in London and HMS *Conway* in Liverpool. However, Chadwick saw other British schools that were nothing more than reformatories for juvenile offenders. "The great defect of the mercantile training system now in use in England is that too many of the vessels are mere reformatories which send into the service boys with bad antecedents. Too great a supply of such boys tends to cast a stain upon the profession and cause it to be looked upon as a refuge for the destitute, worthless, and vagabond class. The great aim ought to be to elevate it as a reputable calling.... [T]here surely is no profession which calls for higher or more manly traits."[36]

Drawing on the opinions of naval officers such as Chadwick and concerned citizens, the Pennsylvania General Assembly voted on April 18, 1889, to establish the Pennsylvania Nautical School.[37] Charles Lawrence was named the first president of the Board of Directors, a fitting honor for a longtime advocate of maritime education in Philadelphia. Lawrence had served in the Union Navy as a sail maker and then pursued commercial shipping interests in Philadelphia. He was an active member of the Vessel Owners and Captains Association and in

1887 had taken the job of Philadelphia's harbor master.[38] Commander Francis W. Green reported as superintendent of USS *Saratoga*, an 882-ton wooden sloop-of-war built in the Portsmouth Navy Yard in 1842.[39] On board with him were Lieutenant Commander Edward T. Strong, Lieutenant B. O. Scott, Ensign Williams S. Sims, and Passed Assistant Surgeon W. H. Rush. Green personally wrote to recruit Sims for the position as the two had served together on the *Yantic*. "The whole details of the school are left to me," wrote Green, "and I think it will be a very comfortable place."[40]

From the onset, the Board of Directors and the naval officers worked to dispel the notion of the school as a reformatory. Instead, the school ship intended to offer a practical and technical course of study in seamanship and navigation. The school's prospectus promised to give boys between the ages of sixteen and nineteen "ample opportunity to advance to the highest position offered by our Mercantile Marine," and Lawrence promised to help them obtain jobs in the Philadelphia shipping industry.[41] The fact that U.S. naval officers acted as instructors was highlighted to assure parents and prospective students that they would be well cared for and "taught the proper courtesies and respect for official position, which will not only render them good citizens, but is essential between men and officers on shipboard."[42]

Given the nature of USS *Saratoga*, the Pennsylvania Nautical School continued to stress aspects of traditional seamanship including a transatlantic training cruise under sail. Cadet-midshipmen engaged in sail handling exercises such as reefing and furling; climbed aloft; maintained and repaired lines; mended sails; practiced lifesaving techniques such as lowering, maneuvering, and raising lifeboats; and tended to the general upkeep of the vessel. The lure of visiting foreign countries in Europe, South America, and the West Indies offered an added attraction to cadets. During the early 1890s, the Pennsylvania school ship made transatlantic trips to England and Portugal as well as Caribbean voyages with stops at St. Thomas, Guadeloupe, St. Kitts, Barbados, and Jamaica.[43] The exercises in practical seamanship allowed boys to discover for themselves whether or not they were suited for careers in the merchant marine.

In addition to seamanship, the Pennsylvania Nautical School's curriculum included navigation. The cadet-midshipmen were fortunate to have William S. Sims as their first navigation instructor. Sims had graduated thirty-third in a class of sixty-two from the Naval Academy in 1880 and had served on a variety of wooden sailing ships equipped with steam auxiliary including the *Tennessee, Colorado, Swatara,* and *Yantic*.[44] Thirty-one years old at the time, Sims discovered that he had a natural aptitude for teaching and threw himself into the assignment with energy and enthusiasm. Starting from scratch to design his own navigation course, he found the common textbook on navigation, Nathaniel Bowditch's *The American Practical Navigator*, too difficult for his cadets. Instead, he wrote his own textbook for their use. By 1892 Sims has amassed some 500 pages of navigation notes and compiled them into a notebook with 144 pages and 60 diagrams.[45] Sims's navigation textbook, although never published, gained wide circulation among merchant mariners. Before graduating from the Pennsylvania Nautical School, cadets made their own copy to take with them.[46] When Alfred Puekey expressed an interest in attending the Pennsylvania Nautical School, Sims responded by succinctly summarizing the aims of maritime education: "Tell him that life on the school ship is not all beans and skittles [and] that he will have to work hard if he wants to accomplish anything. That he will have to sleep in a hammock, eat plain food, wash his own clothes, and help take care of the ship and keep her clean. That in two years he can be a very fine navigator. That after that he must go to sea as a sailor and work his way up by learning to be a thorough seaman. Then his knowledge of navigation will get him the position of an officer if there is anything in him."[47]

The Pennsylvania Nautical School cadets benefited greatly from Sims's navigation instruction. Apparently, so too did the crew hired to serve on board the school ship. Like its New York counterpart, the Pennsylvania Nautical School hired approximately twenty men as petty officers and seamen. With the exception of those relating to William M. Dreilick (boatswain on the New York Nautical School during 1885–1922), few records exist of these sailors, certainly older than the cadets, already with seagoing experience, and many foreign-born. A New York Nautical School cadet-midshipman, Class of 1897, remembered Dreilick as "a real seaman from keel to truck, and who had the respect of all the boys and all the officers."[48] Felix Riesenberg, who had been cadet, instructor, and superintendent at the New York Nautical School, also recalled the Boatswain's extensive influence: "For many years Dreilick was the only man on board who rated visits from admirals. And this is not fiction, for a number of those old whales would come on board, and after a decent remark or two to the negligibles, would ask for Dreilick, the real object of their visits. All of them had served on the school ship as junior officers, and remembered the sea dog's work during those great storms and gales that punctuate the cruises and always give the boys something to remember through life."[49] Sims made it clear that many of the crew took the opportunity to use the nautical schools to study navigation on the side in preparation for licensing exams for first, second, and third mate positions in the merchant marine. In 1892 he wrote his family, "You can imagine that it is a great satisfaction to me to have given these men a chance to raise themselves from the ranks of common sailors."[50]

Throughout the 1880s the merchant marine's decline and its relationship to the U.S. Navy was a constant topic of discussion in naval circles. It figured prominently in articles appearing in *The United States Naval Institute Proceedings*. In 1882 the prize for the best entry in the United States Naval Institute Essay Contest went to Lieutenant J. D. J. Kelley and coauthors for the essay "Our Merchant Marine: The Causes of Its Decline and the Means to Be Taken for Its Revival." The article criticized the federal government for failing to allow foreign-built steamships to enter the American registry and advocated a policy of "Free Ships," allowing any vessel owned by an American to enter the U.S. registry regardless of where it was built.[51] There were several contributing authors including Carlos B. Calkins, who urged the navy to create under its jurisdiction a bureau of mercantile marine and assume responsibility for merchant marine inspection and licensing.[52]

While Green and Sims worked on developing the Pennsylvania Nautical School, Congress passed two key pieces of legislation aimed at strengthening both the merchant marine and the navy. The first Naval Appropriations Act, supported by Secretary of the Navy Benjamin F. Tracy, was passed on June 30, 1890. It provided financial backing for a long-term naval building program. Twenty armored battleships were approved to give the new U.S. Navy greater offensive capability.[53] With the assistance of Secretary of State James G. Blaine, the Merchant Marine Act of 1891 (also known as the Ocean Mail Act of 1891) attempted to offset the higher construction and operational costs of American steamships. Federal mail subsidies were provided to steamship lines using American-built vessels. The act disappointed Free Ships advocates, and given the high price tag at American shipyards, only well-established firms such as the Pacific Mail Steamship Company, the Red D Line, and the Ward Line could take advantage of the legislation.[54] The Merchant Marine Act of 1891 also provided an important provision for those proponents of maritime education. To be eligible for subsidies, a steamship company had to man those vessels with American officers and carry one cadet per one thousand tons.[55] At the beginning of the 1890s, both were heralded as important steps toward the renaissance of the merchant marine and the navy. However, in reality, it was the U.S. Navy that would rapidly eclipse the U.S. Merchant Marine over the next twelve years.

On June 11, 1891, the Commonwealth of Massachusetts created the Massachusetts Nautical Training School.[56] The chairman of the Board of Commissioners, John C. Soley, was determined to shape maritime education in the Bay State in response to a service transformed by steam propulsion. Soley set high standards for the institution and pledged "to render this Massachusetts Nautical Training School in respect to practical seamanship equal to the Naval Academy at Annapolis."[57] He set about achieving this goal by requesting a naval vessel with a steam engine for use as the school ship and succeeded in obtaining the bark-rigged steam gunboat USS *Enterprise*. Thus, the Massachusetts Nautical Training School was the first to add engineering and mechanical courses to its maritime curriculum. When Commander John F. Merry arrived to assume the position of superintendent, he brought with him not only executive officer Lieutenant C. A. Foster, senior instructor Lieutenant F. R. Brainard, mathematics instructor and ordnance officer Ensign William G. Miller, and surgeon J. W. Baker but also chief engineer George R. Salisburg.[58]

The naval officers designed a new maritime curriculum by grafting courses in engineering and mechanics to those in seamanship and navigation. They continued the traditional academic subjects such as mathematics, English, geography, and foreign languages. Since USS *Enterprise* was bark-rigged, cadet-midshipmen learned how to knot and splice rope and wire, handle yards and sails, maneuver small boats, and respond to emergencies. Navigation was required for all cadets. Students calculated latitude and longitude using dead reckoning, lead and log lines, deep-sea sounding, sextants, octants, compasses, and chronometers. In keeping with the navy's desire to use merchant sailors as a manpower reserve in wartime, cadets also drilled in the use of ordnance, including broadside batteries and rapid-fire guns, and were exposed to infantry and artillery tactics.[59]

The biggest difference between the Massachusetts Nautical Training School and the other school ships was the emphasis on engineering and mechanical courses. The Board of Commissioners expected the cadet-midshipmen to understand "all the duties of firemen and engineers on sea-going vessels."[60] Cadet-midshipmen studied mechanics and engineering, which included understanding the theory and practice of steam engines, machinery repair, and boiler maintenance both in port and at sea, mechanical drawing, and the inspection of coal and lubricants.[61] The Board of Commissioners approved: "The demand upon the seaman of to-day, for a fair knowledge of that portion of seaman's work now so largely done by machinery, from weighing anchor and hoisting in and out cargo and boats, to the proper handling of the main engines of his ship, makes it highly important that some attention be given this branch of education."[62] Eventually the New York Nautical School and the Pennsylvania Nautical School would also add engineering and mechanics to their school curriculum, but not until 1908, when the navy sent two bark-rigged steam gunboats, USS *Adams* and USS *Newport*, to Philadelphia and New York, respectively.

In the summer of 1893, USS *Enterprise* made a transatlantic training cruise with Cadet Robert Livermore among the 150 on board. The itinerary included stops in Portsmouth, England; Lisbon, Portugal; and Funchal, Madeira.[63] Livermore and his fellow cadet-midshipmen were kept busy at sea with a myriad of tasks necessary to keeping a twenty-four-hour watch system and a full complement of officers, crew, and cadets. Scrubbing the decks, tarring the rigging, setting sail, working the ship, and finding the position helped drive home aspects of practical seamanship. Still, Livermore's favorite task was steering: "I took to the helmsman's job naturally and looked forward to my trick at the wheel. There was a feeling of power and accomplishment in keeping that bulk of wood and canvas to her course, by day to see every sail drawing cleanly when the course was 'full and bye,' and by night when the sails were dark masses blotting out the stars to watch the compass needle swing true in the binnacle light, and feel the ship respond to the turn of the wheel."[64] The transatlantic voyage was a rite of passage from boyhood to manhood that few cadets ever forgot.

In many ways, the Massachusetts Nautical Training School was the most successful of the three nautical schools. Thanks to the combined efforts of the Board of Commissioners and the naval officers, it had shed the stigma of the Massachusetts State Reform School, which established in 1860 a Boston school ship for delinquent boys.[65] Rather, the Board of Commissioners tried to describe accurately the demands of the school and the advantages that such training could give boys interested in a career in the merchant marine: "This school ship is in no sense a reformatory, a sanitarium, or a craft for pleasure sailing. Boys who are not rugged in physique and resolute in spirit, or boys who are at all afraid of work or wet or cold or the general privations that may accompany a seafaring life, are not suited to become members of this school."[66]

The fact that the Massachusetts Nautical Training School filled its cadet classes to capacity, averaging around one hundred during the 1890s and 1900s, indicated that the cadets understood not only the risks but also the benefits of maritime education. By 1898, the Board of Commissioners reported that "it has been the custom in past years to advertise in the newspapers, notifying young men of vacancies in the school; but for the first time this proved unnecessary this year, as it was found that a sufficient number of applications was on file to fill up the school."[67] Although the majority of school ship graduates were too young to apply immediately for a third mate's license (federal guidelines established the minimum age as twenty-one), they already possessed the skills to pass the exam.

Interest in the Massachusetts Nautical Training School undoubtedly resulted from its ability to wed a seamanship curriculum to an engineering curriculum at a time of technological change in maritime affairs. However, it certainly helped to have a home port with a deep sense of maritime culture. The Board of Commissioners echoed this line of thought and wrote that "Massachusetts has excellent material: our young men have a natural inclination for the deep sea."[68] With an extensive coastline and a long tradition of seafaring activity in the fisheries industry, merchant shipping, and naval service, Massachusetts looked to its young men to continue in sea service.

The outbreak of the war with Spain in April 1898 brought an opportunity to test the new American navy. It also brought numerous challenges for the state nautical schools, as active-duty naval officers were detached from the school ships. All five naval officers on board the Massachusetts Nautical Training School were ordered on active duty during the first two weeks of April 1898. This occurred just before USS *Enterprise* was scheduled to depart for its annual transatlantic training cruise, causing considerable concern among the Board of

Commissioners. They hired Commander Andrew J. Iverson, USN (Retired), to act as interim superintendent and continued an abbreviated summer cruise along the New England coast while the war continued in the Caribbean.[69]

The New York Nautical School suffered the same hardships. The Executive Committee appointed Lieutenant Howard Patterson, New York State Militia, as superintendent of USS *St. Mary's*; he assumed command of the ship on May 10, 1989. Patterson also had to revise substantially the summer cruise itinerary so as to give the cadets some practical experience at sea without venturing too far into the Atlantic Ocean. James D. Laird and Isidor L. Ach, teachers in the New York City public schools system, reported as instructors, with Dr. Robert Smart acting as physician. Henry Campling was appointed as executive officer in July, but a lingering illness caused Patterson to instead appoint boatswain William Dreilick to the position.[70] Despite the trial and tribulations, Patterson proudly reported to the Executive Committee "that from the day I took command, up to the return of the ship from her cruise, the studies of the sections in spelling, reading, history, arithmetic, geography, composition and punctuation were incessantly maintained, in addition to all the professional work."[71] No annual reports exist for the Pennsylvania State Nautical School during this time, but it is reasonable to assume that the same problems plagued USS *Saratoga*.

America's victory over Spain seemed to justify not only Alfred Thayer Mahan's theories of sea power but also the superiority of the new navy. With a new overseas empire to govern, the navy began to rethink the policy of sending active-duty officers to state nautical schools. Although they returned to the schools in November 1898, the disruption caused by the war signaled a change in policy. The merchant marine continued its downward slide, while the navy experienced a renaissance with technologically new and modern vessels. Instead of viewing the merchant marine as a potential manpower reserve, the navy became convinced that it would need to look elsewhere to find enough men to fill its berths. Even if merchant mariners had been available, the navy recognized that they would not have the technological skills necessary for battleships and cruisers. Instead, navy recruiters moved away from major port cities, such as Boston, New York, and Philadelphia, and reached into interior states with new advertising campaigns that promised young men the chance to learn engineering skills.[72]

Despite their best efforts, the state nautical schools never achieved their ultimate goal of becoming "the Annapolis of the merchant marine." The small number of nautical schools limited the number of cadet-midshipmen who entered the merchant service, and other avenues for advancement to ratings of master and mate reflected the division within the maritime community as to the best method of educating future merchant marine officers. In 1902 the Board of Commissioners of the Massachusetts Nautical Training School reported that "the pressing need of the Navy Department for officers for the new ships lately put into commission has resulted in the enforced withdrawal from the various school ships of all the officers detailed for that duty."[73] Attempts were made by the New York Nautical School to fill the vacant position from the navy's retired lists, with limited success.[74] A concerted effort was also made to attract civilian merchant mariners and engineers to the school ships. These men, some of them former nautical school graduates themselves, would continue the job of maritime education in the twentieth century.

This outcome does not diminish the role of the U.S. Navy in introducing maritime education to merchant mariners. Luce and his fellow officers offered a blueprint for the United States Merchant Marine Academy. They viewed nautical schools as a means to strengthen the merchant marine service and solve the social and economic problems of both the commercial and military fleets at the end of the nineteenth century. The State University of New York Maritime College and the Massachusetts Maritime Academy are living legacies to those efforts. Many graduates of these nautical schools went on to serve with distinction during World Wars I and II and demonstrated the tremendous capability of the merchant marine as a naval auxiliary.

Notes

Many thanks to The Citadel Foundation for the generous travel and research support necessary to complete this essay.

1. John D. Hayes, "Stephen B. Luce, Class of 1846, Educator of the Navy, Founder of the Maritime College," *Shipmate* (November 1956): 3.

2. John D. Hayes and John B. Hattendorf, "The Man: Stephen Bleecker Luce," in John D. Hayes and John B. Hattendorf, eds., *The Writings of Stephen B. Luce* (Newport, RI: Naval War College, 1975), 8–13.

3. Robert Seager II, "Ten Years before Mahan: The Unofficial Case for the New Navy, 1880–1890," *Mississippi Valley Historical Review* 40 (1953): 501.

4. Stephen B. Luce, "The Manning of Our Navy and Mercantile Marine," *The Records of the United States Naval Institute Proceedings* 1 (1874): 23. The address was first delivered at the U.S. Naval Academy, Annapolis, Maryland, on November 13, 1873.

5. Lawrence C. Allin, "The Civil War and the Period of Decline: 1861–1915," in Robert A. Kilmarx, ed., *America's Maritime Legacy: A History of the U.S. Merchant Marine and Shipbuilding Industry since Colonial Times* (Boulder, CO: Westview, 1979), 66–67.

6. Stephen B. Luce to George M. Robeson, Secretary of the Navy, November 12, 1872, Stephen B. Luce Papers, Library of Congress, Washington, D.C.

7. Charles Todorich, *The Spirited Years: A History of the Antebellum Naval Academy* (Annapolis, MD: Naval Institute Press, 1984), 35–37, 52.

8. Ibid., 68, 165.

9. Stephen B. Luce to C. P. R. Rodgers, Commandant of Midshipmen, February 26, 1861, Stephen B. Luce Papers, as quoted in John D. Hayes and John B. Hattendorf, "The Man: Stephen Bleecker Luce," in Hayes and Hattendorf, *The Writings of Stephen B. Luce*, 8.

10. Hayes, "Stephen B. Luce, Class of 1846," 4.

11. Stephen B. Luce, *Seamanship: Compiled from Various Authorities and Illustrated with Numerous and Selected Designs, for the Use of the United States Naval Academy*, 2nd ed. (Newport, RI: Atkinson, 1863).

12. *Shipping and Mercantile Gazette*, August 26, 1861, Minute Books, 1861–1867, HMS *Worcester* Collection, National Maritime Museum, Greenwich, England.

13. Frederick H. Stafford, *The History of the "Worcester": The Official Account of the Thames Nautical Training College, H. M. S. Worcester, 1862–1929* (London and New York: Frederick Warne, 1929), 17–18.

14. Thames Marine Officers Training Ship *Prospectus*, 1863, HMS *Worcester* Collection.

15. Stephen B. Luce, "Training Ships: Educating Boys for Seamen," *Army and Navy Journal* 1 (December 19, 1863): 260.

16. Stephen B. Luce, "Nautical Schools," *Army and Navy Journal* 4 (December 22, 1866): 281.

17. Luce, "Manning of Our Navy and Mercantile Marine," 25.

18. Norman J. Brouwer, "Stephen B. Luce and the Federal Act of 1874," *Sea History* 57 (Spring 1991): 12.

19. Executive Committee on Nautical Schools of the Board of Education of New York City to Stephen B. Luce, August 20, 1873, Luce Papers.

20. Stephen B. Luce to Presidents of the General Boards of U.S. Trade, February 12, 1874, Luce Papers.

21. Stephen B. Luce, "... Organization of New York Nautical School," n.d., Luce Papers.

22. Hayes and Hattendorf, "The Man: Stephen Bleecker Luce," 3–5.

23. Luce, "Training Ships: Instruction of Ship's Boys," 277.

24. Luce, "... Organization of New York Nautical School," n.d., Luce Papers.

25. Stephen B. Luce, "Rough Draft of a Bill to Promote the Efficiency of Masters and Mates in the Merchant Service, and to Encourage the Establishment of Public Marine Schools," n.d., Luce Papers.

26. Brouwer, "Stephen B. Luce and the Federal Act of 1874," 13.

27. Luce to Presidents of the General Boards of U.S. Trade, February 12, 1874, Luce Papers.

28. Marine Act of 1874, *U.S. Statutes at Large* 18 (1874): 121.

29. Board of Education of the City and County of New York, *Thirty-third Annual Report of the Board of Education of the City and County of New York for the Official Year Ending December 31, 1874* (New York: Board of Education of the City and County of New York, 1875), 441.

30. William H. Rideing, "The Nautical School Ship *St. Mary's*," *Harper's New Monthly Magazine* 59 (1879): 340–49.

31. Board of Education of the City and County of New York, *Thirty-fourth Annual Report of the Board of Education of the City and County of New York for the Official Year Ending December 31, 1875* (New York: Board of Education of the City and County of New York, 1876), 403.

32. Ibid., 400–402.

33. Washington L. Rodman diary, December 19, 1876, January 3, 1877, New York Nautical School Collection, SUNY Maritime College, Bronx, New York. See Stephen B. Luce, *The Young Seaman's Manual, Compiled from Various Authorities, and Illustrated with Numerous Original and Select Designs, for the Use of the U. S Training Ships and the Marine Schools* (New York: D. Van Nostrand, 1875).

34. Washington L. Rodman diary, July 5, 1876, New York Nautical School Collection.

35. French Ensor Chadwick, *Report on the Training Systems for the Navy and Mercantile Marine of England and on the Naval Training System of France Made to the Bureau of Equipment and Recruiting, U.S. Navy Department, September, 1879* (Washington, DC: U.S. Government Printing Office, 1880), 114, 149.

36. Ibid., 149.

37. Nautical School Act of 1889, *Laws of the General Assembly of the Commonwealth of Pennsylvania* (Harrisburg, PA: State Printer, 1889), 347.

38. "Lawrence Chosen," May 11, 1891, and "Charles Lawrence Wins," May 12, 1891, *The Evening and Sunday Bulletin* News Clipping Collections, Temple University Urban Archives, Philadelphia, Pennsylvania.

39. Cecil Davies, Raymond Eisenberg, and William Wichert, *Chronicle: A History of Pennsylvania's Schoolships and Those Graduates Known to the Association* (Philadelphia: Pennsylvania Schoolship Association, 1956), 5–6.

40. Francis W. Green to William S. Sims, November 18, 1889, Williams S. Sims Papers, Library of Congress.

41. Pennsylvania Nautical School *Prospectus*, 1889, Pennsylvania Nautical School Collection, Independence Seaport Museum, Philadelphia, Pennsylvania.

42. Ibid.

43. Ibid.

44. David F. Trask, "William Sowden Sims: The Victory Ashore," in James C. Bradford, ed., *Admirals of the New Steel Navy: Makers of the American Naval Tradition, 1880–1930* (Annapolis, MD: Naval Institute Press, 1990), 282–84.

45. William S. Sims to Louisa Sims, February 14, 1892, Sims Papers; Williams S. Sims to Sims family, March 13, 1892, Sims Papers. A copy of the navigation textbook reposes in the Nimitz Library, United States Naval Academy.

46. Elting E. Morison, *Admiral Sims and the Modern American Navy* (Boston: Houghton Mifflin, 1942), 32.

47. William S. Sims to Lou Sims, February 27, 1891, Sims Papers.

48. "Memories of the *St. Mary's*," 1897, New York Nautical School Collection.

49. Felix Riesenberg, "About William M. Dreilick," n.d., New York Nautical School Collection.

50. William S. Sims to Sims family, April 1, 1892, Sims Papers.

51. J. D. J. Kelley, "Our Merchant Marine: The Causes of Its Decline and the Means to Be Taken for Its Revival," *United States Naval Institute Proceedings* 8 (March 1882): 28–33.

52. Allin, "Civil War and the Period of Decline: 1861–1913," 75.

53. Ronald Spector, "The Triumph of Professional Ideology: The U.S. Navy in the 1890s," in Kenneth J. Hagan, ed., *In Peace and War: Interpretations of American Naval History* (Westport, CT: Greenwood, 1978), 175–77.

54. René De La Pedraja, *A Historical Dictionary of the U.S. Merchant Marine and Shipping Industry, since the Introduction of Steam* (Westport, CT: Greenwood, 1994), 452–53.

55. Board of Education of the City and County of New York, *Fifty-third Annual Report of the Board of Education of the City of New York for the Year Ending December 31, 1894* (New York: Board of Education of the City of New York, 1895), 292.

56. *Acts and Resolves Passed by the General Court of Massachusetts* (Boston: State Printer, 1891), 1009–10.

57. John C. Soley to the Governor of Massachusetts, December –, 1892, Massachusetts Nautical Training School Collection, Massachusetts Maritime Academy, Bourne, Massachusetts.

58. Massachusetts Nautical Training School, *USS Enterprise Prospectus* (Boston: Massachusetts Nautical Training School, 1894), 11–12, Massachusetts Nautical Training School Collection.

59. Ibid., 8–10.

60. Ibid.

61. Ibid.

62. Commissioners of the Massachusetts Nautical Training School, *Massachusetts Nautical Training School Terms of Admission, Course of Study, Daily Routine, and Code of Discipline* (Boston: Commissioners of the Massachusetts Nautical Training School, 1908), 6.

63. Robert Livermore, *Bostonians and Bullion: The Journal of Robert Livermore, 1892–1915*, ed. Gene M. Gressley (Lincoln: University of Nebraska Press, 1968), 11–13. Robert Livermore's diary is at the Massachusetts Historical Society, Boston.

64. Libermore, *Bostonians and Bullion*, 9–10.

65. Norman J. Brouwer, "Centennial History of the S.U.N.Y. Maritime College at Fort Schuyler, 1874–1974" (Master's thesis, State University of New York College at Oneonta, Cooperstown Graduate Program, 1977), 8–9.

66. Board of Commissioners of the Massachusetts Nautical Training School, *Annual Report of the Commissioners of the Massachusetts Nautical Training School* (Boston: Board of Commissioners of the Massachusetts Nautical Training School, 1897), 8.

67. Board of Commissioners of the Massachusetts Nautical Training School, *Annual Report of the Commissioners of the Massachusetts Nautical Training School* (Boston: Board of Commissioners of the Massachusetts Nautical Training School, 1898), 6.

68. John C. Soley to the Governor of Massachusetts, December –, 1892, Massachusetts Nautical Training School Collection.

69. Board of Commissioners of the Massachusetts Nautical Training School, *Annual Report of the Commissioners of the Massachusetts Nautical Training School* (Boston: Board of Commissioners of the Massachusetts Nautical Training School, 1899), 3–4.

70. Department of Education of the City of New York, *Annual Report of the Department of Education of the City of New York for the Year Ending July 31, 1898* (New York: Department of Education of the City of New York, 1899), 34–36.

71. Ibid., 37.

72. Frederick S. Harrod, *Manning the New Navy: The Development of a Modern Naval Enlisted Force, 1899–1940* (Westport, CT: Greenwood, 1978), 3–6.

73. Board of Commissioners of the Massachusetts Nautical Training School, *Eleventh Annual Report of the Commissioners of the Massachusetts Nautical Training School* (Boston: Board of Commissioners of the Massachusetts Nautical Training School, 1903), 7.

74. Department of Education of the City of New York, *Annual Report of the Department of Education of the City of New York for the Year Ending July 31, 1902* (New York: Department of Education of the City of New York, 1903), 340–41.

4
THE AMBASSADOR'S TROOPS
U.S. MILITARY ATTACHÉS AND MILITARY INTELLIGENCE, 1885–1920

John F. Votaw

PRIOR TO THE WAR WITH Spain in 1898, officers of the U.S. Army were members of a parochial and slowly modernizing professional group. Recent scholarship has challenged the long-held opinion that the officer corps was severely isolated from civilian society during the late nineteenth century, as suggested by Samuel Huntington and others.[1] A small group of American officers serving as military attachés in the last fifteen years of the nineteenth century and the first two decades of the twentieth century experienced the internationalism that other sectors of American society had made routine.[2] As Graham Cosmas has written, "the basic agenda for Army reform was set well before the outbreak of war with Spain."[3] The military attachés were part of that reform impulse. At their foreign posts, the American officers responded to the needs of the resident U.S. minister or ambassador but also worked according to task lists provided by the Military Information Division (MID) of the War Department. Specifically, they developed contacts with military officers of their respective host nations and other military and naval attachés of nations posted to that same host country. Normally, the senior attaché, regardless of nationality, functioned in the capacity of coordinator in both official group and social situations. This international, cosmopolitan outlook was absorbed by American officers and carried back to their units and subsequent staff assignments in the United States. The work of the American attachés did not produce much direct transfer of information from foreign military establishments to the U.S. Army and U.S. Navy, but it did create an awareness of how other military systems dealt with problems and issues confronting the American military. In a reciprocal way, officers of foreign nations were posted as attachés in Washington, D.C., so the same cross-cultural dissemination of ideas and practices occurred there as well. This is not to discount the obvious intelligence-gathering function of the military attaché when he was serving abroad.[4]

John Greenwood, in his study of military observers in the Russo-Japanese War, concludes that not much of importance happened within the American military establishment as a result of the observers' reports to the MID and the Office of Naval Intelligence (ONI) of the Navy Department. He was certainly correct that no important policy or doctrinal issue was implemented or changed as a result of what had been learned by American observers in Manchuria.[5] However, the American observers and military attachés who witnessed in Manchuria the new technology of war—machine guns, rapid-firing field artillery pieces, functional logistics, and tactical intelligence operations—did convey that information back to the MID and the ONI. Some of the information found its way into technical bulletins and pamphlets; other information was shared within the bureaus of government. What has not been proven to date is whether any such activity had a direct bearing on improved technology or operational procedures in the American army or navy. The water had been poured in the trough, but the horses may not have drunk any of it.

Beginnings

An inward-looking nation for the first seventy-five years of its existence, the United States had no pressing need for military information from abroad. Aside from identifying textbooks needed at the U.S. Military Academy and an occasional study of foreign fortifications, American contacts with other military systems were infrequent and in response to specific requests.[6]

After the Civil War, it was common for American officers to seek opportunities outside the normal routine of life within the service or garrison. Some sought adventure overseas with foreign armies, but most regular officers either stuck it out or resigned in favor of civil life. For those who were not fighting Indians, there were opportunities for education, both civil and professional.[7] In the late 1880s the military services, other agencies of the federal government, and business corporations were adding intelligence bureaus to their organizations. Henry J. Reilly Jr., son of the famous commander of Reilly's Battery in the China Relief Expedition, even served as a foreign correspondent for the *Chicago Tribune* while a member of the Officer Reserve Corps (ORC) of the army. He served as an attaché in the Philippines twice and as an artillery regimental commander in the American Expeditionary Forces (AEF) in World War I.[8]

In 1873 Ulysses S. Grant was in the White House, the United States was reeling from the economic panic of that year, and the country had begun to emerge from its tradition of dispersed power and informal management of public affairs.

The Plains Indians and the Apaches of the Southwest engaged the post–Civil War army as roads and railroads began to advance west of the Mississippi River. A sense of community was beginning to extend from local to national focal points in social, economic, and political affairs. As Robert Wiebe has observed, Americans sought "continuity and predictability in a world of endless change" by the end of the nineteenth century. Government was becoming more familiar and perhaps less onerous, if not less intrusive. It was "America's initial experiment in bureaucratic order, an experiment that was still in process as the nation passed through the First World War."[9]

But in the 1870s this transformation had only penetrated slightly into the institutions of the army and navy. In 1873 the U.S. Naval Institute was founded to provide naval officers with a forum to examine current issues of policy and strategy apart from the formal bureaucracy of the navy. Five years later, Major General Winfield Scott Hancock founded the Military Service Institution of the United States to "promote writing and discussion about military science and military history." But the prevailing routine in both military services was conducted apart from society at large and moved at a formal, and often a slow, pace. Some officers in both services, particularly those inclined to things intellectual, took advantage of the hiatus in military operations to reflect on their profession. It was largely among this group of self-motivated men that the army and navy found their attachés. The navy established its intelligence service in 1882, followed in 1885 by a similar agency in the army within the Adjutant General's Office. The first five army officers posted to attaché duty took their stations in 1889.[10] They were young and exuberant. In 1909, when Major T. Bentley Mott returned to France for another tour of duty as military attaché, he observed that the "new military attachés I found in Paris were a much older and more serious lot than the gay blades who had been used to assemble at the Café de Paris for our monthly dinners."[11]

It is difficult to say exactly when military and naval attachés began serving the United States and who they were. Richard Delafield, Alfred Mordecai, and William B. Hazen, to take only a few examples, all performed "attaché-like" duties in the decades preceding the war with Spain.[12] We also know that naval officers on cruises to foreign stations, such as Matthew C. Perry who visited to Japan in 1853, engaged in diplomatic negotiations and made technical reports to the Department of the Navy.[13] But the beginning of organized formal military and naval intelligence activities in the United States coincided with the reform of the government bureaucracies that began at the end of the nineteenth century and was capped by Elihu Root's reorganization of the War Department General Staff in 1903.[14] The navy did not have a comparable staff, although Secretary John D. Long created the General Board of the Navy in 1900 to provide professional advice to the secretary.[15] It is clear that intelligence operations existed long before there were coherent, effective organizations to plan and manage them. The navy in 1882 and the army in 1885 took those first hesitant steps toward a systematic approach to the gathering and analysis of information from abroad. Yet we cannot firmly establish a connection between the activities of the early intelligence gatherers and any permanent codification and rationalization of intelligence and attaché procedures and institutions in the formative period before the National Defense Act of 1920.

Only a few studies of American officers engaged in attaché and intelligence work prior to 1920 have been published. Jeffery Dorwart and Peter Karsten, in books about the Office of Naval Intelligence and the professionalization of naval officers, have studied the work of U.S. naval officers. More recently, Thomas Mahnken explored the craft of intelligence and those who practiced it between the two World Wars.[16] John Greenwood was certainly correct in concluding from his study of the military observers of the Russo-Japanese War that no significant institutional reforms flowed directly from their reports and recommendations. My own study of the larger story of the development of a military attaché system for the U.S. Army shows that the work of army officers who served as military attachés through World War I contributed to the growth of the American army as an internationally sophisticated force disproportionate to their numbers, which were small compared to the size of the officer corps of that period. Their role in the development of the army's intelligence agency was one of leadership and competence. Both of these points still appear valid, but little if any organizational or procedural reform occurred in the War Department as a result of their service.[17]

Some questions about attaché service in the United States remain to be examined. Did the army create the position of intelligence staff specialist prior to 1920? How did the military and naval department leaders view intelligence gathering in the four and a half decades before 1920? Did military and naval attachés talk with each other? How did military and naval attachés view themselves? What did they think they were doing? Can we assess the worth of the early attachés' efforts vis-à-vis any improvement in national intelligence operations prior to 1920?

The Early Attachés

A number of army officers who rose to high rank and responsibilities during World War I served as observers and attachés prior to 1917. Captain Tasker H. Bliss was the U.S. military attaché in Madrid in 1897–98, just prior to the war with Spain. In March 1895, Bliss wrote to Lieutenant General John M. Schofield, commanding general of the army, to remind him that Bliss had proposed a process for gathering information from foreign stations that "exists scattered through the various Bureaux of the War Department." Bliss anticipated the kind of information that would have military value to the War Department nearly twenty-five years before it was codified in a manual for American military attachés. His early attaché experience contributed to his appreciation for the value of accurate, timely information about foreign armies while he served as acting chief of staff of the army in 1917–18 and as senior U.S. military representative with the Supreme War Council in France in 1918.[18]

Henry Tureman Allen is best remembered for his command of the 90th Division in World War I, but he had several early military attaché assignments that were important to his development as a professional U.S. Army officer. He served in Russia from 1890 to 1895, in Germany in 1897 and 1898, and briefly in Korea early in 1904 along with Andre W. Brewster, later the inspector general of the AEF. Allen commanded the U.S. forces in Germany from 1919 until those forces were returned to the United States in 1923. During that same time he was a member of the Inter-Allied Rhineland High Commission, with considerable diplomatic responsibilities. In the 1920s, Allen published two books, retired from active duty (1923), and was a staunch supporter of the League of Nations until his death from a stroke in 1930.[19]

Peyton C. March, army chief of staff from 1918 to 1921, and John J. Pershing, commander in chief of the AEF during World War I, both served in Manchuria in 1904–5 during the Russo-Japanese War. Writing about Pershing's opportunity to serve as a military attaché, Frank Vandiver notes that "attachés in proper places learned much and enjoyed more." As Vandiver writes, Pershing was convinced that the war between Japan and Russia "would teach much about modern methods."[20] With friends in high places, Pershing was soon on his way to Tokyo with a new bride. His tour of duty from March 1905 to September 1906 was in Tokyo itself, but he managed to get to the front in Manchuria. Observing the Russian artillery in action in July 1905, Pershing noted that their indirect fire was "not efficient against attacking troops," a point that he did not forget as a field army commander in France in the fall of 1918.[21]

Captain March was one of four officers selected to accompany the Japanese field army in Manchuria. Colonel Enoch H. Crowder, who would become judge advocate general of the U.S. Army in 1911, was in this same group; its senior officer was British Lieutenant General Sir Ian Hamilton.[22] Later, when March was appointed acting chief of staff, he recalled that the daunting task of organizing the War Department General Staff for efficient operations was made easier by the things that he had learned as a military attaché.[23]

There is a significant body of evidence that service as an attaché provided a number of American officers with experiences that served them well professionally as they rose in rank and took on greater responsibilities. An example is Thomas Bentley Mott, arguably America's most experienced and effective military attaché before World War II. In addition to repetitive assignments to the American Embassy in Paris before and after World War I, Mott had accompanied former Secretary of war Elihu Root and his party on a specially constituted mission to Russia in 1917, days before Pershing, Mott's friend and West Point classmate, offered him a position with the new AEF in France. Mott explained his dilemma, and the new general in chief understood his friend's professional judgment in choosing to remain with the special mission. It was why he had offered Mott the position in the first place. "As soon as you return from Russia," said Pershing, "I will ask for you to come to France."[24]

Lieutenant Colonel Mott developed a close working association and personal friendship with Ambassador Myron T. Herrick in Paris from 1909 to 1913. Mott had served in the Paris post from 1900 to 1905 and was familiar with Paris and the French system of military organization. In 1918 Pershing sent him, along with Lieutenant Colonel Stuart Heintzelman, to the Italian front to report on progress in that peripheral theater. After the armistice of November 11, 1918, Mott returned to the American Embassy in Paris, where he served from 1919 to 1930, part of the time under Ambassador Hugh Wallace and most of the time as personal assistant to Herrick, who replaced Wallace as ambassador in 1921. No other American military attaché had a record of important diplomatic assignments and significant military liaison duties that equaled those of T. Bentley Mott. As he admitted in his memoirs, "it was pleasant to walk about Paris in Uncle Sam's boots."[25]

Attachés Reflect on Their Service and Training

More than any army officer before him, General William Tecumseh Sherman appreciated, in the years following the American Civil War, that education and training in the officer corps was essential to a heightened condition of professional competence. He lent his name and energy to the establishment of army schools of practice and collateral ventures such as the Military Service Institution of the United States. The curriculum at the army's first modern school for officers at Fort Leavenworth, Kansas, stressed Sherman's belief that "broad military and educational experience" was essential for "every officer, particularly those aspiring to high command and staff positions." But this comprehensive educational experience, while innovative for its time, did not include special training in intelligence, attaché staff work, or subjects (other than military geography) that were even tangentially related to such study.[26]

Arthur L. Wagner, a teacher at Leavenworth where he wrote *The Service of Security and Information* (1893), was an exception in that he was very interested in staff work and its application to the American military system. Wagner's interest resulted in his assignment as chief of the MID of the Adjutant General's Office in 1896. He made significant contributions to planning in the Spanish-American War, but the idea of a great general staff was still in the future. It was closer to reality for the army, however, than for the navy. This is not entirely surprising, because European staff procedures at the end of the nineteenth century seemed alien and inapplicable to the American condition even though selected American officers admired the German military system and, to a lesser degree, the French military system.[27]

Even as late as 1919, when U.S. military attachés were invited to submit critiques of the attaché service to their parent agency, it was evident that much of the preparation and training of officers selected for this duty was ad hoc and uneven. Cavalry Lieutenant Colonel R. M. Campbell reported from Mexico City that he "was sent to this Embassy without being called to Washington and without receiving any instructions whatsoever as to the duties . . . [he] was expected to perform [there]." This, he explained, was probably due to the "existence of an emergency" (i.e., World War I) and thus "was an exceptional case." But it was not. In some cases, attachés "representing different branches of our Government evidently arrived with instructions which conflicted with the policy which the United States was trying to carry out" at the legation in Cuba during the Great War.[28]

Specialization as an attaché, or even as an intelligence staff technician, was not a part of staff duty, which was by detail from one's regiment or place of permanent assignment and was limited as to the time an officer could be absent from his unit. Even after the creation of the War Department General Staff in 1903, positions were filled by company and field officers on a part-time basis. Colonel W. F. H. Godson, the military attaché at Berne, Switzerland, suggested in a long letter to the MID in February 1919 that "a section of M.I. [should be] devoted entirely to the work of the Military Attachés, under charge of an officer, who has had experience as a Military Attaché and who understands the possibilities as well as the drawbacks of the position." This knowledgeable chief should have "two assistants who could travel, one to be always on the road." Military attachés should be chosen from "a card index of all the officers in the army" qualified by virtue of language ability, character, and experience. Godson concluded by insisting that all newly appointed attachés undergo "at least one month's course" under the supervision of the master attaché at the MID. "The value of this cannot be overestimated," he emphasized.[29] At a 1996 conference on leadership challenges for the army, one participant mentioned that a system was needed to identify individual officer talent at the macro-level so that appropriate assignments for complex but temporary and ad hoc tasks at the micro-level could be made efficiently. It is the same problem that Colonel Godson identified and essentially the same solution he recommended, albeit without the aid of computers.[30]

Godson was ringing a familiar bell. Well before 1919, officers on station in legations and embassies were lamenting their lack of guidance and training in the specific duties of attaché work. In some ways—which may be characteristic of the times—the work was believed by the officer corps at large to be of marginal value, both personally and institutionally, and to be intuitively simple, something any competent line officer with enough personal wealth could do easily with little or no training. The detached service law of 1911, the so-called Manchu Law, reflected that sort of attitude. Interestingly, both the army and the navy used ad hoc recruiting of bright college graduates and professors by granting them reserve commissions as intelligence officers to fill those rapidly expanding spaces in the MID and the ONI. Some of those men became assistant military and naval attachés, but most became intelligence staff officers. In the same way that John C. Calhoun and Emory Upton imagined an "expansible army" in the nineteenth century, the intelligence agencies employed that technique to meet the rapidly growing demands of World War I. Upton also had called for a cadre of trained professional officers to organize and train the rapidly mobilized filler troops. In the case of the MID and the ONI, a few of those trained cadre existed, but not enough to staff and train their whole organizations. While a specialized body of knowledge (one of Huntington's characteristics of a professional group) emerged from World War I attaché work, officers were not considered—and did not consider themselves—professional attachés.[31]

As the MID geared up for service in World War I and as the intelligence staff office (G-2) of the AEF was being fitted out, the technical requirements for officers filling attaché assignments became more complex, partly because the attaché could "no longer look for his information among military" sources alone. Brigadier General David L. Brainard, U.S. military attaché in Lisbon, Portugal, reported to the MID in March 1919 his opinion that qualified officers should receive three months of training. On their own they should receive refresher training in the language and history of the country where they were to be posted. They should also be trained in codes and ciphers as well as in photography, "especially in methods of photographing documents." Some tutoring in how to get along with the chief and secretaries of the attaché's mission would also be helpful, Brainard believed.[32]

As might have been anticipated, one of the army's most experienced and thoughtful attachés, Colonel Edward Davis, noted the deficiencies of the attaché system prior to and during World War I and then advised that "we are now dealing with the Future and we are responsible for it because we know what ought to be done and how to do it." He advocated educating the army at large via a document "containing a concise and guarded statement of the scope of Military Attache's work with a definite word of official appreciation" to stimulate interest and support. He further suggested "annual courses of lectures" on intelligence and attaché matters "as part of the curriculum at the War College; Army Staff, Signal, Line and Field Engineering schools; Coast Artillery School,

Mounted Service School; schools of fire, musketry and engineering and all other schools for officers." His report included several schemes to raise the morale and visibility of the unsung, unheralded attaché, such as encouraging "some popular magazine" to craft an article "with an air of mystery" and "an element of fiction . . . to arouse interest in the Army" for attaché work. Anyone who had served during World War I as an attaché, he said, should be required to submit a detailed report before being demobilized. Noting that superficial training was given to new attachés during the war, Davis added that "I know from my own experience and the experiences of others, that there was really no training at all." He concluded his report with some detailed advice on subjects and methods of training. Some of this advice was implemented in the reorganization of the courses at Fort Leavenworth in the early 1920s, and some of the recommended lectures were delivered at the Army War College by officers who had been in G-2, the AEF, or the MID during World War I.[33]

Similarly, before the war with Spain in 1898 the typical post-academy education for U.S. naval officers was on-the-job training with the fleet punctuated by short tours with the various Navy Department bureaus. For some, such as Lieutenant Commander French Ensor Chadwick, there were more stimulating assignments: collecting information from abroad and dealing with the representatives of the seal harvesting and other industries. Naval officers, more than army officers, "aided and abetted businessmen abroad" as part of a joint U.S. Navy–Executive Department policy of boosting American industry in the 1880s. Chadwick, an early member of the United States Naval Institute and the ONI's "first permanent naval attaché," was the epitome of an intelligent, versatile, and extraordinary commissioned officer who, unlike Alfred Thayer Mahan, was also a competent line officer. Chadwick became chief of naval intelligence in 1892, a time when morale was plummeting, but "his brief tenure never produced the expected rejuvenation of ONI."[34]

Like their army counterparts, naval attachés were saved from misuse at the end of the nineteenth century by the wars involving Japan. As Dorwart observes, "the U.S. Navy initiated its most comprehensive intelligence exercise in the nineteenth century during the Sino-Japanese War" of 1894. The ONI's attaché network performed well, but the analysis, collation, and sharing of information in Washington were rudimentary and imperfect. During the period before and after the war with Spain, Lieutenant William S. Sims made a name for himself as a "brash and enthusiastic" naval attaché. Similarly, Lieutenant William H. Beehler, from his post in Berlin, alertly monitored the international traffic in arms following the Spanish-American War. But while these officers longed for promotion and responsibilities they saw as possible only in service with the line, the ONI was an acceptable holding pattern for them. As the nation matured "as an expansive world power, ONI emerged finally as an accepted and official part of the naval establishment."[35]

During the lull prior to America's entry into World War I as a belligerent, attachés and intelligence officers of the army and navy observed the German military establishment's rise to power and prominence in Europe. Joseph E. Kuhn, prior to his promotion to brigadier general and his assignment as chief of the War College Division, War Department General Staff, early in 1917, reported from Berlin from 1914 to 1916, first as a military observer and then as a military attaché. By 1913, the ONI had almost abandoned its naval attaché system for an ad hoc system of special missions, but the approaching European war and the energy of naval officers such as Sims and Lieutenant Commander Dudley Knox revitalized the interest in intelligence.[36]

Interservice Cooperation

Addressing the necessity of reorganizing the army in his annual report for 1899, Secretary of War Root suggested that the "proposed [army] war college acting in cooperation with the existing naval war college, that is, the union of the army and the navy in the collection and utilization of information, studying and formulating plans for defense and attack, and the testing and selection of material of war[,] . . . could not fail to be of great value to both services, and to make easier and more certain that perfect cooperation which is so essential both in forming and executing the plans which involved the operations of both forces." Even with so strong a suggestion so early in the process of modernization, in actual practice effective coordination between the army and navy intelligence agencies depended on professional officers to overcome interdepartmental suspicions and petty rivalries to accomplish often overlapping responsibilities.[37]

The less-than-effective cooperation by the Joint Army and Navy Board on matters of policy and strategy that were of interest to both services provided almost no information to attachés who were on their own in overseas legations and embassies and had to obtain information from other government agencies. For example, in January 1919 Colonel Walter F. Martin, the acting chief, Positive Branch, MID, in Washington, wrote to Lieutenant Colonel Thomas F. Van Natta Jr., the military attaché assigned to Madrid, in response to Van Natta's suggestion that attachés be given a briefing on U.S. policies in the region to which the new military diplomat was to be posted. Martin provided some accurate but irritating advice: "Of course, the War Department does not handle the question of policy, and all we can do is to try to interpret the situation to the best of our ability." He went on to explain that it would be "very confusing" if the War Department staff tried to "learn the policy of the State Department" to explain same to their various attachés. They would be better served if such information was sought from the minister or ambassador. Martin accepted Van Natta's advice on seeking information directly from other agencies of government and encouraged him to do so because the MID, with its heavy workload, could not provide such information in a timely way: "The trained officer should not hesitate to ask for what he needs."[38]

The Department of State and its ambassadors abroad received the military and naval attachés with uneven confidence. Some, such as Mott and Chadwick, fit smoothly into the "country team" and were consulted regularly by the ambassador, while others were treated as unwanted intruders. It was very much a personality determinant system in which the novice attaché had to learn quickly or become an ineffective ornament. During World War I, Ambassador William Graves Sharp developed a strong, effective, professional relationship with the military officers in his embassy and elsewhere in France. In most cases, the exigencies of the war put on hold most of the more petty bureaucratic incongruities of attaché duty.[39]

Of course, military and naval attachés posted to the same legation or embassy knew each other and cooperated in obtaining information when it made sense for them to do so, but each group of officers and their assistants, while sharing similar information collection problems, responded to two different agencies in Washington and to questions often divergent and not coordinated between the departments. The ONI under Captain Roger Welles in 1917 did try to "develop policies to collaborate with other branches of government and with the intelligence networks of the Allied powers." Likewise, the MID recognized the necessity of coordination in intelligence matters, but its efforts fell far short of effective joint staff action. In a rare bit of cooperative work at the end of the Paris peace negotiations in 1919, partly by way of fiscal subterfuge, a joint War Department–State Department Black Chamber was established in New York City under Herbert Yardley's direction.[40]

At the highest level of government, the military intelligence agencies coordinated and cooperated only marginally and operated very parochially in discharging their respective departmental intelligence tasks. By the time of the armistice of November 1918, the MID had twenty-one officers maintaining contact with sixteen War Department and thirty-three outside agencies including the ONI and the State Department. Yet liaison and the unilateral movement of information did not constitute effective cooperation. It was here that the work of the military and naval attachés, so arduously performed at foreign stations, came to naught. Training was defective throughout the military and naval intelligence systems, not just at the level of the attachés.[41]

Based on the examination of a recently published guide for naval attachés, Captain Wilson P. Foss Jr. of the MID's Positive Branch informed Colonel Martin by memorandum on March 6, 1919, that a similar guide would benefit the new military attachés: "I believe that such a book, if thoroughly studied, would prove of infinitely more value in generally enlightening Military Attaches about to enter upon their duties, than does the present method of instruction." Another example of cooperation at the MID-ONI level was the willingness of the departments to cover for each other in the event of an unexpected vacancy in a particular embassy. Occasional consultations on matters of the moment did not, however, substitute for institutionally sound procedures designed to coordinate matters of intelligence policy and operations, both of which affected U.S. attachés abroad.[42]

The Eye of the Beholder

What did U.S. Army and U.S. Navy officers think they were accomplishing when on attaché or observer duty abroad? Eric Fisher Wood had been studying in Paris when war broke out in the summer of 1914. On Tuesday, August 4, he reported to the American Embassy and offered his services to Ambassador Herrick. Wood was uncertain of his duties: "I cannot say whether I am a doorman or an Attaché. At present the duties of the two seem to be identical."[43] The letter orders posting attachés to foreign missions were administrative in nature; essentially, they directed the officers to gather information about the host military establishments and report periodically according to the accepted format. Each attaché was told that his superior was the U.S. minister or senior civilian official charged with representing the nation at that location. Implied, but not always explicitly stated, was a requirement to keep the respective military departments informed of significant developments that were of military interest to the United States.[44]

From ad hoc postings in the 1850s to highly institutionalized intelligence operations by 1920, American officers stationed abroad tried to provide the information their departments requested. Occasionally, exceptional officers went beyond the defined boundaries of their duties to comment on larger issues of national security. In 1858 Alfred Mordecai reported to Secretary of War John B. Floyd that he regretted the "imperfect" quality of his report on the Crimean observation mission, which he blamed on the intrusion of other work. Richard Delafield, on the other hand, had been more direct in his report two years earlier to Secretary of War Jefferson Davis. Somewhat awed by the large standing armies in Europe, Delafield noted that "our preparation in material, equipment, knowledge of the art of war, and other means of defense, is as limited and inefficient, as theirs is powerful and always ready." He even postulated that those European powers might "steam across the Atlantic" and put ashore "disciplined armies that could land in six hours after anchoring" and cripple the American republic. Europe was on the threshold of a series of wars of national consolidation and looked far more threatening to American witnesses than was warranted.[45]

William B. Hazen, as well as Philip H. Sheridan, observed the events leading up to and during the Franco-Prussian War of 1870–71. Hazen admired the German people, "who have accomplished so much by rational and persistent labor," and tried to be "just in . . . [his] criticisms upon French character and methods."

Neither Sheridan nor Hazen was a military attaché in the institutional sense because their assignments preceded the establishment of the attaché system, but each performed tasks commonly associated with attachés and military observers.[46]

The group of naval officers referred to in the 1880s as Young Turks included officers interested in reorganizing naval administration and procedures, and many of them wrote for publication. Known as doers, by the eve of World War I many were rising to positions of authority in the new navy. The creation of the ONI in 1882 stemmed directly from the lobbying of a group of reform-minded junior officers; the early attachés included some of this class, the "leading naval activists of the day." The ONI's many publications gave voice to the "activist naval strategy," which often called for active war planning and a general staff for the navy.[47]

During the Balkan Wars that preceded the outbreak of war in Europe in 1914, a number of perceptive army officers reported the approaching storm from abroad. As might be deduced, the navy's interests concerned mostly Great Britain, Japan, and the sea lines of communication with both countries. Although overtly apolitical in the execution of their duties, those young army officers serving abroad were nonetheless politically astute, some more than others. The U.S. military representative in St. Petersburg in 1917 was First Lieutenant Sherman Miles, the son of General Nelson Miles; he was followed without overlap by Second Lieutenant E. Francis Riggs. There was a shortage of American officers qualified to serve in Russia, and Miles did not speak Russian. On the other hand, Captain Newton A. McCully, the U.S. naval attaché, was more experienced. None of this group, which also included Lieutenant Colonel (later Brigadier General) William V. Judson, had "a decisive influence on the course of events in Russia during their tours of duty," but Judson "did help to establish a basis for cooperation between the Bolsheviks and the United States government." At the conclusion of World War I, several conferences "to improve intelligence procedures and provide for a better coordination of effort" were scheduled for American military attachés, but many were dropped when the army and navy began to feel the squeeze of downsizing in personnel and budgets.[48]

Serving a Democracy Abroad

The National Defense Act of June 4, 1920 — had it received support from Congress, an otherwise apathetic public, and a Republican president committed to economy in government — might have allowed the codification and rationalization of our military and naval intelligence agencies on a permanent basis. Brigadier General Dennis E. Nolan, the War Department's assistant chief of staff (G-2), had argued strongly for "a military intelligence reserve element within the structure of the newly created Officers Reserve Corps." This feature — authorized on August 4,

1921, by War Department special regulation—was designed to provide those intelligence specialists who had been difficult to find and train prior to World War I. It was one of those good reorganization ideas that died of neglect. Most important institutional innovations are created under the pressure of dire necessity or impending threat to the nation, and neither condition existed after 1918. Officers with wartime experience left the service because of age or disinterest; meanwhile, training money dried up. The value of intelligence staff work, however, bubbled up during the discussions on naval armaments and particularly during the Washington Naval Conference of 1921–22. As late as 1939, the army's chief of staff was convinced that the training of reserve intelligence officers should be done by detail, just as it always been in the Regular Army.[49]

The impulse to demobilize, while it did not result in the disappearance of the MID or the ONI, did decelerate their modernization initiatives that resulted from rigorous self-analysis at the end of World War I. Reform of an institution seldom receives its impetus from within the institution; normally, it is precipitated by outside events. Recent research has suggested that "the demobilization of intelligence was not nearly as drastic as is commonly thought," and those agencies made intelligent modifications in order to survive in an era of diminishing resources. The Department of State, on the other hand, underwent a "dramatic transformation" toward a true career organization in the decade following 1914. However, the process of modernization in the military departments was delayed until 1938, when the threat of foreign aggression again raised the visibility and importance of intelligence and, by extension, attaché work.[50]

Returning to my general questions, some tentative answers are possible. World War I experience in attaché work showed that intelligence specialists were desirable and could be accommodated in the force structure. The National Defense Act of 1920 gave the intelligence agencies the opportunity to accomplish their objectives, but parsimony and lack of a foreign threat retarded modernization. By the end of World War I, the chiefs of intelligence in the navy, the army, and the State Department realized that intelligence operations involved a body of specialized knowledge requiring professionally trained officers. The military and naval attachés who served in the interwar period benefited from the work and thoughtful reflection of their predecessors, but the agencies that oversaw their deployment and guided their activities languished on the shoals of neglect born of complacency.

Notes

1. See Graham A. Cosmas, *An Army for Empire: The United States Army in the Spanish-American War*, 2nd ed. (Shippensburg, PA: White Mane, 1994), preface, xi (nn. 1–2). This version of "The Ambassador's Troops" is adapted from two unpublished conference papers delivered in 1995 and 1996.

2. The MID of the War Department began posting military attachés in missions and embassies abroad in 1889. The numbers were always very small, but in the thirty-five years following its establishment in 1885, the MID sent approximately 250 officers on attaché duty. Most served a single tour of duty, but a few served recurring assignments.

3. Cosmas, *Army for Empire*, xi.

4. Alfred Vagts, *The Military Attaché* (Princeton, NJ: Princeton University Press, 1967), 15, 18, 33–35.

5. See John Thomas Greenwood, "The American Military Observers of The Russo-Japanese War (1904–1905)" (PhD diss., Kansas State University, 1971).

6. John F. Votaw, "United States Military Attachés, 1885–1919: The American Army Matures in the International Arena" (PhD diss., Temple University, 1991), 3–4; Russell F. Weigley, *History of the United States Army* (New York: Macmillan, 1967), 281–92.

7. Edward M. Coffman, *The Old Army: A Portrait of the American Army In Peacetime, 1784–1898* (New York: Oxford University Press, 1986), 215–86, passim.

8. Reilly Jr. graduated with the West Point class of 1904, served on attaché duty in the Philippines in 1905 and during 1909–11, and then resigned as a first lieutenant. In 1914 he was commissioned a lieutenant colonel in command of the 149th Field Artillery regiment of the 42nd ("Rainbow") Division. Later he commanded the 83rd Infantry Brigade of that division in World War I. He was the youngest brigade commander in the U.S. Army in that war. He was commissioned in the Officer Reserve Corps (ORC) as a brigadier general, serving from 1920 to 1948, when he retired. He reported on events in Poland in 1920 as the Russian Bolshevik army closed on Warsaw. See Lloyd Wendt, *Chicago Tribune: The Rise Of A Great American Newspaper* (Chicago: Rand-McNally, 1979), 472; Association of Graduates USMA, *2000 Register of Graduates and Former Cadets* (West Point, NY: Association of Graduates, USMA, 2000), sect. 4, p. 83; Votaw, "United States Military Attachés," 2, 239.

9. Richard B. Morris et al., eds., *Encyclopedia of American History*, 7th ed. (New York: HarperCollins, 1982), 299–300; Oliver Lyman Spaulding, *The United States Army in War and Peace* (New York: Putnam, 1937), 353–68; Robert H. Wiebe, *The Search for Order, 1877–1920* (New York: Hill & Wang, 1967), xiii–xiv.

10. See Elizabeth Bethel, "The Military Information Division: Origin of the Intelligence Division," *Military Affairs* 11 (1947): 17–18; Colonel Bruce W. Bidwell, *History of the Military Intelligence Division, Department of the Army General Staff: 1775–1941* (Frederick, MD: University Publications, 1986), 53–55, 58; U.S. Army War College Staff Paper, "History of the M. I. D." (created for the use of a board of officers on G-2 records pursuant to G-2 Memorandum No. 38, November 25, 1924), U.S. Army Military History Institute Carlisle Barracks, Pennsylvania (hereafter cited as USAMHI); Kenneth J. Hagan, *This People's Navy: The Making of American Sea Power* (New York: Free Press, 1992), 183–85; Weigley, *History of the United States Army*, 274; and Coffman, *The Old Army*, 222, 234, 246–47, 250–52, 268–86, passim.

11. Colonel T. Bentley Mott, *Twenty Years As Military Attaché* (New York: Oxford University Press, 1937), 148–49.

12. Richard Delafield, *Report of Colonel R. Delafield, U.S. Army . . . on the Art of War in Europe in 1854, 1855 & 1856*, House of Representatives Executive Document, 36th Cong., 2nd sess. (Washington, DC: George W. Bowman, 1861); Major Alfred Mordecai,

Military Commission to Europe in 1855 and 1856, ibid. Delafield was the senior member of a military commission sent abroad by Secretary of War Jefferson Davis; Mordecai was a member of the same commission. Nowhere in the language of the appointing orders is the word "attaché" used, although the tasks assigned were typical of those given to attachés later. See William B. Hazen, *The School and the Army in Germany and France, with a Diary of Siege Life at Versailles* (New York: Harper, 1872). See also Michael Lee Lanning, *Senseless Secrets: The Failures of U.S. Military Intelligence from George Washington to the Present* (New York: Carol Publishing Group, 1996), 100–103, 114–17, for a narrative view of some of those information-collecting missions.

13. Hagan, *This People's Navy*, 147–51.

14. Robert D. Schulzinger, *The Making of the Diplomatic Mind: The Training, Outlook, and Style of United States Foreign Service Officers, 1908–1931* (Middletown, CT: Wesleyan University Press, 1975), passim; Richard D. Challener, *Admirals, Generals, and American Foreign Policy, 1898–1914* (Princeton, NJ: Princeton University Press, 1973), introduction; James E. Hewes Jr., *From Root to McNamara: Army Organization and Administration, 1900–1963* (Washington, DC: Center of Military History, 1975), 3–50, passim; Weigley, *History of the United States Army*, 190–96.

15. Hagan, *This People's Navy*, 132; Jeffery M. Dorwart, *The Office of Naval Intelligence: The Birth of America's First Intelligence Agency, 1865–1918* (Annapolis, MD: Naval Institute Press, 1979), 40, 71, 89, 97; Weigley, *History of the United States Army*, 320, 405.

16. Votaw, "United States Military Attachés," 3–4; Dorwart, *Office of Naval Intelligence*, 40, 71, 89, 97; Jeffery M. Dorwart, *Conflict of Duty: U.S. Navy's Intelligence Dilemma, 1919–1945* (Annapolis, MD: Naval Institute Press, 1983); Peter Karsten, *The Naval Aristocracy: The Golden Age of Annapolis and the Emergence of Modern American Navalism* (New York: Free Press, 1972); Thomas C. Mahnken, *Uncovering Ways Of War: U.S. Intelligence and Foreign Military Innovation, 1918–1941* (Ithaca, NY, and London: Cornell University Press, 2002). See also Jeffrey T. Richelson, *A Century of Spies: Intelligence in the Twentieth Century* (New York: Oxford University Press, 1995); Lanning, *Senseless Secrets*, chap. 6; Ralph E. Weber, ed., *The Final Memoranda: Major General Ralph H. Van Deman, U.S.A. Ret., 1865–1952, Father of U.S. Military Intelligence* (Wilmington, DE: Scholarly Resources, 1988).

17. Greenwood expanded on his study of military observers in the Russo-Japanese War in "The U.S. Army Military Observers with the Japanese Army during the Russo-Japanese War (1904–1905)," *Army History* 36 (Winter 1996): 1–14, 16. He notes that army officers after the Spanish-American War were eager to learn from their experiences in Manchuria, but a precise assessment of the value of those experiences "defies accurate appraisal." No American army, and perhaps no army, "could risk major doctrinal or organizational changes on slim and ambiguous evidence that often contradicted its own basic institutional beliefs and established organization and doctrine." Moreover, the lessons of the fighting in Manchuria, Greenwood cautioned, were far more apparent "after 1918 than they were before 1914." Votaw and Greenwood agree, though, that the career army officers who experienced the duty in Manchuria did benefit professionally from that duty even though the institution of the army may have been oblivious to the information they provided.

18. Memorandum of March 22, 1895, Tasker H. Bliss Papers, 130–33, USAMHI. Although the MID issued administrative orders to its officers posted to foreign missions and legations beginning in 1889, those instructions were very brief and usually directed the officer to collect information of military value and report it to the MID. No detailed standard operating procedure existed before 1921. The Tasker H. Bliss Papers in the Library of Congress (LC) contain "little or no trace of his [attaché] activities during that period [1897–1898]" (LC finding aid). Some information about Bliss's service in Spain is provided in Frederick Palmer, *Bliss, Peacemaker: The Life and Letters of General Tasker Howard Bliss* (Freeport, NY: Books for Libraries Press, 1970), chap. 5, passim.

19. "Allen, Henry Tureman," in Allen Johnson and Dumas Malone, eds., *Dictionary of American Biography*, vol. 21, supplement 1 (New York: Scribner, 1944), 22–23; biographical note from the Henry Tureman Allen Papers, LC, showing assignments from 1859 to 1930; Heath Twichell, "Allen, Henry Tureman," in Roger J. Spiller et al., eds., *Dictionary Of American Military Biography*, 3 vols. (Westport, CT: Greenwood, 1984), 1:19–22. See also Twichell's *Allen: The Biography of an Army Officer, 1859–1930* (New Brunswick, NJ: Rutgers University Press, 1974). The Allen diary, 1904, in the Allen Papers, Box 1, describes his time as military attaché posted to Korea to observe the Japanese army.

20. Frank E. Vandiver, *Black Jack: The Life and Times of John J. Pershing*, 2 vols. (College Station: Texas A&M University Press, 1977), 1:344.

21. Votaw, "United States Military Attachés," 108.

22. Ibid., 100; Edward M. Coffman, *The Hilt of the Sword: The Career of Peyton C. March* (Madison: University of Wisconsin Press, 1966), 27–38. On the threshold of World War I, March observed: "I had served in three arms of the line, the Field Artillery, Infantry and Coast Artillery; and had been part of the War Department Organization both as an Adjutant General and a General Staff officer. All this was rounded by observation in the field of the greatest war of modern times up to that period—the Russo-Japanese War. Few officers of my time had the good fortune to have any such varied experience." Quoted from a 1928 memoir in Coffman, *Hilt of The Sword*, 38.

23. Coffman, *Hilt of The Sword*, 53; Peyton C. March, *The Nation at War* (Garden City, NY: Doubleday, Doran, 1932), 40.

24. Mott, *Twenty Years As Military Attaché*, 191.

25. Ibid., 18; T. Bentley Mott, *Myron T. Herrick, Friend of France: An Autobiographical Biography* (New York: Doubleday, Doran, 1929), 258.

26. Timothy K. Nenninger, *The Leavenworth Schools and the Old Army: Education, Professionalism, and the Officer Corps of the United States Army, 1881–1918* (Westport, CT: Greenwood, 1978), 22–23, 64 (the material quoted here is Nenninger's paraphrase of Sherman's language in the latter's letter of November 22, 1881, to General Philip H. Sheridan); Boyd L. Dastrup, *The U.S. Army Command and General Staff College: A Centennial History* (Leavenworth, KS: J. H. Johnston III; Manhattan, KS: Sunflower University Press, 1982), 14, 31–36.

27. Carol Ann Reardon, "The Study of Military History and the Growth of Professionalism in the U.S. Army before World War I" (PhD diss., University of Kentucky, 1987), 219–27. This work was published as *Soldiers & Scholars: The U.S. Army and the*

Uses of Military History, 1865–1920 (Lawrence: University of Kansas Press, 1990.) See also Nenninger, *Leavenworth Schools and the Old Army*, 24, 31, 37, and John W. Masland and Laurence I. Radway, *Soldiers and Scholars: Military Education and National Policy* (Princeton, NJ: Princeton University Press, 1957), 79–87.

28. MID 2461, Military Attaché Suggested Improvements File, Record Group (RG) 165, Box 1387, p. 2, National Archives (NA), Washington, D.C. See also the report of Lieutenant Colonel Thomas Van Natta Jr., Cavalry, from the U.S. Embassy in Madrid, February 21, 1919, file 2461.2, ibid.

29. MID 2461-17, Report No. 1326, Colonel W. F. H. Godson, Cavalry, to Acting Director of Military Intelligence, "Suggested Improvements to the Military Attaché System," February 14, 1919, RG 65, p. 6, ibid.

30. Oral remarks made at Cantigny, Wheaton, Illinois, March 29, 1996, during the Symposium on Leadership Challenges of the 21st Century Army.

31. MID 2461-17, Report No. 1326, Colonel Edward Davis to D.M.I. [Director of Military Intelligence], "Suggestions As to Improvement of Military Attache System (Your Circular Letter No. 27, Dec. 30, 1918)," April 30, 1919, RG 165, p. 2, NA. Colonel Davis uniformly praised the young, temporary assistants who worked as part of his staff in the Netherlands at the end of World War I: "No group of foreign military intelligence officers in Holland acquitted itself with more credit than did my own staff of assistants, five gentlemen from the Atlantic seaboard . . . of New York City and . . . Boston. They were all temporary officers—not regulars—and had no previous experience in this kind of work. But they all had the first essential, that is to say, complete and unquestioning loyalty to their leader. This and their industry, talents, devotion to duty and general grasp of the situation constituted the foundation of all the success in Holland which was attributed to me by the authorities in Washington, of that period" (Davis diary, 414, US-AMHI). Dorwart, *Office of Naval Intelligence*, 103, 108–12, 141; Lanning, *Senseless Secrets*, 150; Samuel P. Huntington, *The Soldier and the State: The Theory and Politics of Civil-Military Relations* (New York: Vintage Books, 1964), 8–9, 12–13.

32. MID 2461-12, Report No. 944, Colonel Paul W. Beck to Director of Military Intelligence, "Manual," April 17, 1919, RG 165, p. 3, NA. Lanning, *Senseless Secrets*, 155, claims that "the AEF received little or no intelligence assistance from [Major Ralph] Van Deman and his Military Intelligence Section back in Washington" and points to hostility in the relationship between Major Van Deman and "Major" Dennis E. Nolan, the AEF G-2, as the principal reason for ineffective staff-line cooperation. Actually, in June 1918 Colonel Van Deman joined the AEF staff, leaving Colonel Marlborough Churchill in charge of the MID, War Department General Staff, in Washington. Nolan and Churchill were promoted to brigadier general at the end of the war, and Nolan was given command briefly, during the Meuse-Argonne campaign, of the 55th Infantry Brigade of the 28th Division. During this period, Van Deman was the G-2, AEF. Nolan's "personal relationship with Ralph Van Deman and Marlborough Churchill made the coordination of intelligence [and attaché] matters with the War Department reasonably smooth, even though the bureaucratic organization of both agencies was not well developed." See Votaw, "United States Military Attachés," 138; Votaw, "Dennis Edward Nolan," in Anne Cipriano Venzon, ed., *The United States in the First World War: An En-*

cyclopedia (New York: Garland, 1995), 416–17; and Bidwell, *History of the Military Intelligence Division*, 116–17, 136, 138–40. See also MID 2461-14, Report No. 391, Brigadier General D. L. Brainard to Director of Military Intelligence, "Suggestions for Improvement of Military Attaché System," March 24, 1919, RG 165 pp. 4, 6, NA.

33. MID, Davis Report, 2461-17, p. 4, RG 165, NA; Dastrup, *U.S. Army Command and General Staff College*, 63–65, 70, 74–75. In Brigadier General Hanson Ely's reorganized Command and General Staff School (1922), officers were taught that they were managers of violence and "team players," not nineteenth-century warriors. Leavenworth instructors were not out to mold Alexanders and Napoleons; they were making average officers into a skilled staff team that an Alexander or a Napoleon could rely on. But the emphasis at Leavenworth was still on the applicatory method of teaching command, doctrine, and tactics, with little room for specialized subjects such as intelligence techniques. On October 23, 1919, Colonel C. H. Mason gave a lecture titled "The Doctrine and Practice of General Staff Intelligence" at the General Staff College, Washington, D.C. Lieutenant Colonel D. C. McDonald gave a speech titled "The Military Attaché System" to the Army War College Class of 1927–28. There are other examples that some attention was paid to the lessons of staff work in France.

34. Karsten, *Naval Aristocracy*, 192; Dorwart, *Office of Naval Intelligence*, 17, 19, 31–37, 46–49.

35. Dorwart, *Office of Naval Intelligence*, 51, 54, 60, 67–68, 70.

36. Ibid., 94–96. Joseph Ernst Kuhn graduated first in his class (1885) at West Point and entered the Corps of Engineers. He had been an observer during the Russo-Japanese War in 1904–5 and in Germany during the maneuvers of 1906. After his assignments in Germany during 1914–16 and service as chief of the War College Division, War Department General Staff, he was promoted to major general and given command of the 79th Division. His performance as a division commander was not stellar. He retired in 1925 and died ten years later, at age seventy-one. Kuhn was one of the most competent and versatile officers to serve in the intelligence service before and during World War I. *Annual Report of the Association of Graduates, USMA* (West Point, NY: Association of Graduates, USMA, June 11, 1937), 125–27.

37. Elihu Root, *The Military and Colonial Policy of the United States: Addresses and Reports*, ed. Robert Bacon and James Brown Scott (Cambridge, MA: Harvard University Press, 1916), 359–60.

38. MID File 2461-2/3-1, Colonel Walter F. Martin to Lieutenant Colonel Thomas F. Van Natta Jr., "Instruction of Attaches," January 22, 1919, RG 165, NA.

39. Votaw, "United States Military Attachés," 17–19, 39–41; William Graves Sharp, *The War Memoirs of William Graves Sharp, American Ambassador to France, 1914–1919* (London: Constable, 1931), 214–15, 348–50.

40. Dorwart, *Office of Naval Intelligence*, 107–8; Bidwell, *History of the Military Intelligence Division*, 132, 253–54. Yardley's code and cipher group had been factored out of the reorganized Second Division, War Department General Staff, owing to a "lack of any special intelligence funds." The intelligence directors of the War Department, the Department of the Navy, and the State Department conferred and determined that all but the code and cipher functions of M.I.8 would have to be absorbed elsewhere in their

organizations. One hundred thousand dollars was found to conceal Yardley's operation in unauditable contingency funding. Codes and ciphers were the lifeblood of attaché communications.

41. Bidwell, *History of the Military Intelligence Division*, 134; Colonel C. H. Mason, in a lecture to the General Staff College, Washington, D.C., October 23, 1919, took the position that the system of military attachés "is the basis of collection" of information, but "liaison with American international business firms, with the State Department, Navy Department and other official bureaus, . . . the information furnished by the Attaches is supplemented and checked." Copy 133 of 210 on file at USAMHI.

42. MID File 2461-4, Foss to Martin, RG 165, NA; Votaw, "United States Military Attachés," 39. The suggested guide for military attachés was published by the MID on April 21, 1921.

43. Eric Fisher Wood, *The Note-Book of an Attaché: Seven Months in the War Zone* (New York: Century, 1915), 3. In 1917 Wood published a companion volume, *The Note-Book of an Intelligence Officer*, after serving briefly in Germany as an intelligence staff officer of the then-neutral United States. Fisher's experiences as an attaché and intelligence staff officer illustrate the close relationship of the two functions in the American military.

44. MID File 2507-2, Captain M. J. Lenihan, Lecture to Officers of the Second Section, General Staff, and the Army War College, November 14, 1908, RG 165, pp. 10–18, NA; MID File 349-47, Lieutenant Colonel D. C. McDonald, Memorandum for the Commandant, Army War College, "The Military Attaché System," March 31, 1928, RG 165, p. 4, NA.

45. Mordecai, "Report, Watervliet Arsenal, March 30, 1858" (cover letter of transmittal to "Hon. John B. Floyd, Secretary of War"), *Military Commission to Europe in 1855 and 1856*; Delafield, *Report of Colonel R. Delafield*, 2–3. Alfred Mordecai graduated first in his class of thirty-five graduates of the U.S. Military Academy in 1823. Commissioned in the ordnance branch, he transferred to the Corps of Engineers. Following assignments at West Point and the Office of the Chief of Engineers, he commanded, prior to the outbreak of the Civil War, the federal arsenals at Frankford, Pennsylvania; Washington, D.C.; and Watervliet, New York. He resigned his commission as a major in 1861. He died in Philadelphia in 1887 at age eighty-five. Richard Delafield was first in his class of twenty-three graduates at West Point in 1818. He was appointed to the Corps of Engineers and served as superintendent of his alma mater from 1838 to 1845 and again during 1856–61. Brigadier General Delafield was chief of engineers during 1864–66 and retired in 1866 as a brevet major general. He served as a regent of the Smithsonian Institution from 1865 to 1871. He died in 1873 at age seventy-five.

46. Votaw, "United States Military Attachés," 32; Paul Andrew Hutton, *Phil Sheridan and His Army* (Lincoln: University of Nebraska Press, 1985), 201–6; Hazen, *School and the Army in Germany and France*, 382. William Babcock Hazen graduated twenty-eighth in a class of thirty-four at West Point in 1855. Commissioned in the infantry, he served in the Indian-fighting army before the Civil War, commanded an Ohio regiment in that

war, and was breveted five times including to the rank of major general. He was the chief signal officer of the army from 1880 to 1887. He died in 1887 at age eighty-seven.

47. Karsten, *Naval Aristocracy*, 300.

48. Samuel J. Lewis, "American Military Attachés in Russia, 1914–1917," in Joachim Remak, ed., *War, Revolution and Peace: Essays in Honor of Charles B. Burdick* (Lanham, MD: University Press of America, 1987), 59–87; Bidwell, *History of the Military Intelligence Division*, 254–55; Dorwart, *Office of Naval Intelligence*, 140–42.

49. Weigley, *History of the United States Army*, 400–405; C. Joseph Bernardo and Eugene H. Bacon, *American Military Policy: Its Development since 1775* (Harrisburg, PA: Stackpole, 1961), 384–87; Bidwell, *History of the Military Intelligence Division*, 293–98; Dorwart, *Conflict of Duty*, 19–29; Hagan, *This People's Navy*, 261–69.

50. Bidwell, *History of the Military Intelligence Division*, 252; Robert G. Angevine, "Gentlemen Do Read Each Other's Mail: American Intelligence in the Interwar Era," *Intelligence and National Security* 7 (1992): 1–29; Schulzinger, *Making of the Diplomatic Mind*, 59–64. Congress was "persuaded . . . to reform the Foreign Service" in the aftermath of World War I. Schulzinger notes that in 1924 a bill, initiated by U.S. Representative John Jacob Rogers of Massachusetts, fusing the consular and the diplomatic services, passed Congress. The Rogers Act improved salaries for foreign service officers and tied those salaries to rank, not position. A retirement plan, a foreign service school, and a recruiting service were implemented (76). See also Richard Hume Werking, *The Master Architects: Building the United States Foreign Service, 1890–1913* (Lexington: University Press of Kentucky, 1977). Werking has studied the foreign service bureaucracy by carefully examining its internal operations, to include the attitudes of those who worked therein. He concludes that "the 'master architects' themselves were the men chiefly responsible for planning and building the modern foreign service" before World War I. Their "attitudes and personal concerns" and their "tactical considerations in the process of reorganization were key determinants of why the system evolved as it did" (preface, xi). Some progress toward modernization had been achieved under the Stone-Flood Act of 1915, particularly a recognition that promotion be by merit and appointment to grade in the classification of consuls and diplomats (248). See also Challener, *Admirals, Generals, and American Foreign Policy*, 45.

5
LEADERSHIP PREREQUISITES
COLONEL CONRAD S. BABCOCK AND COMMAND DEVELOPMENT DURING WORLD WAR I

Douglas Johnson

THE PRESENT CHIEF OF staff of the U.S. Army, General Peter J. Schoomaker, tells anyone who asks that the U.S. Army's Core Competency today is to develop leaders.[1] Prior to the Vietnam War, leadership training, like most military training, was based upon what the Military Academies taught, augmented by what the branch schools thought was needed for their particular branch expertise. Even at the Army War College, leadership was the subject only of occasional lectures by distinguished general officers and tended to be mostly about personal wartime experiences.[2] Leadership as a science had to wait until the training revolution of the latter 1970s was well under way. That is not to say that leadership was not studied in industry, business, and the military, but the shortcomings of the war in Vietnam demanded a complete relook at everything in the army, in particular at what it was being taught and how it was being led.

One thread of thought that emerged early in the process was the concept that every officer should know as well as, if not better than, any soldier how to perform the soldier's duties. While that might have been appropriate for the Civil War, and barely possible for World War I, by 1972 that possibility was beyond reality. Furthermore, there have been very successful leaders in many realms of endeavor who have come to a profession from the outside and have performed exceptionally well while knowing little of the details of the laborer's duties. In fact, there is some demonstrated validity to the proposition that some of the U.S. Army's best leaders rose to deserved fame by not following the traditional path at all. Arguably, these men were not qualified to perform the duties ultimately thrust upon them by circumstances, yet they succeeded and surpassed many or most of their fellow soldiers who had sought to rise through the ranks by the traditional process. Colonel Conrad Stanton Babcock did not have the benefit of the type of leadership training available today, yet he led three different infantry regiments in battle in the final five months of World War I.

Colonel Babcock entered upon his first command of a regiment of infantry some seven hours before that regiment jumped off in the main attack of the XX French Corps, which was, in turn, the main attack of the French Tenth Army on July 18, 1918, near the town of Soissons, France.[3] Babcock was a cavalryman, but he had sailed to Europe in search of a combat command, and that meant infantry. The twists and turns of his struggles to obtain a command are told compellingly in his unpublished memoir "From This Generation to the Next."[4] But it was his contention, written in an acerbic tone, that command of an American infantry regiment in combat should not be given to just anybody, especially not to those who lacked intimate familiarity with that organization, which was unique in its size and even more so in its internal complexity.

A Civil War infantry regiment had consisted of ten companies, each nominally of one hundred men, usually armed with a rifled musket of one design or another and all operating in essentially similar fashion. The 1917 prewar U.S. Army infantry regiments were larger on paper but manned at much lower levels, and they were armed with the bolt-action, magazine-fed Model 1903 Springfield rifle. The officers carried the M-1911 45-caliber pistol. Peacetime company strength was 58 soldiers, while wartime strength was 150 soldiers. The regiment that Babcock was straining to command was composed of approximately 3,600 soldiers formed into three battalions, each made up of four 250-man companies, plus a machine-gun company, a supply company, and a headquarters company. Some of the regiment's rifles were capable of being fitted with projectors that made them grenade launchers. The soldiers, unless members of a machine-gun, a Stokes Mortar, or a 37-milimeter one-pounder gun team, also carried hand grenades.[5] None of these weapons were standard issue in the prewar U.S. Army. This new regiment also included signaling equipment, a mess section, medical units, and a supply section.[6]

The complexity of the basic infantry company had multiplied perhaps tenfold over its predecessors. It was big, bulky, and lethal but somewhat awkward to handle and difficult to manage, especially when the next layer of support was equally awkward and the echelons above divisions had not been thought through in the rush to get men to the battlefield. Tellingly, soon after the arrival of American troops, then-Colonel (later Brigadier General) Fox Connor, one of the bright lights of the American Expeditionary Forces (AEF), observed that "notwithstanding our enormous military expansion, our weakness is not in our junior officers, soldiers or small units, but in the higher command and staff. Only by actual work in divisional units can we remedy this weakness."[7] All of this is to suggest that there may well have been some merit to Babcock's argument that it is not efficient to put a man in command of the most complex combat organization the army ever had without requiring him to become intimately familiar with its internal workings. It was not efficient, and it might not even have been morally sound.

Babcock would find that despite his own extensive experience with these monsters, commanding one in combat was a huge challenge. He came to France as a cavalryman on detail as an inspector general assigned to the 1st Division. So long as he was stationed with that unit, he was charged principally with inspecting training, a perfect position to observe the inner workings, strengths, and failings of the infantry regiment. He subsequently performed tours of duty as commandant, AEF Heavy Tank School, in Wareham, England, and as headquarters commandant, General Headquarters AEF.[8] Eventually, he was assigned as to fill a lieutenant colonel vacancy in Colonel Frank Parker's 18th Infantry.[9] In due course, Babcock got his wish and was assigned command of an infantry regiment, the 28th, some seven nighttime hours before leading it into combat.[10]

To be perfectly frank, Babcock did not perform brilliantly in that first command and, for all intents and purposes, was relieved after the battle. What he did in light of the circumstances, however, was fully creditable and deserving of far better treatment than he received. He barely had the regiment in hand when it crossed the jump-off line into the attack. He focused first, and properly, on the orientation of the troops who would attack in column of battalions—assault, support, and reserve—per the 1st Division "normal formation."[11] Actually, the reserve battalion, in this case, was not under his control, being assigned to the division reserve, again per divisional standard operating procedure. In the time he had available, he apparently had no opportunity to see to the matters of support and found his second-in-command, who should have been attending to such matters, shirking every hint of responsibility.[12] Nevertheless, over the next four days Babcock's regiment took not just its own objectives but the expanded division objective, albeit at terrific cost.

Sent off, but not actually relieved, by a petulant division commander, Babcock landed on his feet and commanded successfully two more regiments, both in the 89th Division: one, the 353rd, in a support role during the St. Mihiel Operation, and the other, the 354th Infantry, in a assault role in the Meuse-Argonne Campaign. His latter performance was so good that the division commander recommended that Babcock be promoted to brigadier general. The Armistice, however, forestalled that.[13]

Babcock's memoir is that of a bitter man who never came to closure over three issues in particular: as ardently as he sought command, it was denied him until the worst possible circumstances obtained; he was essentially fired by a man whose concept of leadership was singular and inflexible ("Do as I say or die trying!"); and officers deficient in the prerequisites of combat leadership, as he defined it, were promoted to general officer rank, while he was not. His postwar memoir reveals all this bitterness with complete frankness. However, it goes beyond mere petulance to argue professionally for more sensible officer development as well as better tactical systems and other apparently sound alternatives to what he saw as unnecessary soldier irritants. He returned to the issue of qualification for command on several occasions and without much reflection except for the continuing theme that some officers retired as major generals who were not trained for command in combat or who had little or no combat experience. He remained frankly bitter about their success, while he clearly felt that he had met all the better criteria.

He complained about the manner in which General Headquarters directed training, and in this he was very much on the mark. Training either in the continental United States or in France left a great deal to be desired.[14] As a consequence, an entire training and school system was developed in France for the AEF. The training system was quite rigid, frequently unrealistic in expectation, and in some aspects destructive of unit cohesion. Notwithstanding its several faults, it accomplished a great deal in imposing a uniformity of practice, if not a formal doctrine, on the AEF. That relative uniformity was instrumental in enabling the AEF to function as well as it did:

> [Paul B.] Malone and [Harold B.] Fiske were graduates of the Fort Leavenworth school; but all of them were totally and completely ignorant concerning how to train an American Division, 28,172 strong; and so they preceded to issue training schedules, prescribing in great detail just exactly what type of training was to be given, how often each week, and how many minutes a day. A time schedule was issued for each branch of the service in the Division.
>
> Well, like all training schedules of this nature—and in our army they never fail to be published—it was often utterly impossible to live up to an hourly, daily schedule when the Division was constantly called on to give a Review or demonstration for some distinguished French General, or due to the almost constant rain or snow of that hideous climate of 1917–18. Furthermore, even had the weather and the ground been ideal each day, no organization or any size (squad to brigade) should be held to a rigid program of drill and instruction; too much depends on the ability of the instructor or drill master to tie everyone to the same time schedule.[15]

It is fair to note here that Fiske never did command any unit in combat, whereas Malone, who had been chief of the AEF Training Section at GHQ, took command of the 23rd Infantry, 2nd Division, not long before he too found himself leading a regiment of infantry into combat at Soissons on July 18, 1918. He retained command for a fairly long time thereafter and was as bitter as Babcock about being promoted later than many of his peers, but at least he did attain general's rank before the war ended only to lose it after the Armistice, as did so many others.[16]

Babcock's attitude toward command is echoed quietly by another near contemporary, Robert L. Bullard. Senior to Babcock, Bullard worked through his misgivings in a slightly different fashion. He headed for France "convinced that the key to success in the war would be an officer's ability to expand his vision to fit the size of his mission and his command."[17] Vision is now one of the mandatory subjects of current leadership training. Bullard could not have known what that would mean any more than did Babcock at the time. Both men arrived in France before the complete reorganization of the AEF was decided upon. Following the completion of General John J. Pershing's organizational project in July 1917, the changes noted above, and many more, were implemented. Bullard, however, reached France in command of a newly formed brigade of two infantry regiments, the 26th and 28th. Both of these would be reorganized and reequipped in France in response to the changes demanded by the organizational project. His two regimental commanders were Regular Army officers, George B. Duncan and Beaumont B. Buck. Duncan would progress steadily; Buck would progress and then fall prey to shortcomings evident early in his career. Allan R. Millett describes Buck as "a short, dogmatic, inflexible, and not very bright officer" and notes that he had been required to take an extra year to graduate from the Military Academy because of academic failure.[18]

It is worth noting that Bullard's staff contained two other officers who would also rise to prominence in the AEF: Harold B. Fiske—damned by Babcock, above—and Arthur L. Conger. Bullard disliked Fiske but felt obliged to admit his abilities.[19] As Millett describes Bullard, his "claim to attention is that he was a successful officer by the army's standards and that he was an intelligent and articulate student of his own career and officership in his army. Bullard held every officer rank, commanded every tactical formation in his arm (infantry) from platoon to field army, and seldom served away from troops. When he did, however, his assignments and experiences conform to Morris Janowitz's theory that the army's generals often have unconventional opportunities which dramatize their adaptability and intellectual sophistication."[20] This last comment is another avenue for investigation that has yielded some fruit and is presently an issue of serious discussion. The U.S. Army's current operational tempo is such that there is so much to be done that general officers rarely remain in any assignment for very long, and fewer yet remain with troops for any prolonged period of time.

Perhaps more in line with Babcock's objections was the 1st Division commander, Major General William L. Sibert (USMA, 1884), "who had served all but six years as an Engineer. He had performed with distinction in the Philippines . . . [and] then became one of the organizers in building of the Panama Canal."[21] Millett's evaluation is that while Sibert "had shown drive and imagination in running summer training camps... his selection to command... was somewhat mysterious since he had never led combat troops, was not a product of the Line's schools, and was little known outside his immediate staff."[22]

Despite Babcock's additional bitterness at the manner in which this officer was eventually removed from command, he typified the problem that Babcock addressed. His situation was aggravated by an evident lack of the all-essential drive that Pershing demanded of all his officers. In contrast, the following are Bullard's takes on some of the better-known officers who passed through the 1st Division, succeeded there, and were promoted:

Hanson Ely: "An unpleasant man, a large, heavy, humorless, overbearing officer who made every statement a threat... in the Philippines." Ely had impressed him as "self-assertive, pugnacious, almost disrespectful in manner and tone."

Campbell King: "Educated at Harvard and in the family law firm... [and] quickly established a reputation as one of the army's ablest officers, serving as a student and instructor at Leavenworth and the Army War College."

Ulysses Grant McAlexander: Bullard found him impervious to new techniques and relieved him.

Frank Parker: A "widely experienced officer but also a former student of the *Ecole de Guerre*, spoke French fluently, and had been an observer with the French army before the American intervention."

Malin Craig: "Another prize student of warfare on the Leavenworth model... [and] a forceful intelligent officer, but [he] unsettled division commanders with his quick decisions and his habit of giving orders in [Major General Hunter] Liggett's name."[23]

These men were a prized collection. Parker, who gave Babcock his first step toward command, arrived and remained in command of troops throughout the war. Ely served as a battalion commander under Babcock until wounded and then continued to rise through successive troop commands. King became division chief of staff, as did Craig. They demonstrated enormous competence as managers of increasingly larger formations, most of which had not existed before the war.

As is too often the case in any war, the demands of combat make a mockery of the long-revered adage that an army should "train as it will fight." To a certain point that is an admirable and necessary aim, for all too often armies are accused of training for the last war and consequently failing to take note of developments in the technology and art of war. Most damaging, however, are the oft-repeated practices of failing to train as combined arms teams and of training according to branch requirements only. Really effective training is extremely difficult to achieve, as one is seldom able to assemble in a suitable place all the elements that will come together in combat with a suitable training scenario that will exercise all elements and do so without incurring enormous costs. But that serves to place this issue in the spotlight. Who knows what the next war will be like? Jean Bloch divined the outlines of World War I, and others have seen some of the shapes of coming wars through a glass dimly, but rarely has anyone done so with enough foresight to make the prewar training fit the event that ultimately emerges. Similarly, no man is invulnerable, and all too often the training that does take place does so with an unrealistic continuity of leadership. Leaders are killed, wounded, or fail and must be replaced. It is very hard to train a staff to deal with this situation in the first place, but it is even more difficult when the available qualified officers are so few to begin with.

One system would be for a second-in-command to be exactly that, the man of the moment who can step forward and fill the shoes and roles of the fallen or replaced or promoted leader, but it is seldom so. The consequence is that leaders are replaced from the ranks of those deemed able to move in and take charge by virtue of their past overall performance, with little or no specific preparation. And in the absence of combat experience, that performance must be judged from success in other realms. In the case of Major General Sibert, the appointment to command an infantry division was made on the basis of his superior performance as an engineer officer, and the assumption was that organizational and motivational skill was considered inherent in the successful execution of those duties. As matters developed, that same division eventually passed into the hands of an artilleryman, Charles Pelot Summerall, on an essentially similar basis. In Summerall's case, he had at least been serving with that division since shortly after it arrived in France, and fire support of an infantry formation demands some understanding of how infantry units maneuver and fight.

Babcock groused in detail: "As noted, all these officers retired as major generals, and apparently made good as combat commanders, although none of them could have known anything at all about how a modern combat infantry regiment moves up into a combat sector; occupies it, patrols in front of it, fights in it, goes over the top in an offensive movement, or withdraws from the front to rest in billets. How they functioned before acquiring this absolutely essential information, I do not know; but the point is that, although GHQ must have known or should have known that these officers, and many others, were completely and blissfully ignorant of all modern combat knowledge, still they were placed in command of the none too well trained combat infantry organizations of our National Army or National Guard."[24] Babcock simply skips over the fact that initially no one knew how to command organizations that changed enormously while under their command. Parker at least arrived in command and had more opportunity to learn than any of the others except Ely.

Many officers in the AEF advanced through several echelons of command, usually moving from one organization to another in order to fill gaps as they appeared. Some of the gaps were caused by the creation of entirely new echelons. Men such as John L. "Birdie" Hines and Robert L. Bullard commanded every echelon from platoon to field army, in some cases creating the very bodies they were elevated to command. The bedeviling question is whether there was some alternative to throwing men into command at the last minute, and the answer seems to be that there was not. The British practice of styling the second senior officer in a unit as the second-in-command is at least a strong suggestion that the Number Two officer had best prepare himself to take the reins and the corollary suggestion that he has been placed there by virtue of his apparent fitness to do so. The American army was not so organized, and in most organizations the second-ranking officer was designated the chief of staff or executive officer. Both of these positions are staff positions with duties varying as organization and circumstances require. Philosophically, the staff positions are designed to manage the execution of the plan, which is a control function. The command position, however, has always been seen as one that deals with the art of command, the function of leading that differs substantially from staff management. That many men are able to master both is a compliment to them and the society and system that develop them.

Bullard had the good fortune of having spent "twenty-two years with troops, four years on Colonial service, four years in educational assignments, one year on staff duty, and one year on detached service."[25] When scanning the Regular Army officer roster for a man fit to command, it was unlikely that one better fit than himself would be found despite the fact that neither he nor anyone else in the U.S. Army—other than Pershing—had ever commanded a unit as large as a division. But Bullard, reflecting in his diary upon the notice that he was going to be given command of a division, wrote: "November 3rd, 1917. I am trying hard to prepare myself to command it. I feel it that it is to be a very difficult thing." Three days later he confided once again to his diary: "I do not believe that I have the ability to make good; I feel that I am weak in knowing how."[26] He resolved to get to work and performed very well in the end, but through the sanctity of his diary he let us know that he was not ready.

Elevating officers to command of corps and armies was also a gamble, as those organizations had not existed in the U.S. Army since the Spanish-American War, and the roles and functions of the new organizations were immeasurably different from those of their predecessors. Looking at some of the officers to whom Babcock pointed in wonderment or disdain, it is difficult to suggest that they did not put in creditable performances even though their assignments could well be interpreted as moves calculated to both reward their dedicated staff performance and assure them of continued success in an organization that values successful combat command above almost everything else. As Babcock wrote, "I used to wonder why everyone in Chaumont seemed to consider [that] the handling of troops in battle was something one never had to learn or consider; but to function as some junior staff officer took weeks of study at a special school."[27] He also stated that "General Pershing authorized the appointment of brigade and regimental commanders from officers who had not had any combat training what-so-ever."[28]

These officers had never participated in, or even seen, a modern battle, but, unlike the older and more senior officers of the 1st Division, none of them had commanded an organization larger than a peace-strength battalion of infantry or a battery of field artillery: "Lieutenant Colonel Lesley J. McNair had served in the Ordnance Department for three years and seven months of his thirteen years since graduation from West Point. This officer is now a temporary lieutenant general and Chief of Staff of Army General Headquarters."[29]

Babcock picked out four officers as additional examples of how things ought not to be done:

> To me, the appointment of an officer, untrained in modern combat principles to command and be responsible for the life or death of hundreds of fighting soldiers is incomprehensible. There are many incidences, and I shall briefly cover four of them:
>
> Colonel Blanton Winship (1898), now a retired Judge Advocate General with the rank of Major General, was appointed Commanding Officer of the 110th Infantry of the 28th Division and served as such from October 4th to November 25th 1918. This charming gentleman and distinguished army lawyer had had no service with troops since January 1904 when he was made a major and judge advocate from a first lieutenant of infantry.
>
> Colonel B. Frank Cheatham[,] ... now a retired Quartermaster General with the rank of Major General, was appointed Commanding Officer of the 104th Infantry, 26th Division and served as such from September 28th 1918 to April 28th 1919. This officer had a distinguished combat record prior to 1901 in the Philippine Islands; but had been in the Quartermaster Department since February 1901.
>
> Colonel Frank R. McCoy (WP1897) Cavalry, now a retired Major General, was appointed Commanding Officer of the 165th Infantry, 42nd Division and served as such from May 7th to August 25th 1918. When he assumed command of his regiment, he had been Secretary of the General Staff in Chaumont since his arrival in France. He was a second lieutenant of cavalry during the Spanish-American War, and after that he served on the staff of General Leonard Wood or on the General Staff for nearly all the years up to the World War. He was a major of cavalry when the World War came to the U.S.

Colonel William D. Connor (WP1897), now a retired Major General, was appointed a Brigadier General in the National Army on July 11th 1918 and commanded the 63rd Infantry Brigade, 32nd Division from July 22nd to August 4th 1918. He was an officer of the Engineers, and prior to his promotion had been the Assistant Chief of Staff, G-4 in Chaumont.[30]

In order to verify Pershing's judgment or validate Babcock's, the above-named officers need to be examined in light of their battle command performance, but that performance needs to take the following into consideration: the quality of their predecessor (Was that person relieved or promoted because of stellar performance? How did the unit perform under this officer's command versus how had it performed beforehand?) and the condition of the enemy (wherever mention is made of them), precommand and postcommand, to include the relative support they received from flanking units. In short, to be fair, as many of these matters as possible should be factored into making this judgment.

Before embarking on this analysis, however, it would be well to recall that all of these officers, including Babcock, had served in what we today would consider to be dead-end assignments for various periods. Yet that was almost normal in the period of their lieutenancies, which spanned the Spanish-American War and its aftermath. Malone, as an example, served as an instructor of chemistry at West Point; commanded the headquarters guard in Marianao, Cuba; and was appointed provost marshal and later judge advocate general, Army of Cuban Pacification.[31] To his credit, he did serve in active operations in the field during the insurgency period in the Philippines, but clearly he had no troop assignments for the seven years that followed.

All but two of the seven officers whom Babcock mentions—Fiske, McNair, Malone, Winship, Cheatham, Duncan, and Connor—were assigned to units that, by the time these officers joined them, had experienced some combat. Fiske, although initially assigned to Bullard's brigade in the 1st Division, did not command at all but was quickly moved into the G-5 Training Section of GHQ, where he spent the remainder of the war. McNair came to France on the staff of the 1st Division and was likewise transferred to the GHQ G-5 Training Section. He became the youngest brigadier general in the AEF and received a Distinguished Service Medal for his work as the senior artillery officer in the Training Section.[32] He never exercised combat command.

Malone, as previously indicated, took command of the 23rd Infantry, 2nd Division, leading it at the army's companion battle to Belleau Wood at Vaux, adjacent to the Marine Brigade.[33] This action was followed almost immediately by the division's participation in the Aisne-Marne Operation, in which Malone's 23rd Infantry, having barely digested a large number of replacements, was hurled against the German lines near Soissons. Coming into action essentially from the march and without many of its supporting elements, the 23rd reached its first day's objectives with admirable speed. The division was withdrawn two days later, having accomplished its initial purpose but becoming badly disorganized in the process. Malone would eventually command the 10th Brigade, 5th Division.[34]

We now turn to the four highlighted officers. Winship served in action with the 28th Division, which saw its first combat in July. However, he joined the 28th in October in time for the second phase of the Meuse-Argonne offensive. The division saw action in the Château-Thierry Campaign, the Champagne-Marne Defensive, the Aisne-Marne Offensive, the Fismes Sector, and the Oise-Aisne Offensive, suffering some 8,623 casualties in the process.[35] It next served in the Clermont Sector and then attacked on September 26 as part of I Corps in the Meuse-Argonne Campaign. It was a combat-experienced unit when Winship joined it.

There was a pause in the action on October 2–3. Winship joined during this lull. On October 9, the division was relieved by the 82nd Division.[36] Between September 26 and October 3, the division suffered 2,921 casualties.[37] On October 7, the day Winship took command of the 110th Infantry, the 28th Division was again ordered to attack, at 0525 hours. The 55th Brigade, of which Winship's 110th Infantry was a part, was to assist the 56th Brigade; however, the 110th, on the far right flank, was also charged with maintaining contact with the 1st Division. The 110th fought as best it could during the next two days. It made limited progress but was unable to advance as directed on October 8 and was relieved, along with the rest of the division, on October 9 and was moved into Army Reserve.[38]

The principal enemy formation the 110th fought was the 2nd Württemburg Landwehr Division, but that command was periodically intermingled with elements of the 1st Guards and 5th Guards Divisions. Even though the Württemburgers were ground down to 25-man companies and finally classified as a fourth-class division, they lost only 795 prisoners of war, indicating qualities of stoutness and self-sacrifice.[39] During this period the 110th Infantry suffered 281 casualties, of whom 75 were killed or died of wounds.[40] It would be best to categorize the 110th as a battered or worn unit. A change of leadership evidently served little purpose, and Winship's experience was limited.

The 28th Division relieved the 37th Division, IV Corps, in the Thiaucourt sector on October 16 after a six-day rest. It patrolled until the Second Army began its offensive on November 10.[41] The 110th had closed September with a strength of 1,600 men, its low point. Replacements brought it back to 2,576 by October 31, and it ended November with 3,065. Clearly it had suffered from serious combat before Winship arrived, and the fact that it did not last beyond five days after he took command should not necessarily reflect adversely on his command abilities.

We may infer that whatever Winship's qualifications for command of an infantry regiment, he managed reasonably well for two days of the worst fighting of the war. Taking command of an essentially shattered unit and leading it immediately into the attack took courage. How much skill was required to lead it for a day before it stalled is uncertain. How many replacements the 110th received between the end of September and the initiation of another attack phase, October 4, almost does not matter. The leadership issue was severe, and evidently Winship's superiors felt that he met it. The 110th Infantry did about as well as its sister units in those brutal days of combat.

Cheatham served with the 26th Division, which likewise was first employed in offensive operations in July. Cheatham joined in late September. The 26th saw defensive action in the Pas Fini Sector and then participated in July's Aisne-Marne Offensive. It took part in the St. Mihiel Operation during September 12–16 as part of the V Corps reserve. When Cheatham joined the 104th Infantry, 52nd Brigade, it was recovering from the St. Mihiel Operation. It had suffered few casualties in that fight: 30 were killed or died of wounds, and 131 were wounded. It was overstrength as of September 30, with 3,433 soldiers and officers on the rolls.[42] It attacked again, as part of the second phase of the Meuse-Argonne Offensive, on October 16. Stalled that day, it took over a sector from the 29th Division but did not attack again until October 23. Between November 1 and 6 it side-slipped, coming under the command of the French XVII Corps, then attacked again on November 9–10.[43] Thus, Cheatham saw offensive combat for only about three to five days, much of which appears to have been in the pursuit phase, but the unit was in the line for over a month, and that was taxing enough. In an interesting parallel with Babcock's career, Cheatham was also assigned to occupation duty following the Armistice although he remained only until late spring 1919 (Babcock remained until September).[44] Cheatham's record appears unremarkable. It may not mean anything, but the 26th Division's history lists Cheatham in the new and final chain of command but makes no mention of him, and only scant mention of the 104th Infantry, in its 245-page account.[45]

McCoy served with the 42nd Division but joined it in May during "active battle service," as Leonard P. Ayres puts it.[46] That service was initially under French control and is more correctly described as training in a relatively quiet sector. McCoy's two predecessors had been relieved for their inability to handle this "Irish" unit: the 165th Infantry, better known as the New York National Guard's "Fighting 69th."[47] The 42nd remained in this quiet sector until June 21, at which time it was moved to the Champagne region near Rheims and was assigned to the French Fourth Army.[48]

The 42nd Division initially occupied defensive positions. On July 15, the date of the beginning of the final German offensive, it occupied the second position behind the French 170th and 13th Divisions. The French units were holding the front lines in anticipation of the poorly concealed German attack. The 42nd Division's conduct of the defense was exemplary even though the division staff had refused to believe that an attack was imminent.⁴⁹ McCoy's outfit participated in the defense of the sector but was withdrawn to participate in the coming Allied Aisne-Marne counteroffensive. Moving into line on July 25, the division attacked three days later, crossed the Ourcq River, and continued the attack until July 31. It then pursued the withdrawing Germans until relieved on August 4. It remained in reserve until completion of the offensive on August 6.⁵⁰ Close reading of the battle accounts suggests that the 165th performed about as well as most American units at that time, advancing until halted by heavy machine-gun fire and then retiring to consolidate. Its undistinguished performance cost a total of 1,358 casualties.⁵¹

Babcock failed to note that McCoy also commanded the 63rd Brigade, 32nd Division, from September 1 until November 25. This brigade had five commanders between July 22 and November 25, 1918, including Connor (McCoy's predecessor was promoted to command the 77th Division).⁵² McCoy saw action with the brigade through the end of the fighting. The division's commemorative pamphlet states that it had engaged eleven German divisions.⁵³

Connor was assigned to the 32nd Division in April 1918. The 32nd Division participated in the offensive along the Ourcq from July 28 to August 2. It relieved the tired 3rd Division on the night of July 29–30 in front of the Bois des Grimpettes. The 28th and 3rd Divisions had struggled for two days to reduce this position. The 3rd had been in line since early June and had suffered sixty-six hundred casualties.⁵⁴ The 32nd Division relieved the 28th during the night of July 30–31 after the latter had cleared the Bois des Grimpettes and had also taken part of the town of Cierges. The 32nd Division's attacks over the next two days were stumbling affairs. On both days, initial attacks made some progress only to be hurled back by German counterattacks. After falling back both times, the division made another effort and recovered the lost ground. The combined pressure of the 28th Division and the French forces farther to the west caused the Germans to withdraw during the night of August 1–2. The divisions followed the enemy until they reached the Vesle River.⁵⁵

Connor commanded the 63rd Brigade for a total of twelve days, of which three or four were in combat near Cierges. During that time the unit's performance was no more than adequate.⁵⁶ A 32nd Division commemorative pamphlet lists three enemy divisions as opponents at this time; one was the 4th Guards Division, which was carried as a first-class division throughout its service.⁵⁷

Connor's service won him a second Silver Star; he had been awarded his first for combat action in the Philippines. He had been dipped in combat and was withdrawn again to command the Bordeaux District, Base Section No. 2, Service of Supply. However, he had served as 32nd Division's chief of staff from April 1918 until promoted and given this combat command.⁵⁸ He had come to France in command of the 26th Infantry.⁵⁹ He was later assigned to head the 77th Division but was too ill to assume command.[60] Upon recovery, he commanded the 82nd Division. It may therefore be said that he did not come into combat command as largely uninstructed, as Babcock suggests. Of all the officers about whom Babcock complained, Connor was least deserving of criticism, especially Babcock's charge that he was ignorant of the forces he was assigned to command in battle. That notwithstanding, Connor appears to have been intentionally dipped in combat command.

This brief survey of the combat performance of seven American officers produces a mixed picture. Two never saw combat command, something that Babcock felt was the principal stepping stone for promotion. Ironically, this perspective was shared in large measure by General Pershing, who fulminated against Army Chief of Staff Peyton C. March's handling of general officer promotion lists.[61] Malone's name was passed over in favor of several officers who had not served a day in combat. March, on the other hand, was charged with operating the other half of the army—what today is called the Institutional Army—charged with raising, training, equipping, and deploying forces for employment by combatant commanders. Such tasks could not adequately be performed by majors, lieutenant colonels, or colonels. The scope of their duties, although free of combat in the most direct and physical sense, nevertheless involved combat of a different nature and demanded general officer authority in order to be effective. McNair and Fiske were both promoted to general officer rank without commanding in combat, and their promotions were likewise appropriate given the scope and scale of their responsibilities. That Malone was not initially selected was an injustice but also a necessity given the limitations on numbers of general officers and the tasks to be accomplished by the entire establishment.

Of the others who saw only a limited exposure to combat, favoritism of the kind that so upset Babcock does not appear to have come into play. Several officers of the GHQ staff were dipped in combat, seemingly to validate them but also in response to their oft-repeated desire to command. Just like Babcock, they had sought out combat command. Their motives seem to have varied between the certainty that promotion would come first to those who met that challenge (although Malone's case would argue otherwise) and the genuine understanding that this was what they were in the army for in the first place. This later motive may seem old-fashioned or suspect, but it exists today with considerable force as it has throughout our history. To paraphrase the author's company tactical officer in 1963, "You don't join a fire department to watch things burn."[62]

Of the other officers, each had demonstrated his abilities in other realms of action, and, importantly, each was known to General Pershing and had been selected by him to accompany the AEF to France on the basis of his evaluation of their past performance. All were adrift in a foreign sea and none—not even Pershing himself—had experience in the tasks they were about to undertake or in the formations and procedures that evolved during the course of the war. Pershing's performance was less than perfect and at one point even brought forth a strong recommendation by his French and British colleagues that he be demoted or replaced.[63]

In the postwar writings of the senior officers of the AEF, there is unanimity over the merits and quality of all the officers who populated Pershing's inner circle, those he took with him to France and many of those who passed through the 1st Division. All were products of Pershing's selection system, and it would have been a brash individual who said anything against the general's choices.[64]

The very best of the leaders who rose to high command of operational forces during World War I climbed the ladder of successive command slots. Among the most respected of these were Hines and Bullard. Each served at every level of command from platoon to field army, and in this they were unusual. Summerall became army chief of staff, but he was an artilleryman and only ascended the combat command ladder when moved from field artillery brigade commander to command of the 1st Division. Hines, Craig, Douglas MacArthur, and, of course, Pershing and George C. Marshall also rose to become army chiefs of staff, but only Hines climbed every rung in the ladder.[65]

When Dwight D. Eisenhower was promoted to general officer, he had never commanded anything larger than a battalion. Marshall never commanded a tactical formation larger than a brigade. MacArthur, as in all things, had the most unusual career, twice becoming a field marshal in a non-American army and then reverting to a mere theater commander. He made a miserable captain but a superb regimental and brigade commander.

And what of Babcock? His command of the 353rd and 354th Infantry Regiments lasted from mid-August until he left Germany to command Pershing's special parade unit. Babcock had commanded the 28th Infantry in four days of intense combat (July 18–22), then took over the 353rd Infantry on August 7 and commanded it through a month of defensive and follow-in support action. He finally received command of the 354th Infantry on September 7, leading it in combat during November 1–11 and later on occupation duty in Germany. His unit performed so well throughout that the division commander recommended that Babcock be promoted to brigadier general.[66]

It would appear that men of talent are well able to take a situation rapidly in hand and make the best of it. Those who can be thrown into difficult situations and meet their challenges are the bright lights of any organization. Sometimes they are styled as hatchet men and are employed to get the difficult done without regard to personal feelings; regrettably, it is much the same in war. Other men, particularly those who rise to the highest levels and succeed there, have internal balance. They are able to discern the central issue, quickly sort through the facts, and gain and maintain consensus and/or cooperation from without as well as within the organization. The list of essential qualities can be long, but only now and then does one possess a full grasp of the tactics and techniques that are essential.

Only one of the sixteen chapters in *Global Leadership: The Next Generation*, a recent multiauthor effort to address the challenges of leadership in the emerging global marketplace, addresses proficiency with the "tools of the trade." The chapter titled "Developing Technological Savvy" takes note of the rapidly changing world of technology but asks the future leader to "understand how technology, used appropriately, can benefit their organizations."[67] The argument can be made that Eisenhower and Marshall learned the tools of their trade at battalion level and below. Babcock would have argued that the regimental level was the essential base because there more than rifles came into play. His description of the complexity of a regiment is accurate, but even at the company level things had changed drastically by the time he took command. In either case, however, the mission of the infantry was well understood by everyone in that army: to close with and kill the enemy. This meant that the infantry had to go forward, and this, in turn, meant leading men into danger. The skillful leader did so with the full orchestrated support of machine-gun fire, artillery, perhaps tanks, and, on rare occasions, combat aircraft.

How the artillery brought accurate fire upon the enemy was of no direct concern to the infantry leader. His job was to keep close to the barrage and call for additional support when required. He did not care in the least how an aerodrome operated or how to plan close air support. He was concerned that ammunition, food, and water were moved forward to his soldiers on the front line and that his wounded were evacuated; how the supplies got shipped, sorted, assembled, and transported to the rear area was more than he could devote time or worry to. Bullard, again, provides a brief insight into this business. While the latter commanded a division, "General Pershing . . . asked my opinion about some British movement: 'General, I know nothing about it, I never heard of it; I have no time or chance to know of anything but that which is before me.'"[68]

Bullard worked hard at learning as much of his profession as possible, but simply because an officer was serving in some GHQ staff position did not mean he was utterly ignorant of the requirements of command and leadership. Yet the situation in France meant that the really difficult business of maneuvering a large formation was only rarely required. The axis of advance was almost always straight ahead. The artillery plan was prepared and executed by the artillery commander; any air plans were developed and executed by the airman in charge. What an infantry commander had to do at battalion and regimental levels was keep the troops moving forward. Brigade and division commanders had essentially the same responsibility. The latter had the ability to influence matters somewhat with their artillery resources but only if communications held up, which they seldom did in the offense. The tactical employment of the organic weapons of the infantry regiments was the purview of the battalion commanders to whom most of them belonged or to whom they were distributed.

Was it hard to command a regiment? Certainly it was difficult to see to it that the three principal moving parts, the battalions, were moving forward and reducing the enemy wherever encountered, were regularly supplied, and had their wounded evacuated. There were few opportunities to seek or obtain additional fire support, and the utility of that weapon was always dependent on the often elusive ability to locate the front line. The regimental commander must know this, if he knew nothing else. His rear area must be in proper working order to facilitate the bidirectional flow of people and supplies, and he must find a way to report regularly to higher headquarters on the progress (or lack of same) his units were achieving. In Pershing's army, forward progress mattered most.

Babcock was only partially right. The better one knows the instrument one is wielding, the more effectively he should be able to employ it. But officers who have demonstrated their ability to get a variety of jobs done may not need to know all the particulars. They need to know just enough about how the organism functions in order to control and direct it, and they need to have the fortitude to try—despite the personal reservations Bullard expressed—to get the job done. As Bullard put it, the key to success lay in "an officer's ability to expand his vision to fit the size of his mission." That faculty mattered more than tactical or technical proficiency.

Notes

1. General Peter J. Schoomaker, CSA, in *Army Strategic Planning Guidance, 2004* (Washington, DC: Department of the Army, 2004), unnumbered page.

2. Harold R. Winton, "Toward an American Philosophy of Command," paper delivered to the Society of Military History Symposium, Quantico, Virginia, April 28, 2000.

3. Douglas V. Johnson II and Rolfe L. Hillman Jr., *Soissons 1918* (College Station: Texas A&M University Press, 1999).

4. Conrad Stanton Babcock, "From This Generation to the Next," typescript, ca. 1943, Hoover Institution Archives, Stanford, California.

5. General Headquarters, American Expeditionary Forces (AEF), "Tables of Organization and Equipment, Series A, January 14, 1918 (corrected to June 26, 1918), Part I, Infantry Division, Maximum Strength"; Center of Military History, *U.S. Army in the World War*, vol. 1, *Organization of the American Expeditionary Forces* (Washington, DC: U.S. Government Printing Office, 1988), 335–88.

6. Center of Military History, *U.S. Army in the World War*, 1:95, 115, 118, 121–22.

7. Brigadier General Fox Connor, "Memorandum for the Chief of Staff," Headquarters AEF, Office of the Chief of Staff, Chaumont, France, December 16, 1917; Center of

Military History, *U.S. Army in the World War*, vol. 3, *Training and Use of American Troops with British and French* (Washington, DC: U.S. Government Printing Office, 1948), 7.

8. Babcock, "From This Generation to the Next," 443–44, 447–78.

9. Ibid., 481. Babcock had applied and had even been asked for as early as January 1 but was deemed essential to the functioning of the General Headquarters. He finally escaped the GHQ Commandancy on June 19, 1918.

10. Ibid., 506.

11. Ibid., 507–10. In these pages, Babcock critiques the "normal formation" as deadly and unnecessarily wasteful of men. He subsequently devised an alternate formation, which he tested and then employed successfully in the 89th Division's 353rd and 354th Regiments. In this, Babcock was consistent. He was always seeking ways to preserve soldiers' lives and to relieve them of unnecessary burdens.

12. Ibid., 513.

13. Ibid., 657.

14. Douglas V. Johnson II, "A Few 'Squads Left' and Off to France: Training the American Army in the United States for World War I" (PhD diss., Temple University, 1992); James Victory, "Soldier Making: The Forces That Shaped the Infantry Training of White Soldiers in the United States Army in World War I" (PhD diss., Kansas State University, 1990).

15. Babcock, "From This Generation to the Next," 416–17.

16. Malone to Hines, September 23, 1921, in the John L. Hines Papers, Library of Congress, Washington, D.C., reads in part: "If the sum total of my service . . . is believed by you to be worthy, I request that you transmit to the Secretary of War your recommendation that I be promoted to the grade of brigadier general. . . . Already nine juniors have been promoted over my head since the armistice. . . . [T]hese include successful commanders of regiments in the 2nd Division except Upton and me."

17. Allan R. Millett, *The General: Robert L. Bullard and Officership in the United States Army, 1881–1925* (Westport, CT: Greenwood, 1975), 310. Ironically, this issue is before the American army today in the form of what is known as the Agile Leader Study. The purpose of the study is to determine how to bring an officer to the point of instruction and education so that he is proficient in the basic principles of his profession yet able to adapt quickly to changing circumstances such as those that have been thrust upon the American army in the past decade.

18. Ibid., 310–11.

19. Ibid., 311.

20. Ibid., 10–11. See also Morris Janowitz, *The Professional Soldier: A Social and Political Portrait* (New York: Free Press, 1960), 151–72.

21. Millett, *The General*, 310.

22. Ibid.

23. Ibid., 333, 335.

24. Babcock, "From This Generation to the Next," 446.

25. Millett, *The General*, 12.

26. Robert L. Bullard, *Personalities and Reminiscences of the War* (Garden City, NY: Doubleday, Page, 1925), 97.

27. Babcock, "From This Generation to the Next," 446–47.

28. Ibid., 444.

29. McNair subsequently became the army's principal trainer, only to be killed by American bombs while observing the 30th Division's attempt to break out of the Normandy hedgerows in July 1944.

30. Babcock, "From This Generation to the Next," 444–45.

31. George W. Cullum, *Biographical Register of the Officers and Graduates of the U.S. Military Academy at West Point, New York, since Its Establishment in 1802*, supplement, vol. 6-A, 1910–1920, ed. Wirt Robinson (Saginaw, MI: Seeman & Peters, 1920), 518.

32. James L. Collins, "McNair, Lesley James (1883–1944)," in Anne Cipriano Venzon, ed., *The United States in the First World War: An Encyclopedia* (New York: Garland, 1995), 368–69.

33. Edward M. Coffman, *The War to End All Wars: The American Military Experience in World War I* (Madison: University of Wisconsin Press, 1986), 222, briefly describes the contrasting publicity issue.

34. Ibid., 222, 277.

35. American Battle Monuments Commission (hereafter cited as ABMC), *28th Division Summary of Operations in the World War* (Washington, DC: U.S. Government Printing Office, 1944), 35.

36. Ibid., 40.

37. Ibid., 71.

38. Ibid., 58–70.

39. U.S. War Department, *Histories of Two Hundred and Fifty-One Divisions of the German Army Which Participated in the War, 1914–1918* (London: Stamp Exchange, 1989), 63. See p. 21 for a mixed evaluation of the 1st Guards during this period and p. 107 for the 5th Guards suffering severe casualties in the Argonne and being reduced to one-company battalions.

40. Ibid., 71.

41. Ibid., 73.

42. ABMC, *26th Division Summary of Operations in the World War* (Washington, DC: U.S. Government Printing Office, 1944), 46–47, 66.

43. Ibid., 51.

44. Babcock, "From This Generation to the Next," 764.

45. Harry A. Benwell, *History of the Yankee Division* (Boston: Cornhill, 1919).

46. Leonard P. Ayres, *The War with Germany: A Statistical Summary* (Washington, DC: U.S. Government Printing Office, 1919), 33.

47. Andrew J. Bacevich. "McCoy, Frank Ross (1874–1954)," in Venzon, *United States in the First World War*, 362–63.

48. ABMC, *42nd Division Summary of Operations in the World War* (Washington, DC: U.S. Government Printing Office, 1944), 5.

49. Center of Military History, *U.S. Army in the World War*, vol. 5, *Military Operations of the American Expeditionary Forces* (Washington, DC: U.S. Government Printing Office, 1988), 166–71.

50. Ibid., 18.

51. Ibid., 32.

52. William G. Haan, *In Commemoration of the Foreign Service and Home Celebration of the 32nd Division* (Milwaukee: Broadway Press, n.d.), 23.

53. Ibid., 11. The divisions, less two, are found in U.S. War Department, *Two Hundred and Fifty-One Divisions of the German Army*, and include the 3rd Guards and the 13th, 28th, 37th, 39th, 52nd, 115th, 123rd, and 236th Divisions. Of these, the 13th was carried as First Class but was badly worn by the time it was employed in the Argonne; its 13th Regiment closed October with two hundred effectives (227–28). The 37th was always carried as a "first class shock division" (428), the 52nd as weak (503), the 115th as Third Class after the Argonne (608), and the 236th as Third Class. Of the two divisions noted above, one was never listed as being in the Argonne sector; the other is not listed at all.

54. ABMC, *American Armies and Battlefields in Europe* (Washington, DC: U.S. Government Printing Office, 1938), 67–69.

55. ABMC, *32nd Division Summary of Operations* (Washington, DC: U.S. Government Printing Office, 1943), 8–17.

56. Ibid., 12.

57. Haan, *In Commemoration of 32nd Division*, 7; U.S. War Department, *Two Hundred and Fifty-One Divisions of the German Army*, 91.

58. James L. Collins Jr., "Connor, William Durward (1874–1960)," in Venzon, *United States in the First World War*, 166–67.

59. Coffman, *War to End All Wars*, 137.

60. Ibid., 258, 323.

61. Edward M. Coffman, *The Hilt of the Sword: The Career of Peyton C. March* (Madison: University of Wisconsin Press, 1966), 58–59, 81–82, 110–13. On the other side, see John J. Pershing, *My Experiences in the World War*, 2 vols. (New York: Stokes, 1931), 1:124; 2:99, 101.

62. Lieutenant Colonel André Lucas was killed by a rocket attack as his unit was evacuating Firebase Ripcord in 1971. For an account of his actions, see Keith W. Nolan, *Ripcord: Screaming Eagles under Siege, Vietnam, 1970* (Novato, CA: Presidio, 2000).

63. Coffman, *War to End All Wars*, 172–75.

64. Johnson Hagood, *Services of Supply: A Memoir of the Great War* (Boston: Houghton Mifflin, 1927), 179: "Frank McCoy telephoned me from Chaumont on May 1st that there was to be a big shakeup there. General Harbord was to take command of the Marine Brigade of the 2d Division, General Doyen having been found physically disqualified. Major General J. W. McAndrew, who had been commanding the Army school at Langres, was to replace Harbord as Chief of Staff, GHQ McCoy himself was to get a regiment and was to be replaced as Secretary of the General Staff by Major James L. Collins, formerly one of General Pershing's aides. Colonel W. D. Connor was to be Chief of Staff of the 32nd Division and was to be replaced as G-4, GHQ, by Colonel George Van H. Mosley. Colonel Le Roy Elting, Cavalry, was to assume the new duty of Deputy Chief of Staff. General Alford E. Bradley had been found physically disqualified and was replaced as Chief Surgeon by General M. W. Ireland. General Benjamin

Alvord, the Adjutant General, was to be replaced by Colonel R. C. Davis. I lost a lot of my friends at GHQ by this change, and it did not seem to me that it was wise to keep things so stirred up during this formative period."

65. A complete list of the U.S. Army chiefs of staff is available at http://www.army.mil/CMH-pg/faq/FAQ-CSA.htm.

66. Babcock, "From This Generation to the Next," 507–636.

67. Marshall Goldsmith et al., *Global Leadership: The Next Generation* (Upper Saddle River, NJ: Financial Times/Prentice-Hall, 2003), 51.

68. Bullard, *Personalities and Reminiscences*, 195.

6
THE BATTLE FOR UNIFORM VOTES
THE POLITICS OF SOLDIER VOTING IN THE ELECTIONS OF 1944

Christopher DeRosa

IN 1944, FOR THE FIRST TIME since the Civil War, the United States faced a presidential election during a major war. The call to arms had once again swept large numbers of voters far from the districts and wards in which they were eligible to vote. In 1864, state legislatures had to devise the means for soldier voting from scratch. Eighty years later, the absentee ballot machinery was hardly more advanced. Existing state measures, claimed the sponsor of a soldier voting bill, could not meet the needs of personnel overseas when "a fellow down in Florida can hardly vote in Illinois."[1]

It was not only the process of absentee voting that was underdeveloped but also the political commitment to the citizen's right to vote and to the soldier's identity as a citizen. By no means had the Civil War experience settled the issue of whether a soldier's franchise was an immutable right or one of those personal freedoms suspended by military service. During World War II, both advocates and opponents of government-facilitated absentee voting claimed to be defending the rights and wishes of the American citizen-soldier. Yet the argument over soldier voting was so contentious that the *New York Times* called it "one of the most bitter debates" in recent American politics as well as "one of the strangest and most politically dangerous situations . . . in modern political history."[2]

During the Civil War, Republicans in each state legislature tried to amend state laws to permit soldiers to vote on the grounds that an American did not surrender his citizenship by becoming a soldier. They argued that not enabling the soldiers to vote when they were fighting for the existence of the country amounted to the worst sort of betrayal. Democrats opposed soldier voting on the grounds that men in uniform could not render an independent political judgment. They would be herded along by their comrades and commanders to support their commander in chief, becoming a veritable "bayonet vote." As Republicans held majorities in most legislatures, they were able to enact short-lived laws to permit soldier voting. After the war, states took the trouble to strike down their soldier voting laws, and a few states even banned future voting by soldiers. In the end, there was little consensus over whether a soldier was or was not reduced to the status of a quasi citizen while in the service when it came to voting.[3]

Rather than establish guiding principles, the Civil War soldier voting experience previewed controversies that the nation faced anew in the next wartime presidential election in 1944. States had done little in the interim to facilitate out-of-state voting. Although continuing the war to victory was not an issue in dispute in the election, once again the opposition party wondered if the troops would somehow be influenced to vote for their commander in chief as if by default. Some Republicans suspected that the War Department was all too comfortable with the devil it knew. Like Abraham Lincoln before him, Franklin D. Roosevelt was considered a dictator by his fiercest critics, bent on concentrating power in his own hands. Furthermore, he was less vulnerable politically than Lincoln had been in 1864. Republicans did not repeat the blunder of the Civil War Democrats by alienating soldiers, but they displayed little enthusiasm for bringing the election to the front. Liberals who saw soldier voting as a vehicle to attack Jim Crow voting impediments (such as the poll tax then in use in eight Southern states) also spurred conservative Democrats to join Republicans in states' rights arguments against centralized planning for the soldier vote.

Representative Robert L. Ramsay (D-WV) sponsored a bill that would create a standard (i.e., federal) postcard application that soldiers could mail in to their home states to request a ballot. The standardized postcard would eliminate the time-wasting step of having to write in for a ballot application, only to receive it and send it right back to ask for a ballot. The act required the states to create a streamlined war ballot suitable for airmailing. It also required them to accept ballots from soldiers regardless of whether or not they had paid their poll tax, if they were otherwise qualified to vote. The logic was that if the nation wanted soldiers to retain their right to vote in absentia, it made no sense to disenfranchise them because they had not been able to register or pay the poll tax in person.

The soldier vote found its chief obstacle and the poll tax its tireless champion in Congressman John E. Rankin (D-MS). "This measure," he claimed, "is a monstrosity, shoved through in the name of the American soldier, who did not ask for it. It is an attempt to wipe out the election laws as well as the registration laws of the various States. It is part of a long-range communistic program to change our way of life and to take the control out of the hands of white Americans in the various states and turn them over to certain irresponsible elements.... I warn those members from other states who think they are merely nagging the white people of the south with this legislation that they will find, probably after it is too late, that they have commended this poisoned chalice to the lips of their own people."[4]

Edgar G. Brown, director of the National Negro Council, saw matters differently. Calling the bill the nation's first enforcement of the Thirteenth, Fourteenth, and Fifteenth Amendments, he noted that "the 400,000 Negro soldiers from poll-tax states will have an opportunity to participate for the first time ... and have a vote in the democracy for which they are fighting and dying."[5]

Congress passed the Ramsay Act, albeit too close to the election for it to have much effect. Few soldiers availed themselves of the war ballot in the 1942 midterm elections, and fewer still were actually able to vote. The states reported only 136,686 applications for ballots, but even this small figure was inflated by the 58,000 ballots sent out to New Jersey's soldiers on the state's own initiative. Overall, a mere 28,051 soldiers managed to cast votes that counted.[6]

Congress Debates the Soldier Vote

The poor showing inspired Senators Theodore Francis Green (D-RI) and Scott W. Lucas (D-IL) to replace the Ramsay Act with a more effective law. The bill they offered, S1285, retained the Ramsay Act's anti-poll tax language but provided for larger federal and military roles in soldier voting. It called for a federal ballot that soldiers could use to write in candidates' names for national offices and the establishment of a War Ballot Commission that could alleviate from the services the administrative burdens of running the election in the field. Previews of the Green-Lucas Bill predictably aroused the ire of states' rights advocates. A chief source of opposition to liberalized, federalized voting rights was the forty-eight secretaries of state. The secretary of state was the state's chief enforcer of election laws. He generally saw himself not as a promoter or a facilitator of voting but as a wary guardian of the franchise who doled it out only under proper legal conditions.

The secretaries saw Congress's soldier-voting proposals not as a means of doing justice to the soldiers but as a dangerous, ham-fisted stab into their world of strict regulations on voter registration, absentee ballots, publication of candidates' names, and all manner of deadlines pertaining thereto. Anticipating that the Green-Lucas Bill would be enacted, the services sent representatives to the annual conference of the National Association of Secretaries of State in St. Louis in October 1943 to see how the services could work with the disgruntled state officials.

Frederic W. Cook, secretary of state for Massachusetts, opened the session on war voting by noting that the Green-Lucas Bill was "very, very unsatisfactory to many Secretaries" and that they had been particularly alarmed by a provision in an early draft of the bill for soldiers' ballots to be opened, microfilmed, and v-mailed back to the United States. Although this proposed breach of secrecy had been dropped, it left a suspicious thought in the minds of the secretaries, several of whom referred to it in their criticism of the latest version of S1285.[7]

Colonel Robert Cutler, a lawyer in civilian life, represented the army. He described the difficulties that servicemen faced in obtaining ballots under the Ramsay Act but explained that the War Department was officially neither for nor against the Green-Lucas Bill. The services simply wanted to figure out how to carry out the requirements of the law should it be passed. Nevertheless, the secretaries vented their frustration on Cutler.[8]

Secretary Dwight Brown of Missouri questioned the federal ballot's implied prioritization of national over state elections. "I am taking the position very vehemently that servicemen and women are just as interested in the affairs of their states, and their local communities." Secretary Walker Wood of Mississippi emphasized that "we only have one party down there, required to nominate presidential electors. We know if a ballot comes in there for perusal with a name on it, they would declare that ballot illegal and not count it." He seemed to be implying that Mississippi would throw out ballots inscribed with the names "Roosevelt" or "Dewey" rather than the names of the obscure electors. Moreover, allowing soldiers to vote without having paid the poll tax was a "direct conflict with the Mississippi laws."[9]

Secretary John B. Wilson of Georgia also objected to the circumvention of the poll tax and defended (if vaguely) the practice of collecting it. "That is a sore spot in a lot of places. But, I will tell you one thing, 999 out of every thousand voters in Georgia, wherever they are, will gladly pay that dollar poll tax and you know the reason why." Soldier voting, he argued, would be a "simple proposition" if the federal government would "make available only the facilities of the names and last-known addresses of all of those in the armed forces and bless God we will do the rest." In fact, it was anything but a simple proposition to put eleven million soldiers in mixed-state units in touch with officials from their home state in order to get them a ballot in the short window between the determination of who was running for the various offices and election day. These difficulties went a long way toward explaining the failure of the Ramsay Act in the first place.[10]

Secretary Sidney Latham also defended the poll tax, saying, "We still think it is worth $1.75 to vote in Texas," but he pointed out that in his state soldiers were disqualified to vote merely by entering the service. Texas had a law against soldiers voting. Cutler acknowledged that the Green-Lucas Bill could not surmount such a disqualification. Rather, it enabled soldiers to vote if they were otherwise qualified, but military service prevented them from registering or paying poll tax. The bill, he explained, drew a distinction between a voting qualification such as being a citizen, having established residence, or being of a certain age, and a voting requirement such as presenting a poll tax receipt or having to

...struction on this point came not only from the Southern st... ...st insistent in denying that registration was a mere procedural "requirement" was the secretary of Connecticut. That voters appear before an election board, identify themselves, and recite five lines of the state constitution was not a disposable step, he contended, but the essence of their qualification to vote.[11]

In fact, secretaries from all over the map took up the states' rights banner. Michael Holm of Minnesota informed the military representatives, "We have our own laws. . . . A man in England or Europe cannot vote and the vote be counted so far as the state of Minnesota is concerned. . . . I am not in favor of Washington usurping any more rights." Congress was on a course to obviate the very need for state government and "control the whole set-up in the United States," he warned. "As far as Nebraska is concerned you can throw it out the window," declared Secretary Frank Marsh. "Somebody is trying to take away from the states the states' rights to control their elections. We resent it in Nebraska." If the purpose of their meeting was to help implement the Green-Lucas Bill, said Secretary Gene D. Smith, "you can just count Pennsylvania's cooperation out because we will not aid and abet Congress in invading our rights and as sure as there is a God in heaven, that will be thrown back in our teeth in the very near future."[12]

The secretary of Kentucky admonished the states' righters that soldier voting was only a temporary measure in response to extraordinary circumstances. Smith replied, "I certainly hope we are not going to lose our senses merely because this happened to be a soldiers' vote bill. The fundamental things we are fighting for is states' rights, whether it is the soldiers' vote, poll tax, or whatever it may be. If we are going to permit an onrush of alleged patriotism to let us go blind to some of the problems facing us at this time, then God help all of us."[13]

In the face of this intransigence, the military representatives could only note that they were not advocating the bill. Cutler at one point said for himself, "I defy anyone to be a stronger states' rights man than a yankee from Massachusetts." At the same time, he tried to persuade the secretaries that the military simply could not administer elections under forty-eight different sets of rules. Doubts on this score persisted as Congress debated the Green-Lucas Bill.[14]

Little more than a week later, Frederic W. Cook went to Capitol Hill to register the secretaries' complaints but also their willingness to be placated with modifications in the bill. Again, he brought up the discarded plan, laid out in S1285, to microfilm ballots overseas before returning them to the states. The secretaries, he said, were "deeply incensed . . . and very, very much in objection to the idea that there could be a record of how every man in the services voted . . . [,] that is, the secrecy of the ballot taken away."[15]

The Senate's Subcommittee on Privileges and Elections, chaired by Green, met twice, on October 29 and November 5, to debate the Green-Lucas Bill to alter the Ramsay Act. Green op[...] [re]gister in person. O[ther?] fellow-citizens have entered the [...] [St]ates. Among the m[...] world in the bitter struggle to defen[d...] [...] of democracy, and they ought to have the opportunity to exercise individually the rights for which they were fighting. In any case, "as a group they constitute such a large part of the electorate that any national election in which they did not participate could hardly be called representative."[16]

Yet there remained formidable obstacles to soldier voting. "Many states," Green reminded his colleagues, "require applications for absentee ballots to be made and ballots to be sent out and returned within so short a period of time that compliance by the great majority of the members of the armed forces is virtually impossible." Young soldiers casting their first ballots would not be able to register to vote, and some states required a voter who had missed an election to register anew. Reminded of the states' existing absentee ballot laws, cosponsor Lucas dismissed them: "They just can't vote. A fellow down in Florida can hardly vote in Illinois as an absentee voter," much less from an overseas war zone.[17]

Committee members asked Lucas if he had studied the Civil War's experience with soldier voting. He mentioned that in 1864 soldier votes provided the margin for victory only for a "few minor State officers" and "a solitary Congressman" from Michigan. Perhaps trying to minimize the potential consequences of what he urged his fellow senators to undertake, he argued that "except in the State of Maryland soldiers' votes had substantially no effect on the election." Maryland troops were decisive in the ratification of a new state constitution abolishing slavery. However, this one exception put a fine point on the unspoken fears of some of the bill's opponents, conjuring as it did the image of a wave of liberalized young voters bearing on their bayonets an agenda of sweeping social change.[18]

Senator Abe Murdock (D-UT) asked if the bill did not create two standards for voter qualification by enfranchising soldiers from both states that charged poll tax and those that did not. Murdock reported that in the Senate Judiciary Committee the sponsors of an anti-poll tax bill had identified their bill with the soldier voting law. The Ramsay Act, they argued, meant that the right to vote unfettered by a poll tax was already the law of the land in regard to soldiers. Murdock implied that if this interpretation gained currency, it would be harder to pass a new soldier voting bill in time for the election.[19]

The authors of the bill defended their circumvention of the poll tax by noting that such devices were requirements for voters but not actual qualifications. The law would not interfere with the states' ability to define who was a voter and who was not, only with their ability to enforce procedural rules upon those voters casting votes from the armed forces. Of course, the distinction between qualifications and requirements was exactly the fiction upon which the antiblack voting measures in the South relied. Poll taxes and arcane registration rules were barriers to the immediate casting of a ballot rather than direct challenges to a citizen's constitutional identity as a voter, although they disenfranchised the citizen all the same.

Senator Hugh A. Butler (R-NE) was the committee member most skeptical of the bill. He argued against it on the grounds of military inefficiency: "I am wondering, Senator Lucas, if the boys are more interested in getting a right to vote or in getting a sufficient amount of supplies to finish the war quickly and then get home and vote." Butler never tried to prove that providing and retrieving ballots from soldiers would materially impair the war effort. Rather, the argument was that because the election required any resources or effort whatsoever and did not contribute to military victory it was, by definition, wasteful. Lucas retorted that he did not state "that the boy wants to vote, but I do say that the opportunity ought to be presented to him."[20]

Elections caused a lot of excitement and upset everyday civilian life, Butler persisted: "Would something like this create the same furor in the Army and Navy and the Marines and Air Corps, where we are out trying to win some battles?" Critics of soldier voting painted unlikely pictures of battles abandoned and patrols neglected as soldiers dropped their weapons to argue politics and line up for voting, although the reality of absentee voting was that it required no additional assemblies of troops.[21]

Butler's arguments were undercut in particular by the fact that the army and the navy had dropped their original logistical objections and were prepared to cooperate in the balloting. Nevertheless, he alleged that the very fact that army, navy, and merchant marine representatives had to testify before the committee meant that they were "already interfering with the war program" and might ultimately "interfere tremendously with something far more important than voting." Army and navy officers at the hearing testified to the contrary, that the bill in its revised form would ease the difficulties placed on them by the 1942 version.[22]

Butler argued against the bill from every side. Lucas explained that the ballots would contain no information about the candidates other than their name, their party, and the office for which they were running. Butler asserted that it would be unfair for soldiers not to have information on where a candidate stood on "increases in wages, strikes, and about a million other things." No doubt, the senator knew that a bill permitting a government mailing to describe the positions of competing politicians would be such an obvious vehicle for partisan propaganda that it would have no chance of passing.[23]

Butler's probe did raise the question of how voters overseas, under military security, could make informed choices. The army's *Guide to the Use of Information Materials* instructed editors of military newspapers to extend equal time and treatment to any political party that fielded a candidate in at least six states. Soldiers also had access to political news through civilian associations, personal mail, and newspapers at base libraries. As in any population of American voters, those who did not actively follow the news could still form political opinions based on word of mouth. Like their civilian counterparts, many uniformed voters cast ballots based on established party loyalties rather than the late-breaking news from the home front. In the end, there was no compelling reason for the framers of the bill to hold a soldier to a higher standard of political awareness than the civilian voter.[24]

Lucas based his argument for the bill not on the immutable or universal rights of citizenship but rather on the special circumstances of world war. Doubting the constitutionality of laws, in some states, that prohibited soldier voting altogether, he nevertheless sought to avoid the argument. "There is a difference," he remarked, "between a professional soldier and a citizen soldier, and these are citizen soldiers I am talking about; these boys have gone away from their homes and are ready to return to them the moment this bloody war is over." As his cosponsor Green argued in a later part of the hearings, "the Federal Government has, by drafting these men, taken away from them the opportunity of complying with the registration laws of the states. Therefore, they have disenfranchised these soldiers and sailors. . . . We are simply trying to restore to them a right which we have taken away."[25] In this conception, the right to vote did not follow a citizen who chose a life of travel or an out-of-state career. Lucas said, in essence, that short-term volunteers and draftees ought to be able to vote outside normal means because it was not their fault they were away from their home voting place, whereas a career soldier had chosen to exempt himself as a consequence of his profession.[26]

The volunteers and draftees of World War II were, to Lucas, not merely worthier voters than professionals but also more fit than civilian voters: "If these citizen soldiers defending the Republic are denied a part in the civil administration of this Government, it is time to inquire, who is worthy of it? Most of these men are world wise. They have seen other nations and their peoples first hand. Their opinions and conclusions on social, political, and human problems are being molded through the ordeal of a global war." Later in the hearings, Senator Tom Connally (D-TX) quipped that if soldiers were to receive a write-in ballot, "you had better send the alphabet over there." Lucas answered, "You would find out that the 10,000,000 men in the Army are better qualified and better informed as to what is going on than any 10,000,000 men in America . . . and they could come in here and vote on any ballot more intelligently." As Lucas summarized his argument, there was no more affectionate talk of "the boys." "These men," he said, "will soon control the destiny of this Nation." Here, in 1944, was a signal that the generation of Americans who fought the war would be conceded a status as especially virtuous and competent citizens. While civilians debated whether or not soldiers could vote, they laid the attitudinal groundwork for a near future when only veterans could get elected.[27]

In the full Senate, Republicans and Southern Democrats outfought proponents of the Green-Lucas Bill. Senators James O. Eastland (D-MS), John L. McClellan (D-AR), and Kenneth McKellar (D-TN) managed to attach amendments that turned the bill into a pure states' rights bill, doing away with the federal ballot and the idea of a ballot commission. Lucas called it "the hardest blow that was ever struck against the political rights of soldiers in time of war." Eastland contended that "this vote by the Senate has put an end to any chance for the enactment by Congress of anti-poll tax legislation."[28]

The debate became publicly emotional. Senator Joseph Guffey (D-PA) said that his Southern colleagues had made with Republicans "the most unpatriotic and unholy alliance that has occurred in the United States Senate since the League of Nations for peace of the world was defeated in 1919. . . . It's all right to send soldiers to die for their country, but it's all wrong to let them vote for the officials of their country, that's the effect of the Senate's action." The Southern Democrats retorted with threats to bolt the party and throw the presidential election into the House.[29]

Twenty-five Northern Democrats signed a petition denouncing the Eastland version of the bill, which soon became known as the Eastland-Rankin Bill. Congressman Tom Murray (D-TN) declared that "we all know that Vito Marcantonio [a signer of the petition and a New Yorker who was a member of the American Labor Party] wants to bring about social equality of the races in the South. . . . This is the most important battle that has been made since the Civil War for the preservation of states' rights in the South. . . . We do not intend to let this administration tell us to change our racial problem in the South."[30]

After the states' rights triumph in the Senate, the Subcommittee on Privileges and Elections next met on soldier voting in January 1944. Republicans offered a states' rights alternative to the Green-Lucas Bill, and both Senator Homer S. Ferguson (R-MI) and Senator Millard F. Tydings (D-MD) offered amendments requiring the army to ship each state's official ballot to the soldiers. Colonel Cutler, representing the Office of the Secretary of the Army, testified that it was nearly an impossible task. Official state ballots took up more cargo-carrying capacity than the lightweight federal ballot and, given different preparation schedules, the simple bulk shipping that the military was willing to devote to election materials would not be sufficient. Furthermore, military units were full of citizens from different states, meaning the services would have to provide a great excess of ballots to every unit to cover the possibilities of their composition.[31]

Each state ballot, Cutler argued, would displace twelve hundred v-mail letters, which meant that "the most precious morale factor that the men overseas have, would be seriously curtailed or wholly shut off for a considerable period of time." Delivering the mail was not "a matter of just being nice"; it was "a matter that is vital to the fighting spirit of the American soldier and sailor . . . and we feel that, valuable as the right of suffrage is and much as the soldiers and sailors may desire to vote, that they do not want to have balloting material substituted for their letters from home."[32]

Cutler's assumption that soldiers would rather not vote if it meant an interruption of their personal mail is congruent with historian Robert B. Westbrook's argument that in World War II, Americans fought chiefly for private matters such as their families, their homes, and their job prospects rather than for public, abstract considerations such as democracy. Analysts used to describe the American political system as a civic creed binding together a people without deep roots in a common land, faith, or ethnicity. But Americans' sense of home was not limited to a set of political ideas, no matter how celebrated. It could be founded on appreciation for material plenty, economic opportunity, personal relationships, or just a diffuse sense of the United States being "the good guys." Many soldiers indicated a desire to vote, but Senator Butler probably pegged a large percentage accurately when he supposed that all the men wanted was to get the war over with.[33]

The idea that because the troops were fighting for democracy it was especially important that they be able to vote may not have occurred to many soldiers. World War II's propagandists avoided Wilsonian slogans about making the world "safe for democracy," deeming them counterproductive. GIs saw the war not as a crusade but as an unpleasant but necessary job. Men in the ranks frowned upon explicitly patriotic talk. The preferred pose was one of laconic indifference to the innocent or ignorant pronouncements of the civilian world.[34]

As states' rights alternatives and amendments multiplied, Roosevelt lent his support to the unadorned Green-Lucas Bill. In his January 25, 1944, message to Congress, he described it as a "fact" that the "vast majority" of the eleven million military personnel "are going to be deprived of their right to vote" under the existing system: "The need for new legislation is evident if we are really sincere—and not merely rendering lip service to our soldiers and sailors.... Some people—I am sure with their tongues in their cheeks—say that the solution to this problem is simply that the respective States improve their own absentee ballot machinery. In fact there is now pending before the House of Representatives a meaningless bill, passed by the Senate December 3, 1943, which presumes to meet this complicated and difficult situation by some futile language.... I consider such proposed legislation a fraud on the soldiers and sailors now training and fighting for us and for our sacred rights." What was needed, wrote Roosevelt, was a full overhaul of the absentee ballot machinery, and the new bill, "seems to me to do the job." Noting that the fighting men had no lobbyists to work for them, he claimed that as commander in chief "I am sure I can express their wishes in this matter and their resentment against the discrimination which is being practiced against them."[35]

Republicans in the House booed as they heard Roosevelt's message read into the record and hooted when they heard him describe himself as an "interested citizen." In the Senate, Rufus Holman (R-OR) suggested that Roosevelt withdraw as a candidate so that the debate on the bill could come to an end. Later, Republicans charged the administration with disseminating Roosevelt's caustic message to the armed forces. Senator Robert A. Taft (R-OH) accused Secretary of War Henry L. Stimson and Secretary of the Navy Frank Knox of "running for a fourth term," because their departments had testified to the difficulty they would have getting the forty-eight different state ballots in the hands of the right servicemen, this despite the fact that both men were Republicans who had joined Roosevelt's coalition cabinet in 1940. "It is only natural," said Taft, "that men who have the responsibilities which they have are convinced that their continuance in office is essential to the welfare of the country."[36]

By January, the Senate and House were moving in opposite directions. The Senate groped for a compromise on a revised Green-Lucas Bill, and Representative Eugene Worley (D-TX) sponsored the compromise in the House, where conservatives pushed hard for the Eastland-Rankin states' rights bill. Rankin delivered a fiery attack on Worley's bill, suggesting that its real author was Herbert T. Wechsler of the attorney general's office. In an example of Congress's seniority-driven protocol, the forty-five-minute diatribe occurred on time conceded by the sponsor of the bill, and when Rankin finally finished, reported the *New York Times*, "the House came to its feet, shouting and clapping, none more heartily than his youthful adversary, Eugene Worley."[37]

Rankin's appeal did not translate into the Senate, which defeated the Eastland-Rankin Bill on February 4 to stay on course with a version of the bill that retained the federal ballot and a commission, albeit in reduced roles. To bridge their differences, the two houses convened a conference consisting of five representatives (three-to-two for the states' rights bill) and five senators (three-to-two for the Green-Lucas Bill). Across mid-February, the conferees could agree only that they were deadlocked. Meanwhile, the House passed the Eastland-Rankin Bill. Finally, after two weeks, nine of the ten conferees agreed to retain the federal ballot but to make its use contingent upon the approval of the state and a voter's inability to receive a state ballot. The lone holdout was Rankin, who insisted that "the fight has just begun" on a bill that "might prove dangerous if not disastrous to the welfare of the country in one of her most critical hours." Senator Karl LeCompte (R-IA) admitted with regret that there was nothing to prevent a soldier from purposely applying too late to use a state ballot and then availing himself of the federal ballot. He did not mention that the only reason one might wish to do such a thing was because he or she would otherwise be disenfranchised by enforcement of poll tax or in-person registration requirements.[38]

Green believed that the bill that bore his name had been in essence destroyed. More soldiers, he contended, could vote under the Ramsay Act than under the new bill. He urged Roosevelt to veto the law. Other supporters took comfort in the hope that the presence of any kind of federal ballot in the background would spur states to serious attempts to get ballots to the troops. Despite Rankin's invocation of John Paul Jones, he knew that he had won. He and his allies devoted themselves to characterizing the dual ballot system as a choice for the servicemen in which they had provided a long state ballot with all the candidates' names, as opposed to liberals and subversives who had offered a short bobtailed ballot with no names. By concentrating on the comparison of the ballots, he tried to shift attention from the issue of whether soldiers would be able to vote at all.[39]

On March 14 the compromise bill passed the Senate, and the next day the House followed suit. Southern Democrats were the most conspicuous of the holdouts. In its final form, the law recommended that the states enact their own laws to facilitate soldier voting but provided a blank absentee federal ballot for soldiers who could not obtain state ballots in time. Voters would have to fill in the names of candidates to use this ballot. All the election materials would be mailed free of charge. The United States War Ballot Commission (USWBC), consisting of the secretary of war, the secretary of the navy, and the administrator of the War Shipping Administration, would administer the election for military personnel. The services were prohibited from disseminating any political propaganda, with restrictions on books, newspapers, magazines, movies, and broadcasts.[40]

On March 31, Roosevelt informed Congress that he was "permitting S. 1285 ... to become law without my signature. The bill is, in my judgment, wholly inadequate" to ensure soldiers the right to vote. The compromise law was no better than "a standing invitation to the several States to make it practicable for their citizens to vote." Under the law, soldiers could only vote the federal ballot if they had applied for a state ballot and had not received it or if their governor validated its use. These caveats, wrote the president, made the soldier's right to vote a conditional one. For the challenger's part, Governor Thomas E. Dewey charged that a conspiracy led by "a group with unlimited financial resources"—apparently a reference to the Congress of Industrial Organizations (CIO)—was campaigning to convince New Yorkers to adopt the federal ballot.[41]

The War Ballot Commission

Despite the candidates' misgivings, the newly established USWBC met on April 3, 1944, and selected Secretary of War Stimson as chair and Secretary of the Navy Knox as vice chair. Admiral Emory S. Land, the administrator of the War Shipping Administration, completed the commission. Each service appointed representatives who would carry out the day-to-day functions of the commission. Cutler, the army's point man on soldier voting issues since October, was named the commission's executive officer.[42]

The USWBC's first task was to prepare postcard applications for state ballots and the federal ballots themselves in a form suitable for airmailing. Cutler estimated that printing of the election materials would cost $89,000, and that would be the commission's major budgetary outlay. Most other costs, including the salaries of the services' representatives, were borne by the military departments' budgets. It was not a bad estimate. In the end, the USWBC cost approximately $115,000.[43] The commission had to then consult with the secretaries of states, ascertain whether they would use the federal ballot or not, and collect from them the names, addresses, and party affiliations of the candidates for various offices to post to the soldiers.

It was the job of the War and Navy Departments to deliver applications and federal ballots to all soldiers, sailors, and personnel of the American Red Cross, Society of Friends, Women's Auxiliary Service Pilots, and United Service Organization. The military departments had to post the dates of the primaries and the special and general elections, and then they had to deliver the state ballots requested via postcard application. Individual units had to appoint officers to administer voters' oaths for those using state absentee ballots and collect the federal ones as well as provide an opportunity for soldiers to execute their ballots in secret. Then the military had to ship the marked ballots back to the United States and destroy the unused ones. Throughout the period leading up to the election, Title V of the soldier voting law required the military to eliminate from information provided to soldiers any political propaganda "calculated to affect the result of any election."[44]

By June 15, 1944, the USWBC had printed 37.5 million postcard applications and 7.6 million federal ballots and delivered them to the army and navy. A great deal of the commission's time was spent in consultation with the secretaries of state about the myriad obstacles to soldier voting. On May 30, Cutler and his naval counterpart, Captain E. A. Hayes, addressed the Governors' Conference in Hershey, Pennsylvania, and emphasized that the USWBC was trying to work with the states, not tell them what to do. The deadline for states to authorize the federal ballot was July 15. In the end, only twenty states did so, and each of these restricted its use to personnel serving overseas. Georgia further limited the use of the federal ballot to members of the armed forces, and Florida authorized only the WASPs and members of the merchant marine in addition to members of the armed forces. Liberals hoped that the federal ballot would be a sword that cut through all manner of logistical and legalistic barriers to voting, but the victory of the states' righters guaranteed that it would bear home only a handful of soldiers' votes.[45]

Florida had been the subject of some of the USWBC's most vexing negotiations. On July 10, 1944, the governor certified the use of federal ballots "subject ... to the fact that no specific provision is made by the laws of this state for voting for a presidential or vice presidential candidate by name, but only for presidential electors." To Cutler, it seemed clear that using electors' names instead of the names of the candidates "would be extremely confusing, require much space, and is certainly not in conformity with the statutory procedure for voting by writing in the candidates' names" required by the federal ballot. He flew to Tallahassee and met with the governor and secretary of state to resolve this difficulty, but they informed him that their state ballots would indeed eschew the presidential candidates' names. Because the federal ballot had been reduced to a minor role, Cutler was able at least to extract Secretary Robert A. Gray's promise to instruct the county clerks to count federal ballots with the names of Dewey and Roosevelt written in as votes for their respective electors.[46]

On August 2, Cutler paid a visit to Austin, Texas, to confer with Secretary of State Sidney Latham. Latham explained that Texas, like Florida, listed the names of electors rather than presidential candidates. Despite this practice, he agreed to provide the office-seekers' names in 1944. However, he refused to relax a rule that would require Texas personnel stationed stateside to have their ballot notarized by a notary public rather than witnessed by an officer. The secretary once again questioned whether a Texas soldier who had not paid his poll tax could vote. Cutler referred him to the portion of the Ramsay Act that was still in effect, and Latham indicated that he understood that the federal ballot did in fact circumvent the poll tax. Given the emergency-only nature of the ballot, he could view the situation with equanimity.[47]

In June, the army trained voting officers in Chicago and Washington, D.C. Cutler and two other instructors went over the service's voting manual, and students received a special reinforcement on the ban on political propaganda from Major General Alexander D. Surles, director of the War Department's Bureau of Public Relations (PR). The fact that this indoctrination came from the PR chief indicated that the army considered its handling of the election to be a potential threat to its reputation for political neutrality.[48]

On the last day of the course, future voting officers saw *A Few Quick Facts on Voting for Service Men Overseas*, an animated film intended for the general military audience. The movie began with a cartoon Hitler addressing his troops, "All in favor of me say 'Ja!'" The only objector is plucked away by a giant arm and tossed aside. "It is unanimous," cries the Führer. Cartoon Japanese soldiers herd one of their number "at point of bayonet into a satirical Japanese polling booth, built like a pagoda," as the narrator intones, "One more vote for Tojo."[49]

The narrator then contrasts this treatment with the Americans' practice of wartime democracy, quoting an unidentified Civil War general to the effect that while performing a sacred duty, soldiers "should not be deprived of a most precious privilege." The characterization of the franchise as a privilege rather than a right reserved the individual commander's own right to deem the unit's military situation incompatible with voting. The cartoon goes on to describe the method of voting, contrasting a model GI executing a ballot with the struggles of Private Snafu, "who is making erasures, blobs, smears, and messing up his ballot generally, with a frantic little bird tearing his hair in background."[50]

A Few Quick Facts was only one part of the War Department's dissemination of voting information. It issued numerous circulars, pamphlets, posters, and manuals down to the company level to support the voting officers and even broadcast radio instructions on voting to commanders in the field. War Department circulars formed the basis for "stories in non-formal language" in *Stars and Stripes*, the army magazine *Yank*, and more than one thousand individual unit newspapers. Yet this publicity effort did not bear all the earmarks of a true get-out-the-vote campaign. Neither the War Department nor the Navy Department urged soldiers and sailors to vote. Rather, their materials emphasized that servicemen would not be marched to the polling place, and the decision to vote was strictly up to them. Both departments still considered neutrality not only toward candidates and parties but also toward the act of voting itself consistent with civilian control and military professionalism.[51]

To forestall charges of fraud, the USWBC took extensive security precautions. The ballots were printed on special paper that could be tested to distinguish authentic ballots from counterfeits. Armed sentries monitored the envelope stuffers and guarded the ballots under lock and key. Navy inspectors searched for blank ballots left on the stuffing floor. Once collected, these misplaced or otherwise damaged ballots were incinerated under the supervision of the U.S. Government Printing Office. As the ballots moved from place to place, an officer of the commission reconciled the numbers reportedly shipped and received and resolved discrepancies. In all parts of the process, the commission gave its full attention to the fate of unused ballots, making sure they were destroyed so that they could not be used illegally.[52]

The Federal War Ballot itself was a card within a lightweight envelope inside a larger one marked with red stripes. The purpose of the stripes was to alert the services' mail sorters to the item's high shipping priority. The voters wrote in capital letters their choices for president, senator, and representative on the cards and inserted them into the smaller envelope, on which they reaffirmed that they had tried but failed to obtain a state ballot.[53]

One persistent problem in the election was that the lightweight federal ballots tended to fuse together in cartons shipped to troops in tropical climates. Cutler tried to persuade states to accept ballots that obviously appeared to have been mangled or scraped by soldiers trying to unstick them. Vouching for the sticky ballots was expressive of the military's basic attitude toward enfranchisement. The states jealously defended their right to reject applications and ballots for any number of reasons, and so the USWBC and the departments it represented took the position of accepting voters' oaths at face value and passing along whatever they submitted. The *Navy Voting Manual*, for example, instructed voting officers "to resolve all doubts in favor of the delivery of the postcard as the State is the judge of an applicant's right to use the postcard."[54]

In the field, voting officers had to arrange a place where voters could fill out their ballots in private and had to assist illiterate voters and voters with disabilities. They were supposed to keep loiterers away from the area and prevent anyone from stumping for candidates or polling soldiers on their votes. The rule against campaigning near the polls reflected the prohibition against the military's dissemination of political propaganda under Title V of the soldier voting law.[55]

Title V, based on an amendment attached to the bill by Senator Taft, specified that the 1939 Hatch Amendment against "pernicious political activities" in the armed forces applied to the subject of the soldier vote in the 1944 election. Senator Carl A. Hatch (D-NM) differentiated between the government producing propaganda for soldiers and soldiers having access to information. He complained that the army had construed his amendment to restrict the latter, and he called for the entire amendment to be repealed: "In my mind . . . it is extremely bad legislation. It is bad for the morale of the armed forces to set them apart in a class separate and distinct from the rest of the Nation" and to say to them in effect, "You are patriotic enough, you are intelligent enough, to fight and die for your country, but we cannot trust you to read magazines and literature available to the rest of us." Any law against propaganda, he argued, ought to apply equally to civilians and soldiers, in war and in peace alike.[56]

Taft joined Hatch in condemning the army's interpretation of the law. The War Department, he claimed, had given soldiers the false impression that the government had limited their access to political information. In fact, said, Taft, they were free to receive books, newspapers, magazines, and letters with political content. Even military publications were free to cover the news but could not show partiality to a party or candidate. Indeed, the Army's *Guide to the Use of Information Materials*, published that same year, said as much in regard to service newspapers.[57]

However, claimed Taft, individual officers had overzealously interpreted War Department directives concerning propaganda. He cited as absurd a case in which a company cancelled its subscription to the *Los Angeles Times* so as not to be in violation of the order and another case in which the army had labeled historian Catherine Drinker Bowen's biography of Oliver Wendell Holmes Jr., *Yankee from Olympus*, political propaganda based on a passage in which Holmes and the young Franklin D. Roosevelt exchanged some compliments on each other's liberal credentials. "No reasonable person could make such a decision," said Taft. On the other hand, he believed that the army need not issue booklets with photos of Roosevelt merely because he was commander in chief.[58]

Of course, what was reasonable to Taft was not a universal standard. Some did not find reasonable, for example, his contention that because the War Department had complied with the law that required it to help issue the federal ballots, it had aligned itself with the CIO's political action committee. The army found itself whipsawed by Taft's charges that, on the one hand, it was working openly for Roosevelt's reelection and, on the other, it was being obtuse in its application of the Hatch Amendment. Indeed, the War Department considered that "the statute uses the broadest terms ('literature or material') which include every medium of information and entertainment." Nevertheless, it evolved a workable policy toward general circulation publications such as the *Los Angeles Times*. Overseas service libraries or newsstands could sell newspapers and magazines that had been determined objectively to be among the fifteen most popular with the soldiers before April 1, 1944. Soldiers still had the right to subscribe to any other periodical through their personal mail. Military media could use political speeches and editorials only if they provided equal time to all qualified political parties. As to books in general circulation, the Army's Special Services could select books from a list compiled by a nonpartisan group called the Council on Books in War-Time. In making the selections, Special Services were to "stress readability and masculine viewpoint" while "avoiding ... the mediocre, trashy, and mawkish books with a decided feminine interest." It was not reported whether they eventually deemed *Yankee from Olympus* sufficiently manly for military use.[59]

The Results

When the election officials tabulated the results, both civilian and military, Roosevelt won an unprecedented fourth term as president, defeating Dewey by a margin of 3.6 million popular and 333 electoral votes. Democrats retained majorities in Congress. The armed forces made up 5.6 percent of the overall vote, ranging from a low of 2 percent in Alabama to a high of 10 percent in Georgia, the one state that had lowered its voting age to eighteen. Almost 4.5 million members of the armed forces requested ballots. Of these, the states deemed about 4.4 million to be valid applications. States sent 4.2 million ballots to soldiers, meaning that about 200,000 valid requests went unfulfilled. Of the 4.2 million ballots sent out, soldiers sent back only 2.8 million, and of these votes, states accepted almost 2.7 million, meaning that between ballots sent out and ballots received, there was a loss of an additional 1.4 million potential votes. Given approximately 9 million citizens of voting age in the ranks, the armed forces had an effective turnout of about 30 percent.[60]

There are two chief reasons for the large drop-off between ballots sent out and ballots returned. Some of the 1.4 million unreturned ballots must have been the work of states and patriotic organizations applying for ballots en masse on behalf of many soldiers who never intended to vote. New York, the home state of President Roosevelt and Governor Dewey, staged a drive to send ballots to its soldiers. The American Legion and other civic groups undertook similar work. However, some portion of the unreturned vote must have also been due to the inefficiency of having to request and get back a state ballot rather than vote directly on a universal federal ballot. It is impossible to estimate the relative impact of these factors.[61]

The twenty authorizing states accepted only 84,835 federal ballots. These made up 8 percent of the military absentee vote in those states, ranging from a low of 2.7 percent in Massachusetts to a high of 12.7 percent in Washington. An exception was Texas, where a small number of federal ballots made up 64 percent of the military vote because the state used its poll tax law to disenfranchise most of its soldiers voting the state ballot. Even discounting the 1,343 federal ballots sent to nonauthorizing states, states threw out almost 20 percent of soldiers' votes on the federal ballot. They disqualified less than 4 percent of state ballots.[62]

Roosevelt's margin of victory in the popular vote was larger than the total soldier vote. In information provided to the secretaries of state, the USWBC claimed that the soldier vote provided the winning margin for Roosevelt in New Jersey (sixteen electoral votes) and possibly Michigan (nineteen electoral votes). If true, New Jersey had reversed its role from the 1864 election, when it was the only nonborder state to go for the challenger rather than the commander in chief. The commission also suggested that at least one congressional representative and several local officials owed their seats to soldier votes. It did not, however, reveal how it managed to isolate the impact of the military vote in these cases. If indeed New Jersey and Michigan had turned on the votes from the armed forces, these two states accounted for less than 11 percent of the incumbent's lead in the Electoral College. The soldier vote appears not to have altered the election outcomes in any substantial way.[63]

Even after the election, Rankin sought the last word on the soldier voting debate. He continued to brag about having largely thwarted the federal ballot, and he worked to keep it out of the 1946 midterm elections altogether. The results in 1944, he argued on the floor of the House, proved that the soldiers did not want the federal "bobtailed ballot." When another congressman pointed out that the role of the federal ballot was to provide an emergency means of voting to those who did not get state ballots, Rankin replied that "they had a Federal commission to confuse them last year. If they had not had that Federal commission to confuse them the chances are a great many more of them would have cast their ballots in the election." In fact, it is far more likely that the failure to create a single-mailing war ballot suppressed hundreds of thousands of military votes. Rankin and his allies complained furiously that their opponents had characterized them as enemies of the soldier vote.[64]

Supporting Rankin, Congressman Howard H. Buffett (R-NE) asserted that a doctor at the Washington Naval Hospital told him that they had ceased the practice of medicine for three entire weeks because the hospital was preoccupied with the federal ballot. Congressman Charles W. Vursell (R-IL) added the sensational charge that "many servicemen lost their lives trying to crawl from foxhole to foxhole to personally deliver the short ballot. May I point out that there is nothing in the report that indicates that out of the millions of men who voted the long ballot any soldier was wounded or lost his life." Only moments before blaming American soldiers' deaths on his opponents in Congress, Vursell had characterized criticism of the states' righters as "vicious."[65]

The report to which he referred was that of Secretary of War Stimson. On January 30, Stimson offered a sharp critique of the armed forces' voting system. Given the underuse of the federal ballot, he questioned whether it had been worth the expense and effort. General Dwight D. Eisenhower's report to Stimson on voting in the European theater of operations was Vursell's source for men crawling between foxholes to deliver federal ballots. Eisenhower did note that men braved hazards to deliver ballots. In regard to casualties, however, what the general reported was that the person designated as the voting officer sometimes became a casualty, and untrained voting officers had to carry on their work. Voting officers were not exclusively voting officers; they had other duties including combat. Eisenhower did not specify that voting officers had been killed delivering ballots, but it was true enough that he and Stimson had portrayed voting in the field as disproportionately troublesome.[66]

The 30 percent of military personnel who voted represented a large increase in participation compared to the 1942 elections, but many soldiers were frustrated in their attempt to secure a ballot. The federal government's incomplete challenge to the poll tax in 1944's military voting foreshadowed postwar battles over the meaning of American citizenship. The military's accommodation of the election was a signpost in its own transformation as well. Before World War II, the armed forces had been comparatively homogeneous and intimate organizations. One army interwar citizenship training course instructed troops to fear immigrants. The associated manual instructed them that the United States was not a democracy but instead was a republic. Democracy, it said, was really "Mobocracy."[67]

In the war, these organizations swallowed millions of racially and ethnically diverse citizen-soldiers mobilized under the banner of pluralistic democracy and dedicated to the overthrow of the self-appointed master races. Despite rapid force reductions after the war, the army did not return to its previous insularity. The nation maintained the largest peacetime force—more than a million soldiers—in its history. The peacetime draft helped ensure that the army would continue to consist in large part of short-term citizen soldiers. The majority of these men, whether draftees or volunteers, eager or reluctant, entered the army with an attitude similar to their wartime predecessors in at least one respect. They interrupted their lives to discharge a patriotic duty, not because soldiering was their preferred lifestyle.

In part to adapt to this attitude, the government and other opinion makers promoted the World War II army as "democratic" not only in allegiance but also in culture. Continuing the trend in the late 1940s, the army tried to reduce sources of friction in officer-enlisted relations. Most notably, it softened the more severe aspects of military law with a new Uniform Code of Military Justice that featured legal protections for soldiers based on civilian practices.[68]

This democratic posture appalled many career soldiers. Stimson's and Eisenhower's postelection complaints about having to accommodate the election were consistent with the feelings of the old guard. Embracing democracy fit well, though, with the postwar army's version of citizenship training. This training was more stridently anticommunist than that of the interwar period, yet its approach to citizenship was far more inclusive and positive. In the Cold War, the army asked its soldiers to embrace a public and participatory definition of good citizenship. Its own internal propaganda maintained a scrupulous neutrality between the Democratic and Republican political parties, especially around elections. But the army disposed of its former pride in being above the entire process. The Department of Defense attached great importance to soldiers' participation in the elections. In the organization's concept of citizenship, the act of voting, no matter for which party or candidate, legitimized the soldier's patriotism.

In contrast to the 1940s' assurances that soldiers would not be marched to the voting place, during the Cold War information officers staged registration drives in the camps, promoted elections with get-out-the-vote fanfare, and urged soldiers to participate as a matter of civic duty.[69] The exhortation to vote was only sometimes accompanied by urgings to vote carefully or intelligently. In 1864 and 1944, the opposition parties feared that soldiers would heavily favor the sitting administration. In the Cold War, despite a sizable peacetime army and three wartime presidential elections (1952, 1968, and 1972), neither party particularly feared or counted on the soldier vote. What was important was the ritual of participation. The urge to define democratic values in contrast to communism helped ease fears of a bayonet vote. The Cold War short-term volunteer's or draftee's identity as a citizen was no longer in doubt in the armed forces of what was now most assuredly a democracy.

Notes

1. Senator Scott W. Lucas of Illinois, October 29, 1943, testimony before the Senate Committee on Privileges and Elections, *Voting in Time of War by Members of the*

Land and Naval Forces, Hearings on S1285 (78th Cong., 1st sess.), 1943, 39 (hereafter cited as *Voting in Time of War* Hearings, 1943).

2. "The Nation," *New York Times*, January 30, 1944, E2; C. P. Trussell, "Two Houses Split on Soldier Vote," ibid., E6.

3. On the mechanics of soldier voting and the debates in the state legislatures during the election of 1864, see Josiah H. Benton, *Voting in the Field* (Boston: Plimpton, 1915).

4. "Agree on Details of Soldier Voting," *New York Times*, September 2, 1942.

5. Ibid.

6. *Voting in Time of War* Hearings, 1943, 29–30.

7. "Proceedings of the National Association of Secretaries of State," October 18–20, 1943, File, National Association of Secretaries of State, RG 230, Box 5, p. 17, National Archives, Washington, D.C. (hereafter NA).

8. Ibid.

9. Ibid., 30.

10. Ibid., 42, 46–49.

11. Ibid., 56–57, 78.

12. Ibid., 42, 59, 66.

13. Ibid., 81.

14. Ibid., 51.

15. Frederic W. Cook, October 29, 1943, ibid., 57.

16. Senator Francis Green of Rhode Island, October 29, 1943, ibid., 18–19.

17. Scott W. Lucas, October 29, 1943, ibid., 39.

18. Ibid., 45.

19. Senator Abe Murdock, October 29, 1943, ibid., 22, 28.

20. Senator Hugh A. Butler, October 29, 1943, ibid., 35.

21. Ibid., 38.

22. Ibid., 38, 46; Colonel Robert Cutler, ibid., 80–81.

23. Ibid., 43.

24. Department of War Pamphlet 20-3, *Guide to the Use of Information Materials* (Washington, DC: U.S. Government Printing Office, 1944), 7.

25. Green on January 14, 1944, to the Senate Committee on Privileges and Elections, *Voting in Time of War by Members of the Land and Naval Forces*, Hearings on S1612 and S1614 (78th Cong., 2nd sess.), 1944, 32 (hereafter *Voting in Time of War* Hearings, 1944).

26. Lucas, January 14, 1944, ibid., 35.

27. Lucas, January 14, 20, 1944, ibid., Box 2, pp. 48, 76.

28. C. P. Trussell, "Soldier Vote Bill Shifted by Senate to Let States Rule," *New York Times*, December 4, 1943, 1.

29. "Guffey Condemns Soldier Vote Shift," *New York Times*, December 5, 1943, 48; "Senators Clash on Soldier Vote; Byrd Denounces Guffey's Charges," *New York Times*, December 8, 1943, 1.

30. "Soldier Vote Move Called 'Left Wing,'" *New York Times*, December 20, 1943, 24.

31. Colonel Robert Cutler, January 20, 1944, *Voting in Time of War* Hearings, 1944, 63.

32. Ibid., 64, 69.

33. Robert B. Westbrook, "Fighting for the American Family: Private Interests and Political Obligation in World War II," in Richard Wightman Fox and T. J. Jackson Lears, eds., *The Power of Culture: Critical Essays in American History* (Chicago: University of Chicago Press, 1993), 195–221. On the "American Creed," see Gunnar Myrdal, with the assistance of Richard Sterner and Arnold Rose, *An American Dilemma: The Negro Problem and Modern Democracy*, 2 vols. (New York: Harper, 1944), 1:3–25. On diffuse support for a regime, see David Easton and Jack Dennis, "A Political Theory of Political Socialization," in Jack Dennis, ed., *Socialization to Politics: A Reader* (New York: Wiley, 1973).

34. On the "job," see Gerald F. Linderman, *The World within War: America's Combat Experience in World War II* (New York: Free Press, 1997), 48–51; Samuel A. Stouffer et al., *Studies in Social Psychology during World War II*, vol. 2, *The American Soldier: Combat and Its Aftermath* (Princeton, NJ: Princeton University Press, 1949), 150, 169.

35. "Text of the President's Message on Servicemen's Voting," *New York Times*, January 27, 1944, 13.

36. "The Nation," *New York Times*, January 30, 1944, E2; C. P. Trussell, "Senators Accept Compromise Board on Soldier Voting," *New York Times*, February 11, 1944, 34; C. P. Trussell, "Senate Foes Fight Compromise Plan on Soldier Voting," *New York Times*, January 25, 1944, 1.

37. "House Talk Delays Test on Vote Bill," *New York Times*, February 3, 1944, 26.

38. C. P. Trussell, "'State Rights' Bill for Soldier Voting Beaten in Senate," *New York Times*, February 5, 1944, 1; "Senators Accept Compromise Board," *New York Times*, February 11, 1944, 1; "Soldier Voting Deadlock Broken; Limits Are Put on Federal Ballot," *New York Times*, March 1, 1944, 1, 34.

39. C. P. Trussell, "Conferees Adopt State War Ballot," *New York Times*, March 8, 1944, 13.

40. C. P. Trussell, "Vote Bill Passed; President Wires to All Governors," *New York Times*, March 16, 1944, 26; Ensign Leo Seybold, USNR, "Analysis of Public Law 277, 78th Congress" file, Council of State Governments, RG 230, Box 2, NA.

41. "President's Message," *New York Times*, April 1, 1944, 9; "Dewey Charges War Ballot Plot," *New York Times*, July 19, 1944, 1.

42. U.S. War Ballot Commission, minutes from organizational meeting, April 1, 1944, file, Administrative Meetings, RG 230, Box 1, NA, 1.

43. "Notes Taken at the Original Meeting of the War Ballot Commission Held in the Office of the Secretary of War—1100 Monday April 3, 1944," file, Administrative Meetings, RG 230, Box 1, NA; Report of the United States War Ballot Commission to the Congress of the United States, file, Commission Reports, RG 230, Box 2, NA, 5.

44. U.S. War Ballot Commission, minutes from organizational meeting, Administrative Meetings, RG 230, Box 1, NA, 1.

45. Report of the War Ballot Commission, 10; "Minutes of Meeting 31 May 44 1400," file, Administrative Meetings, RG 230, Box 1, NA; "Report of the United States War Ballot Commission to the Senate Committee on Privileges and Elections and the House Committee on Election of President, Vice President, and Representatives of Congress,"

June 14, 1944, file, ibid.; Memorandum re: Governors' Conference at Hershey, Pennsylvania, May 30, 1944, file, ibid; War Department Bureau of Public Relations, "20 States Make Federal Ballot Available to Servicemen Overseas," July 17, 1944, file, ibid.

46. "Use of Federal Ballot by Eligible Soldiers Having Voting Residence in the State of Florida," file, Secretary of State Meetings, RG 230, Box 5, NA; Robert Cutler, "Notes of the Conference with Honorable F. W. Cook, President, National Association of Secretaries of State," file, Federal Ballot and Instructions, ibid.; Robert Cutler, "Memorandum of Conferences in Tallahassee, Fla. with Governor and Sec of State," July 31, 1944, file, Administrative Meetings, RG 230, Box 1, NA.

47. Robert Cutler, "Memorandum of Conference in Austin Texas with the Governor and Secretary of State of State of Texas," August 2, 1944, file, ibid.

48. "Minutes of Meeting of Administrative Representatives of the Commission at 1400, 24 May 1944," file, Administrative Meetings, ibid.; "Course of Instruction in Overseas Soldier Voting Procedure for Theater Soldier Voting Officers," file, War Department, RG 230, Box 7, NA.

49. War Department, "A Few Quick Facts on Voting for Service Men Overseas," A Few Quick Facts series No. 6 (script), May 1994, file, War Department, RG 230, Box 7, p. 1.

50. Ibid., 4–5.

51. Colonel Robert Cutler, GSC, "Report to the Secretary of War on Action Taken by the War Department with Respect to Soldier Voting in the November 1944 General Election," June 13, 1944, file, ibid., 1, 5.

52. War Department Bureau of Public Relations, memo for the press, October 23, 1944, file, Commission Reports, RG 230, Box 2, NA; War Ballot Commission, Memorandum for the Record, July 21, 1944, file, Administrative Meetings, RG 230, Box 1, NA.

53. Official Federal War Ballot, file, Administrative Meetings, RG 230, Box 1, NA.

54. Cutler to Secretaries of State, "Use of Balloting Materials Stuck Together when Received by Army Voters Overseas," October 21, 1944, file, News Releases, RG 230, Box 5, NA; United States Navy, *Navy Voting Manual*, P-55 file, Commission Reports, ibid., Box 2, pp. 8, 10.

55. United States Navy, *Navy Voting Manual*, P-55 file, Commission Reports, ibid., Box 2, p. 10.

56. Senator Carl A. Hatch of New Mexico, August 15, 1944 (78th Cong., 2nd sess.), *Congressional Record—Senate*, 7013.

57. Senator Robert A. Taft of Ohio, August 15, 1944 (78th Cong., 2nd sess.), ibid., 7014.

58. Ibid.

59. Ibid., 7015; Brigadier General Robert H. Dunlop, Acting Adjutant General, to all commands, "Restrictions in New 'Federal Voting Law,' on Dissemination to Members of the Armed Forces of Political Argument or Political Propaganda," April 27, 1944, file, War Department, Box 7, RG 230, NA.

60. Richard C. Spencer, "Army and Navy Voting in 1944," prepared under the supervision of E. R. Gray, Chief, Governments Division, Bureau of the Census, April 1945, file, Census Bureau, RG 230, Box 1, NA, 2.

61. Ibid. Despite being known to lean toward conservatism, both the American Legion and the Veterans of Foreign Wars (VFW) sided with the soldiers being able to vote and extended support (tentatively in the case of the VFW) to the Green-Lucas Bill (*Voting in Time of War* Hearings, 1943, 93–94).

62. Spencer, "Army and Navy Voting in 1944."

63. "Serviceman Voting [notes for *The Book of the States*]," February 13, 1945, file, Council of State Governments, RG 230, Box 2, NA, 6.

64. Representative John E. Rankin of Mississippi (79th Cong., 1st sess., 1946), *Congressional Record—House*, 2975.

65. Howard H. Buffett of Nebraska, February 2, 1945 (79th Cong., 1st sess.), ibid., 783; Charles W. Vursell of Illinois (79th Cong., 1st sess.), 1946, ibid., 2979.

66. "Stimson and Eisenhower Assail the Federal Soldier Vote Law," *New York Times*, January 31, 1945, 15; Vursell (79th Cong., 1st sess.), *Congressional Record—House*, 11701.

67. War Department Training Manual 2000-25, *Citizenship* (Washington, DC: U.S. Government Printing Office, 1928), 91.

68. See Benjamin L. Alpers, "This Is the Army: Imagining a Democratic Military in World War II," *Journal of American History* 85 (June 1998): 129–63.

69. *A Public Trust*, Troop Information Fact Sheet No. 22, June 21, 1962, file 103-01, Reference Publication Files, Soldier Voting, The United States Army Chief of Information Papers (hereafter CINFO Papers), United States Army Military History Institute Archives, Carlisle Barracks, Carlisle, Pennsylvania (hereafter USAMHI); Lieutenant Colonel Thomas Watt, "Report of MOBDES Training for 1967," August 25, 1967, file 718-10, Soldier Voting Files (67), CINFO Papers, USAMHI, 4–8; Army Voting Award (copy of certificate), file 103-01, Reference Publication Files, Soldier Voting, CINFO Papers, USAMHI.

7
EISENHOWER AS GROUND-FORCES COMMANDER
THE BRITISH VIEWPOINT

G. E. Patrick Murray

MUCH TO THE APPREHENSION of the British Chiefs of Staff (COS) and the disappointment of the British public, on September 1, 1944, the Supreme Commander Allied Expeditionary Force, General Dwight D. Eisenhower, officially took command of ground operations in France. Many in Britain perceived the step as a demotion for Britain's iconic soldier, General Sir Bernard Law Montgomery, the commanding general of the British 21st Army Group, who had commanded the ground forces since the invasion of Normandy on June 6, 1944, and continued to command on the main avenue of approach to the Ruhr and Berlin. The Chief of the Imperial General Staff (CIGS), Field Marshal Sir Alan Brooke, and Montgomery believed that Eisenhower prolonged the war by failing to concentrate against a single avenue of approach into Germany. By December 1944, British Prime Minister Winston Churchill concluded that Eisenhower needed a deputy supreme commander who would control ground operations for him. Ironically, the German counteroffensive in the Ardennes made it politically impossible for Churchill to replace Eisenhower's deputy supreme commander, Air Marshal Sir Arthur W. Tedder, with Field Marshal Sir Harold R. G. L. Alexander. Having mortgaged their future to the Grand Alliance, the British concluded that the price for their strategic partnership with the United States was a succession of American military blunders.

By temperament and experience, Eisenhower was virtually a staff officer. He had heard no shots fired in anger until November 1942. Eisenhower ("Ike" to his close associates) had been graduated in the West Point Class of 1915, the class "the stars fell on" so-named because 57 of its 164 graduates became general officers. According to the closest student of Eisenhower's interwar career, Matthew F. Holland, Eisenhower's assignment to command the army heavy tank school that had been established on the Civil War battlefield at Gettysburg, Pennsylvania, cost him his chance at combat in World War I. Yet it helped him graduate first in his class from the Command and General Staff School in 1926, where all tactical problems were drawn from the Battle of Gettysburg on which Eisenhower was an expert. During the interwar period Eisenhower obtained a political education, working in Washington for the assistant secretary of war and three chiefs of staff of the army. After serving under General Douglas MacArthur for seven consecutive years in Washington and the Philippines, Eisenhower returned to the United States in January 1940 and briefly commanded a battalion. His reputation as one of the top staff officers in the army led to his selection as chief of staff to a division, a corps, and, finally, an army. During the Louisiana Maneuvers of September 1941, Colonel Eisenhower earned national press attention and a promotion to brigadier general for his role in the Third Army's victory over the Second Army.[1]

Immediately after Pearl Harbor, General George C. Marshall, chief of staff of the army, summoned Eisenhower to the War Plans Division, where he so impressed Marshall that six months later he sent Eisenhower to London to command the European theater of operations, coordinating the American buildup for the planned 1943 cross-channel invasion. Eisenhower benefited from President Franklin D. Roosevelt's insistent support of Operation Torch, the November 1942 invasion of Northwest Africa. Eisenhower commanded that campaign through Allied Force Headquarters (AFHQ) with an integrated Anglo-American staff that he made to work in tandem through personal example. Eisenhower's AFHQ went on to supervise the Allied landings in Sicily and the Italian mainland.

Few people in Washington or London in mid-1943 would have picked Eisenhower for the command of Operation Overlord, the campaign against Germany in northwestern Europe. Churchill promised Brooke the job three times, but at the First Quebec Conference of August 1943 Roosevelt asserted an American claim to the supreme command based on the eventual predominance of American manpower. Acquiescing to American demands, Churchill informed Brooke that Marshall would command Overlord, while Eisenhower would assume Marshall's job as chief of staff. Alexander would replace Eisenhower as supreme commander in the Mediterranean, and Montgomery would command the 21st Army Group in England. Roosevelt procrastinated, naming Marshall the commander for Overlord because he was scheming to retain Marshall's political influence within the Combined Chiefs of Staff (CCS), wherein the British COS and the American Joint Chiefs of Staff (JCS) acted in concert. In late October, Churchill rejected naming Marshall commander for both the European and Mediterranean theaters as long as he remained on the CCS. Faced with giving up Marshall's organizational skills and political clout with Congress for what amounted to a theater command, Roosevelt named Eisenhower, his second choice.[2]

Compared to Eisenhower, Brooke was a decorated combat veteran of both world wars and had twice commanded a corps in World War II. Brooke was deeply disappointed by the loss of Overlord command, but by December 1943 he felt that Eisenhower was a better choice than Marshall because Eisenhower had experience "as a Commander and was beginning to find his feet," which was a far cry from his first impression of Eisenhower. While Brooke's war diaries contain many criticisms of Eisenhower as a strategist and a commander, it should be remembered that the American staff officer had gained the position Brooke coveted. One of the British field marshal's most telling comments on Eisenhower came after he attended the final commander's briefing for Operation Overlord on May 15, 1944: "The main impression I gathered was that Eisenhower was a swinger and no real director of thought, plans, energy or direction! Just a coordinator—a good mixer, a champion of inter-allied cooperation, and in those respects few can hold a candle to him. But is that enough? Or can we not find all qualities of a commander in one man?"[3]

Assuming that Marshall would command Overlord, the Operations Planning Division (formerly the War Plans Division) and the American JCS realized there was no American general who could match the battlefield experience of either Montgomery or Alexander; thus, they simply vetoed the notion of a permanent ground-forces commander. According to the original invasion plan, the commanding general of the British 21st Army Group would be responsible for planning and commanding the invasion ground forces "until such time as the Supreme Allied Commander allocates an area of responsibility to the Commanding General, [U.S.] First Army Group."[4] Alexander had been Eisenhower's choice to command the British 21st Army Group and to serve as ground-forces commander, but Brooke named Montgomery.

Graduating from Sandhurst in 1908, Montgomery was wounded at the First Battle of Ypres in 1914, for which he received Britain's second highest award for valor, the Distinguished Service Order. Becoming an operations officer saved his life. Between the wars he taught at the British Staff College at Camberley; served in Ireland, Pakistan, and Palestine; rewrote the British army's basic doctrine; and established a reputation as a first-rate trainer of men. Montgomery returned to France in command of a division in 1939 and left from Dunkirk in June 1940, having taken over Brooke's corps when Brooke was recalled to England. Montgomery gained command of the British Eighth Army when Churchill's first choice was killed. Defeating Field Marshal Erwin Rommel at El Alamein, Egypt, in November 1942, Montgomery was the first British general to win a decisive battle, turning the tide of the war in the desert.

Denied the title of commander in chief of ground forces by the Chief of Staff Supreme Allied Commander plan, Montgomery began lobbying as early as July 7, 1944, to retain command of American ground forces in France. At that time, the 21st Army Group included the U.S. First Army under Lieutenant General Omar N. Bradley and the British Second Army under Lieutenant General Sir Miles Dempsey. In the last week of July, General Henry D. G. Crerar took over the Canadian First Army, and Lieutenant General George S. Patton Jr. received command of the U.S. Third Army. Three weeks prior to the activation of the Third Army on August 1—at which time Bradley moved up to command the 12th Army Group, consisting of the First and Third Armies—Montgomery informed Brooke that Supreme Headquarters Allied Expeditionary Force (SHAEF) factions wanted an American army group, a development that would trigger his loss of the ground-forces command to Eisenhower. Montgomery advised Eisenhower that command of the ground forces was "a whole-time job for one man," and if he insisted on performing that function in addition to his current duties, Eisenhower would have to come to the Continent and *"devote his whole and undivided attention to the land battle."* Concluding his July 7 cable to Brooke, Montgomery claimed that Eisenhower had changed the command organization plan: "He has now decided to form the US Amy Group, with Bradley in command, and to put it under me. I will then command: First US Army Group, Second British Army, First Canadian Army. And I see no difficulty in this."[5] No corroboration of Montgomery's assertion can be found among American archival sources.

Activating Bradley's army group would signal American dominance of strategy and command. Having divulged that there were now two American armies in Normandy during the August 15 press conference he held at his temporary tactical headquarters in Tournieres, France, Eisenhower failed to mention Bradley's army-group command, consisting of the First Army under Lieutenant General Courtney H. Hodges and the Third Army under Patton. One of Eisenhower's aides, however, leaked the story of Bradley's promotion, which somehow passed through the censors and appeared in the next day's newspapers. SHAEF's public relations division in London then denied that Bradley's army group command meant less authority for Montgomery, which, of course, was not true. In response to SHAEF's denials, London's *Daily Mirror* on August 17 ran an editorial accompanied by a cartoon by Philip Zec titled "That's SHAEF—That Was!" Calling SHAEF's news management "amateurish, inconsistent, and confusing," the *Daily Mirror* demanded to know when Montgomery was going to receive his apology.[6]

Command issues reverberated in New York later that day when Hanson W. Baldwin, the military correspondent of the *New York Times*, complained that "each army in France should have its own commander, operating under one supreme command. This is the principle—one for which General John J. Pershing fought—that is as old as the first World War. It should be honored today." Prompted by Baldwin's article, Marshall informed Eisenhower that both he and Secretary of War Henry L. Stimson considered it time for Eisenhower to assume command of "the American contingent" in France. Marshall wanted to prevent congressional debate on the issue of command, which might hurt Roosevelt in a presidential election year. The chief of staff attributed Eisenhower's reluctance to assume the ground-forces command to insufficient communications, but in this instance national political need trumped Eisenhower's communication problems in France.[7]

While both the American and British press were occupied by command issues, Montgomery broke up the 59th Infantry Division to provide infantry replacements; he would likewise break up the 50th Division in early November. Nigel Hamilton, Montgomery's official biographer, concluded that Montgomery's single-thrust plans were attempts to prevent cannibalization of British units through concomitant use of American troops. As Russell F. Weigley points out in *Eisenhower's Lieutenants*, the Anglo-American forces understood that primary and secondary thrusts would be followed eastward toward Germany. "Only on August 15, apparently," writes Weigley, "did General Montgomery move toward a different view." Two days later Montgomery briefed Bradley on a dual army-group advance northward along the Channel coast and then eastward to the Rhine, "a solid mass of some forty divisions which would be so strong that it need fear nothing."[8] Montgomery's claim to Brooke on August 17 that Bradley agreed with his plan — a statement that Montgomery repeated in his 1958 memoir — contradicted the view that Bradley expressed in his 1951 memoir, *A Soldier's Story*. In his second book of memoirs, *A General's Life* (1983), Bradley termed Montgomery's 1958 recounting of their August 17 conference deceitful.[9]

From August 23 to September 21, 1944, Montgomery advanced five additional proposals to command American troops along the northern axis of advance. Extending the date to October 10 brings his proposals requiring American ground forces to six, but the first five may be distilled to the following essentials. On August 23 he asked for twelve American divisions, warned that changing the command structure would prolong the war, and volunteered to serve under Omar Bradley as ground-forces commander. On September 4 Montgomery promoted a single-thrust toward Berlin to "end the German war." On September 10 he proposed Operation Market Garden, crossing the Neder Rijn (Lower Rhine) at Arnhem, thus outflanking the German West Wall, and utilizing the theater reserve, the First Allied Airborne Army. On September 18 he wanted nine American divisions to go on to the Ruhr and then to Berlin. Three days later he asked for both the ground-forces command and the U.S. First Army and warned that Eisenhower's command organization would fail to get to the Ruhr. As for Montgomery's offers to serve under Bradley, Royal Air Force marshal Sir Charles Portal, chief of the Air Staff and a member of the British COS, noted that Montgomery could afford to be magnanimous knowing that his superiors, Brooke and Churchill, would never have allowed it.[10]

Throughout the campaign across northwestern Europe, Montgomery and Eisenhower maintained a dysfunctional relationship. Treating Eisenhower with thinly veiled contempt, Montgomery constantly criticized him to the War Office and refused to attend SHAEF conferences. The chronology contained in *The Papers of Dwight David Eisenhower: The War Years* shows that Eisenhower met with Montgomery fourteen times between August 26, 1944, and May 7, 1945. During that same period Eisenhower met with Churchill ten times and with his West Point classmate, Bradley, nearly fifty times, not counting inspections, ceremonies, and their two-day vacation together in southern France. For more than eight months Eisenhower attempted to exercise command by telex rather than personal visitation, giving rise to Montgomery's 1958 complaint that the army groups acted independently of one another: "We did not advance to the Rhine on a *broad* front; we advanced to the Rhine on *several* fronts, which were uncoordinated."[11]

Calling for an advance "on as broad a front as possible," the SHAEF plan for post-Normandy fighting concluded that multiple thrust lines would prevent the Germans from massing against any single approach; SHAEF planners assumed that the Germans would outnumber the Allies until February 1945. The primary Allied thrust would be north of the Ardennes plateau on the line of Amien-Maubeuge-Liege-the Ruhr; Verdun-Metz was the secondary line of advance south of the Ardennes. Additionally, Eisenhower ordered Patton's Third Army to link up at Dijon with the Franco-American invasion forces that had landed along the Riviera Coast in mid-August, a move that infuriated Churchill, Brooke, and Montgomery by virtually closing down the Italian front. When link-up took place on September 15, Eisenhower assumed operational control of the U.S. 6th Army Group, commanded by Lieutenant General Jacob L. Devers and consisting of the U.S. Seventh Army under Lieutenant General Alexander Patch and the First French Army under General Jean de Lattre de Tassigny.[12]

In regard to the politics of command, Eisenhower adopted the recommendations contained in an August 1944 SHAEF staff study, "Command Organization," that called for the 12th Army Group's First Army to advance north of the Ardennes as part of the main thrust: "In every way it is more satisfactory that U.S. forces should operate under U.S. command, exceptions being made for a limited period, as a result of operational need." While noting a major drawback—two separate commanders splitting the approach to the Ruhr—the study avoided placing a large American force under British command, which was implicit in the War Department's August 17 criticism of Montgomery's continuation as ground-forces commander.[13]

For all of August and the first week of September, euphoria over the collapse of the German Seventh Army in Normandy coincided with developments in the Balkans and eastern Europe. In late August, Romania switched sides and declared war on Germany, the Bulgarians requested terms from the Russians, and the Finns followed suit. British and American observers concluded that this was October 1918, while the July assassination attempt on Hitler's life was analogous to the abdication of Kaiser Wilhelm II and presaged an end to the war before the year was out. SHAEF's G-2 (Intelligence) Section predicted a German collapse: "The August battles have done it and the enemy in the West has had it. Two and a half months of bitter fighting have brought the end of the war in Europe within sight, almost within reach."[14]

At the time the supreme commander took on the ground-forces command, the British chiefs would have preferred what they called a land-forces commander operating under the supreme commander, but as General Sir Hastings L. Ismay, Churchill's military chief of staff, advised the prime minister, "it would not be politic, or even practical to question General Eisenhower's right to assume personal command of the land forces." The CIGS suspected that Eisenhower's move would likely prolong the war by three to six months. In anticipation of Montgomery's "demotion," Churchill arranged for King George VI to make him a field marshal effective September 1, 1944. "I consider this step necessary," Churchill wrote to Eisenhower, "from the point of view of the British nation with whom Montgomery's name is a household word."[15]

Acceding to Marshall's pressure exposed Eisenhower to ridicule by interfering with operational command and control. At the end of August, SHAEF set up its advanced headquarters at Jullouville on Mont St. Michel Bay, about five miles south of Granville on the wrong side of Normandy. At the same time, the Communications Zone (COMZ), the U.S. Army's logistical command connecting the front with the Normandy Base Section, relocated from Valognes on the Cotentin peninsula to Paris, occupying some three hundred hotels in the process. French wags referred to SHAEF as "Societé des Hôteliers Américains en France." Moreover, COMZ's pull-out on September 1 disrupted Eisenhower's telegraphic communications from Jullouville. For example, when Eisenhower sent a four-point message to Montgomery on September 5, parts three and four arrived at 21st Army Group on September 7, and parts one and two arrived two days later.[16] As Montgomery wrote in his *Memoirs*, "This was possibly a suitable place for a Supreme Commander, but it was useless for a land force commander who had to keep his finger on the pulse of his armies and give quick decisions in rapidly changing situations.... There were no telephone lines, and not even a radio-telephone, between his H. Q. and Bradley and myself. In the early days of September he was, in fact, completely out of touch with the land battle, as far as I could see." Moving to Granville put Eisenhower 350 miles from the front; in fact, he would have been closer to the front had he stayed in Portsmouth. Flying back to Granville at dusk on September 2, Eisenhower's pilot made an emergency landing on the beach, and while helping to push the plane above the high-water line Eisenhower was seriously injured and had to spend time in bed with his right knee in a cast.[17]

Meanwhile, optimism ruled. Eisenhower's directive of September 4 sent his two army groups on divergent courses that stretched both operational capabilities and credulity. Eisenhower directed the Northern Group of Armies (21st Army Group) to secure Antwerp, pierce the Siegfried Line blocking the Ruhr, and then take the Ruhr. SHAEF used geographical references for its army groups to avoid national titles. The Central Group of Armies (12th Army Group) had missions from the tip of Brittany to the German frontier. It was to open Brest, guard the southern flank of the expeditionary force, advance on the Saar, and then seize Frankfurt. Brest was taken in October, but the Saar and Frankfurt missions were not realized until March 1945, more than six months later. The Ruhr was encircled on April 1, 1945. Eisenhower's directive allowed Bradley to send the First Army northwest of the Ardennes to assist Montgomery's main effort in confirmation of the SHAEF staff study of August 22.

On September 3, a lone voice, Admiral Sir Bertram Ramsay, Allied Naval Commander-in-Chief Expeditionary Force, warned SHAEF and the 21st Army Group that the Germans would mine the approaches to Antwerp. Neither headquarters paid the slightest attention. British ULTRA intelligence based on decrypted German signals revealed German intentions to hold on to the Scheldt estuary, but both SHAEF and the 21st Army Group were focused on the Rhine to the east rather than on the Scheldt estuary leading west to the North Sea. For example, Eisenhower wrote the following on September 5: "For some days now it has been obvious that our military can advance almost at will, subject only to the requirement for maintenance. Resistance has largely melted all along the front." Eisenhower's forces would take advantage of "all existing lines of communication" by advancing through the Aachen Gap in the north and the Metz Gap in the south. "I see no reason to change this conception," Eisenhower wrote. "The defeat of the German armies is complete, and the only thing now needed to realize the whole conception is speed."[18]

With his right knee in a cast, Eisenhower flew to Brussels on September 10, 1944, to see Montgomery, and the two men met aboard his plane. Their last meeting had been on August 26. Five days before the Brussels Conference, Crerar observed that "Monty . . . is very upset at the loss of operational command over the US Armies and his nomination to Field-Marshal's rank has accentuated rather than eased his mental disturbance." On board Eisenhower's plane, Montgomery waved directives in Eisenhower's face, asking if he had written them. Then Montgomery exploded: "Well, they're nothing but balls, sheer balls, rubbish!" The injured Eisenhower reached out, touching Montgomery on the knee, while saying, "Steady, Monty, you can't speak to me like that, I'm your boss." The incident speaks volumes in terms of their relationship and why they avoided one another.[19]

Eventually Montgomery apologized, and Eisenhower approved Montgomery's Operation Market Garden, an ambitious operation designed to capture bridges over the Maas, the Waal, and the Neder Rijn (Lower Rhine) and enable XXX Corps' armored spearhead to occupy Arnhem and outflank the West Wall. Characteristic of their strategic differences, Eisenhower refused to grant Montgomery's northern thrust "absolute priority" in terms of logistical support. On the same day Bradley divided his maintenance equally between the First Army in the north and the Third Army to the east while assigning the highest priority to the seizure of Brest at the western end of the Brittany Peninsula.[20]

Twenty-five days later, on October 5, Eisenhower and Montgomery met again at SHAEF's new headquarters, the Trianon Palace Hotel in Versailles. In the interim the Germans had turned back the attempted crossing of the Neder Rijn and had retained their hold on most of the West Wall. Normally Montgomery sent Major General Sir Francis "Freddie" de Guingand, his chief of staff, to SHAEF conferences, but Brooke's presence in Versailles guaranteed Montgomery's attendance. By claiming that he could capture the Ruhr without opening Antwerp to shipping, Montgomery raised hackles and earned a lengthy criticism from Ramsay. Even Brooke agreed that Montgomery should have opened Antwerp to shipping before trying to cross the Neder Rijn at Arnhem. The 21st Army Group drew its maintenance from the channel ports of Calais, Dieppe, and Ostend; Boulogne came on line the following week. While the British shared use of Le Havre with the Americans, the bulk of American supplies were still coming through Cherbourg and over Omaha Beach. The Allies desperately needed Antwerp, and Ramsay traced the logistical problems of the French and American armies directly to Montgomery's failure to open the Scheldt estuary. Eisenhower rightfully accepted the blame for Market Garden because he had insisted on it prior to opening Antwerp to shipping despite his memorandum of September 5 citing requirements for maintenance.[21]

During the second week of October, General Marshall toured the Western Front, visiting Montgomery's headquarters with Bradley and Hodges. When Montgomery attributed all difficulties on the Western Front to Eisenhower's command organization, he unwittingly was criticizing Marshall's mandate of August 17: "I told him [Marshall] that since Eisenhower had himself taken personal command of the land battle . . . the armies had become separated nationally and not geographically. There was a lack of grip, and operational direction and control was lacking. Our operations had, in fact, become ragged and disjointed, and we had got ourselves into a real mess."[22]

Two days later, on October 10, Montgomery sent a critique titled "Notes on Command in Western Europe" to Eisenhower's chief of staff, Lieutenant General Walter Bedell Smith, Repeating what he had said to Marshall about geographical and national objectives, Montgomery pointed out that British and

American forces were simultaneously advancing on the Ruhr. Such a compromise, the field marshal warned, was possible in politics but not in military operations. He also criticized Eisenhower's mode of command via telegraphed directives that were out of date by the time they arrived because Eisenhower was too far from the front to exercise timely control. There were only three alternatives: Eisenhower could come forward on the northern thrust line and take command, he could appoint Montgomery to do so, or he could appoint Bradley to command.[23]

In response, Eisenhower told Montgomery that he had to open Antwerp, which was unrelated to the issue of ground-forces command. Noting that the front stretched from Switzerland to the North Sea, Eisenhower exclaimed: "This is no longer a Normandy beachhead!" Having reached the limit of his patience and being infused with support from the visiting Marshall, Eisenhower informed Montgomery that as the senior British officer in the theater he could request Eisenhower to refer his command complaints to the CCS for action no matter how "drastic" that might be. The threat was implied: one of them would have to go. On October 16 Montgomery replied, "You will hear *no* more on the subject of command from me."[24]

Besides directing Montgomery's attention to Antwerp, Eisenhower also pointed out that the 21st Army Group's current mission of mopping up left it too weak to capture the Ruhr. Therefore, he relegated the 21st to a supporting role. Concerning the Brussels's Conference of October 18 among Eisenhower, Tedder, Montgomery, and Bradley, the British official historian says that Eisenhower made a momentous change: "Twelfth Army Group will have charge of operations for the capture (or encirclement) of the Ruhr. Ninth U.S. Army will operate north of the Ruhr and First U.S. Army south of the Ruhr." Furthermore, the supreme commander directed Bradley to locate his headquarters near the U.S. First Army with a direct telephone line to Montgomery. Unfortunately, Bradley placed his forward headquarters in Luxembourg City, some sixty miles from First Army headquarters at Spa in the Belgian Ardennes, sixty-five miles from Third Army headquarters in Nancy, and twelve miles from German lines.[25]

Rebuffed by Eisenhower in October, Montgomery began manipulating his press corps and the CIGS in November. After Montgomery twice visited the CIGS at his office during the second week of November, Brooke's diary summarized Montgomery's motivation: "He still goes on harping over the system of command in France and the fact that the war is being prolonged. He has got this on the brain as it affects his own personal position, and he cannot put up with not being the sole controller of land operations."[26]

Brooke explained to Montgomery that because the Americans were the dominant power, they demanded the right to run operations, which implied putting up with Eisenhower's strategy and command. The CIGS had given Cyril Falls of *The Times* the same explanation only days before, while noting that "Falls had been seeing Monty and there is no doubt that Monty had been rubbing it in hard!" From November 10 through 14 Churchill and Brooke toured France, and Brooke returned profoundly disturbed. In Alsace, de Lattre de Tassigny of the French First Army described how the Americans were assaulting through the Vosges Mountains to his north toward Strasbourg while he readied an attack through the Belfort Gap that would turn the Germans in the Vosges, obviating the Seventh Army's assault through the mountains. "The French realize these errors only too well," Brooke wrote, "and are fretting at being subjected to their results." Brooke and Churchill visited Eisenhower's advance headquarters in the suburbs of Rheims on November 14, and Brooke felt that Eisenhower's briefing was vague. In the postwar annotation for this entry Brooke added: "When we lunched with Ike I was interested to see that Kay [Summersby], his chauffeur, had been promoted to hostess, and sat at the head of the table with Winston on her right. At Versailles she had been promoted to personal secretary and ran the lobby next to his office. Now she has moved one step up the ladder. In doing so Ike produced a lot of undesirable gossip that did him no good."[27]

Back in London, Montgomery's ongoing criticism confirmed Brooke's own apprehension. On November 17 Montgomery told Brooke that he had asked Bradley whether the 12th Army Group had plans to deploy troops from its Metz attack to its Aachen advance and vice versa, but Bradley saw no need for such contingency plans. Gripped by a sense of foreboding about the Western Front, Brooke excused the secretaries from the November 24 COS meeting. The fact that the French had turned the Germans in the High Vosges by forcing the Belfort Gap the day before, negating the broad-front attack over the mountains, must have played into Brooke's growing frustration with Eisenhower's inability to coordinate operations. Brooke considered the Belfort-Vosges business proof of "Eisenhower's complete inability to run the land battle" while serving as supreme commander. He mentioned to his fellow chiefs that Eisenhower was isolated on a golf course outside of Rheims with Kay Summersby. Brooke's point was not that Eisenhower was playing golf or committing adultery but that he was out of touch with the situation on the ground and that changes ought to be made for the benefit of the alliance. The COS recommended that Brooke ask Churchill to request that General Marshall come to London to discuss the ramifications of Eisenhower's dual command.[28]

Two days later Montgomery returned to England to meet with Brooke. Accompanying Montgomery was Lieutenant Colonel Christopher "Kit" Dawnay, his personal military assistant, who recorded their meeting in "Notes on the Campaign in North-Western Europe." Montgomery stated that Eisenhower was "quite useless" as a land-forces commander and would prolong the war through 1945. After their discussion, Brooke believed that they had agreed to do three things: counter Eisenhower's broad-front strategy, reorganize the front into two rather than three army groups to prevent splitting Bradley's army group by the Ardennes, and appoint a land-forces commander. "What we want," Brooke wrote, "is Bradley as a Commander of Land Forces, Montgomery, Northern Group of Armies, with Patton's Army in his group—by substituting Third Army for Ninth Army—and Devers commanding Southern Group."[29]

When Eisenhower stayed overnight at Montgomery's headquarters at Zonhoven, Holland, on November 28, he walked into a trap. The two men had not seen or spoken to each other since October 18, but in the interim Eisenhower had met with Bradley ten times. For several hours the field marshal argued for concentration and for a land-forces commander, but Eisenhower repeatedly said no. Spent, Eisenhower asked to go to bed, and Dawnay showed him to his room. Returning to take down the field marshal's nightly epistle to the CIGS, Dawnay recorded Montgomery's "strategic reverse" message: "Ike visited me today and we have had a very long talk. I put the following points to him. 1st. That the plan contained in his last Directive had failed and we had, in fact, suffered a strategic reverse. He agreed. 2nd. That we must now prepare a new plan and in that plan we must get away from the doctrine of attacking all along the front and must concentrate our resources on selected vital thrust. He agreed. 3rd. That it seemed a pity he did not have Bradley as Land Force Commander to take off him the work of running the operations on land. He did not, repeat, not agree." In 1985 Dawnay described his interaction with Montgomery: "'Get this message sent to the CIGS.' I wrote it down at his dictation and was astonished to discover that he was claiming that Ike had agreed in general with the single-thrust strategy. I read the message back and asked if it was correct. He assented. I said: 'May I say something, sir?' 'Yes, certainly.' 'Ike does *not* agree, sir.' His only comment was 'Send that message, Kit.' And so I did. But Ike had not agreed." The next morning, Montgomery maintained in a message to Brooke that Eisenhower recognized that Bradley had failed him as his chief strategist. Furthermore, Montgomery claimed that Eisenhower would return to the Normandy setup by placing Bradley under Montgomery's operational control and that both his and Bradley's army groups would be north of the Ardennes.[30]

Neither of these messages can be corroborated by an American archive, but they set the stage for a British governmental search for alternatives to Eisenhower's ground command. Yet even before Montgomery's strategic reverse cable arrived on the night of November 28, Brooke recommended to Churchill that they repeat what they had done in Tunisia "when we brought in Alex as deputy to Eisenhower to command the land forces for him." Substituting Field Marshal Alexander for Air Marshal Tedder as Eisenhower's deputy supreme commander suited Brooke; Overlord had been without an air commander in chief since Air Marshal Leigh-Mallory's transfer to South East Asia Command. Alexander could assume Tedder's job when Tedder took Leigh-Mallory's former position. Additionally, bringing in Alexander would leave both Eisenhower and Montgomery in their places. Churchill liked Eisenhower and thought him amenable, but he told Brooke that Bradley was a "sour faced blighter" who might not listen to him.[31]

Churchill harbored doubts about Eisenhower's strategy but did not totally disagree with the war of attrition on the Western Front. In late November, Churchill had responded to Roosevelt's proposal for a joint statement aimed at German morale. Churchill thought that German soldiers would see it as a sign of weakness, and he told the president: "The General Grant attitude, 'To fight it out on this line if it takes all summer' appears one to which I see no alternative." One week later, on December 2, Churchill dictated a message to Eisenhower that Brooke convinced him not to send because it revealed Montgomery's secret comments on Eisenhower. Churchill's withdrawn message recommended dividing the Western Front into two army groups rather than three, putting Montgomery in command of Bradley in the north because the two of them "work together so well," and putting Devers in command in the south. "I am entirely opposed to the interposition of any command between you and the two commanders of fronts which will be under you." Concerning the Western Front, Churchill concluded: "I never expected that the final battle would be won, before Christmas, and I was impressed with the arguments that we were spreading our forces too widely. Nevertheless I am glad that it was fought and the results have carried us another good step towards our goal."[32]

During the Maastricht Conference of December 7, Eisenhower, Bradley, Tedder, and Montgomery met at the headquarters of Lieutenant General William H. Simpson's U.S. Ninth Army. Renewing Montgomery's main effort in the north, Eisenhower characteristically refused to halt Patton's upcoming Saar offensive. Eisenhower reinforced the 21st Army Group with Simpson's Ninth Army but divided the northern advance between Montgomery and Bradley. The Maastricht decisions allowed Bradley to mount Patton's Saar offensive, scheduled for December 19, while the First Army continued to attack north of the Belgian Ardennes. The First Army covered the wooded and hilly plateau with its VIII Corps stretched dangerously thin. Brooke had only Montgomery's description of the Maastricht meeting that "Eisenhower has obviously been 'got at' by the American generals" since their meeting at Zonhoven and Montgomery's prediction that neither thrust would obtain its objective. Montgomery told Brooke: "I played a lone hand against the three of them. . . . [A]ny points I made which caused Eisenhower to wobble will have been put right by Bradley and Tedder on the three-hour drive back to Luxembourg. . . . I can do no more myself. . . . If we want the war to end within any reasonable period you have to get Eisenhower's hand taken off the land battle. I regret to say that in my opinion he just doesn't know what he is doing."[33]

In the second week of December 1944, British dissatisfaction with Eisenhower's land-forces command spread from the secret confines of the War Office and War Cabinet into the public arena of the British press. Clearly disappointed by the progress on the Western Front, Churchill cabled Roosevelt on December 6, repeating Montgomery's strategic reverse phrase and requesting a meeting of the CCS, which Roosevelt declined. A. J. Cummings in the *News Chronicle* on December 8 referred to Eisenhower's strategy of "bulldozing attacks on a wide front" as reminiscent of the Somme and Passchendaele. In the War Cabinet meeting of December 11, Parliament member Ernest Bevin, the minister of Labor and National Service, described considerable concern within trade union circles that the Western Front was not being "properly gripped." Bevin feared that continued stalemate "might have serious effects on the Coalition Government." When Bevin recommended that the War Cabinet ask Eisenhower to report on both the current situation and his plans for future operations, Brooke informed him that Eisenhower was coming to London for just such a purpose.[34]

The next day Eisenhower, accompanied by Tedder, arrived in London to discuss strategy with Churchill and the British COS. Eisenhower had invited himself days prior, and supposition in the War Office was that he would not have done so without Marshall's prior approval of his strategy.[35] Eisenhower intended to split his main offensive in the north between the 21st and the 12th Army Groups from south of Arnhem to north of the Ruhr and to launch a secondary assault by the 12th Army Group in the vicinity of Mainz between Frankfurt and Kassel that would lead "to the heart of Germany." With the Ninth Army assigned to Montgomery, the 21st Army Group would have some twenty-four divisions.

"I wish that the Twelfth Army Group were deployed north of the Ruhr and British forces were in the center," Brooke replied, implying that the reversal of national forces would have produced a concentrated attack instead of split offensives. In so doing he put his finger on the strategic disconnect between American strategy and command. Eisenhower was both the supreme commander and ground-forces commander because the Americans were predominant in the Alliance, but the American thrust line under Bradley was the secondary axis of advance toward the Rhine and Berlin. Brooke "flatly disagreed" with Eisenhower's plan and predicted that of eighty Allied divisions involved, five would have to protect the northern flank in Holland, ten would been needed to contain the Germans in Cologne, five would be required in the Ardennes, and another ten would have to man the Rhine in the south. Of the remaining fifty divisions, Eisenhower assigned only twenty-four to the main thrust. Like a war college instructor, Brooke accused Eisenhower of violating the principle of concentration, arguing that thirty-five divisions were needed for the main attack for flank protection and to replace tired divisions from a reserve. As it was, there were as many divisions opposite Bonn and Cologne as there were on Patton's front. Pointing out that the CCS at the Second Quebec Conference in September 1944 had directed that the northern attack on the Ruhr take precedence, Brooke blamed Eisenhower's failure to reach the Rhine on his constantly shifting emphasis to the center and the south. Brooke conceded that Eisenhower's plan might work and turn into a pursuit if the Allies were able to inflict a heavy defeat on the Germans west of the Rhine. Even that prospect for optimism was dashed by Eisenhower's offhand admission that Rhine River flooding would likely prevent its crossing until May 1945. At the same time, Montgomery's planners listed mid-March as the earliest date for crossing the Rhine.[36]

Impressed by the cogency of Brooke's remarks, Churchill invited the CIGS to repeat them to the War Cabinet on December 13, whereupon Brooke noticed that Eisenhower's estimated May crossing of the Rhine struck a discordant chord. Unable to get Roosevelt to call a meeting of the CCS, Churchill delayed requesting Marshall to come to London. In truth, Churchill was distracted by an incipient communist uprising in Athens and devoted most of his attention that December to the worsening Greek situation, eventually shipping seventy-eight thousand British and Commonwealth troops to Greece in December to put down the insurgency.

Returning to the twin issues of strategy and command on December 30, the prime minister in light of the German Ardennes offensive directed that the COS review its November 24 request and bring it up to date. By January 6, 1945, the British COS requested through the CCS a progress report from Eisenhower for the COS conference in Malta at the end of the month, prior to the meeting of Churchill, Roosevelt, and Stalin in Yalta in early February. The COS requested of the CCS that operations on the Western Front satisfy two conditions: "(a) All available offensive power must be allotted to the Northern Front—i.e. from about Prüm northwards; and (b) one man must have power of operational control and co-ordination of the ground forces employed on this front." Four days later the CCS asked Eisenhower for a progress report and his future plans, which they received on January 20, 1945.[37]

In the midst of the British attack on Eisenhower's conduct of the ground campaign, Hitler launched Operation Herbstnebel (autumn fog). On December 16, 1944, from Monschau, Germany to Echternach, Luxembourg, more than twenty German divisions and almost one thousand tanks smashed into all or parts of six American divisions with a three-to-one numerical advantage. Nine days later, on December 24, the German offensive stopped within three miles of the Meuse near Dinant, Belgium, some seventy miles from its start lines. Originally named the Rundstedt Offensive after the German commander in the West, Field Marshal Gerd von Rundstedt, Hitler's Ardennes offensive envisioned crossing the

Meuse and seizing Antwerp, thus splitting the Anglo-American army groups and producing either a political settlement or stasis, thus allowing Germany to concentrate against the Red Army.

When Brooke first took note of the Ardennes battle on December 18, he was most concerned by the lack of American reserves, which he understood as an outgrowth of the American doctrine of conducting offensives all along the front while operating on exterior lines. Brooke's estimation of the Battle of the Bulge, however, more closely resembled Eisenhower's than Montgomery's. While both field marshals argued that Eisenhower's split offensives brought on the Ardennes offensive, Montgomery believed that it prolonged the war, but Brooke believed that, having been promised a reversal of fortune, German morale would plummet as result of their defeat in the Ardennes. Coincidentally, Brooke and Churchill were in Eisenhower's headquarters on January 3, 1945, when General Charles de Gaulle forced Eisenhower to reconsider a pull-back from recently liberated Strasbourg in order to shorten his line and create a reserve. In his postwar supplemental entries for December 18, Brooke observed the political fallout from Eisenhower's broad-front strategy: "Rundstedt had proved how faulty Ike's dispositions and organizations were. Spread out over a large front with no adequate reserves and no land force Commander to immediately take charge . . . he was compelled to withdraw troops from Strasbourg and in doing so to almost create a crisis in the de Gaulle government."[38]

Brooke, Montgomery, and parts of the British press blamed Eisenhower for the disastrous surprise. But no one was more surprised than Bradley when his advanced headquarters in the Alfa Hotel in Luxembourg suddenly lay 12 miles from the front. "Pardon my French," said Bradley prefacing a question about Hitler, "but where in hell has this son of a bitch gotten all his strength?" With the Germans in possession of the one road connecting Luxembourg City with the First and Ninth Armies to the north, Bradley would have to drive west, north, and east 150 miles to reach Hodges in Tongres, Belgium, and 160 miles to meet Simpson in Maastricht, Holland. Due to the weather, flying was nearly impossible. After Bradley stationed his advanced headquarters midway between the First and Third Armies in October (contrary to Eisenhower's expressed intentions), his ability to communicate with the First and Ninth Armies to his north was soon dependent on telephone lines running all the way to Paris; visiting Hodges and Simpson was impossible. As a result of the German penetration, there were now two fronts, one on the northern shoulder of the Bulge and one on the southern.

Eisenhower saw the counterattack as a chance to defeat the German army west of the Rhine. On December 19 at Bradley's main headquarters in Verdun, France, he told his commanders: "The present situation is to be regarded as one of opportunity for us and not of disaster. There will be only cheerful faces at this conference table." Later that day, Major Chester Hansen, Bradley's aide, wrote in the 12th Army Group's headquarters' diary: "In order to secure the necessary deployment of strength to stop the German attack with British help, I am told the terms prescribed [are] that we turn over control of the First and the Ninth Armies to 21 Group."[39] Therefore, on December 20, when Churchill called Eisenhower to suggest allocating the First and Ninth Armies on the northern shoulder of the Bulge to Montgomery, Eisenhower told him he had done so that morning. Bradley's army group consisted of the Third Army on the southern flank, which he took as a public humiliation.

Due to the inherent controversy of giving Montgomery command of two American armies, Eisenhower demanded strict secrecy, but on January 5, 1945, *Time* broke the story. Therefore, the British press portrayal of Eisenhower falls into two categories, before and after January 5. American military attachés recorded the reaction of the British press in London and on January 26, 1945, wired it to Marshall, who forwarded it to Eisenhower. Six out of the seven enumerated articles before January 5 called for a separate ground-forces commander. For instance, the *Evening Standard* of December 16 recalled that there had been British field commanders for Eisenhower in North Africa and Normandy. Noting that Montgomery and Bradley were conducting operations independently of one another, Morley Richards of the *Daily Express* called on December 30 for a land-forces commander.[40]

Not cited in the attachés' report was Alan Moorehead's article ("A 1914 General Asks Me How Rundstedt Did It") of January 4, 1945, in the *Daily Express*. Moorehead described how an unnamed World War I general asked him why the Germans could move forty miles in ten days while the Allies could only move five, if that. One of Montgomery's favorite correspondents, Moorehead, like Cyril Falls of *The Times*, attributed the German counterattack to Eisenhower's twin mistakes: his assumption of the field command and his broad-front strategy of closing to the Rhine without subtlety or reserves. The *Daily Express* correspondent called for either an American or a British land-forces commander and for a concentration of forces behind a single spearhead sufficient to puncture the German front.

Writing on January 6, 1945, in the *News Chronicle*, A. J. Cummings asserted that "Monty Should be Deputy C-in-C." The problem, as Cummings saw it, was that Eisenhower had too little time to devote to operations. Montgomery was the obvious choice for the job but, as Cummings predicted accurately, "Eisenhower probably knows that neither his own generals nor the Washington War Department nor the American public would acquiesce in the appointment of Montgomery to a vital position on the Supreme Staff." Alexander Clifford of the *Daily Mail* noted on the same date that a British field marshal had to be called in "at the moment of greatest crisis" to command two American armies.[41]

At the same time the British press was calling for a land-forces commander, most likely Montgomery, the field marshal was waging his own campaign to that end. Meeting with Eisenhower for the first time in three weeks on December 28 aboard Eisenhower's train in Hasselt, Belgium, Montgomery again urged his host to put all available power behind his upcoming northern offensive, with one man in command. Montgomery's diary as kept by Dawnay, writing in the third person, had this to say of their meeting: "Finally, after considerable argument, General Eisenhower agreed to both the Field Marshal's conditions, and agreed to give him operational command of the whole northern thrust.... General Eisenhower was very pleasant and friendly, and in a somewhat humble frame of mind, and clearly realized that the present defeat would not have occurred if he had accepted the advice of the Field Marshal instead of that of his American generals."[42]

Their train meeting followed the usual course of their encounters. Eisenhower subsequently refused to change either his strategy or command, but Montgomery informed the War Office that Eisenhower had altered his course. Montgomery's version of events cannot be substantiated by American archival sources. Since Brooke was on leave, Montgomery gave his version of events to then-director of military operations Brigadier Frank E. W. Simpson, who in turn told Brooke that Eisenhower had ceded priority to the northern thrust and that Montgomery would enjoy control and coordination over the 12th Army Group. The next day, December 29, Montgomery requested in writing that Eisenhower make his temporary command permanent and included this sentence for Eisenhower to use: "From now onwards full operational direction, control and co-ordination of these operations is vested in the C.-in-C. 21 Army Group, subject to such instructions as may be issued by the Supreme Commander from time to time."[43]

Eisenhower had refused to return the ground-forces command to Montgomery on August 23, September 21, and October 10. The December 29 demand caused Eisenhower to implement his threat of October 16. Coincidentally, the next day Marshall forwarded the American attachés' report that detailed Fleet Street calls for a land-forces commander. Assuming that Eisenhower would not welcome a ground-forces commander, Marshall informed him that London papers were calling for a British deputy: "My feeling is this," Marshall instructed, "under no circumstances make any concessions of any kind whatsoever.... I just wish you to be certain of our attitude. You are doing a grand job, and go on and give them hell."[44] By "them," presumably, Marshall meant the Germans. Under explicit instructions from Marshall, Eisenhower drafted a message to the CCS carrying out the threat that he had made to Montgomery on October 10: one of them had to go. Eisenhower would seek to replace Montgomery with Alexander, his initial choice to command the 21st Army Group.

Once the threat was in writing, Eisenhower's headquarters phoned de Guingand to come to Versailles. When de Guingand arrived at SHAEF, Bedell Smith showed him both Eisenhower's draft to the CCS as well as Marshall's congratulatory admonition. Certain that Montgomery was unaware of his jeopardy, de Guingand flew to Montgomery's advanced headquarters in abysmal weather to save his master's job and avert a public crisis within the Alliance. Nigel Hamilton argues that owing to Marshall's message and the outrage of his SHAEF staff, Eisenhower had once again changed his mind and gone back on what Montgomery claimed had taken place at Hasselt. Therefore, according to Hamilton, to void his pledge to Montgomery the supreme commander asked the CCS to choose between himself and the field marshal.[45] Hamilton pays no attention to the pattern of falsehoods in Montgomery's messages describing his dealings with Eisenhower. Nor does he recognize the pattern of Eisenhower's subsequent actions. Whenever there was a major controversy between them, Eisenhower's words predicted future actions, and Montgomery's messages did not. Admonished by Eisenhower, Montgomery salvaged his command by sending an apology penned by de Guingand that instructed Eisenhower to dispose of the offending communication.

Certain that his apology had saved his command, Montgomery held a press conference on January 7, 1945, ostensibly to deflect British press criticism of the supreme commander. Calling the Battle of the Bulge "possibly one of the most interesting and tricky battles I have ever handled," Montgomery lauded the American fighting man but not his generals. He told the war correspondents that it pained him to see Eisenhower criticized in the British press, but in November he had made those very same criticisms to Cyril Falls of *The Times*. In response to Montgomery's press conference, Bradley held his own on January 9, stating that Montgomery's command of American armies was temporary and would end when the Bulge was erased. Prior to his press conference, Bradley informed Eisenhower that he would resign rather than serve under Montgomery. His remarks provoked the *Daily Mail* on January 11 to run an editorial titled "A Slur on Monty." Taking the 12th Army Group to task for believing that a German propaganda broadcast modeled on Montgomery's remarks was the BBC, the *Daily Mail* criticized SHAEF for underutilizing Montgomery before the Bulge and for having Bradley declare that the command shift was temporary. "It is unusual, to say the least," the *Daily Mail* observed, "for one commander in the field to tell the world what is to be the future professional status of another officer of equal rank."[46]

That same afternoon, the War Cabinet feared that "public statements made by High Allied Commanders during the conduct of campaign might well lead to some embarrassment, and possibly even to some impairment of friendly relations between the Allies."[47] Three days earlier Ernest Bevin had asked why Montgomery felt compelled to make public speeches, and Churchill admitted that

Montgomery had cleared it with him in advance and refused the War Cabinet's suggestion that he disavow the field marshal's remarks. The minister of information, Brendan Bracken, informed the War Cabinet on January 11 that he had told the editor of the *Daily Mail* to stop editorializing on command issues on the Western Front. Behind the scenes on January 10 Ismay minuted the COS for the prime minister:

> I fear great offense has been given to the American generals, not so much by Montgomery's speech but by the manner in which some of our papers seem to appropriate the whole credit of saving the battle to him.
>
> Personally I thought his speech most unfortunate. It had a patronizing tone and completely overlooked the fact that the US have lost perhaps 80,000 men and we but 2,000 or 3,000. . . . Eisenhower told me that the anger of his Generals was such he would hardly dare to order any of them to serve under Montgomery. This of course may cool down, but also it may seriously complicate his being given the leadership of the northern thrust.[48]

January 1945 was Eisenhower's most difficult month of the war. The German counteroffensive was an embarrassment, and American troops suffered because of it. Now the British had questioned his command and strategy. Eisenhower sent a lengthy apology for his broad-front strategy and his ground command to Marshall on January 10; he also explained the assumptions of future operations. Specifically, he intended to gain an economy of scale by closing to the Rhine along its entirety, which would facilitate concentration at opportune crossing points without worrying about German ripostes. He conceded that his deputy supreme commander, Tedder, was little help in dealing with ground commanders and mentioned as a potential replacement Alexander but concluded that he was unavailable. Marshall's immediate rejoinder mentioned two negatives arising from an Alexander appointment: "First, that the British had won a major point in getting control of the ground operations in which their divisions of necessity will play such a minor part and . . . second, the man being who he is and our experience being what it has been, you would have great difficulty in offsetting the direct influence of the PM."[49]

In addition to justifying himself to Marshall, Eisenhower had to report his conduct of the campaign and his future plans at the meeting of the CCS held in Malta from January 30 to February 2, 1945. Worried about Churchill's influence on Eisenhower, Marshall met with Eisenhower in a château near Marseilles prior to the conference. The chief of staff promised Eisenhower that he would resign before he let the British saddle him with a ground-forces commander; he also agreed with Eisenhower's strategy of closing to the Rhine as the means of defeating the German army west of the river.

Sensing Eisenhower's stress, Marshall told him to skip the meeting in Malta, to which, instead, Eisenhower sent his staff. At the first meeting of the CCS, Major General Harold R. Bull, SHAEF's operations officer, said that it was logistically impossible to support more than thirty-five divisions on the northern thrust line until railroad bridges spanned the Rhine. In the south, where there were no such limitations, up to fifty divisions could be maintained. Bedell Smith, who had a history of standing up to the British, pointed out that the 21st Army Group numbered twenty-one divisions, too small a force for the main assault out of a total of eighty-five divisions. Smith stated that Eisenhower wanted to increase the assault's strength to thirty-six divisions but that the road net in the north would limit the attack to twenty-five, with ten in reserve. Under Eisenhower's plan, twelve divisions would take part in the secondary assault on Kassel-Frankfurt. Brooke demanded clarification, because Smith's description varied from Eisenhower's written plan. In response, Eisenhower wired that he intended to close to the Rhine throughout its entirety but would not hold up a promising crossing of the Rhine in order to do so.[50] Perceiving inherent delay in Eisenhower's split offensives, the British put off ratifying Eisenhower's plans.

The Malta Conference represented a sea change in the Alliance. For the first time in World War II, the British went to a CCS meeting with a split position: the COS wanted a land-forces commander, but the prime minister wanted to trade Tedder for Alexander, which was a ground-forces commander by another name. The prime minister, as early as January 8, told the War Cabinet that Eisenhower would be better off with an army officer as his deputy instead of Tedder. The COS wanted a designated land-forces commander in charge of the main thrust in the north against the Ruhr. Additionally, they wanted secondary exploitation only after the failure of the primary thrust, which ran counter to Eisenhower's strategy.[51]

Ismay had warned the COS against criticism of Eisenhower: "If I were George Marshall I would regard anything of this sort as a vote of no-confidence in Ike. We can't do this sort of thing." In a private evening conversation, Brooke told Bedell Smith that Eisenhower was a "good chairman of the board" but was too easily swayed by the last man he talked to, which was a conclusion based on Montgomery's messages. Smith described the British demands as a vote of no confidence and said that the British should recommend Eisenhower's removal to the CCS. Brooke, however, backed away from the logical conclusion of his own policy, admitting that no one else would be acceptable to Marshall.

The next morning, Smith brought up to the CCS the lack of confidence in Eisenhower inherent in the position of the COS. At that point, February 1, Marshall called for a closed session of the CCS, excusing SHAEF staff officers and secretaries. Marshall then defended Eisenhower by attacking Montgomery as a disloyal subordinate, which was more accurate than anyone knew. Unmoved,

Brooke refused to approve Eisenhower's plans; he merely took note of them. Privately, Brooke was certain that Smith grasped the drawbacks of Eisenhower's strategy and would keep Eisenhower on the rails.

When President Roosevelt approved Eisenhower's plans on February 2, the plans represented a compromise that guaranteed the main thrust on the Ruhr in the north and the continuance of Eisenhower's ground-forces command. Seconding the president's approval, Churchill followed suit but still had one more card to play. He brought up his scheme to swap Alexander for Tedder. At Malta, the American response was to postpone a decision to the Yalta Conference, at which Brooke's entry for February 3 read: "The President and Marshall considered that politically such a move might have repercussions in America if carried out just now. It might be considered that Alex was being put in to support Ike after his Ardennes failure!" The American response was for the British to bring it up again in six weeks.[52]

Knowing that his command was secure following the Malta Conference, Eisenhower wrote to Brooke on February 16 concerning the Alexander-for-Tedder trade. "There can be no question whatsoever of placing between me and my Army Group Commanders any intermediate headquarters, either official or unofficial in character." Citing American resentment of the London press coverage of Montgomery's "temporary command" of two American armies in the Ardennes, Eisenhower promised an immediate public refutation if British papers interpreted Alexander's appointment as the establishment of a ground-forces command. Moreover, Alexander's duties would be confined to the rebuilding of liberated countries. Shocked that Eisenhower's "British deputy was relegated to such non-military functions," Churchill considered the job description a waste of Alexander's experience, and he questioned whether Britain's nearly one million-man war effort was being properly represented on Eisenhower's staff. Churchill clung to this idea. On their visit to Eisenhower in Rheims on March 5, Brooke told Eisenhower that if he objected to Alexander coming to SHAEF, he must tell Churchill. Subsequently, Eisenhower told Churchill that he did not want Alexander. On March 10, Churchill wired Roosevelt, officially withdrawing his proposal.[53]

British fears that Eisenhower would prolong the war by closing to the entirety of the Rhine before crossing proved wrong, as the broad-front strategy demonstrated in March 1945. Hodges's First Army gained a Rhine crossing on March 7 when it captured intact a railroad bridge at Remagen, south of Bonn. Montgomery's set-piece crossing in the north carried the imprimatur of the CCS, and Eisenhower consulted with the field marshal the next day as to reinforcing the Remagen bridgehead. Montgomery informed Brooke: "I considered it to be an excellent move as it would . . . undoubtedly draw enemy strength on it and away from my business in the north."

Scheduled for March 23–24, Montgomery's crossing would become the third of the month: Patton's Third Army had crossed on the night of March 22 at Oppenheim, south of Mainz. Patton's liaison officer at the 12th Army Group reported: "Without benefit of aerial bombing, ground smoke, artillery preparation, and airborne assistance, the Third Army at 2200 hours, Thursday evening, March 22, crossed the Rhine River." Possibly the Ninth Army would have beaten the First and Third Armies, but Montgomery had operational control of the Ninth Army when it reached the Rhine at Neuss on March 2, and the field marshal denied permission to cross the river. Officers at the Ninth Army had expected as much, since Montgomery's original Rhine crossing plan in January had attached one corps of the Ninth Army to Dempsey's Second Army, leaving William Simpson with no command. Following protests from Simpson and Dempsey, Montgomery had expanded the scope of the Ninth Army's mission, but the damage had been done. Russell Weigley argues that American suspicion that Montgomery would spotlight British troops became conviction as a result of the initial plan.[54]

If Montgomery failed to utilize the mobility of the Ninth Army, there was little reason for him to command an American army. Attracting little attention, Eisenhower sent Bradley a new directive on March 13 with copies to Devers and the COS but not to Montgomery. Noting that Bradley's recent operations had gained "an economical defensive position along the Rhine north of the Moselle," Eisenhower sensed that Bradley could begin his secondary assault on Frankfurt "without detracting" from Montgomery's upcoming crossing. In addition, Eisenhower ordered that the First Army be readied to exploit the bridgehead north of the Ruhr with at least ten divisions in support of Montgomery's northern thrust. Twelve days later Eisenhower advanced the date of the link-up of the First and Ninth Armies to April 1. These decisions signaled Eisenhower's independence as a commander. Following the capture of the Ruhr, Bradley, not Montgomery, would command the main thrust "to the heart of Germany" when the Western Allies met the Russians.[55]

The British first learned that Eisenhower intended to alter Malta's perceived agreement on strategy during the March 17–18 visit to SHAEF by the newly appointed Assistant Chief of the Imperial General Staff (ACIGS), Major General Frank E. W. "Simbo" Simpson. For both Churchill and the COS, continued command of American troops was implicit in Montgomery's northern thrust toward the Ruhr. Thus, command of the Ninth Army came to symbolize the main attack. In conferences with Bedell Smith and two British SHAEF officers, Major General John F. M. Whiteley, the deputy G-3 (Operations), and Lieutenant General Sir Frederick E. Morgan, the deputy chief of staff, Simpson learned that Eisenhower would return the Ninth Army to Bradley's 12th Army Group following the encirclement of the Ruhr. What would Whitehall say? Simpson called the move unfortunate and recommended that one general command both army groups enveloping the Ruhr, with Bradley being the obvious choice. When Smith argued that SHAEF would be excoriated by the British press, Simpson replied that only one or two yellow papers would howl. If that was their worry, they should appoint Montgomery—something, Smith said, that SHAEF could not hand the American press.

In this, the third week of March, the British were still pushing the arguments of late August 1944. Counting Churchill's two requests at Malta and Yalta to swap Alexander for Tedder brings to eight the British calls to replace Eisenhower as ground-forces commander. The ACIGS informed Montgomery by letter and personally spoke to Brooke about these developments when he returned to the War Office on March 19.[56]

Churchill, Brooke, and Montgomery drove to Rheinberg, the headquarters of the Ninth Army's XVI Corps, on March 25 to meet with William Simpson, Bradley, and Eisenhower. Brooke and Eisenhower spoke about Eisenhower's employing the First and the Ninth Armies to envelop the Ruhr while the units were under separate army group commanders. Eisenhower then asked Brooke's opinion of his secondary attack on Frankfurt and Kassel. Noting that German resistance was crumbling, Brooke felt that Eisenhower had sufficient strength to double-envelop the Ruhr. In his diary entry for April 1, Commander Harry C. Butcher, Eisenhower's aide described Brooke as having been very generous to Eisenhower, telling him "that his current plans and operations are well calculated to meet the current situation."[57]

While at Rheinberg on March 25, Montgomery briefed Eisenhower and Bradley on his upcoming operational plans. Eisenhower recommended, and Montgomery agreed, that Magdeburg would be in Bradley's sector. Taking that as approval of his plans, Montgomery on March 27 issued twin directives, M-561 and M-562, laying out missions for the Second Army and the Ninth Army despite the ACIGS's cable of March 19 warning of the imminent return of the Ninth Army to Bradley. Both of Montgomery's directives usurped the supreme commander's strategic prerogatives and pointed to Berlin as their final objective.[58]

Apparently validating Montgomery's criticism of October 10 that Eisenhower commanded by telex machine, Eisenhower's Cable FWD 18272 of March 28 confirmed what the ACIGS had learned on March 17–18. When the Ninth Army operation along the northern flank of the Ruhr pocket contacted the First Army coming up from the southern flank of the pocket, the Ninth Army would revert to Bradley's command. At that point Bradley, not Montgomery, would command the primary advance, not on Berlin but rather on the line of Erfurt-Leipzig-Dresden, SHAEF's so-called heart of Germany, which Eisenhower had hinted at in London as early as December 12. Holding out the possibility that the Ninth Army might return to Montgomery's command when the 21st Army Group reached the Elbe to assist it in crossing the river, Eisenhower told Montgomery that his mission was to provide flank protection to Bradley's group. Wiring his former brigade major, the current ACIGS Simbo Simpson, Montgomery referred to Eisenhower's method of turning over the Ninth Army to Bradley as "all very dirty work I fear."[59] Eisenhower made no demur on the banks of the Rhine on March 25 in the presence of Brooke and Churchill; he commanded by telex machine on March 28.

No matter how much Montgomery, Brooke, Churchill, or the COS complained, there was nothing the British could do to alter Eisenhower's decisions at this point in the war. The COS launched a formal protest to the CCS concerning Eisenhower's second message of March 28 to Soviet generalissimo Josef Stalin, which argued that as supreme commander Eisenhower had gone outside his chain of command, the CCS, to communicate directly with a head of state and had changed his plans by altering the main thrust. At Malta on February 2, Marshall had advised the president and the JCS that because it wasted time Eisenhower should not have to go through the CCS in order to communicate with the Soviet General Staff. Subsequently at Yalta, Roosevelt informed Stalin that Eisenhower would coordinate operations between their two fronts directly with Stalin, but no one bothered to inform the British. Writing for the JCS, Marshall pointed out to the COS that the destruction of the German armed forces was more important than any "political or psychological advantages" that might be gained by capturing Berlin in advance of the Russians. Moreover, Eisenhower had addressed Stalin as the Russian commander in chief of Soviet forces, not as a head of state, because experience had shown that addressing anyone other than Stalin led to delays. Marshall's reply concluded that since Eisenhower alone was the responsible authority to conduct operations, no further guidance from the CCS to Eisenhower was necessary.[60]

Brooke accepted the politics of Eisenhower's decision more readily than Churchill. "Most of the changes," Brooke wrote on April 1, "are due to national aspirations and to ensure that the USA effort will not be lost under British command." The prime minister, however, played the aggrieved plaintiff. Not content with phoning Eisenhower on March 29, Churchill cabled the general on March 31 and April 2 and importuned the president on April 1 and 5. The prime minister believed that, minus the Ninth Army, the 21st Army Group was overmatched and lacking in offensive power. Furthermore, Eisenhower had altered the Malta agreements that the northern thrust would have priority, thus affecting more than one million British soldiers without recourse to British governmental authority. Eisenhower had not discussed his change of plans with Montgomery; with Air Marshal Tedder, Eisenhower's deputy supreme commander; or with the British COS. Finally, Berlin was the only internationally regarded objective left in Germany.

Speaking of the Red Army on April 1, Churchill described the obvious geographic facts of the war in central Europe to date and his fears for the future:

"The Russian armies will no doubt overrun all Austria and enter Vienna. If they also take Berlin will not their impression that they have been the overwhelming contributor to our common victory be unduly imprinted in their minds, and may this not lead them into a mood which will raise grave and formidable difficulties in the future? I therefore consider that from a political standpoint we should march as far east into Germany as possible, and that should Berlin be in our grasp we should certainly take it."[61]

Eisenhower was at ease responding electronically to Montgomery's and Churchill's pleadings. He pointed to his long-standing strategy of the northern thrust on the Ruhr and the eastern thrust on Kassel and Frankfurt. He rejected Churchill's charge that his orders relegated "His Majesty's forces to an unexpected restricted sphere" merely because Bradley, not Montgomery, commanded the Ninth Army. Moreover, Eisenhower promised to give Montgomery American troops to aid his crossing of the Elbe. As early as September 15, 1944, Eisenhower had pointed out this very same strategy to his three army group commanders: "Clearly, Berlin is the main prize." In this message he also warned that Allied strategy would of necessity be coordinated with the Russians. The Allies would also have to seize Germany's northern ports of Kiel, Lubeck, Hamburg, and Bremen. Eisenhower's message predicted his final missions of the war months in advance: "Should the Russians beat us to Berlin, the Northern Group of Armies would seize the Hanover area and the Hamburg group of ports. The Central Group of Armies would seize part, or the whole, of Leipzig-Dresden, depending upon the progress of the Russian advance. In any event, the Southern Group of Armies would seize Augsburg-Munich. The area Nurnberg-Regensburg would be seized by Central or Southern Group of Armies, depending on the situation at the time."[62]

At the time the conferees at Yalta were drawing up occupation zones for postwar Germany, American, British, and French forces were closing to the Rhine, and the Russians were on the Oder River, less than 50 miles from central Berlin. Those agreements put Berlin inside the Soviet zone, 110 miles east of the Elbe River, and the British zone, which effectively ruled out Berlin as an objective of Montgomery's northern thrust. When the Western Allies closed to the Rhine in March 1945 they were nearly 300 miles from Berlin, while the Russians on the Oder had mobilized, according to Antony Beevor, 2.5 million men for the siege of Berlin. When the First and Ninth Armies linked up on Easter Sunday, April 1, east of Lippstadt, they had completely encircled the Ruhr pocket and nineteen German divisions. Resistance ceased by April 18, by which time the Allies had captured 317,000 German troops, a number that surpassed German losses at Stalingrad. The Ninth Army returned to Bradley's command on April 4, and on April 14–15 the line held by Ninth Army's XIX Corps stretched 150 miles, with two successful bridgeheads over the Elbe. The Americans were some 70 miles from Berlin when the Soviets began their Berlin offensive on April 16.[63]

Eisenhower asked his chief tactician, Bradley, for an estimate of casualties in a Berlin operation. Bradley calculated that one hundred thousand casualties would be the price to cross the swampy lowlands separating Magdeburg from southwestern Berlin. This was "a pretty stiff price to pay for a prestige objective," Bradley concluded, "especially when we've got to fall back and let the other fellow take over." Bradley referred to the zones of occupation that ceded German territory east of the Elbe to the Soviets; Americans would die by the thousands to gain ground that would be handed over to the Russians. Had Eisenhower ordered Bradley to take Berlin, the mission would have gone to Major General Raymond S. McLain's XIX Corps. At the time, McLain told military historian S. L. A. Marshall, a few American patrols were the most he could have gotten into Berlin. As it was, the Americans and the British entered Berlin in July. "At the cost of not a single life," Stephen Ambrose wrote, "Great Britain and the United States had their sectors of Berlin."[64]

I have no doubt that Eisenhower took the Ninth Army from Montgomery and gave it to Bradley as an act of revenge for churlish behavior, a thesis first posited by the British historian Richard Lamb. Lamb thought that Eisenhower's excuses for doing so were lame, especially the magnification of the so-called National Redoubt in the Bavarian Alps into a Nazi last-stand arena requiring SHAEF's attention. There is no evidence in 1945 that the supreme commander suspected Montgomery of manipulating the CIGS through deceptive cables, but if Eisenhower had suspected that it would have explained his final snub of Montgomery. Clearly Eisenhower wanted all the American armies under American command when they met up with the Russians because he could trust the Americans to follow orders. Eisenhower had told Bradley that he suspected Churchill wanted trouble with the Russians. Coincidentally, Brooke made similar comments in his diary. As David Reynolds points out, by April 18–19 Churchill had changed his mind about beating the Russians to Berlin; he did not admit it, however, in his postwar memoirs. Churchill told Anthony Eden, the British foreign minister, on April 19: "It would seem that the Western Allies are not immediately in a position to force their way into Berlin."[65]

Antony Beevor uncovered new evidence that puts Eisenhower's decision not to go to Berlin in a new perspective. The evidence centers on German uranium ore and the Soviet atomic bomb project. Stalin knew that spearheads of the Ninth Army would enter Berlin over a bridgehead at Zerbst near the suburb of Dahlem, home to the Kaiser Wilhelm Institute for Physics on Boltzmannstrasse, which housed a cyclotron of 1.5 million volts. With the help of well-placed spies the Soviets were alerted, and troops from the Peoples Commissariat for Internal Affairs reached the institute on April 25, 1945. There they found 250 kilograms of metallic uranium, 3 tons of uranium oxide, and 20 liters of heavy water. Beevor contends that Eisenhower was naive to refer to Berlin as unimportant, and Churchill was wrong to think that Stalin would have bargained Poland for Berlin. "If any forces from the Western Allies," Beevor wrote, "had crossed the Elbe and headed for Berlin, they would almost certainly have found themselves warned off by the Soviet air force, and artillery if in range." The Red Army took more than 352,000 casualties, including some 78,000 dead, in taking Berlin and its environs.[66]

The war ended when the Germans surrendered at Eisenhower's headquarters in Rheims, France, on May 7, 1945. Two days later Germany surrendered to the Red Army in Berlin, for Stalin required that Germany surrender there. Montgomery and Churchill never forgave Eisenhower for not going to Berlin even though he had doubtless saved tens of thousands of lives by demurring. When the Russians closed Berlin to rail and road traffic in 1948 and the Berlin Airlift saved the city, these events ensured that the last chapter of every memoir would be about Berlin and that the city would become the Cold War's Holy Grail that Eisenhower had lost. No one, however, could ever determine the difference it would have made except to the pride of British arms to see Montgomery enter Berlin after six long years of war. Russell Weigley argues that Eisenhower's Lincoln-Grant strategy was successful: the war was won in eleven months, and the Alliance was held together by Eisenhower's efforts as supreme commander, which is how Americans continue to regard the outcome. The British, on the other hand, think of Eisenhower as the ground-forces commander who employed a politically correct strategy that violated the principle of concentration and sought compromise and consensus at the expense of ending the war through rapid exploitation. Always attempting to downplay controversies, Eisenhower, in the British view, was a chairman of the board who paid too much attention to the last man to talk to him. That particular canard can be retired based on evidence cited here.

Montgomery closed his headquarters diary on May 12, 1945, with the following entry: "The organization for command was always faulty. The Supreme Commander had no firm ideas as to how to conduct the war. . . . [A]t that particular business he was quite useless."[67] One month later, Eisenhower made a speech at the Guildhall, where he received The Freedom of the City of London. In his address he paid tribute to the Battle of Britain, fought two years before the Americans arrived in Europe. He thanked the British for the hospitality they had shown to the American soldiers who had invaded their country in large numbers, often to the great inconvenience of the locals. And he compared Denison, Texas, and Abilene, Kansas—his birthplace and his hometown, respectively—to London: "To preserve this freedom of worship, his equality before the law, his liberty to speak and act as he sees fit, subject only to provisions that he trespass not upon similar rights of others—a Londoner will fight. So will a citizen of Abilene. When we consider these things, then the valley of the Thames draws closer to the farms of Kansas and the plains of Texas."[68] As Brooke noted in his diary on

June 12, 1945, "Ike made a *wonderful* speech and impressed all hearers in the Guildhall including all the Cabinet.... I had never realized that Ike was as big a man until I heard his performance today!"[69]

Eisenhower had been a "big man" throughout the campaign in northwestern Europe. He held conferences to arrive at compromises in order to hold together what Churchill called the Grand Alliance. Montgomery never understood what Eisenhower was about and plotted and campaigned behind his back. And Brooke, who knew better, did little to control Montgomery's penchant for self-promotion. Churchill thought nothing of hectoring Eisenhower by phone, telegraph, and personal entreaty, thereby adding to Eisenhower's many worries. It is clear that all three believed that Eisenhower was a superb supreme commander, but they had a far less generous opinion of Eisenhower as a ground-forces commander.

Notes

1. Matthew F. Holland, *Eisenhower between the Wars: The Making of a General and a Statesman* (Westport, CT: Praeger, 2001), passim.

2. David Reynolds, *In Command of History: Churchill Fighting and Writing the Second World War* (London: Penguin, Allan Lane, 2004), 386; Stephen E. Ambrose, *The Supreme Commander: The War Years of Dwight D. Eisenhower* (Garden City, NY: Doubleday, 1970), 306.

3. Alex Danchev and Daniel Todman, eds., *War Diaries, 1939–1945: Field Marshal Lord Alanbrooke* (London: Weidenfeld & Nicolson, 2001), 441–42, for the Quebec conference decision. See p. 276 for the first impression of Eisenhower, p. 491 for Eisenhower's appointment, and p. 546 for his May 15 comment.

4. Gordon A. Harrison, *Cross-Channel Attack (United States Army in World War II: The European Theater of Operations)* (Washington, DC: Center of Military History, 1989), 115. See p. 116 for the issue of no permanent ground commander. Later the First Army Group, better known as FUSAG, was renamed the 12th Army Group, to prevent confusion with FUSA (First U.S. Army).

5. M-508, "System of Command in France," Montgomery to CIGS, July 7, 1944, Papers of Field Marshal Viscount Montgomery of Alamein, Reel 11, BLM 126/9, Imperial War Museum (IWM), Lambeth, London. Italics in the original.

6. H. C. Butcher, *My Three Years with Eisenhower: The Personal Diary of Captain Harry C. Butcher, USNR, Naval Aide to General Eisenhower, 1942 to 1945* (New York: Simon & Schuster, 1946); for the leak, see p. 648; "Montgomery," *Daily Mirror* (London), August 17, 1944, 3.

7. Forrest C. Pogue, *George C. Marshall, Organizer of Victory* (New York: Viking, 1973), 425. For Baldwin's and Marshall's reaction, see Larry I. Bland et al., eds., *George C. Marshall: Interviews and Reminiscences for Forrest C. Pogue* (Lexington, VA: George C. Marshall Research Foundation, 1991), 386–87; p. 540 for information on the move to France.

8. Carlo D'Este, *Decision in Normandy* (New York: Dutton, 1983), 253, 254, 262–63, for cannibalization; Nigel Hamilton, *Master of the Battlefield: Monty's War Years, 1942–1944* (New York: McGraw-Hill, 1983), 801–2; Russell F. Weigley, *Eisenhower's Lieutenants: The Campaigns of France and Germany, 1944–1945* (Bloomington: Indiana University Press, 1981), 254; Field-Marshal Bernard Montgomery, *The Memoirs of Field-Marshal the Viscount Montgomery of Alamein* (London: Collins, 1958), 266–67.

9. The Bradley Commentaries, 37-B, S-14, U.S. Army Military History Institute (USAMHI), Carlisle Barracks, Pennsylvania. Bradley dictated responses to questions from his ghost writer, Lieutenant Colonel Chester B. Hansen; Omar N. Bradley, *A Soldier's Story* (New York: Holt, 1951), 396–400; Omar N. Bradley and Clay Blair, *A General's Life: An Autobiography by General of the Army Omar N. Bradley and Clay Blair* (New York: Simon & Schuster, 1983), 313–14.

10. G. E. Patrick Murray, *Eisenhower versus Montgomery: The Continuing Debate* (Westport, CT: Praeger, 1996), 118–122, for chronology and quotations; Montgomery to Bedell Smith, September 21, 1944, Montgomery Papers, Reel 10, BLM, 109/34, IWM; interview with Viscount Portal of Purfleet, February 7, 1947, Office of the Chief of Military History (OCMH) Collection, *Supreme Command*, Pogue Interviews, USAMHI.

11. Dwight D. Eisenhower, *Crusade in Europe* (Garden City, NY: Doubleday, 1948), 286; Alfred D. Chandler and Stephen E. Ambrose, eds., *The Papers of Dwight D. Eisenhower: The War Years*, 5 vols. (Baltimore: Johns Hopkins University Press, 1970), 5:155–90; Montgomery, *Memoirs*, 286.

12. SHAEF Planning Staff, "Post-'neptune,' Courses of Action after Capture of Lodgement Area, Section I-Main Objective and Axis of Advance," April 25 and May 3, 1944, Record Group (RG) 331, Box 74, SHAEF, General Staff, Post-overlord Planning, vol. 1, National Archives (hereafter cited as NA).

13. Memorandum for the Chief of Staff, "Command Organization," August 22, 1944, RG 331, SHAEF, Box 77, Post-overlord Planning, vol. I, NA.

14. Forrest C. Pogue, *The Supreme Command (United States Army in World War II: The European Theater of Operations)* (Washington DC: Office of the Chief of Military History, 1954), 244–45.

15. CAB 106/1106, "The Broad Front versus Narrow Front Controversy," 15, The National Archives, Kew, Surrey, UK; Danchev and Todman, *War Diaries*, 585; Reynolds, *In Command of History*, 448.

16. Montgomery, *Memoirs*, 272–73, for the signal of September 5; for the COMZ affair, see Roland G. Ruppenthal, *Logistical Support of the Armies*, vol. 2, *September 1944–May 1945 (United States Army in World War II: The European Theater of Operations)* (Washington, DC: Office of the Chief of Military History, 1959), 31. For French wags, see Eric Larrabee, *Commander in Chief: Franklin Delano Roosevelt, His Lieutenants, and Their War* (New York: Harper & Row, 1987), 473.

17. Montgomery, *Memoirs*, 271; Carlo D'Este, *Eisenhower: A Soldier's Life* (New York: Holt, 2002), 605.

18. Chandler and Ambrose, *Papers of Dwight D. Eisenhower*, 4:2115–16, for directive; for memorandum quotation, see 4:2121. For ULTRA, see F. H. Hinsley et al., *British Intelligence in the Second World War: Its Influence on Strategy and Operations*, vol. 3, pt.

2 (London: Her Majesty's Stationery Office, 1988), 378–79. For Ramsay's comment, see Ruppenthal, *Logistical Support of the Armies*, 2:50.

19. Nigel Hamilton, *Monty: Final Years of the Field-Marshal* (New York: McGraw-Hill, 1987), 209.

20. Interview with Major General Sir Miles Graham, January 19, 1949, 15/15/48, Chester Wilmot Papers, Liddell Hart Collection, Liddell Hart Centre for Military Archives (LHCMA), King's College, London. For the published version, see Chester Wilmot, *The Struggle for Europe* (New York: Harper, 1952), 488–89; Ruppenthal, *Logistical Support of the Armies*, 2:11.

21. Sir Bertram Ramsay diary, October 5, 1944, 5, CAB 106/1124, National Archives, UK; Danchev and Todman, *War Diaries*, 600.

22. Montgomery, *Memoirs*, 284.

23. Major L. F. Ellis with Lieutenant Colonel A. E. Warhurst, *History of the Second World War: United Kingdom Military Series*, vol. 2, *Victory in the West* (Nashville, TN: Battery Press, 1994), 2:85–88.

24. Chandler and Ambrose, *Papers of Dwight D. Eisenhower*, 4:2221–24. See p. 2225n6 for Montgomery's reply. Italics in the original.

25. Ellis and Warhurst, *Victory in the West*, 2:155; Hugh M. Cole, *The Ardennes: Battle of the Bulge (United States Army in World War II: The European Theater of Operations)* (Washington, DC: Center of Military History, 1993), 424; Bradley, *Soldier's Story*, 432–33; Charles M. Province, *Patton's Third Army: A Daily Combat Diary* (New York: Hippocrene, 1992), 68.

26. Danchev and Todman, *War Diaries*, 619.

27. Ibid., 619–20, 624–25.

28. Hamilton has two sources for switching troops along thrust lines, one from Montgomery and a confirming source from Bradley; see Hamilton, *Monty: Final Years of the Field-Marshal*, 141; Danchev and Todman, *War Diaries*, 628, for Eisenhower being out of touch. For approaching Churchill, see p. 629.

29. Hamilton, *Monty: Final Years of the Field-Marshal*, 145; Danchev and Todman, *War Diaries*, 629.

30. Arthur Bryant, *Triumph in the West: A History of the War Years Based on the Diaries of Field-Marshal Lord Alanbrooke, Chief of the Imperial General Staff* (Garden City, NY: Doubleday, 1959), 258–59; C. P. Dawnay, "Inside Monty's Headquarters," in T. E. B. Howarth, ed., *Monty at Close Quarters: Recollections of the Man* (New York: Hippocrene, 1985), 16, italics in original.

31. Danchev and Todman, *War Diaries*, 628, for Tedder. See p. 630 for bringing in Alexander, p. 632 for Bradley.

32. Franklin D. Roosevelt to Dwight D. Eisenhower, November 25, 1944, Dwight D. Eisenhower Papers, Pre-Presidential, Principal File, Roosevelt, F. D. (1), Eisenhower Library, Abilene, Kansas (capitals in the original); CAB 106/1106, "Broad Front versus Narrow Front Controversy," National Archives, UK. For the document, see Murray, *Eisenhower versus Montgomery*, 97–98.

33. Bryant, *Triumph in the West*, 264, for "got at"; p. 265 for "lone hand." For the Maastricht agenda, see Ellis, *Victory in the West*, 2:167–68.

34. Murray, *Eisenhower versus Montgomery*, 99, for Churchill's cable and Roosevelt's reply; A. J. Cummings, "Strategy in the West," *News Chronicle*, December 8, 1944, 2. For Bevin, see CAB 65/44/163, War Cabinet, December 11, 1944, 136, National Archives, UK.

35. Hamilton, *Monty: Final Years of the Field-Marshal*, 169–71.

36. Eisenhower, *Crusade in Europe*, 371; CAB 79/84, War Cabinet, COS Committee, December 12, 1944, National Archives, UK; Danchev and Todman, *War Diaries*, 634. For 21st Army Group Rhine crossing estimate, see Ellis, *Victory in the West*, 2:170n1.

37. Danchev and Todman, *War Diaries*, 635, for Brooke and War Cabinet; for Greece, see p. 634; John Ehrman, *History of the Second World War, United Kingdom Military Series*, vol. 6, *Grand Strategy: October 1944–August 1945* (London: Her Majesty's Stationery Office, 1956), 57. For Greek deployment, see CAB 79/84, War Cabinet, COS Committee, December 18, 1944, 220, National Archives, UK; CAB 79/84, War Cabinet, COS Committee, December 30, 1944, 323, National Archives, UK; Ellis, *Victory in the West*, vol. 2, pt. 2, 169–70, 207 for quotation, 209.

38. Danchev and Todman, *War Diaries*, 636; Bryant, *Triumph in the West*, 269–70.

39. D'Este, *Eisenhower: A Soldier's Life*, 643, for Bradley; see p. 644 for Eisenhower; Hansen Diary (HD), December 19, 1944, Chester B. Hansen Papers (CBHP), USAMHI.

40. James Shepley, "Estimate of the Situation," *Time* 45 (January 8, 1945): 21; "Criticism Command Organization SHAEF," January 26, 1945, Military Intelligence Division, WDGS (War Department General Staff) Military Attaché Report, RG 165, Operations Division, 1942–45, 384 ETO, Box 1312, Case 46, NA.

41. "Criticism Command Organization SHAEF," January 26, 1945, Military Intelligence Division, WDGS, Military Attaché Report, RG 165, Operations Division, 1942–45, 384 ETO, Box 1312, Case 46, NA. For Moorehead, see "A 1914 General Asks Me How Rundstedt Did It," *Daily Express* (London), January 4, 1945, 3; for Cummings, see Murray, *Eisenhower versus Montgomery*, 22.

42. "Notes on Campaign in North-Western Europe," part VII, December 28, 1944, 5, Papers of Montgomery of Alamein, Reel 7, BLM 79, IWM.

43. Danchev and Todman, *War Diaries*, 638; Charles Richardson, *Send for Freddie: The Story of Monty's Chief of Staff, Major-General Sir Francis de Guingand, KBE, CB, DSO* (London: William Kimber, 1987), 169–70; Montgomery, *Memoirs*, 318, for "full operational control."

44. Eisenhower, *Crusade in Europe*, 356.

45. Hamilton, *Monty: Final Years of the Field-Marshal*, 265, 275–79; Francis de Guingand, *From Brass Hat to Bowler Hat* (London: Hamish Hamilton, 1979), 17; Francis de Guingand, *Generals at War* (London: Hodder and Stoughton, 1961), 107–12.

46. Montgomery, *Memoirs*, 312–14; HD, January 8, 1945, CBHP, USAMHI; "A Slur on Monty," *Daily Mail* (London), January 11, 1945, 2.

47. CAB 65/49, War Cabinet, January 11, 1945, 19.

48. CAB 65/49, January 8, 1945, 10; CAB 65/51, War Cabinet, Confidential Annex, January 12, 1945; PREM 3/341/2, Ismay for COS Committee, January 10, 1945, 185–86; all, National Archives, UK.

49. Chandler and Ambrose, *Papers of Dwight D. Eisenhower*, 4:2415–20; p. 2423n1 for Marshall's response.

50. D'Este, *Eisenhower: A Soldier's Life*, 674–75, for Marshall's promise; Butcher, *My Three Years with Eisenhower*, 749, for Eisenhower's staff; CCS, Conference Proceedings, 3/3, Argonaut Conference, 182nd Meeting, January 30, 1945, 195–99, NA.

51. CAB 65/49, War Cabinet, January 8, 1945, National Archives, UK; Ehrman, *Grand Strategy: October 1944–August 1945*, 87–88.

52. Interview with General Sir Hastings L. Ismay, December 20, 1946, OCMH, *Supreme Command*, Pogue Interviews, USAMHI; Interview with Lieutenant General Walter Bedell Smith, May 8, 1947, ibid.; Bryant, *Triumph in the West*, 301–2; Ambrose, *Supreme Commander*, 586; D'Este, *Eisenhower: A Soldier's Life*, 676; Danchev and Todman, *War Diaries*, 655.

53. Danchev and Todman, *War Diaries*, 669; Chandler and Ambrose, *Papers of Dwight D. Eisenhower*, 4:2480–82; Winston S. Churchill to Dwight D. Eisenhower, February 22, 1945, Pre-Presidential, Principal File, 22, Folder 4—Churchill, Eisenhower Papers.

54. Weigley, *Eisenhower's Lieutenants*, 615; Bradley, *Soldier's Story*, 521; Hamilton, *Monty: Final Years of the Field-Marshal*, 404.

55. Chandler and Ambrose, *Papers of Dwight D. Eisenhower*, 4:2526–27, 2527n3.

56. F. E. W. Simpson to Field Marshal Bernard Montgomery, March 19, 1945, Montgomery Papers, BLM 94/25, Reel 8, IWM; Richard Lamb, *Montgomery in Europe, 1943–1945: Success or Failure?* (London: Buchan & Enright, 1984), 367.

57. Eisenhower, *Crusade in Europe*, 372; Bryant, *Triumph in the West*, 332–33; Danchev and Todman, *War Diaries*, 676; Butcher, *My Three Years with Eisenhower*, 792.

58. M-569, Montgomery to F. E. W. Simpson, April 8, 1945, Montgomery Papers, Reel 8, BLM 94/34, IWM; M-561, March 27, 1945, Montgomery Papers, Reel 10, BLM 112/64, IWM; Hamilton, *Monty: Final Years of the Field-Marshal*, 440–41, for M-562.

59. M-569, Montgomery to F. E. W. Simpson, April 8, 1945, Montgomery Papers, Reel 8, BLM 94/34, IWM; Chandler and Ambrose, *Papers of Dwight D. Eisenhower*, 4:2552, for SHAEF FWD (Forward) 18272.

60. Danchev and Todman, *War Diaries*, 679, for the British; John Toland, *The Last 100 Days* (New York: Bantam, 1967), 64, for Malta; Robert Sherwood, *Roosevelt and Hopkins: An Intimate History* (New York: Harper, 1948), 851, for Yalta; George C. Marshall to Dwight D. Eisenhower, April 7, 1945, RG 331, Box 77, "Post overlord Planning," vol. IV, NA.

61. Danchev and Todman, *War Diaries*, 680; Kay Summersby diary, March 29, 1945, Pre-Presidential, Principal File, Summersby, K., Box 140, Eisenhower Papers; Winston S. Churchill, *The Second World War*, vol. 6, *Triumph and Tragedy* (London: Cassell; Boston: Houghton Mifflin, 1948–54), 463–68.

62. Chandler and Ambrose, *Papers of Dwight D. Eisenhower*, 4: 2572–73, for April 1, 1945. For September 15, 1944, see pp. 2148–49.

63. Antony Beevor, *The Fall of Berlin, 1945* (New York: Viking, 2002), 147; Charles B. MacDonald, *The Last Offensive (United States Army in World War II: The European Theater of Operations)* (Washington, DC: Center of Military History, 1993), 359, 379.

64. Bradley, *Soldier's Story*, 535; Stephen E. Ambrose, *Eisenhower and Berlin, 1945: The Decision to Halt at the Elbe* (New York: Norton, 1967), 94; for McLain, see p. 98.

65. Lamb, *Montgomery in Europe, 1943–1945*, 352–95; The Bradley Commentaries, Berlin, USAMHI; Danchev and Todman, *War Diaries*, 693–95; Reynolds, *In Command of History*, 472n23.

66. Beevor, *Fall of Berlin*, 144, for quotation. For Dahlem, see pp. 138–39; for Soviet seizures, pp. 324–25.

67. Lamb, *Montgomery in Europe, 1943–1945*, 394.

68. David Eisenhower, *Eisenhower: At War, 1943–1945* (New York: Random House, 1986), 823–25.

69. Danchev and Todman, *War Diaries*, 697. Italics in original.

8
Operation Rollup
The U.S. Army's Rebuild Program during the Korean War

Peter S. Kindsvatter

MILLIONS OF AMERICAN SOLDIERS and sailors had cause to celebrate on August 14, 1945. Japan had accepted the Allied terms of surrender, bringing World War II to an end. The surrender also brought sighs of relief, because a costly invasion of the Japanese home islands would not be necessary. The millions of tons of equipment and supplies being stockpiled on islands in the Philippines, the Marianas, the Bonins, and the Ryukyus for that invasion would not be needed. The plan to dispose of that matériel, dubbed Operation Rollup, would initially founder for a lack of shipping and personnel, be revitalized in 1948 as a way to provide equipment for U.S. forces occupying Japan, and finally serve as a major source of matériel, following rebuild and renovation, for fighting the Korean War.[1]

Operation Rollup actually began even before war's end as rollup teams began assessing matériel for disposition in areas of the Pacific, such as New Guinea and the Solomons that by 1945 were backwaters in the war effort.[2] Some matériel could be sold to allies. The Foreign Liquidation Commission (FLC) was established to dispose of surplus property. Countries in the region, notably China, Korea, the Philippines, and former enemy Japan, needed that matériel to rebuild devastated infrastructure. By the end of 1946, the FLC had sold 306,900 long tons of supplies to these and other countries for $190 million.[3]

The FLC disposed of only a relatively small amount of matériel, however, as much of the stockpiled military equipment was not especially useful for economic rehabilitation. Some of this remaining matériel would be needed by U.S. occupation forces earmarked for Japan and Korea. When the war in the Pacific ended unexpectedly, hundreds of ships carrying invasion supplies were en route to Pacific staging areas from the continental United States (also known as the Zone of the Interior). Many of these ships were diverted to Japan on the assumption that their cargoes could be used by arriving occupation forces. The ships arrived to find that few intact piers or storage areas and little cargo-handling equipment remained in devastated Japan to handle the cargo discharge. Supplies were literally dumped pier side or on beaches to free up the holds for other missions.[4]

And there was no lack of other missions for shipping. While the decision to divert ships to Japan was not well thought out, Operation Rollup was otherwise a well-conceived plan to concentrate war matériel and then dispose of it, with the understanding that most stocks would have to be returned to the United States. Other missions requiring shipping, however, quickly overwhelmed this plan, although in early 1946 some supplies did reach the United States. At the Port of San Francisco, for example, 289 vessels returned vehicles, equipment, and supplies in the first five months of 1946.[5] This retrograde began to slacken, however, as ships were diverted to other missions.

One largely unanticipated mission, at least in scope, was the requirement to relocate five million or more Japanese to their home islands from regions in the Pacific that they had occupied and in some cases colonized. Conversely, a million Chinese, Koreans, and other nationals sent to work in Japan during the war had to be repatriated. A number of U.S. Navy landing ships and a fleet of 106 Liberty ships spent most of 1946 accomplishing this mission.[6]

The main diversion of shipping from Operation Rollup, however, was caused by the need to return demobilizing troops to the United States. Pressure from the home front, not to mention from the troops themselves, to "bring the boys home" at war's end did not go unheeded.[7] Army strength on September 1, 1945, the day before Japan's formal surrender, was just over eight million. This strength was reduced by more than six million over the next nine months. By the end of June 1947, the army's effective strength was 925,000.[8]

That a great deal of shipping was needed to transport these demobilizing troops is obvious, but related factors also conspired to disrupt Operation Rollup. The manpower needed to collect, classify, package for shipment, and load out rollup stocks was soon in short supply. Worse, the service troops skilled in these areas were some of the first to go home because they had accumulated more than enough overseas service points in the army's rotation system to qualify for demobilization. In January 1946, the assistant chief of staff for logistics (G-4), U.S. Army Forces Western Pacific, summed up the problem in testimony to Congress: "We do not have the skilled or experienced personnel or the manpower to thoroughly go over a piece of equipment, coat it with thin film greases or similar preservatives and place it in a condition for continued storage."[9]

Operation Rollup sputtered to a virtual halt. Not only were huge amounts of matériel left scattered on the Pacific islands, but much of that equipment was left in the open in hot, humid, tropical conditions. An estimated one and a quarter million tons of property valued at $1 billion was earmarked for rollup at war's end, but FLC sales and retrograde shipments to the United States disposed of only a fraction of those stocks. Furthermore, this figure probably represents only that equipment located at the various Pacific depots and supply bases at war's end and does not include the equipment left behind—to the tune of an additional several million tons—by the more than a dozen demobilizing divisions and their supporting corps and army troops.[10]

Not all of the troops went home, of course, at least not directly. Units from the Sixth and Eighth Armies occupied Japan and the southern half of Korea, while limited numbers remained at various Pacific bases. After several changes, the organization that emerged for U.S. forces in the Pacific was the Far East Command, established January 1, 1947, under General of the Army Douglas MacArthur. In addition to naval and air components, the army forces subordinate to Far East Command were the Eighth Army, occupying Japan (the Sixth Army having been inactivated in January 1946); the U.S. Army Forces in Korea, which would be disestablished in 1949 when U.S. occupation troops left; the Philippines-Ryukyus Command, soon separated into the Philippines Command (PHILCOM) and Ryukyus Command (RYCOM); and the Marianas-Bonins Command (MARBO).[11]

The Eighth Army in Japan contained four infantry divisions and supporting troops scattered about the home islands in occupation zones. The authorized strength of these four divisions had dwindled to 12,500 men each by 1950, compared to a wartime (full) authorized strength of 18,900, and none was filled even to its authorized reduced strength.[12] Furthermore, these divisions had received no new vehicles or major items of equipment since their arrival in Japan in 1945. Indeed, there was no new equipment to receive, as wartime production lines were virtually all shut down in 1945, and the army was relying on its World War II equipment stocks.

With age and usage, the Eighth Army's equipment began to break down with increasing frequency. If old equipment could not be replaced with new, then the normal procedure would be to periodically overhaul, or rebuild, that equipment, but this option was not available to the Eighth Army. Rebuilding of vehicles and major assemblies such as engines and transmissions was fifth-echelon maintenance, known as base-shop or depot maintenance.[13] No substantial fifth-echelon maintenance capability existed outside the United States. The Eighth Army's equipment operators, unit mechanics, and maintenance units could perform the first four echelons of maintenance, but this allowed only for repairs and the rebuilding of minor assemblies such as carburetors and generators. Maintenance units could also replace major assemblies such as engines but did not have the capability to overhaul the old, worn-out ones. Nor, as was the case with vehicles and equipment, were new assemblies being produced in any quantity.

In 1947, the Far East Command's ordnance officer, Brigadier General Urban Niblo, proposed a solution to the Eighth Army's growing equipment problems.

He recommended, in essence, a revitalization of Operation Rollup, only this time the vehicles and equipment still sitting on the Pacific islands would be shipped to Japan instead of the United States. While this equipment was being collected, a fifth-echelon maintenance capability would be established in Japan using Japanese workers and industrial infrastructure, much of which had been idle since war's end. The Department of the Army approved this plan on October 20, 1947, initially for wheeled vehicles, but the program soon expanded to include armament and all matériel. No doubt a key factor in that approval was the cost savings that such a plan would achieve compared to producing new vehicles or shipping the Eighth Army's fifty thousand vehicles to the United States for rebuild and return.[14]

The Eighth Army ordnance officer, Colonel Olaf P. Winningstad, was responsible for implementing the plan in Japan. The program was called BIG-5, short for Base Industrial Group for Fifth Echelon Maintenance, and it was an Ordnance Corps program.[15] Here it is necessary to understand the role of the technical services in logistics matters. There were seven technical services, survivors of the army's bureau system. And like the bureaus, each had a significant degree of autonomy. Each technical service was responsible for research, development, procurement, distribution, and maintenance of supplies and equipment in its designated area of responsibility.

The technical service with arguably the broadest responsibilities was the Ordnance Corps, which provided wheeled transport, armament systems (tanks, artillery, and small arms), and ammunition. The other technical services were the Quartermaster Corps, responsible for food, clothing, fuel, and various services such as graves registration; the Corps of Engineers, responsible for units and equipment used for construction, firefighting, water purification, power generation, and map production; the Army Medical Service, responsible for the equipment and supplies needed to care for patients (not to mention medical treatment, veterinary service, and sanitation); the Signal Corps, responsible for communications and photography and their related equipment; the Chemical Corps, providing smoke, incendiary, and chemical warfare capabilities and equipment; and the Transportation Corps, which operated truck transport units (with trucks provided through Ordnance Corps channels) and railway and waterway transportation and related equipment.[16]

Each technical service within the Eighth Army and, later, the Japan Logistical Command (established August 25, 1950), would operate its own salvage, reclamation, and rebuild program. All of these programs will be touched on, but the Ordnance Corps's BIG-5 program, involving wheeled vehicles, combat vehicles, weapons systems, parts and assemblies, and ammunition, was the most ambitious and would eventually become the most significant to the conduct of the Korean War.

Given the green light to proceed in October 1947, the Far East Command began collecting rollup matériel, regardless of the technical service involved, from its subordinate commands in the Pacific (PHILCOM, RYCOM, and MARBO). The process began in earnest in 1948 and continued well into 1950. In addition to the Pacific commands, equipment from Korea was included in rollup late in 1948 as U.S. occupation forces began leaving the peninsula. This collection effort was lengthy because of limited shipping assets and scarce manpower. Some of the recovered supplies had been in covered storage, and some had been so well packaged back in World War II for shipment to the tropics that they were still in good condition. Most vehicles and equipment, however, had not been prepared for storage and had been left, literally piled up in some cases, in open storage. The condition of this equipment, after three or more years of exposure to tropical heat and humidity without proper maintenance, was poor. Metal was rusted, canvas and wood had rotted, and rubber had deteriorated.

A variety of problems in addition to the shortage of shipping and manpower plagued the rollup process. Much of the manpower for loading out rollup stocks came from local labor, especially Filipinos, supervised by the limited number of available service troops who were themselves mostly inexperienced postwar replacements. This workforce lacked the expertise to properly identify and classify equipment and supplies, with the result that shipments arriving in Japan had to be sorted out and materials sent to the appropriate technical service. Furthermore, supplies and equipment that were not salvageable were not to be sent to Japan, but the inexperienced and overburdened work crews tended to load up everything in sight, resulting in matériel arriving in Japan that went straight to the scrap heap.

Also, while some packaging had held up, much had deteriorated, and many items had to be repackaged. Thus, packing and crating facilities had to be established and materials found to make shipping containers. Too often, equipment was shipped without being properly packaged or supplies were haphazardly loaded, resulting in damage or destruction while en route to Japan. Even nature conspired to hinder rollup when a typhoon hit the Ryukyus in 1948, destroying shops and warehouses. On Guam and Saipan, rollup teams discovered that equipment was infested with the giant African snail, and a fumigation chamber had to be build to disinfect equipment before shipment.[17]

Despite these problems, Operation Rollup continued at a slow but steady pace. No consolidated record of rollup tonnage sent to Japan apparently exists, given the autonomous nature of the technical services' separate programs and the origin of the stocks from four separate commands within the Far East Command, but available statistics indicate that at least 2.15 million tons of matériel was recovered, to include between 55,000 and 63,000 vehicles.[18] While Operation Rollup was ongoing, preparations were under way to establish the fifth-echelon maintenance facilities needed to rebuild the rollup vehicles and equipment, not to mention the overhauling of those Eighth Army vehicles already in Japan. This part of the program, officially BIG-5 but also dubbed Operation Rebuild, made extensive use, with some modifications, of existing Japanese industrial infrastructure and, with some retraining, of Japanese workers.

The Eighth Army's Ordnance Section brought in civilian automotive experts from the United States, with the first arriving in December 1947, to assist in choosing and preparing the rebuild facilities. Some of the Japanese plants selected had previously been used for ordnance production but still needed significant modification. Despite being a modern power, Japan's industries did not use American-style assembly-line production methods. Engineering studies were thus necessary to design assembly lines. To the extent possible, machine tools came from rollup stocks, but Japanese tools, where suitable, were also used. Some specialized tools and machines had to be designed and fabricated from scratch.

Spare parts to support the rebuild program also came from rollup stocks, but throughout the life of the program parts often had to be fabricated in Japan or shipped in from the United States. Japanese subcontractors, for example, provided vehicle batteries, safety glass, and wooden components for the rebuild program. Each rebuild facility established an Engineering and Research Division to prepare the specifications and drawings for these locally procured parts. The Engineering and Research Division also tested and inspected samples of those parts provided by local subcontractors to ensure that specifications were met. In 1948 the Ordnance Corps further allocated an initial $1 million to purchase parts and supplies from the Zone of the Interior to support the program.

While the infrastructure was being prepared, workers were recruited and trained. Many had been left idle at war's end and eagerly sought the jobs. Despite the experience of many of these workers, considerable training was required. The Japanese were not used to working with the close tolerances and allowances required in parts and equipment to permit the degree of interchangeability necessary for assembly-line production. Supervisors and inspectors also had to be trained. American procedures called for far more inspections and tests during the production process than Japanese supervisors were accustomed to. Bilingual inspection checklists, forms, and instructions had to be devised. Finally, Japanese workers had to get used to such basic changes as working on benches, as opposed to squatting on the floor, and using tools such as American wrenches, planes, and saws that worked in the opposite direction (push or pull) than did similar Japanese tools.[19]

By the end of 1948, sufficient rollup stocks were on hand and plants and workers on line to begin rebuilding vehicles. The initial efforts were modest, carried out at four shops plus a tire rebuild plant by 5,425 U.S. and Japanese workers. In

1949, additional shops were opened, and the rebuild program was expanded to include armament as well as wheeled vehicles. Armament rebuild was carried out at the Tokyo Ordnance Depot and automotive rebuild at the Oppama, Nagoya, Sugita, Fuchu, Yokohoma, Koshien, and Hino ordnance shops.[20]

All types of trucks from quarter-ton to heavy tractors and all types of trailers and semi trailers were rebuilt. The process involved the complete teardown and rebuilding of the vehicles. Each ordnance shop was designed to handle a specific type or class of vehicle on its assembly lines. Oppama had lines for quarter-ton, one-and-a-half-ton, and two-and-a-half-ton trucks, for example, while the Nagoya shop rebuilt three-quarter-ton trucks.[21]

The rollup vehicles, often in pitiful condition on arrival, were first inspected for missing parts and components. They were then torn down to the frame. All major assemblies such as engines, transmissions, transfer cases, and axle assemblies went to separate shops for rebuild. Engines, for example, were steam-cleaned and had their cylinders rebored and worn parts replaced. Engine accessories such as carburetors, distributors, fuel pumps, water pumps, and generators were removed and rebuilt. Engines were then reassembled and run for two hours and fifteen minutes on a dynamometer, during which time valves and timing were set and carburetors and governors adjusted.

Meanwhile, the vehicle frame was cleaned in an alkali bath and straightened. Cracks were welded, and the frame was painted. All parts, down to nuts and bolts, were inspected, cleaned, repaired, and sent to shop stock. Cabs and bodies were sandblasted, and corroded spots were cut out and patched. Canvas tops and wooden cargo beds, invariably rotted, were replaced. Tires were repaired and re treaded at the Akabane Tire Shop. Radiators were flushed and welded, and their fins were straightened. Because labor was inexpensive, parts that were not normally economically salvageable were rebuilt, including bearings, brake cylinders, and springs. Finally, each truck was reassembled, painted, inspected, and road-tested. One hundred derelict rollup vehicles yielded about eighty rebuilt trucks. Not counting the time to overhaul major assemblies, a quarter-ton truck took 318 man hours and a two-and-a-half-ton truck 438 man hours to rebuild.[22]

When North Korea invaded South Korea on June 25, 1950, only about three thousand vehicles had been rebuilt but, significantly, plans and preparations were complete for boosting the rebuild program to twenty-three thousand vehicles a year with the intent of replacing all Eighth Army vehicles with rebuilds as expeditiously as possible.[23] Thus, a peacetime program intended to keep the Eighth Army's divisions in Japan functioning with relatively inexpensive rebuilt vehicles and weapons soon became, fortuitously for United Nations forces in Korea, the essential source of equipment for fighting the war.

With the decision to send American troops to Korea, Operation Rebuild and the other technical service reclamation and rebuild programs shifted into high gear. In the first four months of the war, the Ordnance Corps rebuild program turned out 489,000 small arms, 1,418 artillery pieces, 34,316 pieces of fire control equipment, 743 combat vehicles, and 15,000 trucks of various types.[24] This matériel was essential for equipping and resupplying the first U.S. troops to go to Korea, troops who, logically enough, came from the nearby Eighth Army. The 24th Infantry Division, 25th Infantry Division, and lst Cavalry Division from the Eighth Army arrived in Korea, in that order, in July 1950. The last Eighth Army division, the 7th Infantry, was stripped of much of its equipment and personnel to support the deployment of the first three divisions, but it too would arrive in Korea in September 1950 as part of the Inchon landing force.[25]

That these divisions were understrength and ill-prepared for combat is a well-known story. They were also short of important weapon systems such as recoilless rifles and 3.5-inch bazookas; these weapons were not on hand in sufficient numbers in Japan, nor did they arrive as part of Operation Rollup stocks. But without rebuilt Operation Rollup equipment, those Eighth Army divisions deploying to Korea would have been significantly less effective than they were. Almost 90 percent of their weapons and 75 percent of their automotive equipment came from the rebuild program.[26]

The shortage of recoilless rifles and 3.5-inch bazookas became critical when the arriving U.S. troops encountered Soviet-made T34/85 tanks. Bazookas had to be flown in from the United States. Of course, the best weapon to counter an enemy tank is another tank, but the Eighth Army divisions were equipped only with light M24s, no match for the T34 medium tank. Division tables of organization and equipment called for medium tanks, but the M24 had been issued instead because it would not damage the Japanese road system and was light enough to cross Japan's bridges. The call went out from Korea for medium tanks, and again rollup rebuilds proved critical. Sixty-five M4 Sherman tanks, all unserviceable, were available in rollup stocks in Japan. Three weeks after the July 4 call for help, a provisional company of seventeen rebuilt M4A3 tanks with 76-mm guns, manned by crews patched together in Japan, was en route to Korea. All sixty-five Shermans were rebuilt and sent to Korea, thirty-four of them within the first six weeks of the war. All early-model Shermans mounting low-velocity 75-mm guns had been up-gunned with high-velocity 76-mm cannon removed from rollup M18 tank destroyers.[27]

Perhaps even more critical than medium tanks to U.S. forces' survival, if not success, in the early months of the war was the availability of rollup ammunition stocks. No matter how plentiful, ammunition from the United States, except for small amounts of key items such as bazooka rockets that could be airlifted, would take weeks to arrive by ship. Fortunately, enough rollup ammunition from the Pacific had been renovated and stored in Japan to get through the early days of the fighting. Virtually all ammunition to sustain the first three months of fighting came from rollup stocks.[28] After that, stocks from the Zone of the Interior arrived in increasing amounts, but from September 1950 to the end of February 1951, slightly more than 51 percent of the ammunition (88,106 out of 172,466 tons) came from the fourteen ordnance ammunition depots and subdepots in Japan.[29]

To maintain command and control of its deploying forces, Eighth Army Headquarters moved to Korea, leaving a rear headquarters in Japan. As the Eighth Army's forces grew in Korea, responsibility for what was essentially a supporting logistics operation in Japan became increasingly burdensome. The Eighth Army was relieved of responsibility for Japan when the Japan Logistical Command (JLC) was established on August 25, 1950. Reporting to the Far East Command, the JLC was essentially a theater communications-zone organization.[30]

Operation Rebuild continued apace under Brigadier General Gerson K. Heiss, ordnance officer of the JLC. By the end of May 1951, fourteen depots, shops, and subdepots carried out armament and automotive rebuild, employing 1,164 ordnance officers and soldiers, 322 Department of the Army civilians, and 30,464 Japanese workers, not including subcontractor personnel.[31] As the war continued, not only rollup stocks ran through the rebuild process but also worn-out or battle-damaged vehicles and equipment shipped from Korea for overhaul. For example, 6,600 trucks and 11,700 truck engines returned to Japan for rebuild in the first year of the war.[32] Some vehicles and weapons were thus rebuilt two or more times. Later in the war, unserviceable vehicles were shipped to Japan from the United States for rebuild en route to Korea.[33]

By May 1, 1952, 98,831 automotive (general purpose) vehicles and 3,220 combat vehicles had been rebuilt, as had 699,224 automotive assemblies and 45,386 combat-vehicle assemblies. Also, 437,080 tires had been reclaimed through sectional patching and retreading.[34] By June 30, 1953, shortly before war's end, about 148,000 vehicles had been rebuilt.[35] This equipment was essential to the prosecution of the war. Vehicles and equipment did arrive from the United States, including new systems, once production was geared up again in 1952 and 1953, but an estimated 65 percent of the general-purpose automotive vehicles used during the war came from Operation Rebuild.[36] By mid-1952, 60 percent of the artillery, 71 percent of the infantry weapons, and 41 percent of the tanks used in Korea had come from the rebuild plants in Japan.[37]

The reclamation programs of the other technical services in Japan, while not on the scale of the Ordnance Corps' Operation Rebuild, nevertheless played a vital role as well. They, like the Ordnance Corps, established rebuild and renovation programs during the occupation period, then expanded that effort to support the war. The first technical service to establish a reclamation program was the Quartermaster Corps. Beginning in December 1945, the 236th Quartermaster Salvage Collecting Company at Kobe, Japan, began receiving and classifying salvaged matériel, turning over items in need of repair to the 217th Quartermaster Salvage Repair Company. By the end of 1946, these companies had received more than four million items, mostly from deactivating units. In August 1947, the Kobe Quartermaster Depot was established to continue this reclamation work, making heavy use of Japanese workers trained in quartermaster schools in Tokyo, Yokohama, and Kobe.[38]

Quartermaster salvage and reclamation continued during the Korean War. Through October 1952, the program had reclaimed more than 4.7 million pieces of clothing and textiles, 26,966 tents, 5,366 musical instruments, 263,328 pieces of furniture, 54,350 office machines, and 41,656 pieces of matériel-handling equipment.[39]

After the Ordnance Corps rebuild program, the engineer program was the next most extensive. Substantial amounts of engineer equipment were rounded up during Operation Rollup, and while numerically far less than the amount of ordnance matériel, rebuilding engineer equipment presented special problems. Ordnance matériel was fairly well standardized by type, meaning, for example, that all two-and-a-half-ton trucks were the same (although there were some differences based on the company of manufacture). Thus, all trucks of the same type could be rebuilt using the same assembly-line process. Engineering equipment was far less standardized. Engineers, for example, used about 250 models of engines versus about 20 different engines in Ordnance Corps trucks. The engineers needed to stock about 188,000 line items of repair parts to carry out their rebuild process, while the Ordnance Corps automotive rebuild needed only 44,000.[40]

Despite these challenges, in August 1948 the engineers forged ahead with their rebuild program, called BIG-9 (for Base Industrial Group, with the "9" representing the initial nine locations used for the rebuild). As with the Ordnance Corps rebuild program, Japanese workers had to be trained and rebuild facilities established. The engineer rebuild effort initially centered on the Yokohama Engineer Depot, but starting in September 1949 the rebuild was phased into new facilities at Sagami, where a Japanese tank production plant had been converted to engineer rebuild. The effort expanded further at war's outbreak, and by October 1951 more than twelve thousand Japanese workers at seventeen plants conducted engineer rebuild. In Fiscal Year 1951, approximately 60 percent of the engineer equipment and supplies used in Korea came from the engineer rebuild program.[41]

The Signal Corps began its program in 1946, rebuilding a modest 12,000 pieces of equipment such as radars, radios, and telephones.[42] By the end of October 1952, however, that total had grown to 322,579 pieces of equipment. The Medical Service rebuilt or reclaimed 3,175 pieces of equipment in 1946, a figure that rose to 31,419 by the end of October 1952. Because of these repairs and rollup medical supplies, sufficient stocks were on hand to support the first ninety days of the war.

The Transportation Corps' rebuild effort started in 1947 with the repair of 260 harbor craft at the Yokohama Transportation Corps Depot. By the end of October 1952, 2,599 watercraft and 102 locomotives and pieces of rolling stock had been rebuilt, not to mention 1,668 major components such as marine diesel engines and 12,092 subassemblies and navigation instruments. At the Chemical Corps's Chemical Base Depot at Camp Ojima between June 10, 1951, and April 30, 1952, 256,283 gas masks of all types, 205 smoke generators, 578 flamethrowers, 8,588 decontaminating apparatus, 342 gas alarms, and thousands of other items had been renovated.

This equipment was essential not only for the prosecution of the war in Korea; the use of rebuilt equipment proved cost-effective compared to the price of replacement items. Granted, rebuilt equipment did not have the service life of new equipment. Ordnance experts estimated that a rebuilt truck, for example, had 70 to 90 percent of the life expectancy of a new vehicle.[43] On the other hand, to rebuild a cargo truck in Japan cost about $1,560 compared to $6,000 for a new truck in the United States. A new jeep cost about $2,000, while the rebuild price was only $800.[44] The 98,831 general-purpose vehicles rebuilt by May 1, 1952, cost more than $110 million. Replacement costs would have been more than $200 million. The 699,224 automotive assemblies rebuilt by May 1, 1952, cost more than $57 million versus more than $201 million for new assemblies. Similar though smaller savings accrued for rebuilt combat vehicles and the equipment reclaimed by the other technical services.[45]

Beyond saving the United States considerable funds, Operation Rebuild and the other technical service reclamation programs had the additional benefit of boosting the Japanese economy, which had been struggling to recover from World War II. As of March 1951, approximately 135,000 civilians in Japan worked directly in support of the war in Korea, and a significant percentage of that number—about 30,000 in the case of Operation Rebuild alone—worked in the technical services' reclamation and rebuild programs.[46] These numbers do not include the substantial number of Japanese workers employed as subcontractors providing various goods and services in support of the war. For example, the need for trucks was so great that in August 1950, in addition to Operation Rebuild, contracts were let with Japanese manufacturers for sixty-eight thousand cargo and dump trucks for the Republic of Korea's army. Japanese companies produced dynamite and made fifty thousand trip flares. Japanese trucks and drivers transported equipment to the docks, where Japanese stevedores loaded the equipment onto what was often Japanese lighterage for shipment to Korea.[47]

Operation Rebuild and other war-related programs in Japan thus stimulated the stagnant Japanese economy and also, at least in the case of the rebuild and reclamation programs, saved the United States a great deal of money. Most important, however, rebuilt or reclaimed vehicles, weapons, ammunition, equipment, and spare parts were essential for equipping those Eighth Army divisions rushed to Korea to stem the North Korean advance. Follow-on rebuilt equipment was equally essential for replacing the initial heavy losses suffered by U.S. and South Korean forces.[48] Without the equipment from this unheralded logistics rebuild program, given how close United Nations forces came to being driven off the Korean peninsula in the summer of 1950, one can easily imagine a different outcome to the war.

Notes

1. Sources refer to this plan variously as "Rollup," "Roll-Up," or "Roll-up." For consistency, "Rollup" will be used.

2. James W. Hamilton, "Operation Reverse," *Army Transportation Journal* 2 (September 1946): 20; Japan Logistical Command Monograph, "Operation Rollup Operation Rebuild, 14 August 1945–30 June 1952" (Historical Section, Japan Logistical Command, July 29, 1952), 7–8, U.S. Army Military History Institute, Carlisle Barracks, Pennsylvania (hereafter cited as USAMHI).

3. Japan Logistical Command Monograph, 3–4.

4. Ibid., 30–31.

5. Hamilton, "Operation Reverse," 20–21.

6. Japan Logistical Command Monograph, 7.

7. For a discussion of the popular, and hence political, pressure to demobilize, see John C. Sparrow, *History of Personnel Demobilization in the United States Army* (1952; reprint, Washington, DC: Center of Military History, 1994), 141–70.

8. Ibid., 265.

9. Ibid., 273–77. Demobilization similarly disrupted the efforts of the Foreign Liquidation Commission. The testimony quoted here is from pp. 275–76.

10. Japan Logistical Command Monograph, 2, 12–15.

11. Ibid., 8–9; James A. Huston, *Guns and Butter, Powder and Rice: U.S. Army Logistics in the Korean War* (Selingsgrove, PA: Susquehanna University Press, 1989), 56–58, 148.

12. James F. Schnabel, *Policy and Direction: The First Year*, United States Army in the Korean War Series (1972; reprint, Washington, DC: Center of Military History, 1992), 54. The divisions were the 7th, 24th, and 25th Infantry Division and the 1st Cavalry Division, configured as an infantry division.

13. For a discussion of echelons of maintenance, see Peter S. Kindsvatter, "The Evolution of the Army's Echeloned Maintenance Doctrine," *Ordnance Magazine* (Fall 2003): 18–21, specifically p. 21 for echelons of maintenance in the 1950s.

14. Gerson K. Heiss, "'Operation Roll-up': How Japan Became an Ordnance Arsenal for Korea," *Ordnance Magazine* 36 (September–October 1951): 243; Japan Logistical Command Monograph, 37–40.

15. Technically, it was the Ordnance Department until the name changed to Ordnance Corps in 1950, but "Ordnance Corps" will be used.

16. Huston, *Guns and Butter*, 49–51. Technical services responsibilities for research, development, and procurement would largely go away with the establishment in 1962 of the U.S. Army Materiel Command as part of a major army reorganization. See James E. Hewes Jr., *From Root to McNamara: Army Organization and Administration, 1900–1963* (Washington, DC: Center of Military History, 1975), 316–65.

17. Japan Logistical Command Monograph, 15–22.

18. Tonnage statistics derived from ibid. For Korea it was 668,000 tons, "but slightly more than this was moved" (21); for the Philippines, 1.2 million tons (21); for the Marianas, "there were some half million measurement tons of supplies and equipment on Guam, and about half of this was excess to the command's needs [and hence included in rollup]" (16); and no statistics provided for the Ryukyus, although the rollup process there is briefly discussed (22). Brigadier General Gerson K. Heiss, the ordnance officer for the JLC and hence responsible for the vehicle rebuild program, claims that 63,000 vehicles were included in rollup and brought to Japan. See his "New Trucks for Old: Ordnance Assembly Line Rebuilds Vehicles in Japan," *Ordnance Magazine* 36 (November–December 1951): 485. William C. Farmer cites a figure of "more than 55,000 automotive vehicles" in his "Operation Rebuild," *Military Review* 32 (February 1953): 51.

19. For a discussion of Japanese worker train-up and plant preparation, see Japan Logistical Command Monograph, 41–45; Heiss; "Operation Roll-Up," 244; and Japan Logistical Command, "Ordnance Automotive Rebuild in Japan, FY 1951" (Office of the Chief of Ordnance, Headquarters, Japan Logistical Command, August 25, 1951), 84–86, 92–95, USAMHI.

20. Japan Logistical Command Monograph, 40–41.

21. "Ordnance Automotive Rebuild in Japan," 111.

22. A detailed and well-illustrated discussion of the truck rebuild process can be found in ibid., 6–81. The 100 to 80 ratio is from Japan Logistical Command Monograph, 49; the man hours figures are from p. 54.

23. Japan Logistical Command Monograph, 40, 57.

24. Huston, *Guns and Butter*, 137.

25. The arrival and commitment of these divisions is addressed in Roy E. Appleman, *South to the Naktong, North to the Yalu*, United States Army in the Korean War Series (1961; reprint, Washington, DC: Center of Military History, 2000). Although an operational history, Appleman's work is one of the few histories to note the importance of the rebuild program, albeit briefly (379–80).

26. Eighth U.S. Army Korea Monograph, "Logistical Problems and Their Solutions" (Historical Section, Eighth U.S. Army, n.d., covering the period June 25, 1950–April 1951), 7, USAMHI.

27. Japan Logistical Command Monograph, 57. In the Eighth Army Monograph, the statistics are slightly different, claiming that fifty-four (not sixty-five) tanks were available for rebuild (9).

28. Japan Logistical Command Monograph, i and 12–13.
29. Eighth Army Monograph, plate 3; Huston, *Guns and Butter*, 158.
30. Huston, *Guns and Butter*, 59–60.
31. "Ordnance Automotive Rebuild in Japan," 111.
32. Robert O. Shreve et al., "Combat Zone Logistics in Korea" (Operations Research Office, General Headquarters, Far East Command, ORO-T-15, November 10, 1951), 137, USAMHI.
33. Japan Logistics Command Monograph, 72. Unfortunately, no statistics are provided.
34. Ibid., 75.
35. Huston, *Guns and Butter*, 139.
36. Ibid.; Heiss, "New Trucks for Old," 489.
37. Huston, *Guns and Butter*, 140.
38. Japan Logistical Command Monograph, 33.
39. Ibid., 77.
40. Ibid., 34, 45.
41. Ibid., 63–64.
42. These statistics and those that follow for the Signal, Medical, Transportation, and Chemical rebuild programs are taken from charts in ibid., 76–82. See also Huston, *Guns and Butter*, 140–42.
43. Shreve, "Combat Zone Logistics," 136.
44. Heiss, "New Trucks for Old," 489.
45. Japan Logistical Command Monograph, 75. See pp. 76–80 for cost savings in the Engineer, Quartermaster, Signal, Medical, and Transportation rebuild programs.
46. Huston, *Guns and Butter*, 125.
47. Eighth Army Monograph, 12–15.
48. In the first year of the war, ordnance equipment losses alone by U.S. and South Korean forces included more than 2,000 jeeps, 900 three-quarter-ton trucks, 1,200 two-and-a-half-ton-trucks, 340 tanks, 390 howitzers, 3,300 machine guns, 1,600 submachine guns, 2,500 mortars, 3,900 rocket launchers, 500 recoilless rifles, and 43,100 rifles and carbines. See Huston, *Guns and Butter*, 126.

9
"Justice with Courage"
Considerations on the Weakness of British Imperial Power

Adam Norman Lynde

> We are paying very heavily now for failing to face the insurance premiums essential for the security of an Empire! This has usually been the main cause for the loss of Empires in the past.
> —Lord Alanbrooke, February 12, 1942

WARFARE IS COMMONLY DISCUSSED in terms of war aims and strategy, of statesmen and generals.* Yet war aims are not shaped merely by the dictates of international relations, be they political or economic. Nor can the ability to meet war aims through effective strategy be limited to the consideration of generals or campaigns. Whether a combatant is able to either conquer or resist is, in the words of Carl von Clausewitz, "the product of two inseparable facts, viz. *the total means at his disposal* and the *strength of his will*."[1] Thus, any assessment of a nation's war aims, the strategy it develops to attain them, and its success in doing so must take into consideration both the material resources available to that nation and the ability of that nation to mobilize those resources. It was this fundamental relationship between means and will on the one hand and the why and how of war on the other that led Clausewitz to define war as the continuation of politics, both domestic and international, by other means. Clearly, the former dictates the manner in which a war is waged far more than the latter, for it is a nation's domestic political situation that enables it to mobilize the material resources necessary for war. It is not enough to possess material resources, even in abundance. For war to be successfully undertaken, the ability to mobilize these

---

* Spelling, capitalization, and style points in this essay follow British guidelines at the author's request.

resources is equally necessary. This ability, Clausewitz's ominously Germanic will, represents the ability of the state to convince the nation of the necessity to provide these resources.

The military history of the British Empire stands as a testament to this relationship between means and will, and the extent to which an apparent abundance of the former may be negated if the latter is lacking. For three centuries, the geopolitical realities of the Empire, and in particular its strategic potential and limitations, shaped the understanding and decision making of Britain's political and military leadership. The most important of these realities were fiscal, military, and naval weakness. Such an assertion is perhaps contrary to the common perception of British strength in the eighteenth and nineteenth centuries. Britain's only defeat in the eighteenth century was the American War of Independence, and that, it is often argued, was an unwinnable situation akin to America's involvement in Vietnam and thus unique for the period. Moreover, defeat in 1783 was more than counterbalanced by victory in 1763 and 1815. Victory in the Seven Years' War, despite the subsequent loss of the American colonies, confirmed Britain's position as, in the somewhat redundant words of one historian, "the global superpower of the eighteenth century."[2] Historians such as John Brewer see this as a slightly earlier development, Britain having already become by the early eighteenth century "the military Wunderkind of the age."[3] Jeremy Black has chosen to see a later development, concluding that by 1815 "Britain became the strongest military power in the world, arguably the strongest at any time till then."[4] Despite disagreements over timing, what these historians share in common, aside from a triumphant rhetoric that echoes High Victorian historians and propagandists, is confidence in the extent of British economic, naval, and military power and the degree to which that power overshadowed all of the nation's European rivals.

Military and naval historians have generally welcomed these studies, and particularly Brewer's *The Sinews of Power*, for they have forced scholars in other fields in British history to acknowledge the importance of the land and sea forces to the history of the nation and its Empire. If there is a cardinal error that these studies have committed, however, it is the focus on effect to the neglect of cause. That is, they have focused on the dramatic outcomes of war, "the decisive British victories of Trafalgar at sea and Waterloo on land," and not so much ignored the institutional infrastructure of the forces that won these battles as they have assumed that, because these victories exist, the institutional infrastructure on which these institutions were based was fundamentally sound.[5] Yet if the scope of analysis is broadened, it becomes readily evident that such conclusions are hardly justified. It is not merely a matter of turning attention from the muddy plains of Belgium or the rough seas off Spain to the British war effort against Napoleonic France in its entirety. Rather, it is a matter of assessing the British war machine's operation and thus its effectiveness through much of the Empire's existence, and particularly the eighteenth and nineteenth centuries. In undertaking such an examination, based on the facts of British military and naval power—the Empire's ability to both prepare for and wage war—a necessary corrective is offered to those studies that simplistically assert the preeminence of British state power as evident on land and sea, in Europe and beyond.

Ubiquitous sword-bearing heroes camouflage the fact that, fundamentally, Britain's was an empire built on commerce and not armed force. This is not surprising, for its geographic position gave Britain an important advantage over its continental rivals in the overseas trade that fueled European expansion. Geography also meant that as an island group, and thus unlike its European rivals, Great Britain did not have to create large land forces to secure itself against invasion. The necessity for France and Spain to raise vast armies in order to defend themselves against the Prussians or Austrians, which in turn inhibited their ability to mount a successful invasion of Britain, played an important role in the defense of the British Isles, perhaps even a greater one than Britannia's hallowed wooden walls. Geography was a qualified benefit for military purposes, for its isolation, while bestowing physical defenses unrivaled in Europe save for the case of Switzerland, meant that England—even after union with Scotland in 1707 and Ireland in 1801—lacked the population from which to raise the forces necessary to meet such a threat. Geography likewise bred a cultural and thus somewhat unrealistic sense of security and, consequently, a political ideology that downplayed the necessity of maintaining large and expensive defense forces. Intimately related to this was the relationship among geography, overseas trade, and the wealth of the nation and its empire. Britain's geographic location played a central role in the construction of empire and the nation's eventual dominance of world trade. That the wealth thereby generated did not create a heavily armed, centralized state was due to the fact that throughout Britain's history, military and naval power was seen as inimical to mercantile interests. "Commercial men and military men," William Beckford—Jamaica merchant, former Lord Mayor of London, Member of Parliament (MP), and supporter of Pitt the Elder—told the House of Commons, "never did, nor never can agree."[6]

Large armies and navies need money, which means a large and intrusive state apparatus to collect taxes and custom duties. Large standing armies need soldiers, and Britain's abhorrence of large standing armies is well known. Often ignored, however, is the fact that large navies needed sailors, who could only be found in the merchant marine of the Empire. Thus, because of a fundamental distaste for and distrust of the state as much in its civil as its military manifestation, the Royal Navy was as much an object of concern as was the British army. Nor was such concern limited to ministerial opponents or narrow-minded backbenchers. Anticipating Clausewitz, in 1828 the *Naval and Military Magazine* drew attention to the role of state power, as represented by the navy, within "the circle of circumstance" formed by Britain's island status, political liberty, and commercial prosperity: "There wants but its isolation to protect and foster its domestic liberties, and its domestic liberties to support and extend its commerce, and its commerce to supply both the *materiel* and the *morale*—the money and the men—and to assert its flag; and the perpetuity of the dominion of the sea must flow out of the circle of circumstance!"[7]

The consequence of this circumstance that has been pointedly ignored by historians who stress the power of the British fiscal-military state is that the political realities of the British Empire—the will, in Clausewitzian terms, of not merely Whitehall but the political nation—prevented the full mobilization of its manpower resources for war. Nothing perhaps more clearly demonstrates the failure of both Brewer and Colley to truly understand the handicap under which the British government operated, and thus the military and naval weakness of the Empire, than their assertion that Britain implemented conscription in the eighteenth century. "In every major eighteenth-century war," asserts Brewer, "the government used conscription to swell the army's ranks."[8] "To beat the French [during the French Revolutionary Wars]," observes Linda Colley, "the British were obliged to imitate many of the devices of the French revolutionary state, and the challenge this presented to its existing order was a considerable one."[9] Such is perhaps an understandable conclusion to be drawn from the passage of the Supplementary Militia Act of 1796, the Defence of the Realm Act of 1798, and other legislation. However understandable, such a conclusion is incorrect: at no time in the eighteenth or nineteenth century did the British government seek to raise its armies or man its fleets through recourse to conscription. What contemporaries generally saw as "compulsory measures" were introduced. But be they militia ballots or press acts, they were limited in terms of the individuals they were intended to gather into the regular forces, while the life of such legislation was often limited to mere months. They were not conscription measures, nor were they seen as such, and only by recognizing this to be the case can the limits on the British state's ability to raise human resources for war be properly understood.[10]

The French Revolutionary and Napoleonic Wars represented Britain's greatest peril at the hands of a European foe until the twentieth century, and, accordingly, from 1793 successive ministries attempted to reform the recruiting system to better meet the crisis. Yet as late as 1807, the government observed that "the indispensable necessity . . . of adopting, without delay, some decisive measure for the augmentation of our Army; the produce of our present system of raising men not being more than sufficient to counter-balance the casualties of the service." Britain's civil and military leadership were not unaware of the measures necessary to achieve France's success in mobilizing manpower. Yet they were equally aware of the nation's cultural as much as political, and thus insurmountable, opposition to conscription. The same 1807 government memorandum went on to observe: "It is impossible to expect that any measure can be devised adequate to such an object, which shall not be liable to considerable objections, and which shall not excite, more or less, the opposition of some considerable class of interests, both in and out of Parliament."[11]

The reason for this was both clear and long-standing. Throughout Britain's history, regardless of the crisis facing it, the words of James Oglethorpe, penned in 1728 in opposition to the Naval Press, rang true: "[To] be pressed into the service, denied liberty, [is to be] turned to slaves . . . for slavery is nothing but service by force."[12] If Oglethorpe was a philanthropist in time of peace, Henry Dundas, variously Home Secretary, Secretary of State for War and the Colonies, and First Lord of the Admiralty under William Pitt the Younger, was a pragmatist in time of war. Yet even to him it was self-evident that "in a free country personal service cannot be compelled. Expedients to induce must be resorted to."[13] Likewise, the 1807 memorandum, written not only in time of war but when Napoleon was master of Europe, observed of any proposal to be made for alleviating recruiting woes: "taking it always for granted that we are not yet pressed to the adoption of an unqualified personal conscription." That it was always taken for granted that the time had not yet come for conscription illustrates not the shortsightedness of Britain's war leaders or, in the words of historian Richard Glover, that "her statesmen lacked the moral courage to take the men they need for victory by direct conscription for offensive service."[14] Rather, the position of the government demonstrated their understanding—better, it would seem, than that of subsequent historians—of the distinct limitations that domestic politics imposed on their ability to raise forces sufficient for the defense of the realm.

Given the constraints under which the state operated, its success in raising men was in many ways remarkable, for despite such obstacles as effective opposition to conscription, Britain did raise large land forces in wartime. At the height of the War of Austrian Succession, the British army numbered some 76,500 officers and men. By the end of the Seven Years' War, this figure had risen to 111,553. In 1782, the army reached a wartime peak for the century, fielding some 159,520 officers and men.[15] Before such impressive figures are accepted as symbolic of the strength of the British state, however, two important considerations must be attended to. First, these were wartime figures and thus temporary and achieved only under tremendous strain and effort. Second, despite such strain and effort, these numbers proved insufficient to meet Britain's strategic objectives. In May 1745 the British fielded a force of 23,000 under the Duke of Cumberland at the battle of Fontenoy. Although the battle lives on in British military history as one of the army's more glorious defeats, the British contingent was less than half an Allied army totaling 50,000 and even then had managed to take to the field only after the defenses of the Home Islands had been largely denuded. Wrote First Lord of the Treasury Henry Pelham to Lord of Trade Henry Fox two months later: "I think we have not left troops enough in this country to mount a guard at the royal palaces, nor to quell an insurrection or smuggling party of one hundred men."[16] Smuggling was an ongoing problem; insurrection would come later that year.

As with all armies at war, that of Britain suffered from disease and desertion, which accounted for far more loss than enemy fire and which left armies perpetually understrength.[17] Because part of the difficulty in making good such losses was directly related to the inadequacies of Britain's system of recruitment, a system that all involved knew was unlikely to change in the foreseeable future, the best some commanders could do was respond with equanimity and humor. In 1758, Lord Loudoun, commanding in North America, advised subordinates that "if we can get fighting men, we must not at present insist on either size or beauty." By way of consolation, Loudoun observed that reduced standards in America were all the more necessary, whereas in England "they [have] been forced to take all sorts of men to complete the regiments there."[18] Almost fifty years later, the infantry of the line, including Guards, numbered 106,466, all "perfectly efficient, and fit for any service." At the same time, however, the forces in the British Isles were deficient by no fewer than 47,464 men, with a mere 16,000 available divided among "56 skeleton battalions."[19] With Napoleon having defeated Prussia and Austria and cowed Russia, few in London saw any humor in the situation.

The greatest problem confronting British generals and statesmen, although the latter were also willing to factor in whinging on the part of the former, was dispersal. The campaigns of Marlborough had concentrated British military strength in Europe, as had the first Hanoverian war. By the 1750s, however, the increasing demands of the Empire made such concentration increasingly difficult, as evident in the exasperation with which Lord Ligonier, Commander-in-Chief, Great Britain, responded to the impassioned demands for reinforcement that he received from Germany in 1759: "We have prodigious regard for our friends in Germany, and a little in reserve for ourselves as well as America, East and West India, Gibraltar, Great Britain, Ireland, etc., etc., etc., etc."[20] Dispersal likewise affected operations overseas. Finding his command in Nova Scotia 466 men understrength, in 1757 Major General Peregrine Hopson proposed detaining the newly arrived battalion of Fraser's Highland Regiment in Halifax. Loudoun, whose command in New York was, between men "wanting" and sick, 1,800 short, strongly opposed this measure in terms that foreshadowed Ligonier's exasperation two years later: "Other services must be starved by it, and especially [as] I have not only the wide frontiers of the provinces of Virginia, Maryland, Pennsylvania, and New Jersies [i.e., the colonies of East and West Jersey], New

York, Connecticut, Rhode Island, Massachusetts, and New Hampshire to defend, but the offensive war to carry on besides."[21] Nor did the threatened dissolution of the Empire two decades later do anything to alleviate the problem. If anything, the global nature of the American War of Independence made it worse. At the time of its wartime peak in 1782, the British Army fielded its peak number in the Americas, 49,132. These were distributed unevenly between the Canadian command, New York, and what posts were still held in the southern colonies. The remaining 110,000 men in uniform were assigned to the defense of the Home Islands, Gibraltar, and the East and West Indies.[22]

When the French Republic declared war on Britain in 1793, the latter's army mustered 34,262 officers and men. Within a year it had risen to 70,570, and, by century's end, 120,000.[23] However much Revolutionary France may have ideologically threatened Britain's old order, the British Empire benefited materially when war was declared in 1793. Yet territorial acquisitions brought added strain to an already stressed system. In 1794 alone the British army lost 18,596 men killed in active service, the majority among the Leeward, Windward, and Charibee Islands, where Britain added at least a half dozen former French, Spanish, and Dutch colonies to its existing possessions. The majority of these losses were due to disease, which invalided a further 40,000 by 1796.[24] If operations farther north drew less blood, garrisons nonetheless had to be maintained in the Canadas, Nova Scotia, New Brunswick, and Newfoundland, while on the far side of the world, war with the Maratha required the deployment of troops to India. And then there was Ireland, where insurrection erupted on a scale not seen for more than a century, complete with intervention by the French. Although the '98 was brutally suppressed in short order, where two of the British commanders of this operation were soon to find themselves serving—General Gerard Lake in India and General Sir Ralph Abercromby in Egypt—speaks to the number and geographically dispersed nature of the threats confronting the Empire at this time.

More disconcerting than the number and nature of threats were the few resources available to meet them. In May 1799, the Duke of York, the Captain General, advised Dundas that although no fewer than 18,500 men were required to secure the Caribbean, the force then deployed was 8,219 "wanting to complete." If the garrisons of British North America were only some 1,800 short, of greater concern, given General Bonaparte's sojourn in Egypt, were those of the Mediterranean: Minorca was short only some 800 men, but Gibraltar was 1,741 understrength. That in reporting these shortages the Duke of York was not merely reflecting the army's wish list is apparent in the extreme measures taken to deploy what men were available. In England, the Foot Guards numbered 4,472, but for reasons that Henry Pelham would have understood all too well, the guarding of royal palaces was the least of their concerns. Their counterparts in the foot regiments mustered only 4,978. Although insurrection had been rife in Ireland less than a year before, by the spring of 1799 the Guards deployed there numbered only 1,880, the regular foot troops, "including Invalids," 6,139.[25] Nothing, perhaps, demonstrates the strains that the dispersal of its forces imposed on the British war machine more than its commitment to operations in Europe. In June 1799, Britain signed a treaty with Tsar Paul to land 18,000 men in French-dominated Holland, the same number committed by Russia. That is, while the British army of the 1790s in its entirety numbered almost twice that of the 1740s, it deployed fewer men in Europe than had served under the Duke of Cumberland. Not surprisingly, the Duke of York's Helder expedition fared as badly as Cumberland's on the Rhine.[26]

Britain's manpower shortages meant that ensuring the security of the Home Islands and the Empire had to be balanced with possible continental commitments. That this often proved a near-impossible task for the regular forces was well recognized by Britain's war leaders. Like the army, the navy suffered from acute manpower shortages, and for many of the same reasons. Indeed, while the army is often seen as the constitutionally challenged service, for the merchant classes of Britain the manpower requirements of the navy posed a far greater material threat to their prosperity. Influencing Parliament as it did, the merchant interest ensured that the needs of the Royal Navy suffered accordingly. If the French trailed the British in naval combat, they proved progressive, at least in an administrative sense, in their efforts to man their fleets more effectively. As early as 1696, the inscription marine required all French merchant seamen to register with the state for potential call-up in the royal French navy. Being voluntary, the inscription proved a failure, but it was not for this reason that the British Parliament rejected the measure. Rather, it was the view that, in the words of MP Sir John Barnard, were Britain to adopt such a registry, "a sailor and a slave will be terms of the same significance."[27] Although the premier historian of the mid-eighteenth century Royal Navy, Daniel Baugh, has dismissed Barnard's "magnificent nonsense," the fact remains that not only did the 1740 Registry Bill fail to pass Parliament but for the next century and a half the issue of effective naval recruitment remained unresolved.[28]

Culturally, the most resonant image of the Royal Navy is perhaps the press gang. At the time of its operation it was the greatest symbol of the state's power to compel service, yet its effectiveness proved the diametric opposite to the disdain with which it was held. Naval recruitment was crippled by the conundrum that as important as a well-manned fleet was to the security of the nation, an equally well-manned merchant marine was essential to the wealth upon which the operation of the state depended in war and peace. "Our calamity," said the Prince Consort about the Royal Navy's manning problems at the outbreak of the Crimean War, "is our prosperity."[29] Large numbers of experienced and therefore valued sailors, the very men whom a naval registry would have accounted for had ever such been legalized in Britain, were for the most part thus protected from the press. A more cynical age accustomed to the powers of a centralized state might assume that in time of crisis legal niceties would be ignored. The figures, however, tell a different story. Between 1755 and 1757, the Royal Navy raised some 70,566 men. Of these, only 16,953 were obtained through the press, barely enough to make good the losses to the fleet through battle and general wear and tear, as suggested by the fact that in 1757, while 4,295 men were pressed, 5,796 seamen deserted.[30] It was thus for practical reasons, reflecting the failure of the impressment system as much as political, that Lord Auckland, First Lord of the Admiralty, opined in 1848: "The French will have their conscription — we cannot resort to impressment."[31]

Like the army, the navy at war reflected the ability of the British state to raise large numbers in time of crisis. In 1754, the fleet mustered 9,797 seamen, while by 1757 the number had risen to 60,548.[32] The subsequent experience of the navy, however, is also suggestive of the extent to which it shared with the army fundamental recruiting problems. In 1759, the navy mustered 77,265, just over 7,000 short of the number actually approved by Parliament. The latter figure remained stable at between 80,000 and 85,000 until 1763, when it dropped to 75,000.[33] What such figures demonstrate is that after a period of rapid expansion, the navy's ability to raise manpower stalled for want of measures more effective than voluntary enlistment or the press. This fact is of all the more consequence when one considers that the obligations imposed on the fleet by the war did not diminish after the fleet reached its peak strength in 1759. North Americans tend to see the latter year as the climax of the Seven Years' War. While not entirely incorrect, this view ignores the subsequent entry of Spain into the war and the consequent deployment of British naval power in places as distant as the West Indies and the Philippines. Even before this expansion of the naval war, the strains under which the Admiralty operated were evident. Ordered to blockade Brest in 1758, when the entire fleet mustered 70,014, Admiral Edward Boscawen found it necessary to strip first-raters in a vain attempt to man his forty-five-ship squadron. When the squadron eventually sailed, it left twenty-two vessels in port for want of crews.[34]

As in the case of the army, therefore, the failure to raise adequate manpower had a direct bearing upon the operations of what is traditionally perceived to have been Britain's first line of defense. Again as with the army, this situation was not unique to the Seven Years' War. In March 1805 Dundas, now Lord Melville and First Lord of the Admiralty, noted that while the Royal Navy carried 108,000 seamen and Marines, this number was "greatly inadequate to the exigency of the present moment." Although Melville would shortly resign in the midst of a financial scandal, his successor would express similar concerns for the strength of the navy. In August 1805, Lord Barham wrote of his frustration "to see a country like ours disgraced, its trade exposed and its coasts open to the French for want of 20,000 men."[35] Attempting to overcome the difficulties created by these manpower shortages, the Admiralty found that it was forced to neglect the more numerous, and in many ways more important, smaller vessels of the fleet in order to send the larger ships-of-the-line to sea. The consequent shortage of frigates concerned many squadron commanders including Horatio Nelson, who complained that the dearth of frigates severely hampered his operations. Nelson believed that he needed at least eight frigates and three fast brigs in order to properly watch the enemy forces at Cadiz, but he preferred to have ten frigates and four brigs "to do this service well." At the time, he had only two frigates and no brigs, which, he told Secretary of the Navy William Marsden, "makes me very uneasy." Writing at the same time to the Secretary of State for War and the Colonies, Nelson not only complained of the shortage of frigates but also that, of those he had, "not one [was] with the fleet." As a consequence, Nelson was "most exceedingly anxious for more eyes." Without frigates, the Royal Navy was rendered blind, allowing enemy fleets or, as in the case of the French invasion of Egypt, entire expeditionary forces to roam "British dominated" seas unmolested. "The last [enemy] fleet was lost to me for want of frigates," Nelson advised Castlereagh. "God forbid this should."[36]

The outcome of Nelson's predicament is telling in terms of both the extent of British weakness and the extent to which historians have ignored it. Barely two weeks after Nelson wrote to the government, he died fighting the Battle of Trafalgar. It is perhaps a matter of debate whether the latter remains so treasured an event in the English-speaking world because it was so important a victory over Napoleon—especially given the Emperor's particularly notable success in Central Europe later that same year—or because of the spectacle of a hero dying at the moment of victory. Had Nelson survived, it is evident in how his concerns continued to be expressed by other officers, including those who served with him, that he would have continued to berate the government concerning the fleet's weakness in frigates. Three days after Trafalgar, Barham advised Pitt that for "some weeks past" the Admiralty had been struggling to have "two line of battle squadrons at sea." Lord Cornwallis, it was hoped, would soon sail with twenty-five ships, two more than had sailed under Lord Boscawen forty-seven years earlier, although in 1758 Britain had a far smaller fleet to draw upon. "More than this cannot be done," wrote Barham, offering an explanation that the late hero of Trafalgar would have appreciated, "as it would be bad policy to go further than we have done in stripping the frigates."[37]

Nelson's victory and particularly his heroic death have enabled history to ignore the fact that Trafalgar did nothing to lessen the incessant manpower problems that confronted the navy and to ignore the fact that when Lord

Collingwood brought the damaged vessels of Nelson's squadron home for repair, their crews were not feted as heroes but instead were ordered to join ships "now ready in port for any service, but which it has not been possible hitherto to get to sea."[38] It is a matter of speculation whether Nelson, as a professional naval officer, would have welcomed such misplaced attention. As a gentleman interested in his public reputation, and thus not unlike any other officer of the navy or army, Nelson's professional pique would in all likelihood have been assuaged by the extent to which his last great victory, and with it his name, has become part of the foundation of British national identity. Less fortunate at the time and in the judgment of history was Admiral John Byng, whose fleet failed to prevent the fall of Minorca to the French in 1756. Tellingly, in his subsequent court-martial, Byng was acquitted of the charge of unduly delaying the departure of his squadron, on the grounds that he lacked sufficient manpower.[39] Acquittal on this one charge did not prevent his conviction under the Twelfth Article of War, that he failed to do his utmost to either defeat the French fleet or relieve Minorca; his execution on the quarter-deck; or his subsequent condemnation by historians.[40] Yet if, in the words of Voltaire, Byng suffered *"pour encourager les autres,"* it is unlikely that the true audience, sitting proudly in the Commons or squirreled away in their warehouses and counting offices or, for that matter, writing triumphant histories of the Georgian Navy, got the point.

Wartime figures are a misleading gauge of fundamental military strength, for although empires may be won through war, they must be maintained in peacetime. To do so, Britain fielded through the eighteenth century, on average, little more than 40,000 officers and men. Prussia, with something of a quarter of Britain's population, fielded a force almost three times as large. Yet while Frederick the Great concerned himself with the affairs of central Europe, the ministers of the British Crown found themselves responsible not merely for the defense of the United Kingdom but also for that of the East and West Indies and North America. The territorial acquisitions that began at the end of the eighteenth century and continued through the nineteenth necessitated a larger peacetime establishment than had existed before in British history, averaging 250,000 all ranks. It might be assumed that the considerable growth in Britain's male population assisted the state in meeting this challenge, and such might have been the case were not the traditional restraints on the state's exercise of compulsive power as strong in 1860 as they had been in 1760. Thus, while between 1815 and 1910 Britain's male population more than doubled, on average the proportion under arms in peacetime amounted to barely more than 1.3 percent of the adult male population.[41]

The disparity between Britain's wartime and peacetime strength is essential in any assessment of the Empire's military power and is commonly ignored by historians.[42] In making statements concerning the strength of the British war machine, historians have generally cited wartime figures that, given the constraints under which the government operated, were admittedly impressive. Impressive, too, was the rapidity with which the state demobilized these forces with the advent of peace. Averaging some 30,000 officers and men during the 1750s, the army more than tripled in size during the Seven Years' War. Yet, before the ratification of the 1763 Peace of Paris, and despite the fact that in Bengal alone Britain found itself, through its East India Company surrogate, responsible for a population three times its own, the Regular Army had been reduced to just over 45,000. This reduction had its precedent in the conclusion of the Wars of Spanish and Austrian Succession and in turn served as precedent for like policy following the American War of Independence, the French Revolutionary Wars, and the Napoleonic Wars. At the end of the latter, the army stood at approximately 300,000 men. Citing the need to maintain 30,000 in France and replenish exhausted foreign garrisons, not to mention the ongoing war with the Gurkhas and the likelihood of yet another war with the Marathas, the Duke of York recommended the maintenance of a peacetime force of 152,500. While the government was sympathetic, Parliament was not, and the army was reduced to 149,000. By 1817 it had been reduced to 123,000. In 1821 a further 12,000 officers and men were struck from the rolls, with two cavalry regiments disbanded and all infantry regiments reduced in numbers.[43] Four years later the nadir for the century was reached when the effective strength of the army totaled 99,718. This policy of reduction continued into the twentieth century. At the conclusion of the Boer War in 1902, the army stood at 383,547 officers and men. In short order, no fewer than 124,000 were given their discharge.[44] With the end of World War I, the army was reduced from 3.5 million in 1919 to 370,000 by the end of 1920,[45] this despite the fact that the collapse of the Ottoman Empire and the creation of the League of Nations Mandate System meant that the British Empire experienced its greatest single territorial expansion since the end of the Seven Years' War. To maintain the British presence, London deployed some 200,000 men, more than at any time in the eighteenth century but less than in the nineteenth.[46]

A great part of the difficulty in assessing British military strength in peacetime relates to the figures employed when making such a calculation. As an example, we might turn to the reductions that followed the Seven Years' War. At the height of the conflict, the army's regular foot regiments numbered 133 battalions in 126 regiments. At war's end, these had been reduced to 71 battalions in 69 regiments, a reduction by almost half but nonetheless an improvement over the standing of the army at war's outbreak, when it had fielded a mere 49 battalions in 48 marching regiments.[47] Yet at the same time, we find King George III proudly reporting that although Britain fielded twenty more regiments than it had at the opening of the Seven Years' War, the cost to the state was "some hundred pounds cheaper" than at the end of the War of Austrian Succession.[48] How this was the case is evident by considering not the total number of formations but their individual strength. In May 1763, all regular battalions were reduced from an established strength of 700 officers and men to 550.[49] This was not the only reduction during the decade that preceded the American War of Independence, and the continual weakening of the army during this period speaks to both the weakness of the state generally and the hazards of perceiving strength where it does not exist.

The appearance of strength where weakness in fact exists was also evident in the case of Ireland. During the eighteenth century the British government maintained a strategic reserve in Ireland intended to support the Protestant Ascendancy and with it the authority of the British Crown. Parliamentarians in Westminster had little reason to oppose the Irish Establishment, as its upkeep, including its general staff, was paid from Irish revenues. In 1766, the Irish Establishment consisted of twenty-seven marching regiments in addition to a dozen horse regiments. At the same time, nineteen regiments of foot and sixteen of horse were deployed in Scotland and England, forming the British Establishment. There were fourteen foot regiments in North America but none of horse. In comparison to other parts of the Empire, therefore, the Irish Establishment would appear an impressive force, clearly the larger in terms of foot regiments, with only Britain slightly besting it in terms of horse. Yet appearances can be deceiving. The numerical strength of the Irish Establishment was set by statute at 12,000 all ranks (horse, foot, and ordnance). In North America, despite the absence of horse regiments, the army maintained 9,000 officers and men, or three-quarters the manpower, with half the formations, of the Irish Establishment.[50]

The disparity in real numbers between Ireland and North America was a consequence of the end of the Seven Years' War, when regiments in the Irish Establishment were reduced to 297 officers and men per battalion, little more than a third their wartime strength and little more than half the peacetime strength of other foot battalions in Britain and the Empire. The fewer regiments stationed in England, Scotland, and America not only fielded more men than those in Ireland, but the latter were little more than weak cadres that required considerable time to be brought up to strength before being deployed overseas. Inevitably, this posed considerable problems for War Office plans to rotate regiments, a policy necessitated by the unprecedented size of the peacetime deployment of the army after 1763. The solution arrived at, however, only made military sense if the fundamental problems with which British planners had to contend are taken into consideration. In 1769, the Irish Parliament approved the increase of the Establishment to 15,000. However, insurmountable obstacles to effective recruiting remained, particularly for the peacetime army. Thus, while regimental strength in Ireland increased to 484 all ranks, elsewhere in the Empire regiments were reduced to that level from the existing 550.[51] The army was therefore smaller than at the end of the Seven Years' War when, in December 1770, war loomed with Spain over the Falkland Islands. To meet this crisis, all foot battalions were ordered augmented to 737 all ranks. Recruiting parties had barely begun to prowl the countryside, however, when the crisis passed. Despite such a close call, the government did not subsequently take measures to strengthen its peacetime forces. Rather, in March 1771 all foot battalions were ordered reduced to 477 officers and men, a smaller figure than not only the 1763 reduction but also that which had followed the increase of the Irish Establishment in 1770.[52] It was with this force of skeleton battalions that, in five short years, the Empire would confront rebellion in America.

The fact that individual battalions were statutorily weaker in peacetime than in wartime is important in assessing the strength of the British Empire because, regardless of the century, regardless of the empire, peacetime standing armies are as subject to the erosion of manpower as armies in wartime. If death from enemy fire is a risk not run by the peacetime soldier, armies nonetheless suffered from what historian John Houlding presciently described as "the friction of peace": among other factors, losses through death from disease (and also suicide or murder), through incapacitation by injury, and especially through desertion. Medical care in the armed forces improved appreciably over the nineteenth century as it did for the public as a whole. Yet medical knowledge, and thus the quality of health care, remained limited, and death and incapacitation rates due to disease remained higher for both the public and serving personnel than a later age would find tolerable.[53] Desertion, too, remained a problem. Particularly hard struck were garrisons near white, if not necessarily English-speaking, civilian populations. The American colonies proved especially problematic in this regard during the 1760s, while the proximity of the American Republic posed desertion problems for British North America's garrisons for the century thereafter. The friction of peace thus ensured that the vast majority of peacetime regiments, by statute upwards of half their wartime strength, remained below their established peacetime strength.[54] Losses through death, desertion, or discharge meant that it was extremely difficult if not impossible to recruit regiments to even the small numbers allowed by Parliament. In 1862, recruiting and transfer of East India Company troops brought an increase to the army of 24,240 men. At the same time, however, death, discharges, and desertion accounted for the loss of 18,576, meaning a real increase of only 5,664. The calculation, however, was not always in the state's favor: in 1868, an increase of 18,281 was offset by a decrease of 22,535.[55]

Peacetime friction was exacerbated by dispersal, a factor that the British forces, by virtue of their imperial mandate, suffered to a greater extent than any of their European rivals. The notorious American command, the cause of much of the constitutional angst that would destroy the First British Empire, numbered little more than nine thousand souls deployed between Placentia and Pensacola on a north-south axis and the Delaware and the Mississippi on an east-west axis. For much of its existence in the American colonies, the British army found itself dispersed in penny packets of a few companies or less. Reporting the condition of Halifax in May 1776, Governor Francis Legge advised Lieutenant General Thomas Gage that as a result of recruiting shortfalls and the detachment of work parties, the 65th Foot's three companies in garrison fielded only forty-nine effectives among them. Although Legge expressed understandable concern for "the number of troops we have to depend upon in case this province should prove refractory," the state of the American command was not unique but rather was shared with the British Establishment.[56] There, the absence of adequate barrack facilities outside of London or Edinburgh required the distribution of regiments among a number of towns and villages, which made company, let alone battalion, exercise impossible, as did deployment on antismuggling or riot control duties. If during the course of the nineteenth century the construction of barracks and depots enabled a greater concentration of the army at home, at the dawn of the twentieth century the peacetime army still found itself conducting major field exercises with battalions well below their established strength. Such was to be expected of a force that listed some seventeen thousand men dispersed on either permanent or daily casual employments of such military necessity as cooks, waiters, or servants.[57]

Fighting is one thing, preparedness is another, and the impact of the army's insufficient and dispersed manpower resources as well as the consequent ability of the Empire to confront effectively either foreign or domestic threats were evident in a report filed in 1750 by Major General Gervais Parker, who as commanding general in Ireland described a review held at Kilkenny as an event that "would make a dog spew."[58] Even with allowances for a less bureaucratic age, and thus one that permitted colorful if brutal honesty, Parker's observation is suggestive of the extent that through the eighteenth and nineteenth centuries, the British lion proved itself a three-legged beast that invariably encountered defeat at the outset of war. Such defeat, moreover, was the consequence less of the preparedness of the enemy than the weakness of the redcoats dispatched to the field of battle. Peacetime regimental strength being clearly inadequate for war, at the onset of any crisis the government scrambled frantically to raise the necessary forces. The inevitable result was the deployment of formations that consisted primarily of men drafted from other regiments and who thus, if experienced, were nonetheless unfamiliar with their new comrades. By far the majority of these formations, however, consisted of raw recruits who had precious little training and no experience of the horror of war. Rebel victories in the Jacobite Rising of 1745—the Battle of Prestonpans lasted "about five minutes"—were directly attributable to the hastily raised and inadequately trained condition of

Hanoverian forces. A decade later, Major General Edward Braddock was killed in action and his army suffered "bloody defeat and rout" on the Monongahela River for largely the same reasons.[59] In the first decades of the twentieth century, "the perennial shortage of men" continued to hamper the army's ability to prepare for war. During the army exercise of 1913, Sir John French theoretically commanded four infantry divisions and a cavalry division, but in fact only some forty-seven thousand men were present. While an improvement over peacetime training as conducted in previous centuries, it may be reasonably questioned whether such an exercise, being some twenty thousand understrength in infantry alone, adequately prepared the general, staff, and regimental officers for the conflagration into which they would be thrown within a year's time. Expressing a sentiment with which any officer attempting to train soldiers on the eve of the War of Austrian Austrian Succession, Seven Years' War, American War of Independence, French Revolutionary War, or Crimean War would have found sympathy, Sir William Robinson described peacetime training before World War I as "largely a case of trying to make bricks without straw."[60]

Manpower shortages in war and peace formed a major weakness of the British Empire. Yet military power, the total means at a combatant's disposal, is not to be measured in manpower alone. Soldiers and sailors alike must be fed, clothed, housed, and, yes, armed. In this respect, Britain's shortfall in personnel was by no means compensated by reduced cost—or, more to the point, by an increased willingness to meet that reduced real cost—that such a shortfall would perhaps suggest. There can be little doubt that except perhaps for Spain, the British Empire was the wealthiest in history. Yet cash in the city should not be equated with military and naval power at Whitehall. The Commons, having gained authority over the raising of public monies with the Glorious Revolution and being an arena dominated by the nation's landed and mercantile interests, proved a tight-fisted financier of empire in peacetime and only slightly less so in times of crisis or war. With regard to what largely insufficient funds were raised for the Crown's land and sea forces, the Treasury reveled in the role of Grecian chorus, croaking relentlessly and stridently about the need for fiscal restraint and "retrenchment." The desire "to run Imperialism on the cheap" was thus by no means unique to Winston Churchill.[61] The parsimony of both the politicians and bureaucrats was one feature of the British Empire that remained constant through the three centuries of social, economic, and technological change that marked its history. It was the necessity of responding to the monotones of the Grecian chorus that was in part responsible for the Native American insurrection of the early 1760s and, eighty years later, the extermination of an army in Afghanistan.[62]

The material condition of the army merely exacerbated the problem of dispersal. With regiments divided into companies and platoons, drill on the battalion level, let alone the brigade level, proved impossible, while in many cases the simple requirements of daily subsistence—relentless repair to buildings and outworks and the gathering of fuel—made even the performance of platoon exercises a luxury. Not that the equipment with which the army was expected to perform these exercises was in much better shape than the quarters in which they were housed. As befit a nation of shopkeepers, the basic equipment of the soldier—coat, cross belts, and musket or rifle—was replaced only in times of absolute necessity. Perhaps the most extreme example of this was the Black Watch, whose battalions were initially dispatched to suppress rebellion in America with wooden ramrods for their muskets despite the fact that such had not been standard issue for at least forty years.[63] Although iron ramrods were issued before the Highlanders sailed, their predicament speaks volumes of the impact that the necessity to economize had on the fitness of the peacetime army. Even when the arms were serviceable, effective peacetime training was not assured. In the age of linear warfare, ball cartridges were often limited to a half dozen rounds per man per year, while the twentieth-century soldier fared little better. Despite the importance of the Boer War in demonstrating the need for aimed and controlled firepower, the increase in the ammunition allowance per cavalryman from 150 to 300 rounds, and 200 to 300 for each infantryman, "only lasted as long as the surplus stocks of wartime ammunition."[64] Thus, an observation of the Georgian army's premier historian holds true for not merely the eighteenth but subsequent centuries as well: "The arms carried in the regiments—especially in the foot—were frequently unserviceable and often unsafe, while the supply of ammunition in peacetime was quite insufficient for proper training."[65]

The weakness of the army in war and peace would seem to be of little or no matter given the importance of the Royal Navy to the creation and preservation of British imperial power. Britain was, after all, an island group, and therefore its economic and political power was based on seaborne trade. Thus, during not only its height but in the nostalgia that has continued unabated despite the dissolution of the British Empire and the diminution of the nation's status as a world power, the navy has held a prominent place in Britain's cultural identity. As a weapon of a seafaring empire, the fleet played an important role in the expansion and defense of Britain's mercantile trade. Yet as has already been illustrated with regard to the Admiralty's manpower problems in wartime, the relationship between the state and the mercantile interests of the nation was marked by contradiction. Merchants could not but appreciate the protection that the Royal Navy offered and thus voted the necessary revenue measures as the government requested during wartime. As important as it was, however, the navy was also a competitor in the most valuable commodity of the overseas trade: manpower. Thus, these same merchant interests, even as they cheered on the Ministry to conquer more French and Spanish colonies and sang choruses of "Heart of Oak" when in their cups, ensured that Parliament passed measures to protect specific classes of merchant seamen from service in the navy in almost the same breath as they voted the funds required to expand the fleet. Once the crisis of war had passed and it was time to reap the profits from conquest of foreign colonies, the navy was seen not as a friend to the merchant community but as an unnecessary drain on its profits, and not merely in terms of the customs and excise duties levied to pay for it but in its demands for seaman who, in the view of the countinghouses of London, Liverpool, and Edinburgh, could be more profitably employed in the merchant marine. Thus, with the advent of peace the sea service found its numbers cut as did the army, if not more quickly and even more deeply. Reductions following the War of Austrian Succession, which in fact had begun in 1739 as the War of Jenkins' Ear—a trade war with Spain in the truest sense of the term—meant that when the navy began to prepare for war again in 1754, it mustered fewer than 8,000 seamen. Rhetoric about the navy being the constitutionally safe and thus the more valued service is put into perspective when it is remembered that at the same time the army was more than three times as large. At the conclusion of the Seven Years' War, the navy experienced reductions even more drastic than those of the army. In 1762 it mustered 81,929, while by 1764 the figure had dropped to 17,415.[66] As with the army, reductions in personnel and the decommissioning of ships continued through the 1760s, meaning that the navy found itself as unprepared as the army when rebellion erupted in America, to be soon followed by global war. At its peak during the Napoleonic Wars, the fleet mustered some 200,000 men. Manpower reductions began after what proved to be Napoleon's penultimate defeat in 1814, and by 1816 the fleet mustered only 25,196 seamen and marines.[67]

Unlike the army, the strength of the peacetime navy cannot be assessed with reference to manpower alone. As naval historians are fond of noting, for much of its history the Royal Navy was "the largest industrial unit of its day in the Western world." Contemporaries were well aware of this but did not share the glee of subsequent generations, for they also realized, with no small amount of concern, that the navy was "by far the most expensive and demanding of all the administrative responsibilities of the State."[68] The cost of maintaining the navy was felt not only in the pocketbooks of the landed interest in the form of the land tax or the professional and working classes through taxes on everything from windows to cider but was also borne by the merchant classes through customs and excise duties. Out of a desire to reduce government expenditure and with it not only taxation but also the exercise of state power in general, Parliament demanded that the peacetime navy, as much as if not more so than the army, function according to Treasury demands for retrenchment and economy. Thus, the strength of the navy in peacetime is not to be measured in manpower alone but also in pounds sterling. To maintain not merely the fleet but also its necessary support services, the government expended more than £7 million at the end of the Seven

Years' War. By 1766 this figure had been reduced to just under £3 million and by 1769 to £1.5 million.[69]

The characteristics of the sea service meant that the impact of these cuts was particularly severe. In peacetime, battalions of foot and regiments of horse could be dispersed about the countryside and quartered in public houses, thus keeping the expense to the state at a minimum. Mobilization of naval personnel, by contrast, meant concentration with all of its incumbent costs, while dispersal in the manner of the army defeated the purpose of keeping a ship's complement on the pay books. Thus, the reduction of manpower meant the withdrawal of warships from service. Whether sloops or ships of the line, the latter represented costs not found with land forces. In effect, each ship maintained by the navy was, in military terms, a miniature fortress. Each necessitated expenditures covering not only the subsistence and pay of personnel but also the physical repair and the provision of its armament. The policy of reducing manpower as part of an overall policy of economy meant, as one example, that the number of ships of the line dropped from 214 in 1815 to 80 in 1817.[70] Upon becoming First Lord of the Admiralty in 1771 after a particularly severe period of retrenchment, Lord Sandwich launched an aggressive revitalization program for the navy. Yet in the matter of funding, he had to abide by the wishes of Lord North, his prime minister, who reminded him that this was a "time of profound peace" and therefore "this was a time, if ever there was a time, for a reasonable and judicious economy."[71] Thus, despite his best efforts, Sandwich was able to ensure the construction of only twenty-two ships of the line between 1770 and 1777, while twenty-one were removed from service. In the words of his biographer, "Sandwich had more or less kept up with decay."[72] An additional cost that ships created for the navy was the consequence of being built and refitted in yards that not only had to be maintained but also had to be supplied with matériel and skilled artisans. As may be expected of a country that, philosophically at least, was the birthplace of capitalism, the government turned to private yards—outsourcing or, in modern military parlance, contracting—to build and maintain a substantial part of the fleet. Of the ten vessels completed before 1775 under Sandwich's program, five were laid down in merchant yards.[73]

The consequences of the Treasury's quest for savings were evident not merely in the reduction of manpower or ships but also in the establishment and maintenance of overseas bases. The farther from home waters, the fewer existed, and those that did were badly maintained. By 1887, Britain maintained more than 150 naval bases worldwide. The majority of these, reflecting the technological metamorphosis of naval power, were coaling stations, in many cases overshadowed by the presence of commercial interests. At the same time there existed only four naval bases protected by an imperial fortress that, supported by a military garrison, were thus capable of providing succor to squadrons of any substantial size:

Gibraltar, Malta, Bermuda, and Halifax.[74] For the most part, the fortresses were established not as a projection of British imperial power but as a strategic response to enemy threats within what was perceived to be a British sphere of interest. Gibraltar and Malta were important not merely for the security they gave to the British position in the Mediterranean but also because of the importance of the latter to the balance of power in Europe. Halifax, the premier Royal Navy base on the Atlantic coast of North America until the beginning of the twentieth century, was founded in response to the French construction of Louisbourg in nearby Cape Breton. British acquisition of Louisbourg by treaty in 1763 led to the closure and eventual deconstruction of its military and naval facilities. Not that the facilities at Halifax were superior; on the contrary, the movement of the British against New York after the evacuation of Boston was a species of flight-forward dictated by the inability of Halifax's facilities to host the military and naval forces gathering to crush rebellion in the colonies. In the Royal Navy's cruising area on the other side of the world, no facilities on the order of the home bases or even Halifax were established until the prolonged construction of the base at Singapore in the 1920s. Until that time, after nearly three centuries in the eastern seas, the Royal Navy lived vicariously through the modest port facilities of the East India Company or such intermittently friendly powers as Holland and Portugal.[75]

Given this tale of difficulty and woe, anyone familiar with Britain's record of success on land and at sea might reasonably wonder how such was accomplished. The answer is simple: recognizing the limitations that confronted their plans, Britain's war leaders knew they had to be creative. Many options were pursued, some successfully, some not. Yet even when successful, Britain's leaders were limited in their ability to counterbalance the considerable weaknesses of the Empire. One such option was the employment of foreign troops. The German forces employed in the American War of Independence are perhaps the most well-known example, being deployed not only in America but Gibraltar as well. Before then, in the War of Austrian Succession, Hessian and Hanoverian troops had been deployed in England to counter invasion and maintain domestic order, while Dutch soldiers had accompanied William of Orange when he assumed the English Crown in 1688. The King's German Legion (KGL) likewise formed an important part of British forces send to the Peninsula and Belgium during the Napoleonic Wars. The KGL, being made up of refugees, had more in common with the Free French of World War II than the Hessians of the American War of Independence, who, if not mercenaries, nonetheless served on the orders of their prince, who was paid by the British Crown. Thus, the nationalist sentiments unleashed by the Napoleonic Wars meant that foreign troops were rarely an option for British planners after 1815. Likewise, while the Royal Navy was in many ways a floating United Nations, drawing on foreign nationals to a far greater extent than was conceivable in the army, these, while adding a romantic multicultural hue to the fleet, hardly counterbalanced the latter's continual shortages in manpower.

More successful and thus more long-lived was the use of forces from within the Empire. From almost the moment of its inception, the British Empire was both expanded and defended as much by local forces—indigenous and European—as it was by the unemployed of Manchester or Glasgow. Initial English penetration of the Western Hemisphere and the East Indies dated from the early seventeenth century, yet for much of the next hundred years that presence remained limited to isolated, often sick and dying, trading stations clinging precariously to the James or the Ganges. Save for a brief period in the late seventeenth century, the Crown's forces in the American colonies were so few as to be practically irrelevant. Aside from the supporting role played by the Royal Navy and a handful of isolated, underpaid, and badly trained regular "Independent Companies" deployed after the War of Austrian Succession, colonial forces took the lead in such affairs as the Pequot Wars or the capture of Louisbourg in 1745. Several thousand miles away, it was the private army of the East India Company that secured the subcontinent, not the forces of the Crown. It would not be until the mid-eighteenth century, and then in response to perceived European threats to existing possessions rather than in pursuit of territorial expansion for its own sake, that British regulars were dispatched to the Western Hemisphere and the East Indies in any effective strength. In the case of the former, their presence, while leading directly to the expulsion of France from the continent of America, would ultimately fuel the constitutional crises that led to the collapse of the First British Empire. Only with the Great Mutiny of the mid-nineteenth century did the Crown take a direct hand in Indian affairs, which meant that British redcoats actively defended the Jewel in the Crown for barely ninety years of the nearly three centuries of British presence in India. Even then, in 1887, British regulars in India numbered some 73,000 troops, compared to 153,000 Indians. By 1903, of an army of India totaling 218,965 all branches, 174,725 were native.[76]

The importance of colonial forces to imperial defense was emblematic of both the strength and weakness of the Empire. On the one hand, the willingness of the British to employ indigenous peoples and colonials to assist in the maintenance of what appeared to be, to many of these men, a foreign and often oppressive regime, speaks volumes of the perspicacity, if not cold-blooded logic, of the Empire's rulers, not to mention the human failing of a willingness to serve masters whose interests may not necessarily be one's own. Although in marked contrast to the policy of Spain, Portugal, or Belgium, any effort to shroud this policy in the cloak of the civilizing influence of the Empire is at best disingenuous. The employment of Sepoys, West Indian freed blacks, African kaffirs, American provincials, Canadian fencibles, or Native American auxiliaries was far more a matter of necessity than beneficence and of necessity born of military weakness. If the nature and degree of its application was without parallel among its contemporaries, this was not a phenomenon unique to the British Empire. Augustus Caesar had formally organized foreign troops into pseudo-Roman formations, and for much the same reason as would the British more than a millennium and a half later: there were simply not enough Roman citizens available to field the number of legions sufficient to defend the Empire. Yet while only gradually did Imperial Rome's *auxilia* come, in some parts of the Empire, to outnumber if not replace entirely the Legions of the Eternal City, the *auxilia*, and more particularly the *foederati*, predated the arrival of the Legions of London, Edinburgh, and Dublin and generally outnumbered them as well.

In terms of the strategic concerns of the Empire, indigenous and colonial forces performed an invaluable role at the local level. Such was clearly the case on the eve of Britain's Peninsular adventure in 1808. At that time, total effective land forces numbered 210,137 officers and men. When cavalry and the Foot Guards are deducted, the army's marching strength was 174,792. Of these, 129,853 were in "British numbered regiments," which, though impressive, were in fact 45,256 below strength. The remainder of the infantry ranged from Veteran and Garrison Battalions to formations raised in such disparate points of the globe as New South Wales, Africa, West India, Canada, and Ceylon, totaling some 44,939 officers and men or just 300 or so short of the total wanting to complete the regular infantry. Yet these were not regulars, and at best it was expected that local forces would fill the regular manpower gap locally. It was neither intended nor expected that the 1,942 members of the four Canadian fencible regiments or the 3,074 souls merely noted as "Ceylonese" would see service in other parts of the Empire or in the Home Islands.[77]

The intention of local forces, wherever formed and of whatever race, was to maintain order within the imperial possessions, maintain at least minimal defense against foreign rivals, and provide military support for regular forces. The nature of the latter role varied across the Empire. In the Americas, colonials primarily provided logistical support, and native auxiliaries provided military support. Even when committed to combat, European colonial formations, be they from the American colonies, British North America, or Australia, were modeled on the English militia system. Thus, with rare exceptions such as Cartagena or Louisbourg during the War of Austrian Succession, they were intended for primarily a defensive role. The same was true in less hospitable regions of the Empire, where disease posed a far greater threat than any human enemy. Here indigenous forces trained and equipped as Europeans performed primarily a combat role but remained geographically restricted to their specific corner of the Empire. Thirty thousand West Indian blacks served for king and country during the French Revolutionary and Napoleonic Wars, both securing and expanding

British power in the Caribbean, while the Cape Corps, as the Dutch Hottentot Corps was remodeled by the British, participated in the Third Frontier War of 1799–1803, Britain's first war[78] against a black African foe.[79] On the other side of the world, Indian troops in the pay of the East India Company participated in British operations against Arabia (1821), Burma (1824–26), and Aden (1839).[80] Here, too, the participation of Indian troops in gunboat diplomacy was limited to the Company's specific sphere of interest. Aden, once the Union Jack was raised there, was placed under the authority of the presidency of Bombay.[81]

Although limited in their strategic role, local forces within the Empire were important in enabling Britain to deploy effectively its limited regular resources for other duties. Throughout the history of the Empire, it was, in the words of Lord Castlereagh, "desirable to throw the conflict, as far as we can, upon the local force, in which we risk nothing but the expense, without exposing a large British army."[82] Such a policy had formed the logic behind the deployment of only Commodore Peter Warren's squadron in support of colonial operations against Louisbourg in 1745 and the dispatch of only a handful of regulars to America under Major General Edward Braddock in 1755. Although William Pitt is lauded for introducing Britain's "winning" strategy during the Seven Years' War, fundamental to that strategy was a dependence on local resources to buttress weak regular forces. In 1758 the total forces deployed in North America amounted to 51,142 officers and men. Major General Jeffery Amherst commanded a force of 14,815, all of whom, save for some 600 Rangers, were regulars. Technically, Amherst's expedition against Louisbourg was subordinate to Major General James Abercromby, who operated against Canada out of New York. Abercromby's force, which came to grief at Ticonderoga, numbered 27,947. Of that—the largest force in America and under the direct command of the Commander-in-Chief—only 7,947 were regulars. That is, 20,000, almost three times their number, were provincials. Finally, Brigadier General John Forbes would capture Fort Duquense three years after Braddock's debacle with a force of 1,880 regulars supported by 5,000 provincials. In other words, of 51,142 men committed to American operations, 21,000 were local in origin.[83]

Yet Castlereagh did not have to look so far back into British history for an example of the role that local forces played in enabling Britain to deploy effectively the few regulars it had on hand. In 1799, Britain was able to deploy regulars in Holland despite the continued uncertain state of an Ireland recently in rebellion thanks to militia and fencible regiments. The latter, drawn from England and Scotland, numbered some 13,687 officers and men, twice the number of regulars then deployed in Ireland. In addition to these, the English militia deployed 14,798 with another 2,838 under orders, for a total of 28,485 English and Scottish forces that were non-Regular Army. Almost as numerous were the Irish militiamen, who numbered 22,372. Only with regard to cavalry did regulars outnumber fencibles, but not by much: 4,051 to 3,208. Of a total force of 65,963 deployed to maintain order in Ireland after the rebellion, 54,065 were militia or fencibles.[84]

As with foreign sources, imperial sources proved less fertile recruiting grounds for the navy than the army. Until the creation of the Dominion navies in the twentieth century, the Royal Navy's mobilization of imperial resources focused on the recruitment of individual seamen wherever they could be found within the Empire, thus the Admiralty's policy of dispatching undermanned ships to the East Indies with the intention that they muster their full complement once on station. The problem was that as an empire based on seaborne trade, the merchants of Madras were as reluctant to provide experienced seamen for the navy as were their counterparts in Bristol.[85] Although it is an exaggeration to say that "the people of the [American] colonies detested impressments as much and probably more than it was detested in Britain," there can be little doubt that New York or Philadelphia proved to be no better recruiting grounds than did home ports such as Liverpool or London.[86] Despite this, at least one navy success in recruiting in the American colonies helps illustrate the problem posed by the use of local resources for not only specific branches of the service but also British strategy in general. In 1759, Governor Thomas Pownall of Massachusetts provided 240 men for the Royal Navy. While acknowledging that this American reinforcement was "of great service to the ships that were weakly manned," Admiral Charles Saunders noted that when the fleet sailed for home, "they must all be left behind in America."[87]

In setting this limitation to the service of these naval recruits, Pownall was not being innovative but was, rather, pursuing a policy that likewise restricted the service of American provincial forces generally. Although elements of the latter participated in the capture of Montreal in 1760, such an offensive operation beyond the limits of their territorial borders was only justified because, for many from Massachusetts in particular, the war against New France was a war against the Antichrist.[88] Such provincial support was not available for other operations of arguably more import such as those against Louisbourg or Quebec or those directed against the West Indies after Spain's declaration of war. In other words, of an apparent strength of some 50,000 available in North America, more than 20,000 were limited in their immediate area of operations to the colonies themselves. The reason for this is the modeling of the provincial forces on the English militia model, which meant that their role was fundamentally one of local defense, not strategic offense. Not surprisingly, one of the clearest examples of the strategic limitations inherent in the employment of local forces is to be found in that of the militia and fencibles of the Home Islands. The maintenance of more than 65,000 men in Ireland in 1799 is suggestive of the continued uncertainty with which the government viewed matters there. Yet when it is recalled that despite the reduction of regular forces in Ireland, including cavalry and Foot Guards, to a bare 12,070 officers and men Britain was only able to deploy 18,000 men to Holland, we are given an idea of the extent to which the employment of local forces, important as it may have been, was at best a neutral and at worst a negative contribution to transimperial defense. Almost 55,000 men in Ireland were nonregulars, meaning that the most that could be demanded of them by law was service within the Home Islands. They could not be deployed to the continent of Europe, and thus at best they freed regular formations for such operations. This helped secure Ireland, but at the same time one must wonder whether such a large force was deployed in Ireland because it could not be used elsewhere. It is perhaps doubtful whether an additional 20,000 men would have changed the outcome of the Helder campaign, especially if they were militia. Yet the latter, even as they secured the home defenses, exacerbated the manpower problems of the army by drawing into their ranks men desperately sought by regular recruiters.

The employment of local forces was not a luxury but a necessity, and, as might be expected of a necessity, local forces proved both an asset and a hindrance to transimperial defense strategy. Perhaps no organization better illustrated the Janus-face of local imperial defense forces than the East India Company Army. As the property of the East India Company until the mid-nineteenth century, this substantial force's deployment was dictated far more by the pecuniary interest of its capitalist masters than by the strategic interests of the Crown. One of the earliest deployments of "John Company's" forces beyond the shores of India was the capture of the Dutch Cape colony in 1805. While in part reflecting the use of local forces in operations of broader strategic concern, possession of the Cape before the construction of the Suez Canal was of direct concern to the East India Company. This expedition also demonstrated how local interest could work against that of the Empire in general. Throughout its planning and execution, commanders of the Cape expedition were reminded that the "security of our Indian Empire" was "paramount." Accordingly, in addition to the Company forces being sent home as soon as the Cape was secure, arrangements were to be made to send British regulars to India from the Cape in case of emergency, even though this would require their replacement with regulars from Britain, men who could hardly be spared. The defense of India was considered so serious that authorization was given, "in a case of extremity, even to direct the absolute evacuation of [the Cape after its capture], and the transfer of the garrison to India."[89] In short, while Indian resources played an important role in the pursuit of imperial strategic objectives, the former imposed their own demands including, on occasion, the demand that the latter, regardless of the cost in blood and treasure in attaining them, be sacrificed as necessary to local strategic interests.

In military terms, local forces, whether European or indigenous, increased the estimated strength of the Empire but only marginally influenced its effective strength. This is an important point that must be borne in mind when historians review figures of the general military strength of Britain in wartime. Paul Kennedy, for example, gives a figure of 200,000 for the year 1760, a number some 90,000 in excess of what the Regular Army mustered at that time.[90] While the former figure is impressive, to assess accurately Britain's disposable force at the time—those regulars available not merely for the defense of Britain and the Empire but also for offensive operations—the latter figure, as a measure of total strength and therefore inclusive of militia, must be deducted. The dangers of miscalculation are even more evident in Thomas Bartlett's assertion that "by 1809, some 750,000 men were serving in the British army." If correct, this figure meant that upwards of "1 in 6 of the male population of military age may have been under arms of one sort or another."[91] That may well be, but being "under arms of one sort or another" does not mean service in the nation's disposable force, the Regular Army. Rather, it meant service for most in the militia, fencibles, volunteers, and constabulary, formations of minimal value to the Empire's offensive capabilities and not merely restricted in their contribution to its defense but, in the case of the Irish Volunteers of the late 1780s, in no small measure detrimental to it.

The limited value of local imperial forces was of continuing concern to British strategists because they could not ignore the fact that, island though Britain was, it was an island in Europe's front yard. Having reviewed the Duke of York's report on Britain's military commitments and, more particularly, its ability to meet them, Henry Dundas could express confidence in the security of the Empire in 1799. It was clear, however, that such security was only to be maintained by the mobilization of local resources and the reinforcement of regulars overseas from forces then in Britain. The defense of the latter was to be secured by mobilizing home forces in support of the regulars. But these were defensive measures; in order to effectively counter the dangers of the French Revolution, or at least seize their colonies while the French were distracted, Britain had to be able to go on the offensive. Such, in the view of Dundas, was impossible: "We are certainly entitled to conclude that at present there is a force, both in Great Britain and Ireland, adequate to their complete defense, and when the foreign settlements, in the different parts of the world, shall receive these additions, which the statement points out, we are likewise warranted to conclude that the various dependencies of the Empire are placed in a rational state of security. But beyond this our views must not extend, and let the object of *offensive operation* be as tempting as the most glorious imagination can suggest, we must rest with our arms crossed, and see it pass."[92]

It might be argued that given the fact that regulars would soon be dispatched to Holland, Dundas exaggerated Britain's predicament. Yet given the small size of the force dispatched and the ignominy of its retreat, it might be better said that the Secretary's grasp of the problems confronting the nation was profound. Eight years later Lord Castlereagh was more optimistic, observing in March 1807 that "continental diversions" might be undertaken "without endangering too seriously our home defenses." The extent to which he qualified his observation—the Horse Guards must have wondered at how to define "too seriously"—is suggestive of how much, despite his confidence, he was aware of Britain's continuing military weakness, as does his recommendation that the force deployed number between only ten thousand and twelve thousand, smaller than the Helder expedition. Two months later, his tone had changed. Asking the cabinet whether it was in fact advisable to send thirteen thousand men to northern Germany, he observed that such an operation "must, in its nature, be a very hazardous one" and, given its size, risk "giving our allies rather too strong expectations and putting the public to more expense in preparations than is requisite for a mere menace."[93]

Recognition of the severe limitations placed on the state's ability to raise the manpower and monies necessary for the assertion of military and naval power is essential to understanding the logic of British strategy during the eighteenth and nineteenth centuries. Equal to the effort that the government expended to mobilize these resources to the maximum of what British domestic politics would permit was attention to the development of strategies that made the best use of what resources were available. In this way, British war making became "a continuation of political intercourse," as the predilections of domestic politics, by limiting the resources available to the state, profoundly shaped the conduct of the nation on the international stage, not merely in the conduct of war but also of diplomacy.[94] Throughout the eighteenth and nineteenth centuries, the foremost strategic imperative of the British army and the Royal Navy was the defense of the Home Islands. During the Seven Years' War, the American War of Independence, and, intermittently, the French Revolutionary and Napoleonic Wars, the threat of cross-channel attack was serious enough to require the retention of large numbers, at times the majority, of regular regiments in the United Kingdom and the deployment of the majority of the British fleet in home waters. The army was able to accomplish this in large part because of the existence of colonial forces that held the line overseas. The navy, however, could not draw on such resources, and yet a strategy that focused on the home waters, while necessary, was to a considerable extent counterproductive. While it secured Britain, it also weakened the security of the overseas trade upon which the nation's prosperity rested. Commitment of the bulk of the Royal Navy to European waters also reduced its ability to seize the possessions of the nation's foes, as important an element in British economic growth as peaceful trade. If the threat to the Home Islands was to be reduced to manageable levels and the armed forces of the Crown thus given a free if predatory hand about the globe, it was necessary to ensure that Britain's colonial rivals were distracted. For reasons of both security and prosperity, therefore, the maintenance of the European balance of power was a hallmark of Britain's relationship with the Continent. As befit an empire built on traders and not legionnaires, this balance was pursued through alliances that promised gold rather than soldiers.

The diplomacy of guineas and gunpowder, which reached its apogee in the eighteenth century, was a direct response to the last major British commitment to the land wars of Europe before 1914. Beginning with the ascent of the House of Hanover to the British throne in 1714, British diplomacy sought to contain the continental dominance of first royal, then revolutionary, and finally Napoleonic France through the creation of alliances and coalitions for which British gold, rather than blood, formed the mortar. Despite the continental fixation of the Hanoverian kings of England, Britain's commitment of manpower to the Continent during the War of Austrian Succession and the Seven Years' War remained negligible when compared to that of the European powers or Britain's commitment in the War of Spanish Succession. Facing foes in Flanders and on the Rhine, France proved unable either to invade Britain or to protect its overseas possessions adequately. In this regard, the security of London and the conquest of Canada in the Seven Years' War owed more to the efforts of Frederick the Great than to the exploits of Anson or Wolfe. The hagiography of Nelson and Wellington notwithstanding, Napoleon's power was crippled in Russia and given its deathblow in Germany a year later. For Napoleonic France, Waterloo was not so much the last gasp of a dying man but an involuntary postmortem convulsion.

The attention paid to the campaigns of Marlborough and Wellington exaggerates the extent to which traditional continental operations figured in British strategic thought. Far more characteristic of British involvement in the affairs of Europe than Malplaquet or Salamanca were the amphibious operations undertaken against the French Channel ports. While much has been made of the colorful image of tars and redcoats joined together in a dashing cutting-out operation, the British fixation on such expeditions reflected as much military weakness as a propensity for drama. "Rochefort was selected not because it was a naval port," Sir Julian Corbett conceded in his seminal study of the Seven Years' War, "but because it was a point of most value to the enemy that was within the scope and range of the British forces available."[95] Incorrectly, Corbett asserts that amphibious operations were among the most important legacies of the system attributed to William Pitt the Elder. True, Channel raids were strongly advocated by the Secretary of State, while the amphibious operations he ordered in North America, specifically against Louisbourg and Quebec, were responsible for ultimate British victory there. Yet amphibious operations predated Pitt, being undertaken during the Seven Years' War in both America and Europe before his ascension to power and earlier still during the War of Austrian Succession. Amphibious operations likewise formed a cornerstone of British strategic thought throughout the two centuries that followed Pitt's death, from Walcheren in 1809 to the Falkland Islands in 1982. It may even be suggested that Wellington's campaigns in Portugal and Spain were in part little more than a glorified amphibious operation for, as his retreat to the Lines of Torres Vedras demonstrated, he was as dependent on the Royal Navy for survival as was any British force on the banks of the St. Lawrence or on the shores of the Bay of Biscay. When and wherever employed and by whomever ordered, amphibious operations proved among the best ways to make effective use of the considerable weaknesses that formed the foundation of the British Empire's strategic reality.

Being in large part a consequence of weakness rather than strength, amphibious operations possessed an important strategic limitation. James Wolfe enthusiastically described amphibious operations as "one . . . of the most brilliant and most useful strokes this nation can possibly make," and he recommended an expedition against Aix in 1758 in explicit terms as to its purpose, noting that it would be one of "the finest diversions that can be made with a small force."[96] "The term 'diversion,'" wrote Clausewitz, "in ordinary usage means an attack on enemy territory that draws off the enemy's forces from the main objective."[97] Not surprisingly, Clausewitz's examples of this military strategy are drawn from the British experience. Amphibious operations not only made the best of chronic manpower and matériel shortages but also served to answer the demands of continental allies that the British launch a second front. This was particularly the case during the Seven Years' War, when Frederick the Great's demands on this account were especially strident and led to the amphibious operations that formed such an important part of Pitt's system. The intent, therefore, was to occupy enemy territory and threaten enemy facilities only until the enemy was forced to respond, thus drawing pressure off allies hard-pressed elsewhere. "If our motions do not draw some French troops from the side of Germany," a British officer observed in 1758, "the nation's money is ill-expended."[98] In most cases the nation's money was indeed ill-expended, for France knew too well the weakness from which British strategy sprang to be seriously deterred from its operations in Flanders or on the Rhine by raids on the Channel coast. As Clausewitz observed of operations against North Holland in 1799 and Walcheren in 1809, "as diversions they can only be justified by the fact that the British troops could not be used in any other way; yet they undeniably left the French defenses stronger than before, just as a landing in France itself would have done."[99] Indeed, by the simple act of landing in Scotland, as weak a threat to the Hanoverian dynasty as Bonnie Prince Charlie, and precipitating the evacuation of the entire British army serving in Flanders in 1745, the French perhaps demonstrated that they, rather than the British, were masters of the diversionary strategy.

Emphasis on amphibious operations and the deployment of expeditionary forces to Flanders, the Rhine, or Spain when allied complaints became particularly shrill meant that through the eighteenth and nineteenth centuries Britain was able to avoid a serious commitment of manpower to the Continent. Instead, the British focused on waging overseas operations against France, Spain, Holland, or any other power with which London fell afoul and that had colonial possessions. What had been piracy on the part of Sir Francis Drake had become, by the eighteenth century, a pillar of British strategy. Not content to raid Spanish convoys laden with gold and silver, Britain turned to the seizure and occupation of enemy possessions across the globe. By the time of the Napoleonic Wars, the British had mastered what in the twentieth century would be called the peripheral strategy. The French and Spanish sugar islands of the West Indies, the French and Portuguese trading stations of the East Indies, and the Dutch Cape colony all fell to the British, many to be returned at the end of one war in full confidence that they could be as easily retaken at the opening of the next. Despite the great naval engagements of the eighteenth and early nineteenth centuries that so inspired Alfred Thayer Mahan, the Royal Navy remained closer to its piratical roots than is generally recognized.

While successful in securing the wealth of the British Empire, an unintentional contribution to British diplomacy made by men such as Anson, Hood, and Nelson was to ensure the European perception of British perfidy. Lacking the human resources to contribute effectively on the Continent but also, thanks to the extent of its Empire, among the wealthier nations of Europe, it made sense that the British contribution to the balance of power should be in the form of financial support to whichever group of nations confronted the particular diplomatic ogre of the moment. Although logical, this meant that Britain was spared the trauma of the repetitive and increasingly horrific conflicts that afflicted Europe between 1740 and 1815. Because Britain's continental operations during this period were undertaken largely in response to complaints from allies, they remained token commitments, while British fleets swept the seas and scooped into the British net the colonial possessions of the common enemy.

Arguably, the increased wealth of the British Empire would help the allied cause, but few in Berlin, Vienna, and Moscow had any doubts that the ultimate economic benefits would remain in the custody of London. The marriage of the balance of power in Europe to the defense of the Empire thus brought with it its own dangers. Important as British gold was to the maintenance of the balance of power, everyone in debt hates his banker, particularly when, as was often the case with the British, arrogance accompanies the guineas in equal measure. European distrust of England (the "Perfidious Albion") repeatedly threatened the British with diplomatic isolation, and more than any other factor such isolation, in laying bare the weakness of Britain's imperial defenses, accounts for the loss of the American colonies. American independence was not merely the result of the British army's inability to effectively control large tracts of American territory or that of the Royal Navy to close the American seaboard. Rather, Britain's diplomatic isolation following the Seven Years' War, a consequence of an intentional isolationist policy that encouraged rather than assuaged discontent among former allies who witnessed the British Empire's exponential expansion while they gained little, enabled France to confront the British without distraction in Europe. If the absence of a continental distraction meant that France was able to gain local superiority in American waters for only a brief moment, it was enough to secure the surrender of a British army at Yorktown, the collapse of the British government, and the evaporation of the British nation's will to continue the fight against American independence.

That Pax Britannica coincided with the nineteenth century is suggestive of the nature of British imperial power. The American Civil War, Europe's various wars of national unification, and sundry colonial wars notwithstanding, the nineteenth century was appreciably more peaceful than the centuries that preceded or followed it. Nothing stands as a clearer testament to this than the British government's drift away from militant imperialism at midcentury. This was reflected not merely in the renunciation of the mercantilist system represented by the repeal of the Corn Laws but also in the decision to withdraw regular garrisons from the largely white possessions of the Empire. Colonial Secretary Lord Grey placed responsibility for defense on Australian shoulders in the 1850s and was only prevented from doing likewise to the Canadians by the diplomatic tensions caused by the American Civil War. In the end, however, the latter served to encourage London to promote Canadian confederation, accomplished in 1867, that allowed the removal of all British regulars from British North America, save for the naval bases at Esquimalt and Halifax, by 1871. New Zealanders had seen their last redcoat in 1868.[100] The departure of the regiments did not, however, represent a complete renunciation of Britain's right to rule its Empire. Rather, it represented the advantage that innovations in naval technology were believed to have given to the use of local forces. The latter, it was argued, could maintain a successful defense against foreign attack until regulars, transported by the steam-powered vessels that were in ascendance in the Royal Navy, arrived in sufficient time to provide support, if not go on the offensive. It was a time-honored strategy but one prone far more to failure than success. The inability to protect the Home Islands, relieve Gibraltar, and counter French movements in American waters led to the debacle at Yorktown. Almost thirty years earlier, the inability of the Admiralty to mobilize resources in timely fashion was largely responsible for the humiliating loss of one of Britain's most important possessions in the Mediterranean. Despite these and other examples, the strategy of timely response formed a cornerstone of the British response to the threat posed by Imperial Japan in the 1930s. It was perhaps just as well for admirals of the twentieth century that, unlike their counterparts two centuries before, they did not face the possibility of execution for failure.

As the decision to withdraw key garrisons and depend on a timely response to threats suggests, British security during the Victorian era rested ultimately on the fact that at no point was its naval or military power seriously challenged. By the dawn of the twentieth century, however, Europe had placed its house in sufficient order to offer such a challenge. Yet while finding its supremacy threatened for the first time since 1815, Britain's situation in 1914 was distinctly different from that of a century before. Symbolic of the problems for traditional British strategy were the maps of the world that adorned classrooms from Kamloops to Kuala Lumpur and, specifically, the extent of global territory on those maps that, colored red, were marked as territory of the British Empire. Having secured most of the non-European world for itself, the colonial war that loomed in 1914 found Britain on the defensive and allied with its traditional enemy in opposition to Imperial Germany. If such an alliance was confusing to some, the geopolitical circumstances of Germany created more serious problems for traditional British strategy. Far more than either France or Spain, Germany was a landlocked nation with primarily continental aspirations. Dreams of imperial expansion into Africa or the Far East were largely the will-o'-the-wisp fantasies of the Kaiser, while Germany's continental reality ensured that its threat to Britain's overseas possessions remained only potential. Germany's continental reality, while ensuring the security of the British Empire, also meant that Britain's peripheral strategy was largely irrelevant in the continental conflict that unfolded in 1914. Thus, the Empire needed to be defended not on the Irrawaddy but on the Somme. A victim of its own success, the effectiveness of British imperial strategy in the two centuries after 1714 was largely responsible for the rejection of that strategy in favor of a continental commitment in 1914.

The extent to which World War I diverged from traditional British strategy was evident in two circumstances. The first was the introduction of conscription. As late as 1913, Labour MP Keir Hardie had uttered what for two centuries had been the British mantra on the issue: "Conscription is the badge of a slave. Compulsory military service is the negation of democracy."[101] Unprecedented as the introduction of formal conscription in January 1916 was, it was also a temporary expedient, one abolished in 1921. Thus, when the British were finally "obliged to imitate many of the devices of the French revolutionary state," they did so in a manner that reflected British sentiment not only of the twentieth century but of the eighteenth and nineteenth centuries as well, sentiment that hindered the recruitment of the armies of Amherst and Wellington as effectively as it did that of Haig. Not only was conscription introduced, as in Canada, in the second half of the conflict but, as Hew Strachan has observed, it proved a twentieth-century application of the militia draft rather than compulsion on a European model. The former had been a popular measure through the eighteenth century into the Napoleonic Wars and was, like conscription in the twentieth century, "adopted in extremis."[102] Whether conscription proved any more successful than its forerunners is perhaps a matter of debate. What is clear, however, is that given its limited impact on the British army's manpower problems, the unprecedented circumstances that had forced its adoption, and the lateness and thus limited scope of its application, conscription during the World War I had its roots in British tradition rather than the French Revolution.[103]

The second notable diversion from traditional strategy represented by World War I was the fact that imperial forces played a much greater role in transimperial defense after 1914. "Under the pressure of a danger which threatened the Mother Country," observed *The Empire Review* in 1923, "all her daughter nations sprang to her assistance."[104] Yet as with the introduction of conscription, the role of colonial forces in World War I was the exception to the imperial strategic heritage that proved the rule. The deployment of not merely thousands but tens of thousands of Canadians against Germany, and of Australians and New Zealanders against the Ottoman Empire, not to mention the use of Indian and African units against both, demonstrated the tremendous manpower base upon which the Empire could draw in the early twentieth century. Yet this strength was in truth a façade that maintained its integrity due to the peculiar nature of the threat faced by the Empire in 1914. Imperial forces were deployed not merely in traditional support roles but, as at Lens, Vimy Ridge, Passchendaele, and Gallipoli, in primary combat roles due to the fact that Britain, despite the introduction of conscription, could only deploy five million men to confront an Austro-German bloc of more than twenty million.[105] Not merely was the mobilization of the British Empire, at some eight million, impressive, but the extent to which hitherto local forces participated in transimperial defense was without precedent. That colonials came to the defense of the Mother Country's position in Europe, however, had little to do with the inherent strength of the British system and everything to do with the fact that at no time did the Central Powers seriously threaten the Empire and require local forces to assume their traditional role or large numbers of British naval and military resources to deploy overseas. The British Empire's success in World War I was therefore to be attributed not to the extent to which British strategists overcame the long-standing material weaknesses of the Empire but rather to the limited strategic objectives of the Central Powers. Twenty years later, and unfortunately for the British Empire, the Axis would not prove so narrow in its strategic outlook.

An important issue that John Brewer must address in *The Sinews of Power* is how the traditional image of "Little England"—a nation that avoided the trappings of strong, centralized state power—can be reconciled with his model of an aggressive and successful "fiscal-military state." On the one hand, the historical evidence must force him to concede that eighteenth-century Britain lacked the instruments of domestic power wielded by contemporary France, Prussia, and

Russia. Yet Brewer asserts that Britain was not merely one of Europe's major naval and military powers but, in the mobilization and deployment of armed force, outpaced the capabilities of its European rivals. Brewer seeks to resolve this contradiction by arguing that "states are Janus-faced: they look in, to the societies they rule, and out, to those states with which they are so often locked in conflict." He thus concludes, "The British government was able to act effectively against its international enemies but was weak in its dealing with its own subjects."[106] Even among military historians who disagree with Clausewitz, there must be instant recognition of the fallaciousness of such an assertion. How is it possible for a nation to remain domestically weak while asserting sufficient power not only to ensure its national security but also to raise sufficient resources in manpower, money, and matériel to become "the military Wunderkind of the age"? The short answer is that it is not possible. The longer answer, presented by the arguments in this essay, is that it is clearly not possible.

The study of war, but more especially of the institutions that wage it, cannot be limited to campaigns and battles, whether won or lost. Likewise, the study of war cannot be limited to the event itself but must also take into consideration the preparation for its outbreak and conclusion. If, as Clausewitz said, war consists of a series of pulses, then the historian must pay equal attention to the continuo as to the pulses that punctuate it. In other words, Britain's success in war must be placed within the broader context of how the nation prepared for conflict, not merely during wartime but in times of peace as well. When the influence of domestic politics on the British state's ability to mobilize the nation for war is assessed with reference to the actual size and condition of the armed forces in peace and war, it becomes evident that if "a fully effective military is one that derives maximum combat power from the resources physically and politically available," then the extent to which the armed forces of the British Empire proved, if not ineffective, then somewhat less than fully effective may be easily anticipated, and the reasons for this circumstance made readily apparent.[107] Like parliamentary democracy, the manner in which the Mother Country mobilized its resources was emulated throughout the Empire. "What I want to accomplish, if I possibly can," the Canadian Defense Minister, George Graham, explained to the House of Commons in 1922, "is to have a well-organized, snappy defense force that will be a credit to Canada without being too expensive."[108] However much they may have likewise wished to field a "snappy" force, British statesmen, generals, and admirals could not ignore the centuries-old "perennial question of how to better adjust scarce manpower and tight budgets to meet heavy, unpredictable commitments."[109] It did not help that a majority of Britons believed that, in the words of George Frederick Handel's librettist Thomas Morell, "justice with courage is a thousand men."[110] Despite its popularity, this view was pure propaganda, and the fact of its being accepted by not a few historians does nothing to discredit the lie that lay beneath it. In short, due to the sundry restrictions placed on the resources physically and politically available, the regular forces of the Empire proved woefully inadequate for either the purposes of defense or offensive operations against rivals or indigenous foes.

Yet there remains an issue that must be addressed before any conclusion may be offered: what Linda Colley describes, with some accuracy, as "the generally high level of success achieved abroad by Britain's army in this period."[111] There can be little doubt that skill, both in politics and war making, accounts for much of the nation's success. If Britain's warships were generally not of the same high quality as their Spanish and French opponents, the British tar's reputation for skill in seamanship was based far more on reality than myth. Likewise, if British generals were for the most part less able than their comrades in the navy or their colleagues on the Continent, British infantry were masters of firepower, a quality that, as with the experience of the Prussian army, more than compensated for fewer numbers. Yet skill and bravery alone cannot explain success in war. As Lord Barham observed of the Royal Navy's manpower shortages in 1805: "Our skill I think is superior to [the enemy's]; but skill without means can only regret the inactivity that appears to me to prevail everywhere."[112]

As important as skill, therefore, were manpower resources to be found elsewhere. The employment of local forces within the Empire was essential if regulars were to concentrate in a disposable force sufficient to undertake effective operations against the enemy. Yet, as noted, the Empire made its own demands and imposed its own limitations, and thus the best that was achieved for British strategists was equilibrium rather than a substantial increase to the offensive strength. Perhaps more important was the pursuit of alliances in Europe. This was a cornerstone of British diplomacy for more than three centuries, as the distraction of France and Spain by war in Europe enabled Britain to deploy its limited resources against the overseas possessions of its colonial rivals with relative impunity. The importance of this mixture of diplomacy and strategy was apparent, and the limits to British military and naval power were most clearly evident when Britain's European enemies were not distracted, as demonstrated by the outcome of the American War of Independence and also in stressful periods during the Napoleonic Wars when Britain, if not conquered, nonetheless played a minimal role in influencing the affairs of Europe. The importance of diplomacy to buttress British naval and military power may thus be said to form a fourth component to Britain's "circle of circumstance" as described by the *Naval and Military Magazine*. If isolation, liberty, and commerce by turns both strengthened and weakened the military and naval capabilities of the nation, diplomacy, although often unable to overcome the realities of British weakness, remained a valuable tool by which the ill consequences of such weakness might be lessened.

The role of diplomacy in the circle of circumstance is a reminder that in assessing the strength of Britain's effectiveness as a fiscal-military state, due consideration must be given to what is in fact often ignored: the condition of Britain's opponents. For many historians, the Royal Navy's success in building Britain's empire symbolizes how effectively the state was able to both mobilize and deploy its resources. Although this is true in part, in no small measure the success of the Royal Navy in the late seventeenth and eighteenth centuries was due to the fact that Imperial Spain's naval power was in precipitous decline during the same period, while that of a France distracted by affairs on the continent of Europe was never able to rise to the challenge. Likewise, the period of Britain's unquestioned dominance of the world's oceans coincided with a post-1815 Europe reeling from bloodletting of almost twenty years of warfare. The Royal Navy's success during this period very largely rested on the fact that at no time was it as seriously challenged as it had been in the seventeenth and eighteenth centuries. When such a challenge was revived with the naval arms race at the end of the nineteenth century and the coming of war in 1914, Britain was, as ever, hard-pressed to meet it.

Historians of the British Empire have often ignored the fact that Britain's success against Spain during the eighteenth century was directly related to the fact that Madrid's Empire had reached its zenith in the seventeenth century. The Royal Navy's victories in campaigns against an enemy that was generally weaker and less organized, if not exhausted, were inevitable, not because of Britain's war resources but, all things considered, despite them. The condition of Spain therefore highlights a consequence of the fundamental weakness of the British Empire, especially in its twentieth-century dotage and particularly during World War II. By 1941, if not earlier, Japan had recognized in the British Empire what Xenophon had seen in the Persian Empire twenty-three hundred years earlier: "It is strong in respect of extent of territory and number of inhabitants; but it is weak in respect to its lengthened communications of the dispersal of its forces, that is, if one can attack with speed."[113] In effect, Japan did unto Britain in the twentieth century what Britain had done unto Spain in the eighteenth, and in neither case did victory represent an ability to overcome the severe material limitations imposed on both island nations. Rather, victory represented an ability to mobilize effectively those limited resources to overcome an opponent that, despite appearances to the contrary, was substantially weaker. In 1941, as in 1741, the survival of the British Empire depended on the mobilization of colonial resources and the pursuit of foreign alliances as much as, if not more than, its own military and naval strength.

The emphasis that some have placed on the strength and effectiveness of the British fiscal-military state stands as a warning to not only students of the eighteenth century but historians generally. It is not enough to draw broad conclusions from the fact of a handful of victories on land or at sea or even from the record of British imperial expansion, impressive as all of these may be. Serious attention must be paid to the realities of the British state at war, the role of domestic politics in limiting its ability to mobilize resources, and the impact of those limitations on the development of strategy. In the end, the historical record of victory and expansion stands; it is just the explanation for it that must be changed. More fundamentally, the juxtaposition of the reality of British military and naval weakness against the conclusions of historians regarding its fiscal-military power serves not only as a reminder that appearances may be deceiving but that any conclusions concerning state power must take into consideration Clausewitz's two inseparable facts: total means at one's disposal and the strength of will to use them. Had he done this, John Brewer could not have concluded that "judged by the criteria of the ability to take pounds out of people's pockets and to put soldiers in the field and sailors on the high seas, Britain was one of Europe's most powerful states."[114] Aside from the fact that an ability to extract revenues does not mean that a government will to spend them either wisely or on its armed forces, given the perennial problems of specie and manpower shortages suffered by the army and the navy in both war and peace, the opposite conclusion, that Britain was among Europe's least powerful states, is more accurate.

The British experience is also suggestive of the extent to which Clausewitz's two inseparable facts are not time-specific but are, rather, eternal. Save for examples of a political system being fundamentally transformed—as in the case of Rome's transformation from republic to empire—the influence of the relationship between these two inseparable facts will continue to make itself felt in the same manner throughout the history of a nation. In many respects, Victorian Britain was unlike its Georgian predecessor and not least because "the drive for empire in the eighteenth century had distinctive motives and rationales and generated different images and responses within the domestic culture from the imperial project of the nineteenth century."[115] Be that as it may, the contradictory relationship between the resources of the nation and the popular will to use them, on the one hand, and the consequent military and naval weakness of the British state, on the other hand, was a reality confronted not only by Walpole but by Pitt the Elder and the Younger, Lord North, Lord Castlereagh, Palmerston, Disreali, and Lloyd George. As Sir Alan Brooke, Chief of the Imperial General Staff from December 1941 until June 1946, noted in his diary during Britain's darkest hours of the Pacific War, the problems that Britain's military and naval weaknesses posed for the defense of home and Empire were not new in 1941 but had a history stretching back two, if not three, centuries.

Our reexamination of the British fiscal-military state would seem all the more important given that some historians have chosen to apply the fiscal-military state model to other states in other periods. "Britain became the strongest military power in the world, arguably the strongest at any time till them," observes Jeremy Black, "and also the strongest in relative and absolute terms until the American century of the present age."[116] Given the extent to which, largely for reasons of domestic politics, the will of the Anglo-American world has been such as to prevent the creation of armed forces on the order that the total means at the disposal of Britain and America might otherwise suggest possible, such an observation assumes a meaning that the author did not perhaps intend. Indeed, when one considers the role that absence of will, rather than political or military incompetence, has played in the fact that the British and American military experience, while marked by some important victories, contains not a few catastrophic defeats, one cannot help but be left with the sense that such an observation is not as complimentary as at first blush.

Notes

The epigraph is taken from Alex Danchev and Daniel Todman, eds., *War Diaries, 1939–1945: Field Marshal Lord Alanbrooke* (London: Phoenix, 2002), 229.

1. Carl von Clausewitz, *On War*, trans. and ed. Michael Howard and Peter Paret (Princeton, NJ: Princeton University Press, 1984), 77.

2. Frank McLynn, *1759: The Year Britain Became Master of the World* (London: Jonathan Cooper, 2004), 388.

3. John Brewer, *The Sinews of Power: War, Money and the English State, 1688–1783* (London: Unwin, Hyman, 1989), xii.

4. Jeremy Black, *Britain As a Military Power, 1688–1815* (London: University College Press, 1999), vii.

5. See introduction to Lawrence Stone, ed., *An Imperial State at War: Britain from 1689 to 1815* (London: Routledge, 1994).

6. *The Parliamentary History of England from the Earliest Period to the Year 1803*, 36 vols. (London: Hansard, 1804), 15:269.

7. "Prospects of the British Empire," *Naval and Military Magazine* (September 1828): 253. Italics in original.

8. Brewer, *Sinews of Power*, 50.

9. Linda Colley, "The Reach of the State, the Appeal of the Nation: Mass Arming and Political Culture in the Napoleonic Wars," in Stone, *Imperial State*, 180.

10. Neither Colley not Brewer was the first to make this error. Richard Glover, an authority on the British army of the Napoleonic Wars, incorrectly assumes that impressment was the same as conscription. Richard Glover, *Peninsular Preparation: The Reform of the British Army, 1795–1809* (Cambridge: Cambridge University Press, 1963), 215.

11. Measures Proposed for Improving the State of the Military Force, May 12, 1807, in William Charles Vane, Marquess of Londonerry, ed., *Correspondence, Despatches, and Other Papers of Viscount Castlereagh, Second Marquess of Londonderry*, 12 vols. (London: William Shober, 1851), 2nd ser., 8:54.

12. James Oglethorpe, "The Sailor's Advocate," in J. S. Bromley, ed., *The Manning of the Royal Navy: Selected Public Pamphlets, 1693–1873*, Naval Records Society, vol. 119 (London: Naval Records Society, 1974), 95.

13. Notes for speech to Parliament (1799), Dundas Papers, William R. Perkins Library, Duke University, Durham, North Carolina.

14. Glover, *Peninsular Preparation*, 215.

15. General Returns, WO 17/1155, National Archives, Kew, Surrey, United Kingdom.

16. Pelham to Fox, July 22, 1745, in The Earl of Ilchester, ed., *Henry Fox, First Lord of Holland: His Family and Relations*, 2 vols. (London: John Murray, 1920), 1:115–16.

17. Alan Guy, *Oeconomy and Discipline: Officership and Administration in the British Army, 1714–1763* (Manchester: Manchester University Press, 1985), 9; J. A. Houlding, *Fit for Service: The Training of the British Army, 1715–1795* (Oxford: Clarendon, 1981), 9.

18. Loudoun to Major General Peregrine Hopson, January 21, 1758, WO 34/44, National Archives, UK.

19. "Memorandum Respecting the State of the Military Force, May 26, 1807," in Castlereagh, *Correspondence*, 8:62.

20. Lignoier to Lord Granby, November 27, 1759, Ligonier Letterbook, William L. Clements Library, University of Michigan, Ann Arbor.

21. "Troops under Lord Loudoun's Immediate Command," July 24, 1757, WO1/1; Hopson to Loudoun, August 29, 1757; and Loudoun to Hopson, September 16, 1757, WO 34/44; all in National Archives, UK.

22. General Returns, WO 17/1155, ibid.

23. I am grateful to Dr. Gregory J. W. Urwin of the Department of History, Temple University, for these figures.

24. Michael Duffy, "The British Army and the Caribbean Expeditions of the War against Revolutionary France, 1793–1801," *Journal of the Society for Army Historical Research* 62 (Summer 1984): 65–73; David Gates, "The Transformation of the Army, 1783–1815," in David G. Chandler, ed., *The Oxford History of the British Army* (Oxford: Oxford University Press, 1994), 138.

25. Queries from Mr. Secretary Dundas with Answers from the Commander in Chief, May 11, 1799, Dundas Papers.

26. Sir J. F. Maurice, ed., *The Diary of Sir John Moore*, 2 vols. (London: Edward Arnold, 1904), 1:333–58.

27. *Parliamentary History of England from the Earliest Period to the Year 1803*, 11:416.

28. Daniel Baugh, *British Naval Administration in the Age of Walpole* (Princeton, NJ: Princeton University Press, 1965): 234; Bromley, *Manning of the Royal Navy*, passim.

29. C. J. Bartlett, *Great Britain and Sea Power, 1815–1853* (Oxford: Clarendon, 1963), 307.

30. Stephen Gradish, *The Manning of the British Navy during the Seven Years' War* (London: Royal Historical Society, 1980), 212.

31. Bartlett, *Great Britain and Sea Power*, 305.

32. A fact all the more impressive if one considers that despite the mayhem in North America, technically the Seven Years' War did not begin until 1756.

33. N. A. M. Rodger, *The Wooden World: An Anatomy of the Georgian Navy* (London: Fontana, 1988), 369.

34. Gradish, *Manning of the British Navy*, 34–41.

35. Memorandum by Lord Melville, March 5, 1805, and Barham to Pitt, August 3, 1805, in *Barham Papers: The Naval Records Society*, vol. 39 (London: Naval Records Society, 1910), 59, 96.

36. Nelson to Castlereagh, October 5, 1805, in Castlereagh, *Correspondence*, 5:117.

37. Barham to Pitt, October 23, 1805, *Barham Papers*, 3:103–4.

38. Barham (draft letter), November 28, 1805, ibid., 105.

39. Gradish, *Manning*, 34–45.

40. William Laird Clowes, *The Royal Navy: A History from the Earliest Times to 1900* (1898; reprint, London: Chatham, 1996), 3:157; Jack Sweetman, "Survey II: The Line of Battle," in Jack Sweetman, ed., *The Great Admirals: Command at Sea, 1587–1945* (Annapolis, MD: Naval Institute Press, 1997), 145.

41. Edward M. Spiers, *The Army and Society, 1815–1914* (New York: Longmans, 1980), 36.

42. Paul Kennedy, *The Rise and Fall of the Great Powers: Economic Change and Military Conflict from 1500 to 2000* (New York: Random House, 1987), 99; Brewer, *Sinews of Power*, 30.

43. J. E. Cookson, *Lord Liverpool's Administration: The Crucial Years, 1815–1822* (Edinburgh: Scottish Academic Press, 1975), 28–30, 119–20, 341–42.

44. Spiers, *Army and Society*, 39.

45. Brian Bond, "The Army between the Two World Wars, 1918–1939," in Chandler, *Oxford History of the British Army*, 256.

46. Brian Bond and Williamson Murray, "The British Armed Forces, 1918–1939," in Allan Millett and Williamson Murray, eds., *Military Effectiveness*, vol. 2, *Interwar Period* (Boston: Allen & Unwin, 1988), 107; Bond, "Army between the Two World Wars," 257, 265.

47. Houlding, *Fit for Service*, 11.

48. Romney Sedgwick, ed., *Letters from George III to Lord Bute, 175–1766* (1939; reprint, Westport, CT: Greenwood, 1981), 135.

49. Welbore Ellis to Major General Sir Jeffrey Amherst, May 20, 1763, Jeffrey Amherst Papers, William L. Clements Library, University of Michigan.

50. Houlding, *Fit for Service*, 412.

51. Thomas Bartlett, "The Augmentation of the Army in Ireland, 1767–1768," *English Historical Review* 96 (1981): 540–59.

52. Lord Barrington to Major General Thomas Gage, December 11, 28, 1770, March 6, 1771, Gage Papers, English Series, William L. Clements Library, University of Michigan.

53. Peter Burroughs, "The Human Cost of Imperial Defence in the Early Victorian Age," *Victorian Studies* (Autumn 1980): 7–32.

54. Peter Burroughs, "Tackling Army Desertion in British North America," *Canadian Historical Review* 61 (1980): 28–68.

55. Spiers, *Army and Society*, 38–39.

56. Legge to Gage, May 14, 1776, Gage Papers, American Series, 128.

57. Edward Spiers, "Reforming the Infantry of the Line, 1900–1914," *Journal of the Society for Army Historical Research* 238 (1981): 86–87.

58. Guy, *Oeconomy and Discipline*, 36.

59. Houlding, *Fit for Service*, 353–56.

60. Spiers, "Reforming the Infantry," 87.

61. Trumbull Higgins, *Winston Churchill and the Second Front, 1940–1943* (New York: Oxford University Press, 1957), 187.

62. Patrick Macrory, *Signal Catastrophe: The Retreat from Kabul, 1842* (London: Robert Clay/Chaucer Press, 1966); Ian K. Steele, *Warpaths: Invasions of North America* (New York: Oxford University Press, 1994).

63. Lord Barrington to Lord Rochford, August 8, 1775, WO 4/94, National Archives, UK.

64. Spears, "Reforming the Infantry," 87–88.

65. Peter Burroughs, "An Unreformed Army? 1815–1868," in Chandler, *Oxford History of the British Army*, 172–74; Houlding, *Fit for Service*, 152.

66. Rodger, *Wooden World*, 369.

67. Bartlett, *Seapower*, 339–40.

68. Rodger, *Wooden World*, 11.

69. Kennedy, *British Naval Mastery*, 109.

70. Paul M. Kennedy, *The Rise and Fall of British Naval Mastery* (Malabar: Robert E. Krieger, 1982), 156.

71. Thomas D. G. Thomas, *Lord North* (London: Allen, Lane, 1976), 57.

72. N. A. M. Rodger, *The Insatiable Earl: A Life of John Montagu, Fourth Earl of Sandwich, 1718–1792* (London: HarperCollins, 1993), 148.

73. Ibid.

74. Peter Burroughs, "Defense and Imperial Disunity," in Andrew Porter, ed., *The Oxford History of the British Empire*, vol. 3, *The Nineteenth Century* (Oxford: Oxford University Press, 1999), 334.

75. C. Northcote Parkinson, *War in the Eastern Seas, 1793–1815* (London: Allen & Unwin, 1954), 340.

76. T. A. Heathcote, "The Army of British India," in Chandler, *Oxford History of the British Army*, 373, 379; V. G. Kiernan, *Colonial Empires and Armies, 1815–1960* (Kingston: McGill-Queen's University Press, 1998), 23–26.

77. Abstract of the Effective Strength and Establishment of the British Army on the 1st of November, 1808 . . . Adjutant-General's Office, December 8, 1808, in Castlereagh, *Correspondence*, 8:188; R. L. Yaple, "The Auxiliaries: Foreign and Miscellaneous Regiments in the British Army, 1802–1817," *Journal of the Society for Army Historical Research* 201 (1972): 10–28.

78. Although Britain's first such war, it was the third in a series (also known as the Kaffir Wars) between the Xhosa and Afrikaners.

79. Philip D. Morgan, "The Black Experience in the British Empire, 1680–1810," in P. J. Marshall, ed., *The Oxford History of the British Empire*, vol. 2, *The Eighteenth Century* (Oxford: Oxford University Press, 1998) 485.

80. Burroughs, "Defence and Imperial Disunity," in Porter, *Oxford History of the British Empire*, 3:322.

81. Jeremy Black, *The British Seaborne Empire* (New Haven, CT: Yale University Press, 2004), 218.

82. Castlereagh to Chatham, December 31, 1807, in Castlereagh, *Correspondence*, 8:105–6.

83. Disposition of His Majesty's Forces in America, 1758, WO 34/18, National Archives, UK.

84. "Queries from Mr. Secretary Dundas with Answers from the Commander in Chief," May 11, 1799, Dundas Papers.

85. Parkinson, *Eastern Seas*, 340.

86. Baugh, *Naval Administration*, 93.

87. Saunders to William Clevland, May, 18, June 6, 1759, ADM 1/482, National Archives, UK.

88. Fred Anderson, *A People's Army at War: Massachusetts Soldiers and Society in the Seven Years' War* (New York: Norton, 1984), passim.

89. Castlereagh to Cornwallis and Baird, September 10, 1805, in Castlereagh, *Correspondence*, 6:143–48.

90. Kennedy, *Great Powers*, 99.

91. Thomas Bartlett, "Militarization and Politicization in Ireland (1780–1820)," *Culture et practiques en France et en Irlande, XVIe–XVIIIe siecle* (Paris: Centre de Recherches Historiques, 1990), 127.

92. Dundas Papers Memorandum, May 13, 1799. Italics in original

93. Memorandum for the Cabinet Relative to State of the Military Force, March 1807; Memorandum respecting the State of the Military Force, May 26, 1807; both in Castlereagh, *Correspondence*, 8:47, 63.

94. Clausewitz, *On War*, 87.

95. Julian S. Corbett, *England in the Seven Years War: A Study in Combined Strategy*, 2 vols. (London: Longmans, Green, 1907), 1:192.

96. Wolfe to George Sackville, July –, 1758, in *Report on the Manuscripts of Mrs. Stopford-Sackville at Drayton House, Northamptonshire*, 2 vols. (1904; reprint, Boston: Gregg Press, 1972), 2:265–66.

97. Clausewitz, *On War*, 562.

98. Alexander MacDowall to Sackville, August 16, 1758, in *Report on the Manuscripts of Mrs. Stopford-Sackville*, 1:293.

99. Clausewitz, *On War*, 563.

100. Burroughs, "An Unreformed Army," 176–77.

101. Hew Strachan, "Liberalism and Conscription, 1789–1919," in Hew Strachan, ed., *The British Army: Manpower and Society into the Twenty-first Century* (London: Cass, 2000), 7.

102. Ibid., 20–21.

103. Peter Simkins, "The Four Armies, 1914–1918," in Chandler, *Oxford History of the British Army*, 253–54.

104. Wireless Expert, "Wireless and the Empire," *Empire Review* 38 (1923): 853.

105. Marc Ferro, *The Great War, 1914–1918* (London: Ark Paperbacks, 1987), 227; Robert Holland, "The British Empire and the Great War, 1914–1918," in Judith M. Brown et al., eds., *The Oxford History of the British Empire*, vol. 4, *The Twentieth Century* (Oxford: Oxford University Press, 1999), 117.

106. Brewer, *Sinews of Power*, xvii.

107. Allan R. Millett et al., eds., *Military Effectiveness*, vol. 3, *The Second World War* (Boston: Unwin, Hyman, 1988), 2.

108. Desmond Morton, *A Military History of Canada* (Toronto: McClelland & Stewart, 1999), 170.

109. Burroughs, "An Unreformed Army," 169.

110. *Judas Maccabaeus*, written to commemorate the Duke of Cumberland's defeat of Prince Charles Stuart in 1745, was the most financially successful of Handel's works.

111. Colley, "The Politics of Eighteenth-Century British History," *Journal of British Studies* 25 (1986): 362.

112. Barham to Pitt(?), in *Barham Papers*, 3:85.

113. Xenophon, *The Persian Expedition*, trans. Rex Warner (London: Penguin, 1972), 77.

114. Brewer, *Sinews of Power*, xviii.

115. Kathleen Wilson, "Empire of Virtue: The Imperial Project and Hanoverian Culture, c. 1720–1785," in Stone, *Imperial State at War*, 130.

116. Black, *Britain As a Military Power*, vii.

Select Bibliography of Published Works and Conference Papers Written by Russell F. Weigley

Books

Quartermaster General of the Union Army: A Biography of M. C. Meigs. New York: Columbia University Press, 1959.

Towards an American Army: Military Thought from Washington to Marshall. New York: Columbia University Press, 1962. Reprint, Westport, CT: Greenwood, 1974.

History of the United States Army. A title in the Macmillan Wars of America Series, edited by Louis Morton. New York: Macmillan; London: Collier Macmillan, 1967. Enlarged edition, Bloomington and London: Indiana University Press, 1984.

(editor) *The American Military: Readings in the History of the Military in American Society.* A title in the Themes and Social Forces in American History Series, edited by Robin W. Winks. Reading, MA, Menlo Park, CA, and London: Addison-Wesley, 1969.

The Partisan War: The South Carolina Campaign of 1780–1782. Tricentennial Booklet No. 2, Published for the South Carolina Tricentennial Commission. Columbia: University of South Carolina Press, 1970.

The American Way of War: A History of United States Military Strategy and Policy. A title in the Macmillan Wars of America Series, edited by Louis Morton. New York: Macmillan; London: Collier Macmillan, 1973. Paperback edition, Bloomington and London: Indiana University Press, 1977.

(editor) *New Dimensions in Military History: An Anthology.* San Rafael, CA: Presidio, 1976.

(editor, with Nicholas B. Wainwright and Edwin Wolf II) *Philadelphia: A 300-Year History.* New York and London: Norton, 1982.

Eisenhower's Lieutenants: The Campaigns of France and Germany, 1944–1945. Bloomington: Indiana University Press, 1981; London: Sedgwick & Jackson, 1981. Paperback edition, Bloomington: Indiana University Press, 1990.

The Age of Battles: The Quest for Decisive Warfare from Breitenfeld to Waterloo. Bloomington and Indianapolis: Indiana University Press, 1981. Paperback edition, London: Pimlico, 1993.

A Great Civil War: A Military and Political History, 1861–1865. Bloomington and Indianapolis: Indiana University Press, 2000.

Essays and Chapters

"The Elihu Root Reforms and the Progressive Era." In William Geffen, ed., *Command and Commanders in Modern Warfare: Proceedings of the Second Military History Symposium, U.S. Air Force Academy, 2–3 May 1968.* Reprinted in William Geffen, ed., *Commanders in Modern Warfare: The Proceedings of the Second Military History Symposium, U.S. Air Force Academy, 2–3 May 1968* (Washington, DC: Office of Air Force History and U.S. Air Force Academy, 1971), 11–27.

"The Role of the War Department and the Army." In Dorothy Borg and Shumpei Okamoto, eds., *Pearl Harbor As History: Japanese-American Relations, 1931–1941* (New York: Columbia University Press, 1973), 165–88. Translated into Japanese by Iwano Ichiro as "Assmerika Rikugun to Kyukuto Senryaku," in Hosoya Chihiro et al., eds., *Nichi-bei Kankeishi: Kaisen Niitaru June (1931–41),* 4 vols. (Tokyo: Tokyo University Press, 1971), 2:17–70.

"Commentary: From Vienna to Versailles." In Monte D. Wright and Lawrence J. Paszek, eds., *Soldiers and Statesmen* (Washington, DC: Office of Air Force History, 1973), 47–53.

"European Background to American Military Affairs." In Robin Higham, ed., *A Guide to the Sources of United States Military History* (Hamden, CT: Archon, 1975), 40–69.

"Military Strategy and Civilian Leadership." In Klaus Knorr, ed., *Historical Dimensions of National Security Problems* (Lawrence: University Press of Kansas, 1976), 38–77.

"American Strategy: A Call for a Critical Strategic History." In Don Higginbotham, ed., *Reconsiderations on the Revolutionary War: Selected Essays* (Westport, CT, and London: Greenwood, 1978), 32–53.

"The Colonial Militia." In Robert Grant Crist, ed., *The First Century: A History of the 29th Infantry Division* (Harrisburg, PA: 29th Infantry Division, 1979), 17–29.

"The Evolution of Strategic Thought." In Ben Thomas Trout and James E. Hart, eds., *National Security Affairs: Theoretical Perspectives and Contemporary Issues* (New Brunswick, NJ: Transaction Books, 1982), 57–59.

"The Border City in the Civil War, 1857–1865." In Russell F. Weigley, ed., *Philadelphia: A 300-Year History* (New York and London: Norton, 1982), 363–416.

"A War of Posts: The Morristown Encampments and the American Revolution." In *Morristown: A History and Guide, Morristown National Historical Park, New*

Jersey. Produced by the Division of Publications, National Park Service Handbook 120 (Washington, DC: U.S. Department of the Interior, 1983), 14–83.

"The Armed Forces, Strategy, and Foreign Policy." In Richard Dean Burns, ed., *The Society for Historians of American Foreign Relations: Guide to American Foreign Relations since 1700* (Santa Barbara, CA: ABC-CLIO, 1983), 1179–1214.

"Reflections on 'Lessons' from Vietnam." In Peter Braestrup, ed., *Vietnam As History: Ten Years after the Paris Peace Accords—A Wilson Center Conference Report* (Washington, DC: University Press of America, 1984).

"The Modern Army." In William C. Davis, ed., *The Image of War, 1861–1865*, vol. 6, *The End of an Era* (Garden City, NY: Doubleday, 1984), 15–33.

"Discussion and Comments: The Sinews of War—Economic Mobilization in World War II." In James Titus, ed., *The Home Front and War in the Twentieth Century: The American Experience in Comparative Perspective: Proceedings of the Tenth Military History Symposium, October 1982* (Washington, DC: U.S. Air Force Academy and Office of Air Force History, 1984), 119–20.

"American Strategy from Its Beginnings through the First World War." In Peter Paret, ed., with the collaboration of Gordon A. Craig and Felix Gilbert, *Makers of Modern Strategy from Machiavelli to the Nuclear Age* (Princeton, NJ: Princeton University Press, 1986), 408–43.

"European Background of American Military Affairs." In Robin Higham and Donald J. Mrozek, eds., *A Guide to the Sources of United States Military History: Supplement II* (Hamden, CT: Archon, 1986), 5–10.

"The Anglo-American Armies and Peace, 1783–1868." In Joan R. Challinor and Robert L. Beisner, eds., *Arms at Rest: Peacemaking and Peacekeeping in American History* (Westport, CT: Greenwood, 1987), 133–60.

"The Inter-War Army, 1919–1941." In Kenneth J. Hogan and William R. Roberts, eds., *Against All Enemies: Interpretations of American Military History from Colonial Times to the Present* (Westport, CT: Greenwood, 1987), 257–78.

"The End of Militarism." In Harry R. Borowski, ed., *The Harmon Memorial Lectures in Military History, 1959–1987: A Collection of the First Thirty Harmon Lectures Given at the United States Air Force Academy* (Washington, DC: Office of Air Force History, 1988), 539–52.

"Armed Forces." In Eric Foner and John A. Garraty, eds., *The Reader's Companion to American History* (Boston: Houghton Mifflin, 1991), 47–50.

"The Legacy of World War II for American Conventional Military Strategy: Should We Escape It?" In Warren F. Kimball, ed., *America Unbound: World War II and the Making of a Superpower* (New York: St. Martin's, 1992), 73–94.

"The Necessity of Force: The Civil War, World War II, and the American View of War." In Gibon Bard, ed., *War Comes Again: Comparative Vistas on the Civil War and World War II* (New York: Oxford University Press, 1995).

"How Americans Wage War: The Evolution of National Strategy." In John Whiteclay Chambers II and G. Kurt Piehler, eds., *Major Problems in American Military History: Documents and Essays* (Boston: Houghton Mifflin, 1998), 2–6.

"'A Peaceful City': Public Order in Philadelphia from Consolidation through Civil War." In Allen F. Davis and Mark H. Haller, eds., *The Peoples of Philadelphia* (Philadelphia: Temple University Press, 1973), 155–73.

"Strategy and Total War in the United States: Pershing and the American Military Tradition." In Roger Chickering and Steg Forster, eds., *Great War, Total War: Combat and Mobilization on the Western Front, 1914–1918* (Washington, DC: German Historical Institute; Cambridge and New York: Cambridge University Press, 2000), 327–45.

"The American Civil Military Cultural Gap: A Historical Perspective, Colonial Times to the Present." In Peter D. Feaver and Richard H. Kohn, eds., *Soldiers and Civilians: The Civil Military Gap in American National Security—BCSIA Studies in International Security, Triangle Institute for Security Studies* (Cambridge, MA, and London: MIT Press, 2001), 215–46.

"Auf der Suche Nach der Entscheidungsschlacht: Luctzen, 16 November 1632." Matthias Rawert, trans. In Stig Foerster, Markus Poehlmann, and Dierk Walter, eds., *Schlachten der Weltgeschichtc: Von Salamis bis Sinai* (Munich: Verlag C. H. Beck, 2001), 138–53.

Journal Articles

"Emergency Troops in the Gettysburg Campaign." *Pennsylvania History* 25 (1959): 39–57.

"The Military Thought of John M. Schofield." *Military Affairs* 23 (1959): 77–81.

"A Historian Looks at the Army." *Military Review* 52 (February 1972): 25–36.

"Valley Forge and the Strategy of an Army in Being." *The Valley Forge Journal: A Record of Patriotism and American Culture* 2 (1984): 101–10.

"From the Normandy Beaches to the Falaise-Argentan Pocket: A Critique of Allied Operational Planning in 1944." *Military Review* 70 (September 1990): 45–64.

"To the Crossing of the Rhine: American Strategic Thought to World War II." *Armed Forces and Society: An Interdisciplinary Journal* 5 (1979): 302–20. Reprinted in Davis Curtis Skagges and Robert S. Browning III, eds., *In Defense of the Republic: Readings in American Military History* (Belmont, CA: Wadsworth, 1991), 255–73.

"Just Wars and Unjust Means." *Temple International and Comparative Law Journal* 6 (Spring 1992): 7–11.

"The American Military and the Principle of Civilian Control from McClellan to Powell." *Journal of Military History* 57 (1993): 27–58.

"Fighting with Allies: The Debate Fifty Years On." *JFQ: Joint Forces Quarterly—A Professional Military Journal* 8 (Summer 1995): 38–45.

The George C. Marshall Lecture in Military History: "The Soldier, the Statesman, and the Military Historian." *Journal of Military History* 63 (1999): 807–22.

"Response to Brian McAallister Linn by Russell F. Weigley." *Journal of Military History* 66(2) (2002): 531–33.

Introductions and Forewords

In John Morgan Dederer, *Making Bricks without Straw: Nathanael Greene's Southern Campaign and Mao Tse-Tung's Mobile War* (Manhattan, KS: Sunflower University Press, 1983).
In Shelby L. Stanton, *Order of Battle, U.S. Army, World War II* (Novato, CA: Presidio, 1984).
In Basil Henry Liddell Hart, *Great Captains Unveiled* (New York: Da Capo, 1996).
In Hannah Benner Roach, *Colonial Philadelphians* (Philadelphia: Genealogical Society of Pennsylvania Monograph Series, 1999).
In Earl A. Reitan, *Riflemen: On the Cutting Edge of World War II* (Burlington, VT: Merrian, 2001).
In Colin D. Heston, *German Anti-Partisan Warfare in Europe, 1939–1945* (Atglen, PA: Schiffer, 2001).
In Gregory A. Daddis, *Fighting the Great Crusade: An 8th Infantry Artillery Officer in World War II* (Baton Rouge: Louisiana State University Press, 2002).
In Russell H. Conwell, *Acres of Diamonds* (Philadelphia: Temple University Press, 2002).
In Peter S. Kindsvatter, *American Soldiers: Ground Combat in the World Wars, Korea and Vietnam* (Lawrence: University Press of Kansas, 2003).

Reference Work Entries

In *Encyclopedia Britannica*, 24 vols. (Chicago and London: Encyclopedia Britannica, 1972): "Brandywine, Battle of," 4:104; "Chester," 5:471; "Germantown," 10:277; "Haverford," 11:168; "Norristown," 16:580; "Philadelphia," 17:14–22; "West Chester," 23:420.
In John A. Garraty, ed., *Encyclopedia of American Biography* (New York, Evanston, San Francisco, London: Harper and Row, 1974): "Benedict Arnold," 39–40; "Benjamin O. Davis, Sr.," 256–57; "George Dewey," 274; "Nathanael Greene," 351–53; "Joseph Eggleston Johnston," 596–97; "George Brinton McClellan," 705–6; "Samuel Eliot Morrison," 781–84; "Matthew Calbraith Perry," 850–51; "Oliver Hazard Perry," 1086; "Anthony Wayne," 1162–63; "James Wilkinson," 1203–4.
In *Dictionary of American History, Revised Edition*, 7 vols. and index (New York: Scribner, 1976): "Air Cavalry," 1:49; "Philadelphia," 5:277–78.
In John A. Garraty, ed., *Dictionary of American Biography, Supplement Five* (New York: Scribner, 1977): "Frank Down Merrill," 466–76.
In Alexander DeConde, ed., *Encyclopedia of American Foreign Policy: Studies of the Principal Movements and Ideas*, 3 vols. (New York: Scribner, 1978): "Dissent in Wars," 253–67.

In David C. Roller and Robert W. Twyman, eds., *Encyclopedia of Southern History* (Baton Rouge: Louisiana State University Press, 1980): "City Point," 216; "Battle of Cold Harbor," 247–48.

In Jack P. Greene, ed., *Encyclopedia of American Political History: Studies of the Principal Movements and Ideas*, 3 vols. (New York: Scribner, 1984): "Armed Forces," 1:69–82.

In Roger J. Spiller and Joseph G. Dawson III, eds., *Dictionary of American Military Biography*, 3 vols. (Westport, CT, and London: Greenwood, 1984): "Halleck, Henry Wager," 2:421–25; "Mahan, Denis Hart," 2:714–18; "Root, Elihu," 3:938–42; "Upton, Emory," 3:1123–26.

Papers Presented to Professional Organizations

"Military History and Peace Research: A Discussion." Organization of American Historians Joint Session with Conference for Peace Research in History, April 20, 1968.

"The Elihu Root Reforms and the Progressive Era." U.S. Air Force Academy Military History Symposium, May 10, 1968.

"The Civil War Impact on Military Strategy." Pacific Coast Branch, American Historical Association, September 4, 1970.

"'A Peaceful City': Public Order in Philadelphia from Consolidation through Civil War." Temple University Conference on the History of Peoples of Philadelphia, April 1, 1971.

"The Armed Forces and American Foreign Policy since 1898: The Army." Southern Historical Association Joint Session with the American Military Institute, November 19, 1971.

"The End of Militarism." Fifteenth Harmon Memorial Lecture in Military History, U.S. Air Force Academy Military History Symposium, October 14, 1972.

"The Writing of the History of Military Institutions: The Army." American Military Institute, April 3, 1976.

"American Military Strategy." Military Academy Bicentennial Symposium on the History of the American Revolution, April 22, 1976.

"American Strategic Thought to World War II." Inter-University Seminar on Armed Forces and Society, October 22, 1977.

"Washington's Campaign in Northern Chester County in 1777." The French and Pickering Creeks Conservation Trust, Kimberton, Pennsylvania, December 1, 1977.

"A Past in Need of Remembrance: Neglected Paths from Colonial Backgrounds." Society of Colonial Wars in the Commonwealth of Pennsylvania, Philadelphia, March 2, 1978.

"The Middle States Campaign of 1777: A Reappraisal of the Continental Army." Presidential Address, Pennsylvania Historical Association, October 20, 1978.

"The Long Death of the Indian-Fighting Army." National Archives Conference, "Soldiers and Civilians: The United States Army and the American People," May 17, 1979.

"Lincoln and the Strategy of the American Civil War." The Fortenbaugh Memorial Lecture on the Civil War, Gettysburg College, Gettysburg, Pennsylvania, November 19, 1979.

"The Atomic Revolution in Warfare," Air War College, Maxwell Air Force Base, Alabama, September 17, 1981.

"The Condition of Military History: Armies and Air Forces." Pacific Coast Branch, American Historical Association, August 13, 1982.

"Ulm and Vicksburg, Austerlitz and Gettysburg." Shelby Cullom Davis Center Seminar, Princeton University, Princeton, New Jersey, October 1, 1982.

"Reflections on the 'Lessons' of Vietnam." Woodrow Wilson International Center for Scholars Conference on the Vietnam War, January 8, 1983.

"Valley Forge and the Strategy of an Army in Being." Valley Forge Historical Society, Valley Forge, Pennsylvania, December, 18, 1983.

"General Omar N. Bradley: Peace in Europe." The Eisenhower Center, University of New Orleans, May 6, 1985.

"The New Relevance of Southern Chivalry: The South and the Problems of the Control of War." The Walter Lynwood Fleming Lecture in Southern History, Louisiana State University, Baton Rouge, April 16–17, 1986.

"The World War II Legacy in Conventional Military Strategy." Conference on "World War II and the Shaping of Modern America," Rutgers University–Newark, Newark, New Jersey, April 5, 1986.

"World War II: A Retrospective View." The Robert G. Bone Distinguished Lecture Series, Illinois State University, Normal, Illinois, March 4–7, 1986.

"American Warfare in the Evolution of War." Mellon Seminar, Princeton University, Princeton, New Jersey, February 24, 1989.

"The Wound in the Heart: America and the Vietnam Wars." Saint Joseph's University, Philadelphia, Pennsylvania, March 21, 1989.

"D-Day: Flaws in the Most Careful of Plans." Symposium on "D-Day Remembered: The 29th Division and the Normandy Invasion," University of Baltimore, June 9, 1989.

"The Great Transformation: The Military Coming of Age and World War II." The Forty-eighth Coast Guard Academy Lecture of the Newcomen Society of the United States, New London, Connecticut, September 15, 1989.

"Eisenhower in Perspective: Ranking Him among the Great Commanders of American History," Kansas State University, Manhattan, Kansas, October 9, 1990.

"Dwight D. Eisenhower: An American Leader in the Pennsylvania Tradition." Fifty-ninth Annual Meeting of the Pennsylvania Historical Association, Dickinson College, and the Cumberland County Historical Society, Carlisle, Pennsylvania, October 19, 1990.

"On War in Military History." Fifty-eighth Annual Meeting of the American Military Institute, Duke University, Durham, North Carolina, March 22, 1991.

"The Persian Gulf War: The Logical Culmination of American Military History?" The Victor L. Johnson Lecture, Department of History and Phi Alpha Theta History Honor Society, Muhlenberg College, Allentown, Pennsylvania, April 3, 1991.

"The American Way of War." United States Marine Corps Command and Staff College, Quantico, Virginia, September 12, 1991.

"The American War Effort." United States Marine Corps War College, Quantico, Virginia, October 29, 1991.

"The Present and Future of War." National War College, Fort Lesley J. McNair, Washington, D.C., November 14, 1991.

"The Not So Good War: Reflections on the American Conduct of World War II." Conference on "1941, America Enters the War: A Retrospective Analysis of America's Entry into World War II and the Significance of 1941 to World Order." La Salle University, Philadelphia, December 5, 1991.

"The American Military and the Principle of Civilian Control from McClellan to Powell." Conference on "The History of War As Part of General History." Institute for Advanced Study, Princeton University, Princeton, New Jersey, March 12, 1992.

"The Revolutionary War and Its Impact on the Idea of Freedom." Lecture Series on "African-Americans in Antebellum America," Temple University, Philadelphia, April 8–10, 1992.

"The Pennsylvania Provincial Conference of 1776 and the Meaning of the American Revolution." Conference on Pennsylvania's Two Hundred Sixteenth Birthday Celebration, Carpenters' Court, Philadelphia, June 20, 1992.

"The American Army in Europe in World War II: Lessons—The Future of Warfare." United States Army Europe and Seventh Army Officer Professional Development Session, Headquarters United States Army Europe, Heidelberg, Germany, September 16, 1992.

"Keeping the Peace after the Cold War." Temple Association of Retired Professionals, Temple University–Center City, Philadelphia, September 21, 1992.

"The Lessons of World War II for Future World Peace." Conference on "The Military Lessons of World War II: A Public Humanities Symposium," State University of New York at Brockport, October 2, 1992.

"USA: Pershing." International Conference cosponsored by the German Historical Institutes, the Swiss National Foundation, and the Max and Elsa Beer-Brawand Foundation, Schloss Munchenwiler, Bern, Switzerland, October 9–12, 1992.

"The Historian and the Library." Inaugural lecture for the Friends of the Library of Albright College, Reading, Pennsylvania, October 29, 1992.

"The Strategy of Robert E. Lee." United States Marine Corps Command and Staff College, Quantico, Virginia, November 4, 1992.

"The Future of Civilian Control of the Military in the United States." National War College, Fort Leslie J. McNair, Washington, D.C., November 12, 1992.

"Ike and Monty." Lecture series on "Perspectives in Military History," U.S. Army Military History Institute, Carlisle Barracks, Pennsylvania, November 19, 1992.

Select Bibliography 253

"The United States in World War II." United States Marine Corps War College, Quantico, Virginia, December 10, 1992.
"D-Day: The Most Carefully Planned Military Operation in History, and Its Flaws." Lecture series on "America Goes to War: The European Theater in World War II," Camden County College, Blackwood, New Jersey, April 21, 1994.
"The Necessity of Force: The Civil War, World War II, and the American View of War," Gettysburg Civil War Institute, Gettysburg, Pennsylvania, June 27, 1994.
"The Great War in the History of American Strategy." Sixth Annual Great War Seminar, San Francisco, September 27, 1996.
"Weapons of War: The Technological Legacy." Forum on "Issues and Institutions: The Great War—The Shaping of Our Century," the Smithsonian Institution, Washington, D.C., October 25, 1996.
"North Africa and Italy: Preparation for OVERLORD." Advanced Warfighting Seminar, U.S. Army War College, Carlisle Barracks, Pennsylvania, March 8, 1997.
"A Great Civil War." History Books 2001, Greystone American History Store, Gettysburg, Pennsylvania, June 30, 2001.
"Philadelphia in the Gettysburg Campaign." Association of Mid-Atlantic Civil War Round Tables Symposium, October 20, 2001.

Contributors

CHRISTOPHER DeROSA is assistant professor of history at Monmouth University, West Long Branch, New Jersey, and author of *Political Indoctrination in the U.S. Army from World War II to the Vietnam War* (Lincoln: University of Nebraska Press, 2006).

DOUGLAS V. JOHNSON is research professor, National Security Affairs, at the Strategic Studies Institute, U.S. Army War College, Carlisle Barracks, Pennsylvania. He retired from the U.S. Army in 1992 after thirty years of service as a field artilleryman and educator. He has been associate professor of history at the United States Military Academy and is an original member of the faculty of the School of Advanced Military Studies, U.S. Army Command and General Staff College, Fort Leavenworth, Kansas. He coauthored *Soissons, 1918* (College Station: Texas A&M University Press, 1999).

PETER S. KINDSVATTER served in the U.S. Army for twenty-one years, retiring in 1992 as a lieutenant colonel. He is a graduate of the Armor Officers' Basic and Advanced Courses and the U.S. Army Command and General Staff College and holds a Master of Military Arts and Science degree from the School for Advanced Military Studies. He is author of the award-winning *American Soldiers: Ground Combat in the World Wars, Korea, and Vietnam* (Lawrence: University Press of Kansas, 2003) as well as numerous articles for *Parameters*, *Military Review*, *Army*, *Armor*, and *Army Logistician*.

EDWARD G. LONGACRE (coeditor) is a staff historian at Headquarters Air Combat Command, Langley Air Force Base, Virginia. He has written twenty-three books, one hundred journal articles, and more than four hundred reference-work entries on the Civil War and U.S. military aviation. His writings have won the Fletcher Pratt Award, the Douglas Southall Freeman History Award, and the Moncado Prize.

ADAM NORMAN LYNDE has held sessional appointments at the University of Western Ontario, the Memorial University of Newfoundland, Toronto's Humber College Institute of Technology and Advanced Learning, and the Royal Military College of Canada. He is currently assistant professor of history at Delta State University, Cleveland, Mississippi. He is author of the forthcoming *The Mediterranean Theater: British and American Combined Operations, 1942–1945* (Wilmington, DE: Scholarly Resources).

J. BRITT McCARLEY, a former National Park Ranger, has worked in the U.S. Army History Program since 1988 and is now Chief of Field History Programs for the U.S. Army Training and Doctrine Command, Fort Monroe, Virginia. He is the author of *The Atlanta Campaign: A Civil War Driving Tour of Atlanta-Area Battlefields* (Cary, NC: Cherokee Publishing, 1989), and is coauthor of *The Whirlwind War: The United States Army in Operations Desert Shield and Desert Storm* (Washington, DC: U.S. Army Center for Military History, 1998).

G. E. PATRICK MURRAY for the past thirty years has taught history at Valley Forge Military College, Wayne, Pennsylvania. A specialist in World War II in northwestern Europe, he has published three books, *Eisenhower versus Montgomery: The Continuing Debate* (Westport, CT: Greenwood, 1996), *World War II Chronicles: Victory in Western Europe* (New York: Metro Books, 1999), and *Bomber Missions: Aviation Art of World War II* (New York: Barnes & Noble Books, 2006). He has delivered papers at several conferences devoted to World War II and has appeared on A&E's *Biography* series.

JAMES PARADIS, a former licensed guide at Gettysburg National Battlefield Park, is dean of the Upper School at St. Mary's Hall–Doane Academy in Burlington, New Jersey, where he has taught history and psychology. He also teaches history at Arcadia University, Glenside, Pennsylvania. His published works include *Strike the Blow for Freedom: The 6th United States Colored Infantry in the Civil War* (Shippensburg, PA: White Mane Books, 1998) and *African Americans and the Gettysburg Campaign* (Lanham, MD: Scarecrow, 2005).

DENNIS SHOWALTER is professor of history at Colorado College and Past President of the Society for Military History. His most recent monographs are *Patton and Rommel: Men of War in the Twentieth Century* (New York: Berkeley, 2005), and the forthcoming *Mercenary to Citizen*, vol. 2, *Soldiers' Lives through History* (Westport, CT: Greenwood, 2007), coauthored with William Astore.

JENNIFER L. SPEELMAN is assistant professor of history at The Citadel, the Military College of South Carolina. Previously she taught in the Maritime Studies Program of Williams College and Old Mystic Seaport. In 1999 she participated in a United States Military Academy seminar that examined the impact of war on society, and she served as coordinator of the 2005 meeting of the Society for Military History and is now a member of the Board of Trustees. She has authored several entries in *Encyclopedia of War & American Society* (Thousand Oaks, CA: Sage, 2006) and is currently at work on a history of U.S. maritime education.

JOHN F. VOTAW, a graduate of the United States Military Academy, is executive director Emeritus, Cantigny First Division Foundation, Wheaton, Illinois. A retired lieutenant colonel, he commanded U.S. Army cavalry and armored units through the battalion level and served a tour in Vietnam during 1966–67. He is adjunct associate professor of history at Dominican University, River Forest, Illinois, and a trustee for the Society for Military History. He authored *The American Expeditionary Forces in World War I* (Oxford, UK: Osprey, 2005) and is writing a history of the U.S. First Division in 1918.

THEODORE J. ZEMAN (coeditor) received his doctorate in history from Temple University in 2000 and subsequently taught at his alma mater. At present he teaches at Saint Joseph's University, Philadelphia, Pennsylvania and Valley Forge Military College. He is at work on *Partners in Victory: Grant, Meade, and the Army of the Potomac, May 1864–April 1865*.

Index

Aachen, Germany, 160, 163
Abercromby, James, 223
Abercromby, Ralph, 207
Abilene, KS, 180
Ach, Isidor L., 77
Adams, USS, 75
Adjutant General's Office, 85, 88
Admiralty, British, 210, 217, 224, 231
African Snail, 191
Agricultural College Bill: see Morrill Act
Aisne-Marne Offensive, 113–16
Aix, France, 229
Akabane Tire Shop, 193
Albright College, x
Alexander, Harold R. G. L., 153–54, 164–65, 170, 172–74, 176
Alexander, John, xix
Allatoona Mountains, 35
Allatoona Pass, 35–36
Allen, Henry Truman, 87
Ambrose, Stephen, 179
American Expeditionary Forces (AEF), 84, 87–88, 90–91, 105–08, 111, 117–18
American Labor Party, 137
American Legion, 146
American Military Institute, xvi
American Philosophical Society, xvii
American Red Cross, 141
Amherst, Jeffery, 223, 232
Amiens, France, 158
Andersonville Prison, 42
Andrew, John, 14–15
Annapolis, MD, 70, 74, 77
Anson, George, 228, 230
Antwerp, Belgium, 160–62, 168
Appomattox Court House, VA, 47
Ardennes Mountains, 153, 158, 160, 162, 164–68, 174
Armies,
  First Allied Airborne, 157

First (Canadian), 156
First (French), 158, 163
First (U. S.), 156, 158, 160–62, 165, 168–69, 174–76, 178
Second (British), 156, 175
Second (U. S.), 114, 154, 176
Third (U. S.), 154, 156, 158, 161–62, 164, 168–69, 175
Fourth (French), 115
Sixth (U. S.), 189
Seventh (German), 158
Seventh (U. S.), 158, 163
Eighth (British), 155
Eighth (U. S.), 189–91, 193–94, 198
Ninth (U. S.), 162, 164–66, 168–69, 175–79
Tenth (French), 105
Army, Department of the, 190, 195
Army Field Engineering School, 90
Army Groups,
  1st (U. S.), 155–56
  6th (U. S.), 158
  12th (U. S.), 156, 158, 160–62, 165, 168–69, 174–76, 178
  21st (British), 153–56, 159–62, 164–66, 169, 173, 176–78
Army Line School, 90
Army-Navy Game, xi
Army of Arkansas, 29
Army of Cuban Pacification, 113
Army of Mississippi, 36
Army of Northern Virginia, 14, 47
Army of Tennessee, 28, 32–33, 35, 45–46
Army of the Cumberland, 29, 34, 41, 43
Army of the James, 13–17
Army of the Ohio, 29, 36, 38
Army of the Potomac, 6–7, 16–17, 41, 47
Army of the Tennessee, 29, 33–34, 38, 40–42
Army Signal School, 90
Army Staff School, 90

Army War College, xii, xvii, 90–92, 104, 109
Arnhem, Holland, 157, 161, 166
Athens, Greece, 167
Atlanta & West Point R.R., 43–44
Atlanta, Battle of, 40–41
Atlanta Campaign, 26–47
Atlanta, GA, 26–27, 30, 32–36, 38–47
Auckland, Lord, 209
Augsburg, Germany, 178
Austin, TX, 142
Axis Powers, 233
Ayres, Leonard P., 115

Babcock, Conrad Stanton, 104–10, 112–13, 115–20
Baker, J. W., 75
Bald Hill, 40
Bald Hill, Battle of: see Atlanta, Battle of
Baldwin, Hanson W., 156
Balkan Mountains, 158
Balkan Wars, 95
Baltimore, MD, 20–21, 69
Barham, Lord, 210, 235
Barnard, John, 208
Bartlett, Thomas, 226
Bates, Edward, 20
Battery Wagner, SC, 13
Baugh, Dan, 208
Bavarian Alps, 179
Bay of Biscay, 229
bazooka rockets, 194
bazookas, 194
Beauregard, P. G. T., 18
Beckford, William, 202
Beehler, William H., 91
Beevor, Antony, 178–80
Belfort, France, 163
Belleau Wood, Battle of, 113
Bennett, Lerone, Jr., 8
Berlin Airlift, 180
Berlin, Germany, 91–92, 153, 157, 166, 176–80, 230
Bermuda, 220
Berne, Switzerland, 89
Bevin, Ernest, 166, 171
Big-5: see Rebuild, Operation
Big Five Basketball, xi
Big-9, 196
Black, Jeremy, 202, 238
Black Watch, 217
Blaine, James G., 74
Blair, Montgomery, 20

Bliss, Tasker H., 86–87
Bloch, Jean, 110
Board of Education for New York, 68
Board of Steamboat Inspectors, 68
Boer War, 212, 217
Boise desGrimpettes, France, 116
Bombay, India, 223
Bonn, Germany, 167, 174
Bonnie Prince Charlie: see Stuart, Charles Edward
Bordeaux, France, 116
Boscawen, Edward, 209–10
Boston, MA, 69, 76–77, 220
Boulogne, France, 161
Bowditxh, Nathaniel, 70, 72
Bowen, Catherine Drinker, 144
Braddock, Edward, 216, 223
Bradley, Omar N., 156–66, 168–69, 171, 175–79
Bracken, Brendan, 172
Brainard, David L., 90
Brayman, Mason, 19–20
Bremen, Germany, 178
Brest, France, 160–61, 209
Brewer, John, 202, 204, 233–34, 237
Brewster, Andre W., 87
Brice's Cross Roads, Battle of, 42
Brigades, U. S.,
  4th Marine, 113
  10th Inf., 114
  52nd Inf., 115
  55th Inf., 114
  56th Inf., 114
  63rd Inf., 113, 116
  90th Inf., 87
Bristol, England, 224
Britain, Battle of, 180
British Broadcasting Corp., 171
British Chiefs of Staff, 153, 166
British Establishment, 213
British Isles, 206
British Staff College, 155
Brittany, France, 160–61
Brooke, Alan, 153–58, 161–68, 170, 173–74, 176–77, 179–81, 201, 237
Brown, Dwight, 132
Brown, Edgar G., 131
Brush Mountain, 36
Brussels, Belgium, 160
Brussels Conference, 160, 162
Buck, Beaumont B., 108
Buell, Don Carlos, 8

Buffett, Howard H., 147
Bulge, Battle of the, 168–69, 171–72
Bullard, Robert L., 108–9, 111, 113, 118–20
Bull, Harold R., 173
Bull Run, First Battle of, 6, 29, 32–33, 38
Bullivant, William M., 67
Bureau of Equipment and Recruiting, 71
Bureau of Public Relations, 142
Bureau of U. S. Colored Troops, 15
Burleigh, Daniel C., 69
Burnside, Ambrose E., 17
Burton, David, xv
Bush Creek, MO, 12
Butcher, Harry C., 176
Butler, Benjamin F., 12–13, 19, 69
Butler, Hugh A., 135, 138
Byng, John, 211

Cabin Creek, Indian Terr., 12
Cadiz, Spain, 210
Caesar, Augustus, 222
Calais, France, 161
Calhoun, John C., 90
Calkins, Carlos B., 74
Camberley, England, 155
Campbell, R. M., 89
Campling, Henry, 77
Camp Ojima, Japan, 197
Camp William Penn, 14
Canadian Confederation, 231
Cape Breton Island, 220
Cape Corps: *see* Dutch Hottentot Corps
Caribbean Sea, 207, 223
Cartagena, West Indies, 222
Cassville, GA, 35
Castel, Albert E., 27, 46
Castlereagh, Viscount, 210
Center for the Study of Force and Diplomacy, xvii–xviii
Central Goup of Armies: *see* Army Groups, 12th
Central Powers, 233
Chadwick, French Ensor, 65, 71, 91, 93
Champagne, France, 115
Champagne-Marne Defensive, 114
Chancellorsville, Battle of, 40
Charibee Islands, 207
Charles Evans Cemetery, ix
Chase, Salmon P., 9, 20
Chateau-Thierry Campaign, 114
Chattahoochee R., 33, 38–39, 43–44, 46
Chattanooga Campaign, 29

Chattanooga, TN, 30–31, 33, 42, 45
Chaumont, France, 112–13
Cheatham, B. Frank, 112–13, 115
Chemical Base Depot, 197
Chemical Corps, 190, 197
Cherbourg, France, 161
Chicago, IL, 10, 142
Chicago Tribune, 84
Chickamauga, Battle of, 30, 39
Chickasaw Bluffs, Battle of, 33
China Relief Expedition, 84
Churchill, Winston S., 153–55, 157–59, 163–68, 171–72, 174–81, 216
Cierges, France, 116
Cincinnati, OH, 29
Civil War, American, ix–x, xii–xiv, xvii–xix, 5–22, 26–47, 66–67, 71, 84, 88, 104–5, 129–30, 134, 142, 148, 154, 231
Clausewitz, Carl von, 201–4, 229, 234, 237
Clauss, Errol M., 27
Clermont, France, 114
Clifford, Alexander, 169
Coast Artillery School, 90
Cold Harbor, Battle of, 37
Cold War, 148
Colley, Linda, 204, 235
Collingwood, Cuthbert, 210–11
Cologne, France, 166–67
Colorado, USS, 72
Colt .45 pistol, 105
Combined Chiefs of Staff, 154, 162, 167, 170–73, 177
Comello, Jerry, xii
Command and General Staff School, 154
Communications Zone, 159
Confederate Congress, 18
Confiscation Acts, 6–7
Conger, Arthur L., 108
Congress of Industrial Organizations, 140, 145
Connally, Tom, 136
Connor, Fox, 105
Connor, William D., 113, 116–17
Conway, HMS, 67, 71
Cook, Frederic W., 131, 133
Corbett, Julian, 228
Corn Laws, 231
Cornwallis, Charles, 210
Corps,
    I (U. S.), 114
    IV (U. S.), 114
    V (U. S.), 115

Corps, *(continued)*
   VIII (U. S.), 165
   IX (U. S.), 17
   XIV (U. S.), 43
   XV (U. S.), 41–42
   XVI (U. S.), 39–41, 176
   XVII (French), 115
   XVII (U. S.), 32
   XIX (U. S.), 178–79
   XX (French), 105
   XX (U. S.), 41
   XXIII (U. S.), 43
   XXV (U. S.), 13
   XXX (British), 161
Corps d'Afrique, 13
Corps of Engineers, 190
Cosmas, Graham, 83
Cotentin Peninsula, 159
Couch, Darius N., 14
Council on Books in War-Time, 145
Covington, GA, 39
Cox, Jacob D., 27
Craig, Malin, 109, 118
Crater, Battle of the, 17
Crerar, Henry D. G., 156, 160
Crimean War, 94, 208, 216
Crowder, Enoch H., 87
Cumberland, Duke of, 205, 208
Cummings, A. J., 166, 169
Curtin, Andrew G., 14
Cutler, Robert, 132–33, 137–38, 140–43

D-Day, 153, 158, 162, 164
Dahlem, Germany, 179
Daily Express (London), 169
Daily Mail (London), 169, 171–72
Daily Mirror (London), 156
Dallas, GA, 35, 43–44
Dalton, GA, 33–34
Dartmouth College, xi
Davis, Edward, 90–91
Davis, Jefferson, 18, 39, 47, 94
Davis, Stephen E., 27
Dawes, Henry L., 69
Dawnay, Christopher, 163–64, 170
Decatur, GA, 38–40
Declaration of Independence, xiv
decontaminating apparatus, 197
Defence of the Realm Act, 204
De Gaulle, Charles, 168
De Guingand, Francis, 161, 171
Delafield, Richard, 85, 94

Delaware R., 215
DeLong, George W., 69
Dempsey, Miles, 156, 175
Denison, TX, 180
Devers, Jacob L., 158, 164–65, 175
Dewey, Thomas E., 132, 140, 142, 145–46
Dieppe, France, 161
Dijon, France, 158
Dimmock Line, 13
Dinant, Belgium, 167
Disreali, Benjamin, 237
Distinguished Service Medal, 113
Distinguished Service Order, 155
Divisions,
   1st Cav. (U. S.), 194
   1st Inf. (U. S.), 106, 112–14, 118
   2nd Inf. (U. S.), 107, 113
   2nd Wurttemburg Landwehr (German), 114
   3rd Inf. (U. S.), 116
   1st Guards (German), 114
   4th Guards (German), 116
   5th Guards (German), 114
   5th Inf. (U. S.), 114
   7th Inf. (U. S.), 194
   13th Inf. (French), 115
   24th Inf. (U. S.), 194
   25th Inf. (U. S.), 194
   26th Inf. (U. S.), 112, 115
   28th Inf. (U. S.), 112, 114, 116
   29th Inf. (U. S.), 115
   32nd Inf. (U. S.), 113, 116
   37th Inf. (U. S.), 114
   42nd Inf. (U. S.), 112, 115
   50th Inf. (U. S.), 157
   59th Inf. (U. S.), 157
   77th Inf. (U. S.), 116–17
   82nd Inf. (U. S.), 114, 117
   89th Inf. (U. S.), 106
   170th Inf. (French), 115
Dorwart, Jeffery, 86, 91
Douglass, Frederick, 11
Drake, Francis, 230
Dreilick, William M., 73, 77
Dresden, Germany, 176, 178
Drexel University, x-xl
Dublin, Ireland, 222
Duncan, George B., 108, 113
Dundas, Henry, 205, 207, 209, 226–27
Dunkirk, France, 155
Dunn, Richard, x
Dutch Cape Colony, 225, 230

Dutch Gap Canal, 19
Dutch Hottentot Corps, 223

East India Co., 212, 214, 220, 223, 225
East Indies, 211, 221, 224, 230
East Point, GA, 43–44
Eastland, James O., 137
Eastland-Rankin Bill, 137, 139
Echternach, Luxembourg, 167
Ecole deGuerre, 109
Eden, Anthony, 179
Edinburgh, Scotland, 215, 218, 222
Eisenhower, Dwight D., 118–19, 147–48, 153–81
El Alamein, Battle of, 155
Elbe R., 176, 178–80
Electoral College, 146
Ely, Hanson, 109–110
Emancipation Proclamation, 8–10, 12
Emory University, 27
Empire Review, 233
English Channel, 157, 228–29
Enterprise, USS, 74–76
Erfurt, Germany, 176
Ershkowitz, Herbert, xi
Esquimalt, British Columbia, 231
Etowah R., 35, 43
Evening Standard (London), 169
expansible army, 90
Ezra Church, Battle of, 42–43

Falkland Islands, 214, 229
Falls, Cyril, 162, 169, 171
Far East Command, 189, 191, 195
Federal War Ballot, 143
Ferguson, Homer S., 137
Ferrero, Edward, 17
Fifteenth Amendment, 131
First Unitarian Church of Philadelphia, xiv
Fiske, Harold B., 107–8, 113, 117
Fismes, France, 114
flamethrowers, 197
Flanders, France, 228–29
Floyd, John B., 94
Fontenoy, Battle of, 205
Foot Guards, 207–8, 222, 225
Forbes, John, 223
Foreign Liquidation Commission, 187–88
Forrest, Nathan B., 19, 42
Fort Blakely, AL, 21–22
Fort Fisher, NC, 13
Fort Harrison, VA, 14

Fort Leavenworth, KS, 88, 91, 107, 109
Fort Monroe, VA, 12
Fort Pillow, TN, 19–21
Foss, Wilson P., Jr., 93
Foster, C. A., 75
Fourteenth Amendment, 131
Fox, Henry, 206
Franco-Prussian War, 94
Frankfurt, Germany, 160, 166, 173, 175–76, 178
Fraser's Highland Regiment, 206
Frederick the Great, 211, 228–29
Freese, Jacob R., 16
French Channel, 228
French, John, 216
French Republic, 207
French Revolution, 204, 207, 212, 216, 222, 227, 233
Fuchu, Japan, 193
Fugitive Slave Law, 12
Funchal, Madeira, 75

Gage, Thomas, 215
Gallicchio, Marc, x
Gallipoli, Battle of, 233
Ganges R., 221
Garrard, Kenner, 39, 41
gas alarms, 197
gas masks, 197
General Board of the Navy, 85
George III, King, 212
George VI, King, 159
Georgia R.R., 38–40
German West Wall, 157, 161
Gettysburg Address, xiv
Gettysburg, Battle of, xviii–xix, 12, 37, 39
Gettysburg, PA, ix, 154
Gibraltar, Territory of, 207, 220, 231
Glasgow, Scotland, 221
Glorious Revolution, 216
Glover, Richard, 205
Godson, W. F. H., 89
Graham, George, 234
Grand Alliance, 153
Grant, Ulysses S., 17–19, 29–30, 32–34, 37, 41, 45–47, 84, 165, 180
Granville, France, 159
Gravelly Plateau, GA, 35
Gray, Robert A., 142
Great Mutiny, 221
Greeley, Horace, 7
Green, Francis W., 72, 74

Green-Lucas Bill, 131–39
Green, Richard, 67
Green, Theodore Francis, 131, 133–34, 136, 139
Greenwood, John, 84, 86
Gregg, David M., ix
Grey, Lord, 231
Grimsley, Mark, 5, 7
Guelzo, Allen C., 8
Guffey, Joseph, 137
Gurkhas, 212

Hagerman, Edward, 47
Haig, Douglas, 232
Halifax, Nova Scotia, 206, 220, 231
Halleck, Henry W., 29, 38, 43–44
Haller, Mark, xiv
Hamburg, Germany, 178
Hamilton, Ian, 87
Hamilton, Nigel, 157, 171
Hancock, W. S., 85
Handel, George Frederick, 234
Hanover, Germany, 178
Hanover, House of, 228
Hanoverian War, First, 206
Hansen, Chester, 169
Hardee, William J., 44
Hardie, Keir, 232
Harrisburg Civil War Round Table, xiii
Harrisburg, PA, 14
Harvard University, 109
Hasselt, Belgium, 170–71
Hatch Amendment, 144–45
Hatch, Carl H., 144
Hayes, E. A., 141
Hazen, William B., 85, 94–95
Heintzelman, Stuart, 88
Heiss, Gerson K., 195
Helder, Holland, 208, 227
Herbstnebel Operation, 167
Herrick, Myron T., 88, 94
Hershey, PA, 141
Hessians, 200
Higginson, Thomas Wentworth, 11
Hines, John L., 111, 118
Hino, Japan, 193
Hitler, Adolf, 142, 159, 167–68
Hodges, Courtney H., 156, 161, 168, 174
Holland, Matthew F., 153
Holman, Rufus, 139
Holm, Michael, 133
Holmes, Oliver Wendell, Jr., 144

Home Islands, British, 206–8, 222, 224–25, 227, 231
Hood, John Bell, 27–28, 39–42, 44–47
Hood, Samuel, 230
Hooker, Joseph, 41
Hopson, Peregrine, 206
Horse Guards, 227
Houlding, John, 214
House of Commons, 202, 211, 216, 234
Howard, O. O., 41–42, 45
Hunter, David, 9, 11

Immerman, Richard, xvii
Imperial General Staff, 153, 164, 167, 176–77, 179
Inchon Landing, 194
Indian Wars, 85
Institutional Army, 117
Inter-Allied Rhineland High Commission, 87
Irish Establishment, 213–14
Irish Volunteers, 236
Irrawaddy R., 232
Iverson, Andrew J., 77

Jackson, Andrew, 12
Jackson, Stonewall, 40
Jacobite Rising, 215
Jacques, William H., 69–70
James R., 7, 19, 221
Jamestown, USS, 71
Janowitz, Morris, 108
Japan Logistical Command, 190, 195
Jim Crow Laws, 130
Johnson, Andrew, 16
Johnston, Joseph E., 27–28, 32–39, 43, 45–47
Joint Army and Navy Board, 92
Joint Chiefs of Staff, 155, 177
Joint Committee on the Conduct of the War, 17
Jones, James Pickett, 27
Jonesboro, Battle of, 44–46
Jonesboro, GA, 44
Judiciary Committee, Senate, 134
Judson, William V., 95
Jullouville, France, 159

Kaiser Wilhelm II, 159, 232
Kaiser Wilhelm Institute for Physics, 179
Kamloops, British Columbia, 232
Karsten, Peter, 86
Kassel, Germany, 166, 173, 176, 178

Keegan, John, 32
Kelley, J. D. J., 74
Kennedy, Paul, 226
Kennesaw Mountain, 35–37
Kennesaw Mountain, Battle of, 36–38, 43–44, 46
Kennett, Lee B., 27
Kiel, Germany, 178
Kilkenny, Ireland, 215
King, Campbell, 109
King's German Legion, 220
Kingston, GA, 35
Knox, Dudley, 92
Knox, Frank, 139–40
Kobe, Japan, 195–96
Kobe Quartermaster Depot, 196
Kolb Farm, Battle of, 37
Korean War, 187–98
Koshien, Japan, 193
Kuala Lumpur, Malaysia, 232
Kubrick, Stanley, xiii
Kuhn, Joseph E., 92

Laird, James D., 77
Lake, Gerard, 207
Lamb, Richard, 179
Land, Emory S., 140
Lane, James H., 12
Latham, Sidney, 132, 142
Lattre de Tassigny, Jean de, 158, 163
Lawrence, Charles, 71–72
Lay's Ferry, 35
League of Nations, 87, 137
League of Nations Mandate System, 212
LeCompte, Karl, 139
Lee, Robert E., 14, 19, 37, 39, 41, 47
Leeward Islands, 207
Legge, Francis, 215
Legions of the Eternal City, 222
Le Havre, France, 161
Leigh-Mallory, Trafford, 164–65
Leipzig, Germany, 176, 178
Lens, France, 233
Liberty Ships, 188
Liege, France, 158
Liggett, Hunter, 109
Ligonier, Lord, 206
Lincoln, Abraham, 5–12, 14–16, 19–22, 27, 29, 47, 180
Lincoln Prize, xviii
Lines of Torres Vedras, 229
Lippstadt, Germany, 178

Lisbon, Portugal, 75, 90
Livermore, Robert, 75
Liverpool, England, 71, 218, 224
Lloyd George, David, 237
Logan, John A., 41
London, England, 71, 154, 156, 163, 166–67, 169–70, 174, 176, 180, 202, 206, 212, 215, 218, 222, 224, 228, 230–31
Long, John D., 85
Los Angeles Times, 144–45
Lost Mountain, 35
Loudoun, Lord, 206
Louisbourg, Fortress of, 220–24, 228
Louisiana Maneuvers, 154
Louisiana Native Guard, 12
Louisville, KY, 26, 31, 33
Lovejoy's Station, GA, 45
Lubeck, Germany, 178
Lucas, Scott W., 131, 134–37
Luce, Stephen B., 65–71, 78
Luxembourg City, Luxembourg, 162, 168

M4 (Sherman) tanks, 194
M18 tank destroyers, 194
M24 tanks, 194
MA43 tanks, 194
Maas R., 161
Maastrich Conference, 165
Maastrich, Holland, 168
Macon & Western R.R., 39, 41–44
Macon, GA, 42
Madras, India, 224
Madrid, Spain, 86, 92, 236
Magdeburg, Germany, 176, 179
Mahan, Alfred Thayer, 65, 77, 91, 230
Mahnken, Thomas, 86
Mainz, Germany, 166, 174
Malone, Paul B., 107, 113–14, 117
Malplaquet, Battle of, 228
Malta, 167, 172–73, 220
Malta Conference, 173–77
Manassas, Battle of: *see* Bull Run, First Battle of
Manchester, England, 221
Manchu Law, 90
Marathas, 207, 212
Marcantonio, Vito, 137
March, Peyton C., 87, 117
Marianao, Cuba, 113
Marianas-Bonins Command, 189, 191
Marine Act of 1874, 69
Market Garden, Operation, 157, 161

Marlborough, First Duke of, 206, 228
Marsden, William, 210
Marsh, Frank, 133
Marshall, George C., 118–19, 154–57, 159, 161, 163, 166–67, 169–74, 177
Marshall, S. L. A., 179
Martin, Walter F., 92–93
Massachusetts Maritime Academy, 78
Massachusetts Nautical Training School, 65, 74–77
Massachusetts State Reform School, 76
Maubeuge, France, 158
McAlexander, Ulysses Grant, 109
McClellan, George B., 5–6, 8
McClellan, John L., 137
McCoy, Frank R., 112, 115–16
McCully, Newton A., 95
McDonough, James Lee, 27
McKellar, Kenneth, 137
McLain, Raymond S., 179
McMurry, Richard M., 27
McNair, Lesley J., 112–13, 117
McPherson, James B., 29, 34, 36–41, 45
Meade, George Gordon, 17
Medical Service, Army, 190, 196
Mediterranean Sea, 154, 207, 220, 231
Mediterranean Squadron, 66
Meigs, M. C., x
Memphis, TN, 33
Mensa, xvii
Mercantile Marine Association of Liverpool, 67
Merchant Marine Act of 1891, 74
Merchant Marine, U. S., 65, 135, 141
Meridian Campaign, 45
Merry, John F., 74
Metz, France, 158, 160, 163
Meuse-Argonne Campaign, 106, 114–15
Meuse R., 167–68
Mexico City, Mexico, 89
Miles, Nelson A., 95
Miles, Sherman, 95
Military Division of the Mississippi, 29
Military Information Division, 83–84, 88–93, 96
Military Service Institution of the United States, 85, 88
Militia Act, 7, 12
Miller, William G., 75
Millett, Allan R., 108
Milliken's Bend, LA, 13
Minorca, 207, 211

Missionary Ridge, Battle of, 33
Mississippi R., 5, 13, 85, 215
Monongahela R., 216
Monschau, Germany, 167
Montgomery, Bernard Law, 153–81
Montreal, Canada, 224
Mont St. Michel Bay, 159
Moorehead, Alan, 169
Mordecai, Alfred, 85, 94
Morell, Thomas, 234
Morgan, Frederick E., 175
Morrill Act, 68
Moscow, Russia, 230
Moselle, France, 175
Mott, Bentley, 85, 87–88, 93
Mounted Service School, 90
Munich, Germany, 178
Murdock, Abe, 134
Murray, Tom, 137

Nagoya, Japan, 193
Napoleon Bonaparte, 205–7, 210, 218
Napoleonic Wars, xiv, xvi, 202, 204, 212, 218, 220, 222, 227, 230, 232, 235
Nancy, France, 162
Nashville, TN, 30
National Army, 110, 113
National Association of Secretaries of State, 131
National Defense Act of 1920, 86, 95–96
National Negro Council, 131
National Redoubt, 179
Naval Affairs, House Committee on, 69
Naval and Military Magazine, 235
Naval Appropriations Act, 74
naval impressment, 205
Naval Institute, 65, 73, 85, 91
Naval War College, 65
Navy Department, United States, 84–85, 91, 141, 143
Navy Voting Manual, 143
Nelson, Horatio, 210–11, 228, 230
Neuss, Germany, 175
Nevins, Allan, 18
New France, 224
New Hope Church, Battle of, 35, 46
New Hope Church, GA, 35
New Orleans, LA, 9, 12–13
Newport, USS, 75
News Chronicle (London), 166, 169
New York Board of Education, 70
New York Harbor, 71

New York, NY, 69, 71, 75, 77, 93, 156, 206, 220, 223–24
New York State Militia, 77, 115
New York State Nautical School, 65, 68–69, 71, 73, 75, 77–78
New York Times, 129, 139, 156
New York University, xi
Niblo, Urban, 189–60
Nichols, Roy F., x, xv
Nickajack Creek, 38
Nolan, Dennis E., 95
Norfolk, VA, 69
Normandy, France, 153, 156, 158–59, 162
Northern Group of Armies: *see* Army Groups, 21st
North Korean Army, 198
North, Lord, 219, 237
North Sea, 160, 162
Nurnberg, Germany, 178

Ocean Mail Act: *see* Merchant Marine Act of 1891
Oder R., 178
Office of Naval Intelligence, 84, 86, 90–93, 95–96
Officer Reserve Corps, 84
Oglethorpe, James, 205
Oise-Aisne Offensive, 114
Olustee, Battle of, 19
Omaha Beach, 161
Oostanaula R., 34–35
Operations Planning Division, 155
Oppama, Japan, 193
Oppenheim, Germany, 175
Ordnance Corps, 190, 192, 194–96
Ordnance Department, 112
Ostend, Belgium, 161
Ottoman Empire, 212
Ourcq R., 116
Overland Campaign, 20
Overlord, Operation, 154–55

Pacific Mail Steamship Company, 74
Palmerston, Viscount, 237
Panama Canal, 108
Paris, France, 85, 88, 93–94, 159, 168
Paris, Peace of, 212
Parker, Frank, 106, 109–10
Parker, Gervais, 215
Parliament, British, 208–9, 212, 214, 217–18
Parliament, Irish, 213
Pas Fini, France, 115

Passchendaele, Battle of, 165, 233
Patch, Alexander, 158
Patterson, Howard, 77
Patton, George S., Jr., 156, 158, 164–65, 167, 175
Paul I, Tsar, 208
Pax Britanica, 231
Peachtree Creek, Battle of, 39–40
Pelham, Henry, 206–7
Peninsula Campaign, 6
Peninsular Campaign, 220, 223
Pennsylvania Assembly, 71
Pennsylvania Historical Association, xi, xvi
Pennsylvania History, xvi
Pennsylvania State Nautical School, 65, 71–73, 75, 77
Pensacola, FL, 215
Peoples Commissariat for Internal Affairs, 179
Pequot Wars, 221
Perry, Matthew C., 85
Pershing, John J., 87–88, 108–9, 111–13, 117–20, 156
Petersburg, VA, 13, 16–18, 41, 47
Philadelphia Orchestra, xvi
Philadelphia, PA, xi, 14–15, 69, 71–72, 75, 77, 224
Philippine Insurrection, 113
Philippines Command, 189, 191
Philippines-Ryukyus Command, 189
Phythian, Robert., 65, 69–70
Pitt, William, the Elder, 202–3, 228–29, 237
Pitt, William, the Younger, 205, 210, 223, 237
Placentia, Palace of, 215
Poison Springs, AR, 19
poll tax, 130, 133–35, 137, 139, 142, 146–47
Port Hudson, LA, 13
Portal, Charles, 157
Portsmouth Navy Yard, 72
Portsmouth, England, 75, 159
Pownall, Thomas, 224
Prestonpans, Battle of, 215
Privileges and Elections, Senate Subcommittee on, 133, 137
Protestant Ascendancy, 213
Providence College, xix
Prum, Germany, 167
Puekey, Alfred, 73
Pumpkin Vine Creek, 39

Quartermaster Corps, 190, 195
Quartermaster Salvage Collecting Co., 195
Quartermaster Salvage Repair Co., 196

Quebec, Canada, 224, 228
Quebec Conference, First, 154, 167

Rafuse, Ethan S., 5
Ramsay Act, 131–32, 134, 139, 142
Ramsay, Bertram, 160–61
Ramsay, Robert L., 130
Rankin, John E., 130, 139–40, 146
Reading, PA, ix
Rebuild, Operation, 190–91, 193
Red D Line, 74
Red River Campaign, 32
Regensburg, Germany, 178
Regiments,
   1st Kansas Colored Inf., 12
   1st South Carolina Inf. (African Descent), 11
   3rd U. S. Colored Inf., 14
   7th Pennsylvania Cav., ix
   18th U. S., 106
   23rd U. S., 107, 113–14
   26th U. S., 108, 116
   28th U. S., 106, 108, 118
   54th Massachusetts Inf., 13–14, 18
   55th Massachusetts Inf., 14
   65th Foot (British), 215
   104th U. S., 112, 115
   110th U. S., 112, 114–15
   165th U. S., 112, 115–16
   353rd U. S., 106, 118
   354th U. S., 106, 118
Registry Bill, 208
Reilly, Henry J., Jr., 84
Remagen, Germany, 174
Resaca, Battle of, 35, 37, 46
Resaca, GA, 34
Reserve Officers' Training Corps, xiv, 95–96
Revolutionary War: *see* War of Independence, American
Reynolds, David, 179
Rheims, France, 115, 163, 174, 180
Rheinberg, Germany, 176
Rhine R., 157–58, 160–61, 166–69, 172–75, 177–78, 208, 229
Richards, Morley, 169
Richmond, VA, 7, 16, 18, 21
Riesenberg, Felix, 73
rifles, recoiless, 194
Riggs, E. Francis, 95
Robeson, George M., 68
Robinson, William, 216
Rochefort, France, 228
Rocky Face Ridge, 33–34
Rodman, Washington L., 70–71
rollup, Operation, 187–98
Rome, GA, 33
Rommel, Erwin, 155
Roosevelt, Franklin D., 130, 132, 138–40, 142, 144–46, 154, 157, 165–67, 174, 177
Root, Elihu, 85, 88, 92
Rosecrans, William S., 45
Roswell, GA, 38
Rough and Ready Station, GA, 44
Rousseau, Lovell H., 44
Royal Navy, 202, 208–10, 217–18, 220–21, 224, 227, 229–31, 235–36
Ruff's Mill, GA, 38
Ruhr R., 157–58, 160–61, 166, 174–76, 178
Rundstedt, Gerd von, 167–69
Rundstedt Offensive, 167
Rush, W. H., 72
Russo-Japanese War, 84, 86–87, 91
Ryukyus Command, 189, 191

Saar Basin, 160, 165
Sagami, Japan, 196
Saint Joseph's University, xv
Salamanca, Battle of, 228
Salisburg, George R., 75
Saltville, VA, 19
Sandhurst, 155
Sandwich, Earl of, 219
San Francisco, CA, 69, 71, 188
Saratoga, USS, 72, 77
Sargent, Aaron A., 69
Saunders, Charles, 224
Saxton, Rufus, 11
Scheldt Estuary, 160–61
Schofield, John M., 29, 38–39, 43, 45, 86
Schoomaker, Peter J., 104
Scott, B. O., 72
Scott, Winfield, 5
Secretary of State for War and the Colonies, 210
Secretary of the Army, Office of the, 137
Seddon, James A., 18
Sepoys, 221
Service of Supply, 116
Seven Years' War, 202, 205, 209, 212–14, 216, 218–19, 223, 227–29, 231
Seward, William H., 7, 20
Sharp, William Graves, 93
Sheridan, Philip H., 94
"Sherman's Neckties," 44

Index

Sherman, Thomas West, 11
Sherman, William T., 13, 19–20, 26–47, 88
Sherwood, MO, 12
Shiloh, Battle of, 29, 33
Sibert, William L., 108–10
Siegfried Line, 160
Signal Corps, 190, 196
Silver Star, 116
Simpson, Frank E. W., 170, 175–77
Simpson, William H., 165, 168, 175–76
Sims, William S., 65, 72–74, 91
Singapore, 200
Smart, Robert, 77
Smith, Captain, 71
Smith, Gene D., 133
Smith, Walter Bedell, 161, 171, 173–76
Smith, William F., 17
smoke generators, 197
Smyrna Station, GA, 38
Snake Creek Gap, 34
Soap Creek, 38
Society for Military History, xvii
Society of Friends, 141
Soissons, France, 105, 113
Soley, John C., 74
Somme, Battle of the, 166, 232
Sommers, Richard J., xii, xviii
South East Asia Command, 164
Southern Group of Armies, 178
South Korean Army, 197–98
Soviet Army, 168, 177–80
Soviet General Staff, 177
Spa, Belgium, 162
Spanish-American War, 76–77, 83, 85, 89, 91, 111–13
Special Services, 145
Spotsylvania, Battle of, 35, 37
Springfield Rifles, 105
St. Lawrence R., 229
St. Louis, MO, 131
St. Mary's, USS, 69–71, 77
St. Mihel Operation, 106, 115
St. Petersburg, Russia, 95
Stalingrad, Siege of, 178
Stalin, Josef, 167, 177, 179–80
Stanton, Edwin M., 11, 14, 19–20
Stars and Stripes, 143
State Department, U. S., 93, 96
State University of New York Maritime College, 78
Steele, Frederick, 29
Stimson, Henry L., 139–40, 147–48, 156

Stokes Mortars, 105
Stoneman, George, 42
Strachan, Hew, 232
Strasburg, France, 163, 168
Strong, Edward T., 72
Stuart, Charles Edward, 229
Suez Canal, 225
Sugita, Japan, 193
Summerall, Charles Pelot, 110, 118
Summersby, Kay, 163
Supplementary Militia Act, 204
Supreme Headquarters, Allied Expeditionary Force, 156, 158–61, 171, 173–76, 179
Supreme War Council, 87
Surles, Alexander D., 142
Swatara, USS, 72

T34/85 tanks, 194
Taft, Robert A., 139, 144–45
Tallahassee, FL, 142
Tedder, Arthur W., 153, 162, 164–66, 172–74, 176–77
Temple University, x–xi, xv–xvii, xix
Tennessee, USS, 72
Thames Marine Officers Training Ship, 67, 71
Thames R., 180
Thiaucourt, France, 114
Third Frontier War, 223
Thirteenth Amendment, 131
Thomas, George H., 29, 32, 34, 36–37, 44–45
Ticonderoga, Battle of, 223
Time, 169
Times (London), 163, 169, 179
Todorich, Charles, 67
Tojo, Hideki, 142
Tokyo, Japan, 87, 196
Tokyo Ordnance Depot, 193
Tongres, Belgium, 168
Tournieres, France, 156
Tracy, Benjamin F., 74
Trafalgar, Battle of, 202, 210
Transportation Corps, 190, 197
Treasury, British, 216, 218–19
Twelfth Article of War, 211
Tydings, Millard F., 137

ULTRA, 160
Uniform Code of Military Justice, 148
United Nations Forces, 193, 198
United Service Organization, 141
University of Pennsylvania, x–xi, xv

Upton, Emory, 90
U. S. Army Forces in Korea, 189
U. S. Army Forces Western Pacific, 188
U. S. Army Military History Institute, xii
U. S. Colored Troops, 13–14, 16, 18
U. S. Government Printing Office, 143
Usher, John P., 20
U. S. Merchant Marine Academy, 78
U. S. Military Academy, xvii, 84, 88, 108, 112–13, 153
U. S. Military Railroad Construction Corps, 31
U. S. Naval Academy, 65, 67, 69–70, 72, 74
U. S. War Ballot Commission, 131, 140–41, 146
Utoy Creek, 43, 46

Valognes, France, 159
Vandiver, Frank, 87
Van Natta, Thomas F., Jr., 92
Vaux, France, 113
Verdun, France, 158, 168
Versailles, France, 161, 163, 171
Vesle R., 116
Vessel Owners and Captains Association, 71
Vicksburg Campaign, 29, 33
Vienna, Austria, 177, 230
Vietnam War, xiv, 104, 202
Vimy Ridge, Battle of, 233
V-Mail, 137
Voltaire, Francois-Marie, 211
Vosges Mountains, 163
Vursell, Charles W., 147

Waal R., 161
Wade, Benjamin F., 20
Wadleigh, George H., 69
Wagner, Arthur L., 88
Walcheren Island, 229
Wallace, Hugh, 88
Walpole, Horace, 237
War Department General Staff, 85, 87, 89, 92, 112
War Department-State Department Black Chamber, 93
War Department, United States, 83, 86–87, 92–93, 95–96, 130, 132, 141, 143–45, 158, 169
Ward Line, 74
Wareham, England, 106
War of Austrian Succession, 205, 212, 216, 218, 220–22, 228
War Office, British, 157, 166, 170, 175–76, 213
War of Independence, American, 202, 207, 212–13, 216, 220, 227, 235
War of Jenkins' Ear, 218
War of Spanish Succession, 212, 228
War Plans Division, 154–55
Warren, Peter, 223
War Shipping Administration, 140
Washington, DC, 70, 83, 89, 92–93, 133, 142, 154
Washington, George, xiv
Washington Naval Conference, 96
Washington Naval Hospital, 147
Waterloo, Battle of, 202, 228
Wechsler, Herbert T., 139
Weigley, Catherine, xiii
Weigley, Emma Seifrit, x, xiii
Weigley, Francis A., ix
Weigley, Jacob, ix
Weigley, Jared, xiii
Weigley, Russell Frank,
  birth of, ix
  early influences on, ix–x
  early schooling of, x
  early teaching career of, x
  early books of, x
  joins Temple University faculty, x
  teaching philosophy of, x–xi, xv, xviii
  marries Emma Seifrit, xi
  love of sports, xi
  as visiting professor at Dartmouth College, xii
  publishes *History of the United States Army*, xii
  develops military history course, xii
  as visiting professor at Army War College, xii
  personality and character of, xi–xii, xvi, xix
  children of, xiii
  publishes *American Way of War*, xii–xiv
  lecture style of, xiv–xv
  publishes *Eisenhower's Lieutenants*, xv
  edits *Philadelphia: A 300-Year History*, xv
  named Distinguished University Professor, xv
  mentors non-traditional doctoral candidates, xv–xvi
  edits *Pennsylvania History*, xvi
  advises historical committees, xvi
  wins Samuel E. Morrison Prize, xvi
  publishes *The Age of Battles*, xvi–xvii

holds USMC chair, xvii
Masonic affiliation of, xvii
retires from full-time teaching, xvii
world travels of, xvii-xix
co-founds Center for the Study of Force and Diplomacy, xvii–xviii
publishes *A Great Civil War*, xviii
wins Lincoln Prize, xviii
death of, xviii–xix
eulogized, xix
Welles, Gideon, 20
Welles, Roger, 93
Wellington, Duke of, 228–29, 232
Westbrook, Robert B., 138
Western & Atlantic R.R., 30, 33–36, 38, 42
West Indies, 209, 211, 224, 230
Westminster, England, 213
Wheeler, Joseph, 42–44
Whiteley, John F. M., 175
Whitman, Walt, 28
Wiebe, Robert, 85
Wilderness, Battle of the, 34–35, 37
Wiley, Bell Irvin, 27
William of Orange, 220
Wilmington, NC, 13
Wilson, John B., 132
Winningstad, Olaf P., 190
Winship, Blanton, 112–15
Winward Islands, 207
Wolfe, James, 228–29

Women's Auxiliary Service Pilots, 141
Wood, Eric Fisher, 94
Wood, Leonard, 112
Wood, Walker, 132
Worcester, HMS, 67, 71
World War I, xvii, 78, 84–87, 89–93, 95–96, 104–20, 155–56, 166, 169, 212, 216, 232–33,
World War II, xv-xvi, 78, 86–88, 129–48, 153–81, 187–89, 191, 197, 220, 236–37
World War II Studies Association, xvi
Worley, Eugene, 139

Yalta Conference, 167, 174, 176–78
Yank, 143
Yantic, USS, 72
Yardley, Herbert, 93
Yokohama Engineer Depot, 196
Yokohama, Japan, 193, 196
Yokohama Transportation Corps Depot, 197
York, Duke of, 207–8, 212, 226
Yorktown, VA, 6, 231
"Young Turks," 95
Ypres, First Battle of, 155

Zec, Philip, 156
Zerbst, Germany, 179
Zone of the Interior, 187, 192
Zonhoven, Holland, 164–65

www.ingramcontent.com/pod-product-compliance
Lightning Source LLC
Chambersburg PA
CBHW081113160426
42814CB00035B/310